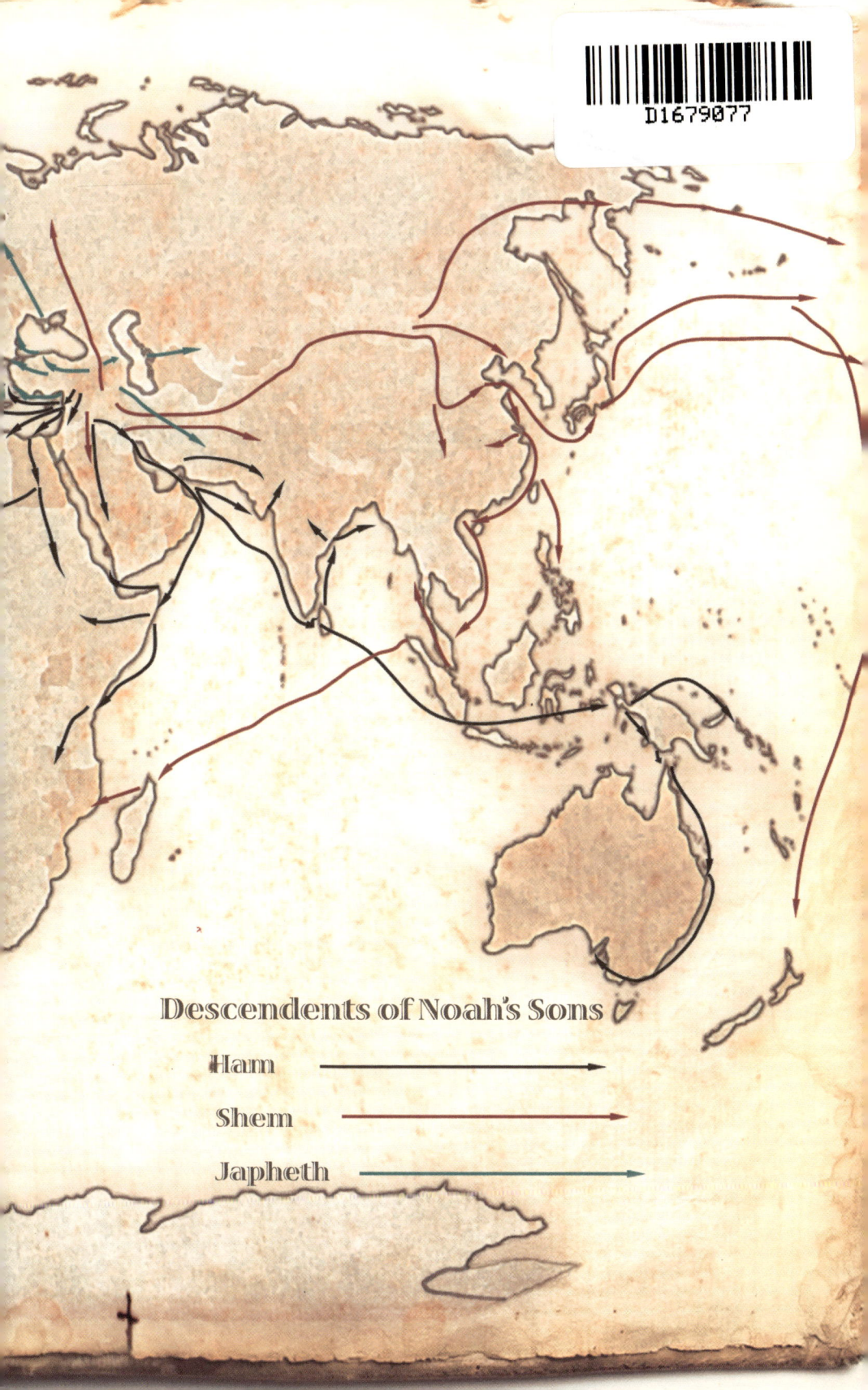

The Archaeological Evidence of

Noah's Flood

CLSP

Copyright 2011 by Philip Ernest Williams
First Edition

Unless otherwise noted, all Scriptures quoted in this book are from the English Standard Version of the Bible

Library of Congress Control Number: 2009909534

ISBN-10: 0979310229
ISBN-13: 978-0979310225

Printed in the United States of America and in other countries
17 16 15 14 12 11 10 PR 9 8 7 6 5 4 3 2 1

Published by the
Christian Leaders & Scholars Press
PO Box 680847 Charlotte, NC 28216

www.christianleadersandscholars.com

Cover background photo of Mt. Ararat from Armenia on a summer day
© by Mikhail Pogosov, image from BigStock.com
Cover foreground photo of Tel Megiddo in Israel by author

Contents

Contents vi
List of photographs, illustrations, and credits viii
Preface xiv
Acknowledgement xvi

Part I Understanding the Problem 1

1   Introduction 3
2   The author 8

Part II The Bible and History 13

3   The Biblical roots of history 15
4   Christian History 24

Part III The Roots of Modern Historiography 33

5   The Enlightenment's rejection of biblical history 35
6   Developing the modern historiography of ancient and world history ... 51
7   Revising biblical history 61
8   The archaeological recovery of biblical history 69

Part IV Scientific Prehistory and the Problem of Noah's Flood 73

9   Jesus and Noah's Flood 75
10   How theologians and geologists have understood the Flood 81
11   Young Earth Creationism, its contributions and its problems 95
12   The light by which we see 104
13   How light can be tested 114
14   The challenge due to the fragmentation of knowledge 123
15   My methodology for searching for the Flood 128

Part V Finding the Flood 133

16	Discovery	135
17	Light from Sir Leonard Woolley's Excavations at Ur	141
18	Flood forensics	147
19	The world before the Flood	154
20	Dating the ancient world and the Flood	158
21	Tracing the Middle Bronze cultures back to their source	176
22	The first international economy on the plains of Shinar	180
23	The new dispersion	185
24	Summing up my search for the Flood	193

Part VI The Flood's Implications for Science and Scholarship 197

25	The Bible and Science	199
26	Climate change and dating the earth's history	211
27	The origins, antiquity, and migrations of man	221
28	Anthropology	238
29	How animals and plants were affected by the Flood	255
30	A geological understanding of the waters of the Flood	262
31	Understanding cosmology in the light of Genesis	269
32	Ancient writing, scripts, and texts	273
33	Higher Criticism of the Bible	280
34	Summary	287

Part VII The Flood's Meaning for Today 291

35	The days of Noah and the Day of the Lord	293
36	What the Scriptures literally say	300
37	Restoring biblical community as a light to a world in trouble	312
38	A bright future for a dark day	320
39	The biblical method for determining truth	335
40	Acknowledging the truth	342

Epilogue Discovery on Mount Ararat 347

Discovery on Mount Ararat 349
Glossary 369
Topical Bibliography 386
Author and Book Information 411

List of photographs, illustrations, and credits

Figure 1   Noah's Ark
Painting by Edward Hicks, 1826. Philadelphia Museum of Art, Philadelphia.

Figure 2   Seekers of God's wisdom for the earth
Photograph of George Washington Carver by Frances Benjamin Johnston, Library of Congress.
Photograph of Ernest Blaine Williams, author's collection.

Figure 3   Writing and preserving history
Photograph © Lune Erickson. Image from Bigstock.com.

Figure 4   The Venerable Bede translates the Book of John
Painting by James Doyle Penrose, 1902. Courtesy of Wikimedia Commons.

Figure 5   Leaders of the Protestant and Catholic Reformations
Painting of Martin Luther from workshop of Lucas Cranach the Elder, 1533. Courtesy of Wikimedia Commons.
Painting of Ignatius of Loyola by anonymous Flemish artist. Courtesy of Wikimedia Commons.

Figure 6   The Enlightenment's Great Chain of Being
Left: Diagram from Didacus Valades, *Rhetorica Christiana* (Petrutius, 1579). Courtesy of Wikimedia Commons.
Rght: Chart from Ephraim Chambers, *Cyclopaedia* (James & John Knapton,1728). Courtesy of Wikimedia Commons.

Figure 7   Founders of anthropology and German folk history
Painting of Immanuel Kant by unknown, 18th century. Courtesy of Wikimedia Commons.
Painting of Brothers Grimm by Elisabeth Jerichau-Baumann, 1855. Berlin State Museum, Berlin. Courtesy of Wikimedia Commons.
Painting of J. G. Herder by Anton Graff, 1785. Gleimhaus, Halberstadt. Courtesy of Wikimedia Commons.

Figure 8   Leading figure of documentary criticism, and founder of the form criticism
Painting of Julius Wellhausen. Courtesy of Wikimedia Commons.
Painting of Hermann Gunkel, Gymnasium Johanneum Hansestadt, Lüneburg, Germany.

Figure 9   Awards Day
Illustration by John Tenniel from Lewis Caroll's *Alice in Wonderland* (Macmillan, 1871). Courtesy of Wikimedia Commons.

Figure 10   Arca Noë
Drawing from Athanasius Kircher, *Arca Noë* (Amsterdam, 1675) in John Hedley Brook, *Science and Religion*, (Cambridge University Press, 1991), 30.

Figure 11   Discoverers of the geological Flood
Painting of Georges Cuvier by François-André Vincent. Whitfield Fine Art, London. Courtesy of Wikimedia Commons.
Painting of William Buckland by Thomas Phillips. National Portrait Gallery, London. Courtesy of Wikimedia Commons.

Figure 12   Opponents of the Flood and creators of modern geology
Photograph of Charles Lyell by David Octavius Hill. United States National Library of Medicine, Bethesda, Maryland.
Lithograph of Louis Agassiz by Antoine Sonrel. Courtesy of Wikimedia Commons

Figure 13   Founders of modern Young Earth Creationism
Photograph of Ellen G. White from Adventist Book Center website.
Photograph of George McCready Price from Price, *The Predicament of Evolution* (Southern Publication Association, 1925) at Creation.org.

Figure 14   Stages of Belief
A. Photograph © Andres Rodriguez. Image from Bigstock.com.
B. Photograph © Dušan Zidar. Image from Bigstock.com.
C. Photograph © Michele Piacquadio. Image from Bigstock.com.

Figure 15   Important philosophers of science
Cover of *Thomas Kuhn*, Thomas Nickles, editor (Cambridge University Press, 2002).
Cover of *Quantum Theory and Schism in Physics: From the Postscript to the Logic of Scientific Discovery*, Karl Popper (Routledge, 1992).

Figure 16   Three kinds of light for understanding ancient history
A. Photograph © Eray Haciosmanoglu. Image from Bigstock.com.
B. Photograph © Jason Cheever. Image from Bigstock.com.
C. Photograph © Ismael Montero. Image from Bigstock.com.

Figure 17   Bristlecone pine, oldest living species of tree
Photograph © Dean Pennala. Image from Bigstock.com.

Figure 18   Special fields in the historical sciences
A. Photograph © Elaine Haykal. Image from Bigstock.com.
B. Photograph © Evgeny Kan. Image from Bigstock.com.

Figure 19   Systems science, telecommunications
A. Photograph © Eimantas Buzas. Image from Bigstock.com.
B. Photograph © Cheryl Alford. Image from Bigstock.com.

Figure 20   The Ancient Near East in the Bronze Age
Mesopotamia by D. Bachmann. Courtesy of Wikimedia Commons.

Figure 21   Kathleen Kenyon's sketch of Jericho
Sketch from Kenyon, *Digging Up Jericho: The Results of the Jericho Excavations, 1952 - 1956*, (Praeger, 1957).

Figure 22   Sir Leonard Woolley with assistant Lawrence of Arabia
Photograph by Heinrich Franke, 1913. Liddell Hart Centre for Military Archives, King's College, London. Courtesy of Wikimedia Commons.

Figure 23   Treasures found in the royal tombs of Ur
Sir Leonard Woolley. Excavations of Ur (1954). British Museum, University of Pennsylvania Exhibition.

Figure 24   Woolley's drawings depicting the royal tombs of Ur
Sir Leonard Woolley, Excavations of Ur (1954). British Museum, University of Pennsylvania Exhibition.

Figure 25   Diagram of Tel Megiddo strata
Author's photograph of display by the Israeli Antiquities Authority.

Figure 26   Early Bronze ruins underlying Tel Megiddo
Author's photograph of Israeli Antiquities Authority photo.

Figure 27   Nawamis of the Sinai
Photograph from Avner Goren, "Nawamis of Sinai: Exploring 5,000-Year-Old Desert Tombs." Archaeology Odyssey 5, no. 1 (January – February 2002), 20.

Figure 28   Neolithic or Early Bronze remains from Israel's Golan Heights
Author's photograph.

Figure 29   Cliff Dwellings at Mesa Verde National Park, Colorado
Photograph © Lonnie Widler. From Bigstock.com.

Figure 30   Metal from European shop buried by the Flood
Photograph from Andrew Sherratt, Barry Cunliffe, editor, The Oxford Illustrated Prehistory of Europe (Oxford University Press, 1994), 57.

Figure 31   Metal hoard found in Israel
Photograph of the Nahal Mishmar treasure, Israel Museum from Amnon Ben-Tor, The Archaeology of Ancient Israel (Yale University Press, 1994).

Figure 32   Mastabas beside the Pyramids
Photograph from Walter B. Emery, "The Tombs of the First Pharaohs." Scientific American 197 (July 1957), 112. Reprinted in Old World Archaeology (1972).

Figure 33   Stonehenge
Photograph © Louise Mahoney. From Bigstock.com.

Figure 34   Burial "ditches" surrrounding Stonehenge
Photograph from "Case of Stone Henge" by James Barton at Virtuescience.com.

Figure 35   Mummies of some who may have perished in the Flood
A. and B. Photographs from Elizabeth Wayland Barber, The Mummies of Urumchi (Norton & Company, 1999).
C. "Mummy from Chacalluta" photograph © Australian Museum, Sydney, Australia.
D. "Ötzi the Iceman" photograph © South Tyrol Museum of Archaeology, Bolzano, Italy.

Figure 36   Dagger wielding beer drinker
Photograph from Andrew Sherratt, Barry Cunliffe, editor, *The Oxford Illustrated Prehistory of Europe* (Oxford University Press, 1994), 252.

Figure 37   Calibrated radicarbon dates from Harappa burials
Chart from Jonathan Mark Kenoyer in R. H. Meadow, editor, *Harappa Excavations, 1986-1990: A Multidisciplinary Approach.* (Prehistory Press, 1991), 42.

Figure 38   Calibrated radiocarbon dates from Jomon burials
Photograph from Keiji Immura, *Prehistoric Japan: New Perspectives on Insular East Asia* (University of Hawaii Press, 1996).

Figure 39   Calibrated radiocarbon dates from Stonehenge
Chart from Michael Pitts, *Hengeworld* (Random House, 2000), 6.

Figure 40   Tracing the source of the culture from Israel's sparsely populated interlude
Map from Amnon Ben-Tor, *The Archaeology of Ancient Israel* (Yale University Press, 1994),111.

Figure 41   Settling down in the mountains of Ararat
Photograph © Mikhail Pogosov. From Bigstock.com.

Figure 42   Pottery and tent platforms sites from earliest settlements after the Flood
A. Photograph from Amnon Ben-Tor. *The Archaeology of Ancient Israel* (Yale University Press, 1994), 110.
B. Photograph from Charles Burney and David Marshall Lang, *The People of the Hills* (Praeger, 1972).

Figure 43   Ruins of Uruk
Photograph by Tore Kjeilen at LexicOrient.com.

Figure 44   The Tower of Babel
Painting by Pieter Brueghel the Elder. *The Tower of Babel,* 1563. Vienna Museum of Art and History, Vienna. Courtesy of Wikimedia Commons.

Figure 45   Geographical Dispersions from the Table of Nations in Genesis 10
Author's illustration based on "Middle East" © Ruslan Olinchuk. From Bigstock.com.

Figure 46   Reunion of Noah's family
Painting by William Hodges. *Resolution and Adventure in Matavai Bay,*1776. National Maritime Museum, London. Courtesy of Wikimedia Commons.

*Figure 47   Charles Lyell's *Principles of Geology*
Photograph from Charles Lyell, *Principles of Geology* (John Murray, 1834) at PBS.org.

Figure 48   Some of the 100,000 burials under the sands of Bahrain
Photograph by Shawn Baldwin in Michael Slackman, "In a New Age, Bahrain Struggles to Honor the Dead While Serving the Living," *New York Times,* September 17, 2009.

Figure 49   Mother and Children buried under the Sahara desert
Photograph by Mike Hettwer in John Noble Wilford, "Graves Found From Sahara's Green Period," *New York Times,* August 14, 2008.

Figure 50 Fathers of scientific sociology
Drawing of Auguste Comte © Getty Images at Bolender.com.
Photograph of Émile Durkheim. Courtesy of Marxist Internet Archive at Marxists.org.

Figure 51 Peaceable Kingdom
Painting by Edward Hicks, 1826. National Gallery of Art, Washington, D. C. Courtesy of Wikimedia Commons.

Figure 52 Floating Islands
Painting by W. Westall. Floating Island in Derwentwater. Carlisle Library, Cumbria in Chet Van Duzer, Floating Islands: A Global Bibliography, (Cantor Press, 2004).

Figure 53 Russian stamp commemorating the Kola Superdeep Borehole
A. Kernosov, USSR Stamp issued November 25, 1987.

Figure 54 The Narmer Palatte
Replica, Toronto Museum, Toronto. Photograph by Captmondo at Wikipedia.com.

Figure 55 "Philip" written in Egyptian hieroglyphics
Author's collection.

Figure 56 Ark of the Covenant
Illustration from Philip Y. Pendleton, Standard Eclectic Commentary (Standard Publishing, 1901), 21-23. Courtesy of Wikimedia Commons.

Figure 57 "As in the days of Noah..."
A. Photograph by National Park Service, September 11, 2001. "9.11.01 Remembrance" at NPS.gov.
B. Photograph by NASA, August 28, 2005.
C. Photograph by Petty Officer 2nd Class Nyxo Lyno Cangemi, August 30, 2005. U.S. Coast Guard.

Figure 58 The Jesus who came in the flesh
Photograph © Kurt Tutschek. From Bigstock.com.

Figure 59 Light on the Scriptures or light from the Scriptures
Photograph © Chris Howells. From Bigstock.com.

Figure 60 Alcuin of York, father of Europe's schools
Carolingian Manuscript (ca. 831- 840), Austrian National Library, Vienna. Courtesy of Wikimedia Commons.

Figure 61 The first New World feast of Thanksgiving
Painting by Jennie A. Brownscombe. The First Thanksgiving, 1914. Pilgrim Hall Museum, Plymouth, Massachusetts.

Figure 62 Ancient threshing floor
Photograph from John H. Vincent, Earthly Footsteps of the Man of Galilee (N. D. Thompson, 1884). Courtesy of BiblePlaces.com.

Figure 63 The End
Photograph © John Solie. From Bigstock.com.

Figure 64 *The NAMI announcement*
Courtesy Noah's Ark Ministries International.

Figure 65 *The discovery*
Courtesy Noah's Ark Ministries International.

Figure 66 *Panda Lee confirms the discovery*
Courtesy Noah's Ark Ministries International .

Figure 67 *Beneath tons of glacier ice and volcanic roks*
Courtesy Noah's Ark Ministries International.

Figure 68 *NAMI's Wing Cheung Yeung with author*
Photograph from author's collection.

Figure 69 *Clara Wei addresses National Conference on Christian Apologetics*
Photograph from author's collection.

Figure 70 *The Ark's decaying remains*
Courtesy Noah's Ark Ministries International.

Figure 71 *The remarkable wooden pegs*
Courtesy Noah's Ark Ministries International.

Figure 72 *Discoverers of history's greatest archaeological find*
Courtesy Noah's Ark Ministries International.

Preface

I am grateful, after many frustrating attempts, to find myself able to write this account of my long search for the biblical Flood and of my subsequent re-examination of history and the natural sciences in the light of what I found. To follow this account it will be necessary to put aside almost everything one has previously heard, read, or seen concerning the matter of the Flood, including what has been said of it by believers and skeptics alike.

Previous searches for a worldwide Flood have mainly concerned *geological* phenomena. In this book you will find a straightforward and systematic search for the biblical Flood in the *archaeological* remains of ancient man. Notwithstanding the general presumption that archaeological searches for the Flood using the biblical chronology of ancient man have proven fruitless, in twenty years of extensive study I have been unable to discover such searches. The Bible has indeed been studied in the light of archaeology and Ancient Near Eastern texts, but archaeology and the ancient texts are rarely studied in the light of the Bible.

In Part I, I explain how the teachings of modern science conflict with the biblical account of the origins of man and the difficult challenge that poses to a faith that is based upon historical truth. In Part II, I point out how historical thinking is rooted in the Bible but how influential Christian theologians have shifted from teaching the historical revelation of the Scriptures to philosophical theology. As I explain, the God of the philosophers is not the God of the Bible. In Part III, I show how Reformed theology gradually developed into the Deist view that challenged the literal words of Scripture. This section also shows how the modern understanding of history cut its biblical roots. Non-specialists may be shocked to learn how the framework for the modern versions of ancient history developed out of the deep racism of the Enlightenment. They may also be surprised to discover just how much the modern historical criticism of the Bible stems from the particular needs of German nationalism.

In Part IV, I review the most influential interpretations of the biblical Flood. I also explain the method of searching for the Flood that I determined to follow. Part V covers what I discovered using this approach. Part VI examines some of the implications of what I have found for related scientific and scholarly fields.

Part VII discusses the relevance this holds for our present world. Though I had not intended to cover archaeological searches for Noah's Ark, as I completed this book I became aware of an exciting new discovery on Mt. Ararat, which I describe in the Epilogue.

This book also chronicles my lifelong search for truth. At some point, this required me to read the words of the Bible as one would read ordinary letters or communications, something often decried as biblical literalism. The same commitment required that I challenge numerous traditional Christian views that threaten to obscure the plain meaning of the Scriptures. I claim no more for what I have written than that I have tried to accurately chronicle my search for truth.

My aim is that this book be accessible to the widest range of readers from the entire spectrums of belief, doubt, and learning. I have written as simply as I am able. Even so, the large amount of material so summarily presented may challenge many readers. Because of the nature of the subject and the number of specialized fields it covers, even the most learned readers may not be familiar with all the concepts and terms. Many of these may be found in the glossary in the back of the book. Some may prefer to move to chapters and sections that concern the discovery of the Flood and as leisure allows return to the topics that seem more difficult.

Making an effort to understand this book and pursuing further study using some of the sources listed in the bibliography will reward the reader with a broader insight into history in the light of the Bible and a deeper understanding of the Bible in the light of this same history. Others may find the book to be a compact but powerful guide to important fields of science and scholarship.

I trust that this book will open many minds as to how simply our world and its history can be understood in the light of a straightforward reading of the Scriptures. The Christian Leaders & Scholars web site listed on the back of this book will keep interested readers informed of news concerning various responses, discussions, and conferences pertaining to this book.

Philip Williams   Charlotte, North Carolina

Acknowledgement

Over the twenty years this book has been in the making, I have received needed encouragement and assistance from many friends, colleagues, members of my family, and others no longer with me in the flesh or with whom I have been unable to maintain communication. Besides those I mention, I have surely overlooked some who helped or encouraged me in this project. Our God knows just how your encouraging words sustained my fire to research and produce this book.

Of those that I specifically mention, first is my late father, who served as my example of faith; and my mother, who was not only the chief financier and servant to this project but also helped me understand how the pioneers that settled uninhabited wildernesses were able to sustain themselves by working together and earning their bread from the ground. Next to note are Mollie Faison, who assisted with expenses as well as travel and meetings with key archaeologists and scholars working in Israel, Italy, and America; Stephen and Claire Pfann, Peter Flint, my editor, Elisabeth Adams, and the Holy Spirit who inspired her to turn this difficult book into something better.

I am much indebted to those archaeologists and scholars everywhere who were willing to share their special knowledge and insights; the numerous scholars and scientists, noted by asterisks in the bibliography from whose publications I learned much; and to an unnamed professor and his friends in biblical archaeology and the media whose encouragement initiated the current version of this book.

I am also grateful to Paul and Alice Chou, Cy Johnston, Claire Bateman, Nancy Kate Gordon, Carole Ardizone, Miller Byne, Michael Jetton, Jim and Kim Edwards, Rebecca Boggs, Mike Crisp, Bill Robinson, Kay Tisdale, Pamela Wester, Mark Williams, Bill Thurman, Milt Baker, Jay Ferris, Bill Fleming, Rusty Maisel, Nell James, Myrtle Grant, Jonathan Campbell, my late uncle Johnnie Williams, and all my colleagues, teachers, ministers, brothers, sisters, and extended family who assisted and encouraged me over the long years that I have been researching and writing this book.

Not least were the labors of Richard Kendall, who spent numerous hours in libraries on behalf of this book, taught me sustainable agriculture, and gave spiritual encouragement; Cephas Tardzer for assistance in the business aspects of this venture; Vlatko Dir, who kept me posted on archaeological news and assisted with the biblical languages; my nephew William Waters for keeping me abreast of technologies useful to my work; those at Gospel Chapel including Billy and Judy Waters, Joel Williams, Linda Torrance, Mel West, and especially Kathy Nelson and my sister Mary Kennally, who so greatly assisted with the conferences for the Ararat Discovery; Kären Stevenson and my son Paul, who kept me stable and down to earth in the midst of so much elevated adventure and discovery.

Finally to mention are the prayers and spiritual advice of Les Schofield, Alan Smith, Dr. Michael Brown, Shelly and June Volk, Ellen Dusault, Robin Boseman, Steve Robinson, Thomas Macon, Sal Citro, the late John McClintock and Jack Myers; and most especially Jeremiah Boseman for his great and constant encouragement and for helping guide the direction of this book towards those hungry for righteousness and truth.

Part I

Understanding the Problem

— 1 —

Introduction

I**N RECENT YEARS**, a surprising number of important archaeological discoveries have been refuting the skeptics as they have been confirming history just as recorded in the Bible. Disappointingly, finds pertaining to the world's earliest history are not among them. Because the argument for the Bible's truth is no stronger than its weakest link, the difficulty in relating the earliest chapters of Genesis to the world of early man is grave.

The problem is not so much the account of Creation in the Bible's first chapter, which gets the most attention today, but the seemingly mythical narratives that follow. I refer to the Garden of Eden, the antediluvian world, Noah's Ark, the worldwide Flood, the great hunter Nimrod, and the scattering of mankind from the Tower of Babel. It is bad enough that the world about which we read in these earliest chapters of the Bible differs so from the one that we know, but according to even conservative biblical references, there are also clear contradictions

Figure 1   *NOAH'S ARK* **BY EDWARD HICKS**

between these accounts and what we now know about the earliest period of man's history. If the opening chapters of Genesis can indeed enlighten what we know about the early history of mankind, conservative scholars fail to use them.[1] These commentaries attempt only to relate a few things in the early chapters of Genesis to what archaeology and scholarship have shown to be the case concerning the wider culture of the Ancient Near East. That reduces these key accounts, so important to the Bible's central teachings, to ordinary ancient culture. Instead of using the Bible as a light on the remains from early man, these references use secular archaeology and scholarship to enlighten the Bible!

The popular Creationists who use Noah's Flood to explain a young earth have even more difficulty explaining the remains from early man. These Young Earth Creationists teach that the Flood destroyed the evidence of those who lived in the antediluvian world, but that only creates another problem. While the Bible puts the birth of Abraham no more than five hundred years after that great interruption, deep and significant archaeological remains underlie the scanty ruins of the time to which conservative scholars date Abraham, the Middle Bronze Age. Even if the scientific dating of human remains to an age far more ancient than Adam is mistaken, how are we to explain the deep Paleolithic deposits from the Ice Age, the numerous Neolithic remains from mankind's first settlements found all over the world, and the massive ruins of the extensive Early Bronze civilizations? Young Earth Creationists want us to believe that most of the remains of early man date to just after the time when the Bible declares that the Flood destroyed the earth's population. That is a better argument against the historicity of the Flood.

Is it any wonder that the most learned evangelicals prefer philosophy to the facts of history when discussing origins? Notwithstanding their sophisticated approach, this implicit concession that the Bible's history of early man cannot be literally believed is but a return to the Deist view of Creation!

One might compare the dilemma created by these early chapters of Genesis to the proverbial elephant in the living room. He has been standing there for so long that folks have become accustomed to his presence. All the same, the elephant does not go away just because learned believers and their friends are too polite to constantly bring up this embarrassing subject. If few believers want to give this matter attention, their brightest children will soon discover the elephant and lose confidence in the Bible. All their children will be influenced by a world ever more confident that it has vanquished the biblical account of man's origins.

If one supposes that I am putting the matter too severely, consider what it might be like were the situation between believers and skeptics reversed. Let us compare the Darwinian view by which our world presently explains origins to

---

[1] e.g. *New Bible Dictionary* (1962), *International Standard Bible Encyclopedia* (1995), *The Wycliffe Bible Commentary* (1962), *Halley's Bible Handbook* (1965), *Archaeological Study Bible* (2006), *ESV Study Bible* (2008).

the Aristotelian science of the late Middle Ages. It is not a bad comparison since Aristotle's philosophy was then the chief contender to the biblical light, and one that the Christian establishment eventually accepted. The great medieval theologian Thomas Aquinas showed how the Christian faith could accommodate itself to the most advanced philosophical thinking. Today, some leaders among the evangelical establishment make the same arguments for Darwinian science, even if that is to reject the truth of these earliest chapters of Genesis. They suppose that science is to dictate the terms by which the Scriptures are to be understood.

Now, let us suppose that some new "Copernican Revolution" somehow reverses this situation by booting the evolutionists into the same position as the Aristotelians at the dawn of modern science. Suppose the elephant was forced by new discoveries and circumstances to walk out of the believers' living room and make a new home in the camp of the Darwinists. Of course this would occur only if researchers were making the most remarkable progress using the light of Genesis to understand matters of science and history, much as Protestants once challenged the Aristotelian orthodoxy formerly used to explain both science and the Bible. Should that happen, the Darwinians who ignore the discoveries will find themselves having to make increasingly cumbersome assumptions to accommodate their evolutionary theory to the latest progress in science and history. The Darwinists would face the same fate as the Aristotelians when the Copernican Revolution took hold. What a wonderful reversal that would be for the fortunes of believers!

For now, that is just a pleasant dream. Today, it is believers who have to make all the concessions and accommodations. This explains why, beginning in the nineteenth century when the contradictions began appearing, so many sincere but thinking Christians ceased believing the Bible.[2] In a world where everyone admires the magnificent accomplishments of science and modern man – mechanization and industrialization, air and space travel, solid-state chips, computers, genetic and robotic engineering, mobile phones, the worldwide web, and the recent marvels of medical technology – the scientific history that we teach today seems far more credible. Those who developed our conception of an ancient world that is so different from what we read in the Bible worked from a scientific understanding. Today, it is unacceptable to quote the Bible to settle matters of truth. Our courts, universities, government agencies, and even the religious leaders and teachers of our modern culture look instead to science and sound scholarship for ascertaining truth.

---

[2] cf James Turner. "The Intellectual Crisis of Belief." In *Without God, Without Creed: The Origins of Unbelief in America* .(Johns Hopkins University Press ,1985).

Part I   Understanding the Problem

Modern Christians who continue in "the faith" claim that these words of the Bible pertaining to mankind's most ancient history cannot or should not be taken literally, that is, as historic. Unfortunately, this removes from the realm of faith the deep importance and meaning that necessarily stems from the truth concerning our origins. Christians have forfeited authority for these most important truths to science.

Even worse, if the plain words of the Bible – formerly regarded as the Word of God – are no longer authoritative, whose interpretation or religious instruction shall we believe? Do not church authorities, theologians, ministers, rabbis, imams, biblical scholars, and individual religious traditions interpret the Bible in different and contradictory ways? Religious traditions continue to serve those who are hungry for spiritual truth, but spiritual matters are now relegated to the private sphere. We may be fortunate that this is now the case because abandoning the straightforward meaning of the inspired words of the Bible licenses these various authorities to interpret the Bible in whatever manner or light suits their purposes. That in turn has led to a complete breakdown of consensus concerning the Bible's most fundamental teachings – about even such things on which Protestants, Catholics, Jews, and Muslims once agreed. It explains the complete loss of the Bible's spiritual and religious authority for the people of our modern Western world.

All this turns on the issue of truth. Biblical scholars tell us that these early chapters of Genesis are a retelling of similar Creation and Flood myths found throughout the Ancient Near East. If so, that is unfortunate because from beginning to end the Bible claims to be about what actually happened in history rather than teaching myths in the manner of the heathen. Just as this sacred book commends those who remain steadfast in the truth, it strongly condemns idle speculation, old wives' tales, superstition, false religion, and wrong beliefs. If these early chapters are meant only to convey important spiritual "truths" as theologians now claim, truth itself is not one of them. They seem to be teaching the very opposite of truth.

Most troubling of all is that Jesus frequently prefaced his teachings with "Verily, I say to you" or "I tell you the truth." He promises that those who trust him will know the truth, and that the truth will set them free. Did that include setting men free from the darkness of myth? More than any prophet or apostle of the Bible, Jesus had the most to say and teach about these earliest chapters of Genesis. He presumed them historical fact. Obviously, the Jesus in which moderns believe is not the Jesus of the Bible but a figure of our own making. In any case, the lack of consensus and trust concerning the plainest teachings of the Bible has resulted in the abandonment of the words of the Bible as the foundation of truth.

Chapter 1   Introduction

The leaders and the learned of our culture have chosen to become modern or progressive. Left behind are the simple and less-educated folks who cling to the Bible – or perhaps those able to leave behind their minds. Reversing its nineteenth century stand against modernism, the Vatican now declares such literal belief in the Bible to be intellectual suicide. To be sure, none of the Catholic Churches ever advocated a fully literal understanding of the Bible. They have always insisted on interpreting the Bible according to their traditions. Protestants became Protestant because they disagreed. Have even the champions of the authority of Scripture alone conceded that the plain words of the Bible are an insufficient guide? It seems that none of the churches want to be left behind as our world marches bravely into the future.

It is true that the God of the Bible hides himself from the wise and prudent and reveals himself to babes. That includes those with humble, sincere, and trusting hearts. For that very reason if the Bible does not mean what it forthrightly says, or if the Holy Spirit failed to communicate truth in a way we can understand, the book can hardly have a spiritual message. Even if it is simply mistaken, it is a deceptive book. However sad, getting to the truth requires being tough-minded and bravely following the evidence wherever and to whatever it may lead. Thus, beginning with the development of the scientific history of the ancient world, many Christians turned entirely from the faith and began trusting science. Those seeking something more spiritual turned to philosophy, literature, music, and art; or nowadays to Eastern religions and to new forms of spirituality. Many did so in what we believed was the pursuit of truth.

7

— 2 —

The author

I AM A former systems engineer and telecommunications entrepreneur. Like many of similar background and age, during my college days I lost my childhood faith as the result of a scientific and humanist education. I had discovered that science and scholarship were more serious than the babble of nonsense that I was hearing from most Christians. Eventually I had to concede: the Bible does not appear true. Sadly, I looked down on simple folks like my father who still believed the Bible. I attributed it to his lack of education. He was unable to attend college, but he was a seeker of truth, especially concerning the God of the Bible. He explained his steady convictions as a matter of faith, but I was convinced that truth lay in the direction of objective science.

Nowadays one may learn as early as primary school that the Bible is literature and not actual history. That is a polite way of saying that the Bible is not true. One should not be fooled by the pretentious nonsense of "two kinds of truth." When their hidden lives and plans are threatened with exposure, some public figures defend two kinds of "truth." Inveterate liars may defend more than two versions. Maintaining separate truths requires us to compartmentalize our lives just as some would have us compartmentalize knowledge and faith. Whether applied to our personal or corporate lives, this reveals a lack of integrity. Of course, different ways of understanding and doing are indeed appropriate for different realms and fields, but the truth on Sunday must be the same as the truth on Monday, or it is not truth.

A world that rationalizes "more than one truth" in order to believe what it wants to believe, or to get what it wants to get for as long as it can get it, has pushed aside its regard for truth. It seems that "two kinds of truth" was only a clever way of getting folks to accept the idea that the Bible does not teach the truth concerning our world. This explains why it is permissible to teach the Bible in the schools of America in the context of the "truths" of other religions, spiritual literature, and myths, but why it is no longer allowed in science and history classes. In areas where our society looks for determining truth, it is only acceptable to teach how the Bible has affected history, including how it once held back the progress of science and human betterment. Today, our wise Courts allow many things to be taught as true, but they protect children from those who might suppose the Bible a source of truth.

From my college days, I was liberated from the outmoded and contradictory teachings of the Bible. To be sure, I knew the Bible more from the teachings of Christians and from critical scholars than from my own serious reading and study. Leaving the faith was an important decision, but it did not mean giving up belief in truth and kindness. I was particularly attracted to the human and humanitarian dimensions of science and engineering. I was a devoted Scientific Humanist, seeking a place in a community that sought justice, prosperity, and peace for all mankind. During the idealistic sixties I went into science and engineering to help make the world a better place.

After some years of actual practice, my understanding and attitude towards science and technology began to change. I learned that the scientific theories that so enthralled me in college scarcely comprehended the real world. That caused me to see science in a purely practical and applied way. As I helped develop new theories that pushed forward the digital revolution and network solutions for telecommunications, I became less awed by scientific theory.

I found myself constantly challenging current thinking, though incurring fierce opposition every step of the way. The word *theory* actually derives from *theology*, and I was beginning to see a great similarity between established scientific theory and the theology used to interpret the Bible. I came to deplore the shallow salesmen who promoted fashionable technologies as ends in themselves. They seem to regard human beings as existing to serve technology and the companies that provide it. After much struggle, I was able to change much of the thinking and many of the practices in my industry, but such things caused me to become suspicious of all forms of scientific theory along with their supposed benefits and promises. I now know this to be simply the mark of a good scientist. At that time it shocked the scientistic view of the world that I held and in which I had been trained.

I was also becoming aware of profoundly disturbing problems in the most fundamental presuppositions of the physical sciences to which, I had formerly supposed, all things could be reduced. The theories of communications with which I worked could not explain something so simple as how human beings can learn one another's language, or even how they learn to speak. Physicalist theories fail to recognize conscious beings as anything but objects whose behavior may be manipulated and observed. Much less can they explain how a human being or soul comes to be.[3] I came to understand that human communications, along with novelty and creativity, are mysterious or unexplainable in terms of physical theory.

Since the era of classical mechanics, every new technology seems to create all-encompassing theories of the world and of human beings and society, along with plenty of boorish advocates for each of these narrow and conflicting views. Theoretical scientists and philosophers build mechanical, chemical, behaviorist, genetic, evolutionist, economic, and other materialist models of human beings and their societies, as well as the universe at large. Because these reductionist systems explain away things that are important to our hearts and for ordinary living, not even their advocates can take these ideas seriously without becoming loony or dangerous, all the more so when they influence popular culture and become political wisdom.

If changing thinking regarding the application of technology was difficult, challenging the scientistic thinking within the theoretical sciences in which our modern world so firmly believes seemed frightening. I knew that questioning things so fundamental could destroy a career within large corporations, and especially in the universities and government institutions that sponsor pure science. Fortunately, I had chosen to work in industry and the applied sciences. There independent thinking was highly prized so long as it could create a successful business.

Those who popularize and crusade for various kinds of science today resemble the shallow salesmen of fashionable technologies with whom I had to contend. The less they know, the more certain they are of scientific claims. Instead of welcoming disagreements in the interest of the discovery of truth, they operate like evangelists or messiahs, while demonizing those who disagree. That is no obstacle to winning such honors as Noble Prizes. Such is scientific "truth" today.

Eventually, I understood how economic interests, institutional politics, ideologies, fashions, and human vanities have more influence on scientific thinking about the big issues in our world than is the pure pursuit of truth on the part of those with relevant experience and knowledge. I was losing my confidence in science.

Though I believed in the sixties' ideal world of love and peace, the kind of world that I actually found was mainly one in which humans exploited and then abandoned one another. Even more disturbing were my disappointments in myself. Despite my humanitarian ideals, I discovered my own inability to al-

---

[3] cf William Barrett, *Death of the Soul: From Descartes to the Computer* (Anchor Press/Doubleday, 1986).

ways do the just and noble thing. I was losing confidence in the innate goodness of man. Reality was beginning to seem more like a living hell than the wonderful new age I was expecting. Such things shook my confidence even more than had my loss of faith. This time I had no obvious community to which I could turn either for loyalty or for truth. Owing to the matter of truth, I could not return to the consoling faith of religion, or to a Bible that I no longer trusted.

As was happening with quantum physicists in those days, these problems pushed me from my narrow interest in technology and my reductionist scientific understanding towards philosophy and literature, and eventually to comparative religion. I even began reading the Bible. Reading the last book was only because of my sister. Aiming to convert me, she handed me a new version of the gospel of John. It was the first publication of a very accessible new translation. I politely accepted it, but I aimed to make short shrift of the book. I wanted to be able to better explain why I could not accept the Bible's various contradictions and moral shortcomings. Before I could refute the book, I had to understand it. That is why I read the Bible as I would any other book. Today this is decried as biblical literalism, but it seemed only fair to try to understand the book in accordance with the plain meaning of its words.

As I began to read, I discovered that little book of John was actually making short shrift of me. Contrary to what I had learned from Christians and critics alike, I could find no contradictions. I found the book to be spiritually profound and intellectually brilliant. Jesus was indeed a great teacher. I wished, however, that he had not said those hard sayings concerning his exclusive messianic calling. Did Jesus really say those things? I wanted him to be a great teacher but I could not or did not want to see him as my Savior. My ego was too large for that. However profound, he was still a man.

On the other hand, contrary to what I had been taught by Christians as well as unbelievers, I discovered that the God of the Bible is deeply compassionate. He takes the side of the humble and the afflicted. I realized that at heart I was a Christian. I wanted my head to believe that there was a God behind the world that we know, and I wanted him to be the wonderful God of the Bible, but sadly, by now I knew too much about the scientific nature of the world and the truth concerning the history found in the Bible.

One day, as I was pursuing these broader interests, I happened upon a passage in a popular book about the former slave and accomplished plant scientist, George Washington Carver. As a young slave, Carver had come to understand plants. He learned how to return them to health and to extract important products from their leaves and oils. Such knowledge was significant for the development of organic chemistry, a field I had admired from my earliest days in the

Part I Understanding the Problem

study of science. Carver had accomplished more than his peers who learned their craft from their scientific training in chemistry.

The passage that I read related an incident near the end of Carver's life. He had just testified before Congress about how much it would help farmers in the South if they turned from growing cotton to growing the lowly peanut. He showed the Congressmen numerous products he had made from the peanut. Soon after his appearance before Congress, some reporters visited Dr. Carver in his Washington, DC office. One of them asked the famous black scientist, "Dr. Carver, what are your secrets?"

Carver pointed to a Bible that lay on the corner of his desk.

"The secrets," he replied, "are in there."

The words of this former slave reminded me of my father and his steadfast faith in the Bible. After reading those words, I heard myself exclaim, "How arrogant I have been!"

The very next instant I discovered that everything about the world that I knew to be certainly false was in fact certainly true. That also meant that everything about the universe that I knew to be certainly true was in fact certainly false. I found this light and truth in the very place I had regarded as the hopeless holdover of darkness owing to a lack of or resistance to better education.

As I returned to awareness of my surroundings and realized what had just happened to me, the corners of my lips turned upward in a painful grin. It was the kind of grin that forms only when one's world is suddenly and surprisingly turned upside down, from the deepest darkness to the most wonderful light. This theophany explains my sudden "Damascus Road" change – from scientism and philosophy to unabashed simple belief. It also explains the boldness and confidence with which I pursue the matters I discuss in this book. I was on the road to recovering the faith of my fathers.

Ernest Blain Williams **George Washington Carver**

Figure 2 SEEKERS OF GOD'S WISDOM FOR THE EARTH

Part II

The Bible and History

— 3 —

The Biblical roots of history

THE CERTAIN KNOWLEDGE that a loving God firmly rules the present day was a far more wonderful truth than I deserved. So mercifully did the Lord reveal himself without condemning this sinful unbeliever that I fixed in my heart never to doubt that moment. As I pondered what I had just experienced, I thought about those early chapters of Genesis. The same God who revealed himself to a man today would have long ago revealed himself to those he created. He would not have failed to tell them something so important as the truth about creation. The Bible firmly records these facts, but it seemed astonishing that the modern world could have made such great mistakes as I recounted in the first chapter.

I had just encountered the Jesus of the Scriptures. I should have understood and immediately accepted that he was also confirming the Bible. I am ashamed to say that regardless of my doubts concerning science and despite this wonderful revelation, I was unconsciously wedded to the gross darkness that our modern world accepts as light. It would take years for me to gain complete confidence in all that the Bible teaches. But from that moment I began my education anew, this time passionately preferring Jesus and the Scriptures as my source of light. This experience launched my long search to better understand what the Bible teaches about our beginnings, about history, and about itself. I wanted to compare *that* with what Christians since the time of the Bible have been teaching. Then I planned to find out what mistakes the modern world had made and just how those mistakes came about.

Our beginnings have to be continuous with the history of man whether the beginnings of man are taken from the Bible or from modern science. This is hardly the case today as the history of native peoples and modern nations fail to be integrated with the beginnings of man either as taught by the Bible or by modern science. While modern science has numerous suppositions for man's beginnings, whether for believers or secularists the intermediate history of man is hidden in confusion and darkness. In this chapter, I will briefly outline some things the Bible teaches about our beginnings and about history. I will also point out a few things this sacred book teaches us about God and Heaven that both transcend and determine history. The Bible makes it clear that mankind is not alone in determining or directing the events of history.

The first thing to note is how not only history but even the very concept of history is grounded in the God of the Bible. This makes the Bible vitally important for preserving mankind's sense of history and our knowledge of the most ancient past. Before I explain why this is so, I must address the common myth that the ancient Greeks were "the fathers of history." Some say that the Greeks were at least the first to employ a *critical* sense of history. The latter is only because they have confused being skeptical with being critical.

While Rome dominated the government of the world into which Christianity was born, the Greek language dominated its culture. Christians preserved the writings of the Greeks and Romans, as they also preserved their languages. This does not mean that other nations possessed fewer or less excellent documents and histories. It does explain why almost all the surviving pagan texts possessed by Europeans were by Greek and Latin authors and why Greece and Rome have seemed disproportionately great in the modern recovery and understanding of ancient history.

The Greeks had good reason to be critical about their own widely conflicting accounts of the past. Moderns tend to forget that what we see as their poetry was to the Greeks their sacred history. The moral shortcomings of their gods together with the incoherence of their myths explain why some Greeks sought to discover the more profound truths by means of philosophy. It is true that some of the Greek historians surveyed various myths and legends and gave their opinion as to what they regarded to be true. This is not, as some seem to think, "critical thinking." The Greeks had no chronicles of their ancient past by which to test various claims. Had they somehow preserved a reliable history among their conflicting accounts, they did not know or agree which of those stories that might be. The Greeks could not make sense of history because the events of history contradict philosophical systems pertaining to society and these contradictions must be constantly explained away. This explains why no nation has ever despised *un-philosophical* history so much as the Greeks.

Owing to his exceeding greatness, the God of the Bible can be comprehended neither by philosophy nor by theology. Instead, he reveals himself in history and through history, as he alone is the ground and root of history. Only he instills a sense of history into mankind, including our critical sense of history. In the rest of this chapter, I will enumerate some reasons why this is so, though the matter will become clearer in the rest of this book.

Chapter 3   The biblical roots of history

First, as I noted in the first chapter, the God of the Bible is the God of truth. Concern for truth is part of the defining character of biblical faith. Critics of the Bible point out that the sense of history used by the writers of the Bible is not the same as that of moderns. This is true, but as will become clear, it is true in the very opposite of the way they imply. Contrary to these implications, the people of the Bible had a deep understanding of history. Don't be misled by modern conceit. Those who wrote the Bible understood better than modern scholars the meaning of factual history in contrast to legends and myths.

Second, the Bible gives an account of important matters of history. These range from things that we could never know aside from revelation by the Creator to events in mankind's early history that most have forgotten. The Bible also includes prophecies, all of which are rooted in the historical circumstances of the people of the Bible. As oracular utterances, many prophecies transcend the ancient circumstances in which they arose.[4] Their full meaning had to await the Messiah – the Christ who fulfills them in the Kingdom of God.[5] Other prophecies ordain a time of growth and struggle for the faithful until the Day of the Lord, the Second Coming of Jesus. However dark that Day, it is accompanied by restoration and resurrection of those who have righteously devoted themselves to God, and is followed by a long era of earthly justice and peace. After a final trial, the world ends with the resurrection of all who have lived so as to appear before Jesus to answer for everything done while in their earthly bodies, whether good or bad.[6] These "last things" of history, also known as *eschatology*, provide hope to the people of God and meaning to history. As historians know, this arrow of history – usually referred to as "the linear sense of history" – is unique to the Bible. The scientific "arrow of time," as opposed to either eternalist or cyclical views of the world, stem from the historical views of natural history that, as I will explain, developed from the Bible.

Third, the God of the Bible is himself the creator of history. Natural history began when the Lord created the heavens and the earth by commands he gave during the six days of Creation. God changed the earth and made new history by his expulsion of man from the Garden of Eden, by his saving of one family from the Flood, and by his scattering of mankind from Babel. The accounts of the chosen people from the time of Abraham are likewise faith-defining and history-creating acts of God. The faith of the Bible is uniquely an historical faith.

Fourth, God intended that his people remember this important history. The Ark of the Covenant (or the Testimony), which preserved this history, was the throne where God met those who came to worship him and receive his bless-

---
[4] 1Peter 1:10-12
[5] Matthew 13:17; Luke 10:24; 24:24-27
[6] Acts 24:15; 2Corinthians 5:10

ings. No less today, meeting with the living God requires seeking him among those who acknowledge his historical revelation, the Bible. The Lord God gave the Sabbath as a day to remember the Creator, all that he had done, and all that he had taught and commanded. The important feasts of the Bible such as Passover and Pentecost were instituted to remember specific events in Israel's history: from Israel's mighty deliverance from Egypt to their famous entry into the Promise Land. At the Last Supper, the Lord made the Passover a remembrance of his death until his Second Coming. Remembrance of divine history is at the very center of biblical life and worship. It is closely associated with faith and faithfulness. Calling non-biblical religions other "faiths" misleadingly ascribes to them the characteristic that distinguishes biblical faith from other religions.

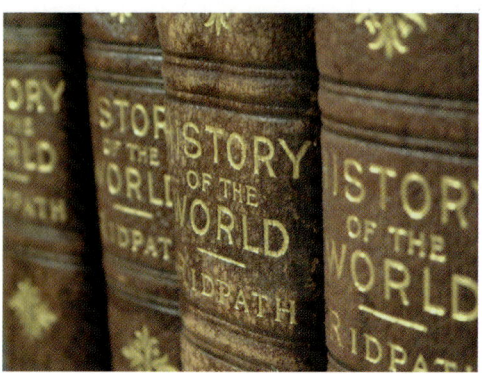

Figure 3   WRITING AND PRESERVING HISTORY

Fifth, the only way that history can be reliably preserved is for eyewitnesses and those who experience history and God's revelation to write it down; hence, the Bible is full of references to the chronicling or the recording of history and revelation. Detailed records of historical persons and important events are rare in pagan nations and civilizations. Not only do written documents allow faith to be preserved, but also to be published, spreading the message of faith throughout the world. Christianity is the faith of a book. God even refers to a book that he himself wrote, and to records that he himself keeps.[7] This is not an anthropomorphic view of God. God made man in *his* own image. Books are among the things that distinguish God and man from the rest of Creation. God and man uniquely possess a sense of history, and books of some type are essential to this purpose.

The Bible creates interest in history. Those who chronicle and carefully preserve history, and those who are even much interested in history, have been mainly those grounded in the Bible. As the world loses its biblical roots, it also loses its interest in history and truth. We see this happening today.

Most ancient nations and native peoples preserve some account of history however mixed with legendary and mythical accretions. Many are interesting and worth remembering. These nations may have retained some ancient

---

[7] Exodus 32:32-33; Daniel 7:10;10:21;12:1; Philippians 4:3; Revelation 3:5; 20:12,15; 21:27

knowledge of the Creator and of the events recorded in the Bible up to and following a short time after the Flood. Whatever they remember, we would know hardly anything about these legends, myths, or bits of history were it not for Christians who valued and preserved them. Christian missionaries do the same today. Missionaries have put most of the world's languages into writing. As servants of the God of all mankind, Christians preserve languages. We have the language and writings of the pagan Greeks and Romans only because Christians preserved them. Karaite[8] and Rabbinic Jews preserved the Hebrew text of the Old Testament and their own commentaries and traditions, but Christians preserved the Bible in the other ancient languages and the extra-canonical histories and writings of the ancient Jews.

> **As the world loses its biblical roots, it also loses its interest in history and truth.**

Sixth, truth is in the details. All good accounts of history are concerned with the specific people, events, and places that tie these reports to their time and place in history. In contrast to the abstractions of philosophy and the theoretical sciences, and to the vague legends of pagan religions, the Bible anchors its history to specific individuals, nations, events, eras, and places. Even spiritual concepts in the Bible are embodied in the life of historic individuals. Abraham embodies Faith. Moses embodies the Law. Jesus embodies Salvation.[9]

Dislike of the Bible by those who prefer philosophy owes to this "scandal of particularity." They do not like the fact that biblical faith is grounded neither in ideas, nor abilities, nor worldly accomplishments, but as is always the case where there is love – it is anchored to special persons. Like all relationships, this one with the living God requires respect, fidelity, and vigilant maintenance. For the God of the Bible, faith and faithfulness springing from the heart are more important than outward religious activities however scrupulous or "correct" the latter. Because biblical faith is intrinsically personal, the God one knows – and more importantly, whether God knows you – is more essential to biblical faith than *what* one knows. With regard to faith, this puts the wise on the same level as the simple. Because knowledge puffs up, the humble have an advantage in discovering wisdom and in getting to know the living God.

Because God is still making history, biblical faith combines new things with old. At the same time, it is wonderfully grounded to the past. It is the faith of pilgrims on a journey until they reach their promised City. New situations and experiences appear along the way. The faith of Abraham is a faith of knowing

---

[8] I will explain the Karaite Jews in Chapter 4.
[9] cf Ben Witherington III, November 9, 2005 interview with Mark Galli of *Christianity Today* regarding Witherington, *The Problem with Evangelical Theology* (Baylor University Press, 2005).

and being led by a living God. It is faith that will continue to make history after everything not based on love and truth has failed.

Systems of philosophy and non-biblical religions, along with Christian departures from strict biblical faith, attempt to escape the unpredictable or unfathomable acts of history for some or another fixed, permanent, and safe order.[10] Perhaps this is because change most often seems to be for the worse. Usually societies try to enforce some proper order, or they desire to return to some golden age of the past. Joyful endurance of present difficulties with confidence and hope for a wonderful future – even absent the expectation of earthly rewards – belongs almost exclusively to biblical faith.

Non-biblical religions look to some ultimate order or to the world itself rather than to a personal God as the ground and root of all. The pagan gods were themselves either born or created, or they were part of some eternal or chaotic cosmos. These gods are less than the great cosmos where they exist, but the God of the Bible is the Rock upon which the cosmos itself is built. He has stretched out the heavens and the earth as a tent.[11] The world can be explained. The God of the Bible can be experienced, but he cannot be explained. Neither does he need to be explained.

The million-year cycles of Hindu religion do not provide an absolute ground for history. Hindus were influenced by the competition for antiquity among the nations when Alexander the Great conquered India but, as I will explain in Part III, many of their myths of antiquity are rooted in modern Aryan studies. The Eastern religions not only deny the arrow of history but even the reality of the created or temporal world. As do speculative philosophies, the Eastern religions reduce reality whether seen or unseen to some or another permanent order – even if it be a permanent order of nothingness or change. Plato's demiurge or "God" created the visible world, but he did so according to eternal ideas or forms that belonged to an eternal transcendent reality. Aristotle's "God," his First Cause, existed within an uncreated visible cosmos and his "Final Cause" gave direction to an eternal world, but history is absent from the worlds taught by both Plato and Aristotle.

In contrast to the easily domesticated pagan religions, the God of the Bible is the "Troubler" and Savior of mankind. He involves himself in the visible world and in what mankind is doing. The governments or powers of the present world cannot domesticate him. Neither will he go away. History is his creation, and no one commands him concerning the work of his hands.

---

[10] *cf* Mircea Eliade, *The Myth of the Eternal Return: Cosmos and Religion* (Princeton University Press, 1954).
[11] Isaiah 42:5; 44:2; 8:13

The God of the Bible is a God of revelation, but he is not the "God" of the philosophers. Disappointingly, most Christian theologians have preferred the philosophers' "God." They prefer their systems of theology to the very words of Scripture. Though theologians interpret the Bible through theology, though they prooftext their theology with isolated passages of the Scriptures, and though the word *theology* was available in the first century Greek language, that word never appears in the Bible.[12] This Greek way of explaining rather than meekly hearing and obeying God's teachings and commandments seems to have been introduced into Christianity by Clement of Alexandria (c.150-215).

God has provided a firm foundation and a secure order to the world, though without stopping the move of history. The boundaries of the sea and skies are fixed. The days and seasons are regular. The animals procreate after their own kind. Here the Bible is on the side of those who see a real order to the world, and is against those who claim there is no higher order or meaning. Contrary to the teachings of the evolutionists, the earth and the creatures that live here were completed at the end of the sixth day of Creation. God also provided a moral order to the world. Long before the Lord God gave the Ten Commandments, he put the tree of knowledge of good and evil in the Garden of Eden.

Just as God's Creation, what is sometimes called his *general revelation*, is complete, so now is his *special revelation*, what we know as the Bible. It is the faith once and for all time entrusted to the church, those called out from the world to be God's holy people.[13] Nonetheless, God continues to make history by his judgments and restorations, and by fulfilling his promises. He also makes history by giving life to individual humans, each with unique personalities. The philosopher Alfred North Whitehead (1861-1947) understood that history and creativity could only come through the agency of a transcendent God. To explain new personalities or the emergence of a higher order, he found it necessary to postulate eternal objects that exist in a transcendent realm. Whitehead was not God and therefore could not conceive of creation as the Bible records – of qualitatively new entities that exist nowhere until God creates them. Regardless of what philosophers have thought, God does not need inspiration or ideas aside from his love in order to create unique things.

As did the Greeks, many suppose a general, scientific, or philosophical understanding superior to the knowledge of particulars, which belong to "the contingencies of history." This explains why those who understand the world in terms of some philosophy or ideology have difficulty regarding individuals as essential and precious. Many prefer ideas and the institutions supposed to em-

---

[12] The Apostle Paul's reference to *philosophy* in Colossians 2:8 would have chiefly included what we now call *theology*.

[13] Jude 3

body them to individuals. Ideologists like Marxists seek their ideals for *humanity* and *justice* at the expense of individuals, but none of the children of the God of the Bible are expendable. The Great Shepherd leaves the ninety-nine safely in the fold to search for the single lost sheep.

Our problem is that sin corrupts that which God has created, reducing the unique personalities of individuals to the ordinary and destroying that which gives life meaning – the life we share with those who are special. Through repentance his straying children may receive mercy and grace through the blood of God's Son, his wonderful Spirit confirming that we are adopted as God's own children. Whereas the world, along with Christianity patterned on the world, only creates clones, the Lord regenerates each of his children with a unique personality befitting to his divine family and kingdom. Unlike the original Creation, the New Creation formed from former sinners is incorruptible because it is entirely the product of God's mercy and grace. There faith, hope, and love endure for Eternity.

Like human history, natural history is also grounded in the personal God of the Bible. God has dominion over his Creation and governs it through unseen principalities, even if philosophers and scientists have falsely imagined his Creation as their impersonal Nature. The *principles* that philosophers suppose and scientists discover as governing the present world are but the rule of unseen principalities. God commands these principalities, and when he gives new orders, he changes the very nature of "Nature." God's Creation is hardly the disenchanted world of physical processes as supposed by scientists and lamented by the poets.

History cannot be explained by scientific or philosophical principles. Attempts to reduce history to philosophy are known as *historicism*. History can only be understood by discovering the personality, purposes, and work of the God of history and the same of the individuals who with him create history by their specific acts. Those with a natural understanding may learn *what* or *how* things happened, but a deeper and spiritual understanding is to know *why* they happened. Pedagogues who teach only the events of history have created an unpleasant subject because they fail to convey the relevance of their history. Understanding the aims and purposes of those who have created history, whether from Heaven or earth, turns the subject into a matter of great interest as it allows us to understand the marvelous world into which we are born.

However great God's interest in the earth and human history, this in no way diminishes the reality of invisible Heaven where God dwells. Regardless of what some think and teach, the spiritual things of Heaven are neither abstract nor shadowy. Theologians may tell us that the descriptions of God and Heaven in the Bible cannot be literally believed, but the living God of the Bible is no abstraction. Nor is he so transcendent and unconcerned with the current earth as they suppose. The Lord sits on a throne whose foundations are literally the righteousness and justice by which he governs the earth.[14] Physical thrones, as with the other material things visible to our physical senses, only dimly reflect the richness and meaning of invisible Heaven. Hardly the impersonal place supposed by philosophers, Heaven is in fact deeply personal. God and Christ are persons and their interests are in individuals.

Some are eager to go to Heaven, but Heaven is even more eager to come to earth. It is here that God's purpose in Creation will be revealed both to the powers in Heaven and to those living in the earth. This explains the great spiritual conflict that centers on the history and future of mankind in the earth. Fleeing from God's historical revelation to some or another religion, philosophy, scientific worldview, or system of theology is fleeing from God and from truth. In the next chapter, I will explain how Christians have often been tempted to join the world in its flight from history and truth – the truth of the present, the truth of the past, and the truth concerning the future.

---

[14] Psalm 89:14, 97:2

/ – 4 –

Christian History

As early Christians spread the good news of the Kingdom of God, they had also to re-acquaint Gentiles with true history. The Scriptures that Christians introduced to the pagans are not just about Christian history or Jewish history. Preserved by the chosen servants of the Creator, the Bible contains the most ancient history of all mankind. Both Old and New Testaments contain history as well as warnings and promises concerning the future, including its good news for all mankind. The light of the gospel freed those who worshipped idols, who believed pagan myths, and who were bound by destructive spirits. Large numbers joyfully left the kingdom of darkness where their ancestors had wandered to become part of the great family of God and the kingdom of light.

Jews and Christians were among the most learned in the ancient world. The Jewish historian Josephus (32-c.100) and the early Christian historians Sextus Julius Africanus (third century) and Eusebius of Caesarea (263-339) sought to relate the history of the nations both to the Bible and to their own times. Christians quickly surpassed the pagan world in learning. The decline and death of ancient paganism after Christianity obtained prominence was accelerated due to the pagans' embarrassment over their former beliefs and behavior.

As Christians prospered and became preeminent in the present world, their attention turned from the world to come to the present one. No longer expecting Jesus' Second Coming to establish his reign in the earth, they reckoned the church in the present world to be the promised Kingdom of God. A political institution replaced what was formerly a loving spiritual family. To explain this, theologians turned from the God of the Bible to the God of the philosophers. Ignoring the plain meaning of the words of Jesus and the Apostles, they turned the Scriptures pertaining to the church into allegories for the spiritual journey of individuals. Senses of the Scriptures other than the plain meaning served to rationalize the Church's developing traditions. As theology replaced the Scriptures, history went into eclipse.

One should not confuse the historicist vision that Augustine of Hippo (354-430) put forth in his *City of God* either with factual history or with God's revelation in the Bible. Augustine's book was a story of two cities: the City of God and the City of Man. Augustine traced these two cities throughout their "history," finally identifying them with the Catholic Church and the earthly City of Rome. The citizens of Augustine's earthly city were those who pursued fleshly pleasures. The citizens of his heavenly City of God were those who forsook such things to serve the Catholic Church. Augustine taught that the Catholic Church consists of a mixture of these two kinds of men. These "wheat and tares" in the Catholic Church would be sorted on the Day of Judgment. This is philosophy, it is poetry, it is theology, it is *historicism*, and it reflects Augustine's personal history, but it is neither revelation from God, nor is it history. Unlike the Gnostics, Augustine declared his teachings to be found in the canonical Scriptures, but no less than the Gnostics did his vision replace the Bible's historical faith with philosophy.

Though the earliest Christians expected that Christ was returning to inaugurate the reign of saints on the earth., Augustine taught that the Church had already entered the Millennium, the thousand-year reign of the saints promised in the book of Revelation.[15] Instead of appearing as the Savior of presently afflicted Christians when he brings the Kingdom of God to earth, Augustine maintained that Jesus would next appear as the Great Judge on the Last Day. This is how the joyful Christianity of the Apostles turned into the long faces of orthodox Christianity. In Augustine's theology, the arrow of Christian history points backwards from the Great Judgment.

In line with the growing asceticism and celibacy of his day, Augustine regarded an earthly Millennium as a "fleshly" hope. He taught that original sin was passed from Adam and Eve to their children by the concupiscence necessary for procreation. His monkish hatred of Creation came from Cynic and Neoplatonist philosophies. The Gnostics, Manichaens, and certain Eastern religions teach such things, but the Bible does not. The Scriptures teach against allowing fleshly desires or worldly ambitions to control one's behavior, but though the flesh may be weak and stained by sin, it is not evil. To the contrary, the Scriptures teach that all things created by God are good.[16] Worshipping God means sacrificing one's fleshly life on behalf of the Kingdom of God, but not because the flesh is intrinsically evil.[17] To the contrary, sacrifices of flesh must simply

---

[15] Revelation 20
[16] 1 Timothy 4:1-5
[17] Romans 12:1

be clean to be acceptable. Indeed, the Lord himself became flesh. To promote asceticism and celibacy, these theologians conflated God's Creation with the sinful world under the sway of Satan. But far from advocating a spirit of philosophical resignation and contemplation, Jesus taught us to pray to see God's will done in the earth as in Heaven.

Interestingly, Augustine taught that light goes forth from the eye to enlighten the object of vision. Likewise the light of Augustine's *City of God* isn't coming from the Bible, from the living Jesus, or from the facts of history. His famous book was a projection of the light of his mystical philosophical theology onto history and onto the Bible. Everyone who interprets the Bible through his own philosophy or theology does the same thing. Unfortunately many Christians defend practices and teachings that are contrary to the Bible by appealing to some famous Christian theologian or church tradition. Whether Catholic or Protestant, many great theologians remain popular because they serve as reputed Christian authorities for things that contradict the plain sense of the Bible's words.

Augustine had trouble reconciling the historical Creation, the miracles, and the exceptional history recorded in the Bible with his preference for the eternal truths of philosophy. Noting that the miraculous powers seen in the days of the Apostles seemed to have disappeared from the Church, he sought to explain the earlier miracles as part of some higher philosophical order that is not presently understood. As times became more perilous, Augustine and churchmen such as Pope Gregory the Great became fascinated with contemporary miraculous claims. Augustine could accept them as part of his philosophical understanding for the very reason that he now understood them as ordinary.

The miracles of the Bible were never ordinary. They witness God's intervention to change the world and the course of history. Accepting unsubstantiated claims and seeing miracles as part of the ordinary Christian life only debases the coinage or meaning of miracles. Rather than causing wonder and hope, strange "miracles" are just strange. But supposing that spiritual "powers" are carried by ecclesiastical offices or present in relics and ordinary sacraments reduces them to ordinary religious patterns of the present world. What should be charismatic is instead dead ritual. This explains why the miracles of the Bible were done for exceptionally good or righteous purposes or were done to confirm something new that God was introducing into history. It also explains why they were so wonderful, so public and so well attested that even the enemies of the prophets, the Apostles, and Jesus could not refute them.

The Dark Ages, which began around this time, were an era of deep superstition and sensational claims. Miraculous powers were attributed to the relics of martyrs and to famous saints and church officials. Reflecting pagan customs and local culture, the focus of these miracles shifted to venerating saints and their legends more dearly than the universal faith passed down from the Apostles. The doctrine of transubstantiation relegated supernatural powers taught as essential for salvation to the control of the established church. As had been the case in ancient Israel, the institutions of Christendom were often corrupt, and just as Jesus taught, those who were faithful experienced persecution from their Christian brothers. From the Council of Ephesus in 436, chiliasts, those who expected Jesus Second Coming to establish the Millennium, were persecuted as heretics. Also persecuted as heretics were those who taught that the church should be a community of the righteous. The orthodox who persecuted them preferred seeing the church as chiefly a school for sinners.

Notwithstanding such troubles that must continue until Jesus returns, through the suffering and service of the faithful the peaceful fruits of Christian community extended across the warring kings and nations of Europe. Though Augustine's mystical philosophical vision dominated the theology of the Medieval Church, it did not completely stop the chronicling of history. During the darkest of the Dark Ages, Gildas (516-570) wrote the history of early Britain in the manner of an Old Testament prophet. The Venerable Bede (672-735) wrote a detailed history of the English Church. The Anglo-Saxon Chronicles were probably written during the era of Alfred the Great (847-899). However imperfectly, these exceptions to the Medieval flight from history used the Bible rather than philosophy as their guiding light.

FIGURE 4   THE VENERABLE BEDE TRANSLATES THE GOSPEL OF JOHN

While biblical faith persisted through the Dark Ages, beginning with Augustine timeless Neoplatonic philosophy competed with the Bible and with the sense of history that is grounded in the Bible. Neoplatonism explains creation and history as emanations from a philosophical hierarchy of being. This theology of the philosophers is given biblical clothing by assuming that the abstract "One" at the top of the hierarchy is the God of the Bible. Following the suggestion of Augustine, theologians supposed the philosophers' way of reason to be superior to the way of authority found in the Scriptures. Not only does this contradict the irreducible historical character of the biblical revelation, it implies that the writings of the philosophers, even pagans such as Plato, are superior to the inspired Scriptures.

A similarly high view of philosophy arose within Islam, a new religion appearing during the seventh century. By the end of the eighth century, it had conquered great regions of the Christian world. Likely, because Mohammed did not embrace the world-denying asceticism and celibacy so prized in medieval Christianity, Muslims preferred the this-worldly philosophy of Aristotle to the otherworldly philosophy of Plato. The fact that Mohammed did no miracles as did Jesus and the prophets of the Bible and that Islam conquers through the worldly sword rather than spiritual power that comes from the weakness of the cross also favored Aristotle's scientific world view. But in distinction from modern science, Islamic science also encompassed astrology, alchemy, and magic.

Though Western Christians were initially isolated from these developments in Islam, they more immediately affected Judaism. The rabbis had also to confront a Karaite movement that first asserted itself in Baghdad with the rise of Islam. These were Jews who rejected the Talmud and sought to a return to the Old Testament as the sole basis of Jewish faith. The new attention these Karaites gave to the Hebrew text of the Scriptures would profoundly shape modern biblical scholarship and understanding.

Since the ignominious failure of the Bar Khochba revolt of the second century, rabbis had suppressed teachings about a Jewish messiah and Zionism, the expectation that Jews might one day return to the ancient land of the Bible as promised in the prophecies of the Old Testament. Christians taught the destruction of Jerusalem in AD 70 and the failure of a worldly kingdom to appear in the land of the Bible as evidence of the truth that Jesus was the Messiah who had fulfilled these prophecies. Though the complete fulfillment of the Kingdom of God on earth would have to await his Second Coming, I have explained how Christian theologians allegorized the Scriptures to proclaim the present Church as the promised Kingdom of God. The rabbis had even more reason to declare a spiritual and allegorical interpretation of these Scriptures. Since the worship proscribed by the Torah required the Temple, the rabbis turned to the Talmud, which accommodated Judaism to life outside the ancient land of Israel. With the new attention that Karaites gave to the Old Testament, the dilemma presented by the Torah and the proper understanding of the Old Testament prophecies returned.

Though affirming the Talmud, rabbis among the Askenazi Jews,[18] such as Rashi (1040-1105) and Abraham ibn Ezra (1089-1164), discovered in this Jewish revival of interest in their ancient Scriptures an effective anti-Christian polemic against the pressure of Jews to convert to Christianity that occurred during the Crusades. Challenging the excessive allegorizing and spiritual understanding that had accompanied earlier Rabbinic and Christian exegesis, they learned to apply the prophecies as pointing to historical circumstances of the ancient Jews. They denied that Jesus had fulfilled the Old Testament Scriptures concerning the restoration of Zion, pointing instead to their need to be fulfilled when a future earthly Jewish messiah leads Jews back to Zion. The Christian Crusader kingdom in the ancient land of the Bible, following centuries of Islamic rule, made such an interpretation seem all the more credible. Ignoring the apocalyptic and supernatural aspects of the messiah and the Kingdom of God as found in the Prophets, the *Judaica exposito* turned towards an earthly interpretation of Israel, Zionism, and the future Jewish messiah.

Sepharadi rabbis,[19] many of whom prospered in service to Islamic rulers, viewed the Karaite movement as a serious threat to the very existence of Rabbinic Judaism. Their concerns seem not so much the revival of Zionism, but the stricter ethical teachings of the Torah and the unphilosophical character of the Hebrew Scriptures. These rabbis preferred the Aristotelian teachings of their hosts to the historical view of the world found in the Scriptures and favored by the Karaites. A series of Sepharadic rabbis culminating in the famous Moses Maimonides (1132-1204) developed ways of accommodating the Old Testament Scriptures as teaching a version of Aristotelian philosophy. Though allowing that God had created the matter he used in forming the world, these theologians taught a system of the world along the lines of Aristotelian science. Maimonides used allegories to explain away the historical and "anthropomorphic" character of biblical revelation similar to the way early Christians had accommodated the Scriptures to Plato's philosophy.

Aristotle's philosophy entered Western Christianity from Islamic philosophy by way of Jewish intermediaries and was first embraced by the faculties of the arts teaching in the medieval universities. Seeing its essential contradiction to the Bible, the proponents of Scripture vigorously opposed the system of Aristotle. Yet having become an established part of the present world, Roman Catholicism was ready for a theology that attributed the presently visible world to the design of God. Following Maimonides, Thomas Aquinas (1225-1274) modified Aristotle's philosophy to accommodate Creation and resurrection. According to his philosophy, Heaven, Hell, and the earth, the present, the future,

---

[18] *Askenazi* Jews were those living in Christian lands.
[19] *Sepharadi* Jews were those living in Islamic lands.

and the past all belong to a timeless static hierarchy of Christian society such as depicted in Dante's *Divine Comedy*.

If indeed the visible order of the world and society never changes, earthly progress and hope disappear together with the arrow of history. In truth, the feudal society depicted in Aquinas' philosophy was but a continuation in Christian dress of the class system and order of the pagan Roman world. It conflicts with the family of God in which all men are brothers and where there is always hope for God's deliverance, but this was neither the first nor would it be the last time by which some theology or philosophy would be used to rationalize an unjust "Christian" society that a literal reading of the Scriptures plainly condemns.

Aquinas declared that his Aristotelian philosophy of Nature was complementary to the special revelation of the Bible. He taught that God was limited in what he could create by the universal ideas of philosophy, ideas that God held in his mind. Theologians such as Duns Scotus (1266-1308) and William of Ockham (1288-1348) saw its incompatibility with the greatness and sovereignty of the God of the Bible. So superior is God to men and so free is his will, that the things God chooses to create can never be predicted or encompassed by any system of philosophy or science conceived by the human mind. Rather than through philosophical speculation, one can only know the world by discovering and analyzing the individual things that God did create. This focus on the particulars of God's Creation led to the beginnings of empirical science. This sense of discovery suggested reading ancient texts for what they actually said rather than as proof texts for systems of scholastic theology. Scholars turned their attention to the proper methods for the study and reading of texts.

Because they needed a definite reading of the original texts to serve as the basis of new translations of the Bible, humanist scholars returned to favoring a literal understanding of the Bible. This change stimulated Reformers to turn from philosophy and to look anew at the church, society, and history in the light of a more literal reading of the Bible. The Reformation was not caused by a return to the authority of the Bible. The Catholic Church had never denied the authority of the Bible. It was rather a return to the authority of a literal understanding of the Bible – the Bible understood by the Holy Spirit, by reason, by philology, or by common sense.[20] Some light accessible outside the control of a religious hierarchy is necessary if the Bible is to serve as the authority for a priesthood of believers.

The return to history stemming from the Reformation was also due to a revived interest in biblical prophecy that developed when Martin Luther declared

---

[20] Roland H. Bainton, "Sola Scriptura." In *The Cambridge History of the Bible*, Vol. 3, *The West from the Reformation to the Present Day*, edited by S. L. Greenslade, 1-6 (Cambridge University Press, 1965).

the book of Revelation a foretelling of Christian history. He taught that the evil City of Babylon that persecuted the saints was not the pagan City of Rome but the Roman Catholic Church. As Protestant and Catholic scholars searched church history to prove or challenge whether the Papacy and Catholic Church fulfilled prophecy concerning the antichrist, they gained a better knowledge and understanding of the Christian centuries. Though not unaware of the challenge that the *Judaica exposito* posed to the Christian interpretation of the Old Testament, Luther and other Reformers were deeply affected by the rabbis' literal and historical interpretation of the Old Testament prophecies. Aside from those who followed Theodore Beza (1519-1605), who interpreted Romans 11 as a restoration of a future Israel composed of converted Jews, most Reformers saw the Zionist prophecies as pointing to a restoration of a latter day light from the church.

Reformed Protestants and Puritans saw their reforms in the church and society as leading to a brighter day. They identified this progress of the church with the Latter Day Glory found in the Old Testament prophecies – the time when Zion would give forth her light. This view shared by John Cotton (1585-1652), America's first pastor, informed the hope of early Americans that the church in the New World would become "a city on a hill" and "a light to the nations." America's characteristic optimism grew out of the expectation that the Kingdom of God would soon appear in history. Some believed the community of faith in America was divine preparation for that appearance. Such optimism is rare in human history, but whenever it appears one will discover it to be rooted in the Bible.

It was natural that American Christians would adopt the view of those such as Cambridge University's Joseph Mede (1586-1639) that the latter-day light would bring about the Millennium promised in the book of Revelation. Teaching that the church had not yet entered the Millennium challenged the Augustinian view that had long dominated Christian theology. Joseph Mede's students also noticed in the book of Daniel that in the last days, knowledge would increase. They embarked on a program of establishing international scientific organizations and societies for the promotion of knowledge. Some of these students became founding members of England's Royal Society for the promotion of science. The Puritans held to the view begun by Renaissance humanists that the medieval era was a time of degeneration. They called these centuries of Catholic darkness "the Dark Ages." They contrasted this darkness with the latter day light of the church – what would become known as the Enlightenment.

A more accurate understanding of ancient history developed from efforts to determine just when the seventy weeks in the prophecies of the books of Daniel took place.[21] Anchoring the historiography of ancient nations to the Bible, to the current calendar, and to mathematically-calculated astronomical events led to better chronology and dating of ancient times. Very popular during this era was the four-monarchy system of history developed from the images in the book of Daniel. This influential view understood history to be dominated by four great monarchies or kingdoms: the Assyrian-Babylonian, the Persian, the Greek, and the Roman. The kingdom of Christ was understood to be the fifth monarchy.

Because the Greeks seem not to have known any Ancient Near Eastern kingdom earlier than the Assyrians, the four-monarchy system was accepted during the Enlightenment as the basis of ancient history. But challenging those who wanted to see Greeks and Romans as having the most accurate version of ancient history, the French Huguenot Joseph Scaliger (1540-1609) pointed to the more ancient civilizations of the Ancient Near East, about which the ancient Greeks and Romans knew little. The most famous of the chronologies that connected the ancient pagan nations to the Bible was that of the Anglican Bishop of Ireland, James Ussher (1581-1656).

Interest in ancient history during the era of European exploration was stimulated by the discovery of new accounts of the Flood possessed by people from around the world. Though some believed that the great period of time that had elapsed since the Flood made linking modern peoples to the family of Noah impossible, linguists such as the Irish doctor James Parsons (1704-1770) could see commonalities among the languages of Europe. He explained that these nations had their origin in the family of Japheth, son of Noah. Sir William Jones (1746-1794) discovered that India's Sanskrit language belonged to the same Japhetic family. These observations led to the development of the science of historical philology, and to a new scholarly version of ancient history based upon it.

---

[21] Daniel 9:24-27

Part III

The Roots of Modern Historiography

— 5 —

The Enlightenment's rejection of biblical history

IN THE LAST chapter, I explained how the Enlightenment arose from looking at the history of the church in the light of biblical prophecy. Of course today we see the Enlightenment as a turning from rather than a looking to the Bible as a source of light. Though the men of the Enlightenment ceased literally believing the Bible, this did not happen as currently supposed – through an attack upon Christianity by secularists. The anachronistic understanding possessed by our current world stems from viewing the Enlightenment through the lens of the French Revolution and Darwinian science, as if secularists are more the children of the Enlightenment than are evangelicals. All the men of the Enlightenment delighted in championing Intelligent Design as proof of a Creator.

A more historical understanding of the Enlightenment is important for several reasons. First, certain views held by many evangelicals, including Reformed theology and a high regard for science and natural theology (Intelligent Design), are similar to those held by Christians of the Enlightenment that led to the apostasy of Deism. Those holding these views today may be on the same road. Second, believers may however need to ponder whether there may be truth to the view of some of these Reformers and of America's first Christians that the Scriptures do in fact point to a latter day light from the church. Third, secularists should not be credited with forging the notion of progress that in fact developed out of biblical prophecy. Fourth, the shift of the Enlightenment from a biblical to naturalistic basis was much driven by the desire of European colonialists to avoid the inconvenient biblical teaching that all mankind are of one race and must therefore be treated as potential Christian brothers and sisters. Most today would probably not suppose the racism accompanying the Enlightenment's move from a biblical to a philosophical basis to be progress towards a more enlightened age.

The Enlightenment's shift away from the Bible started in England in the wake of the Puritan Revolution and was inspired by the progress in understanding Creation – now known as the scientific revolution – that the Puritans expected to accompany the imminent advent of the Millennium.[22] Impressed by these accomplishments, many were coming to believe that social progress could be better accomplished through philosophical advances than by religious means. Convinced that truth should be established by reason alone, they came to see the Bible, in the words of Isaac Newton, as a text "written for the vulgar who were incapable of a nice philosophical understanding." Following this shift in meaning, the keynote of the Enlightenment came to be its fierce opposition to a literal understanding of the Bible.

The Enlightenment thinkers were opposed neither to God nor to his revelation, but whether as a matter of practice or principle, they were more impressed with his general revelation found in Creation than the special revelation given in the Scriptures. Voltaire, the Enlightenment's most radical thinker, possessed a reverent piety for the Creator and was frightened by the thought that men would throw off moral constraints and respect for authority due to the very doubts about the Bible he himself was raising. Had he lived to experience it, the French Revolution would have confirmed his fears.

The Scriptures do teach a revelation of God in Creation that has always been available apart from the Scriptures.[23] The Bible further declares that because men have turned from acknowledging God their hearts and minds are darkened. The Apostles proclaimed the need for repentance and for the special revelation of Jesus to restore the light of God to man. The gospel preached by the Apostles and the Early Church to those formerly in pagan darkness was then understood as a new age of enlightenment. But whether from unconscious practice or conscious principle, those bringing the message of the modern Enlightenment repudiated the biblical teaching about the profound effects of sin, affirming instead the rationalist view that sin, whatever that might be, is caused by a lack of understanding. Their opinion, popular to this day, is that the solution to mankind's problems lies in his education (enlightenment).

The Bible disagrees with Socrates and the modern Enlightenment that we sin because we are in darkness. Rather, the Scriptures declare that we are in darkness because we sin. Sin stems from not trusting the Word of God, and darkness comes from embracing that which is not true. Above all books, the Bible assigns the highest importance to righteousness and declares the deepest concern for sin. The Scriptures depict the light of God more as righteousness than as cogni-

---

[22] Chapter 4, p 31
[22] Psalm 19:1; Romans 1:20

Chapter 5 The Enlightenment's rejection of biblical history

tion. According to the Bible, repentance and meekly accepting God's Word is the first step and the only way to man's true enlightenment.

The Enlightenment's deflection of the issue of sin and its high regard for human reason were both rooted in opinions from the earliest period of the "Age of Faith" and from the very beginning of the back-to-the-Bible Reformation. It is important in this regard to note that the Reformers were Augustinians. Though they replaced Augustine's teaching that salvation is to be obtained through the sacraments with the declaration that it comes by faith alone, the Reformers embraced his teaching that sin belongs to the cosmic condition of man more than to one's own sinning. The Enlightenment's high regard for reason was also true of Augustine's intellectualist view of the faith. It was present from the beginning of the Reformation – at Martin Luther's trial for heresy when he famously declared that he would recant "only if convinced by Scripture or by reason." Luther's appeal to reason concerned an internal witness possessed by all believers. Trained as humanists, professors, and lawyers, the Reformers tended to identify the Holy Spirit with reason.

Catholics challenged Luther's assertion of the sufficiency of Scripture by pointing to the fact that Protestants could not agree about all that the Bible taught. Taking a cue from the influential humanist Desiderius Erasmus (1466-1536) they also challenged Luther's confidence in reason. Luther was a schoolman, but Erasmus was a humanist. The humanists despised the schoolmen's preference of theology, philosophy, and endless logical disputation above letters and languages.[24] Though he had enthusiastically supported Luther's appeal to the Scriptures, Erasmus was skeptical of Luther's arguments against freewill and he was unsure of his own defense of the same. He opined that such matters are best left to the wisdom and decisions of the ancient Catholic Church.

Radical skepticism is not infrequently a weapon used by conservatives to combat good arguments against the status quo. Mounting an aggressive assault against reason, Catholic partisans revived ancient arguments for skepticism from newly translated writings of the pagan skeptic Sextus Epiricus (160-210) and the agnostic Pyrrho (360-270BC). The Catholic authorities were inclined to wink at speculations that were implicitly skeptical of the Bible from good Catholics such as Michael Montaigne (1533-1592) because it made the authority of the Church the essential grounding of faith.

Though never denying the authority of the Bible, Catholic faith in practice is defined by rules of faith, traditions arising over the long history of the church. They taught that the Bible was itself a product of the Church and only the Church could interpret it. The founder of the Jesuit order, Ignatius of Loyola,

---

[24] The humanists used the term *dunce* to refer to the fine logic used by the school of Duns Scotus. These schoolmen did not sit facing a corner, but they did wear tall pointed caps.

Part III   The Roots of Modern Historiography

      Martin Luther (1483-1586)　　　　　　　　Ignatious Loyola (1491-1556)

Figure 5   Leaders of the Protestant and Catholic Reformations

made this point in the most radical way: "If the Pope declares white to be black and black to be white, both are to be believed regardless of what one's own eyes might see." Such blind faith in the Catholic Church is called *fideism*. Aside from pious dissidents like Blaise Pascal (1623-1622), Catholic fideists tended to be indifferent to skeptical arguments against the Bible so long as they did not challenge Catholic authority over matters of faith. This attitude helped create the climate of skepticism toward the Bible that would come to be associated with the Enlightenment.[25]

From the late Middle Ages, there had been a distancing and then a *de facto* independence of learning from faith as Christianity's finest thinkers, fearing censure, avoided entangling their studies with the teachings of the Church. This produced the increasing focus on man and study of the visible order of the world independently of and sometimes in conflict with the Scriptures that we currently identify with the Renaissance. Legal proscriptions against secular studies hardly protected the faith because as the prestige of secular learning in-

---

[25] cf Richard H. Popkin, *A History of Skepticism from Erasmus to Spinoza* (University of California Press, 1979).

creased, officials of the Church gradually incorporated secular learning (such as Aristotle's science and biblical criticism) into the Church's teachings.[26]

The Reformation occurred at a time ripe for skepticism as Crusaders and merchants were bringing writings of the infidel Turks and Sepharadi Jews into Europe and as scholars were acquainting Western Christians with literature of the ancient pagans never before translated into Latin, Europe's language of learning. The most popular works concerned the practical sciences: astronomy, algebra, chemistry, and medicine. Some were enshrouded in the mystical speculations and philosophical rationalizations of Muslims and Jews. Others were mixed with astrology, alchemy, and magic. Because the Scriptures condemn the dark arts, Western Christianity had long banned or ignored them. The "knowledge is power" maxim put forth by Francis Bacon (1561-1626) had special meaning in the light of the seductive power claimed for these arts. Separated from a learned understanding of the Scriptures by their increasing secularization, the practical arts gave forbidden knowledge a foothold in Western Christianity.

The Copernican Revolution, which closely followed the Reformation, brought with it the notion that there might be other planets like the earth and other stars like the sun. This led to speculation about peoples or worlds that might not be known from the Bible. Adding to the perplexities, explorers and merchants were acquainting Europeans with the non-Christian civilizations of Africa and Asia and with previously unknown peoples of the New World and the Pacific. Some wondered how all these isolated and distant peoples could have descended from Noah's family.

Answers Isaac La Peyrere (1596-1676) gave to this question launched a revisionist history of the text and composition of the Bible. Coming from a wealthy New Christian[27] family, La Peyrere appeared to have been acquainted with rabbinic apologetics that viewed Christians as heathens rather than as God's true Israel. Following the rabbis, he supposed the Old Testament to be a Rabbinic rather than Christian book and interpreted the Old Testament according to the Zionism of the *Judaica exposito* developed by medieval rabbis. He believed these Jews would see Jesus as their still-to-come messiah if restored to their ancient homeland by the messiah's regent, the present king of France. Aiming

---

[26] As soon as they became established, Europe's Protestant churches developed their own form of fideism. Neither for them would faith mean fidelity to the Scriptures alone, but allegiance to their confessions and creeds. By separating faith from the search for truth and both from the plain words of the Bible, fideism enforced by religious censorship only spurred the rejection of biblical faith in all the European nations both within and outside their official churches. Ironically, as a substitute for biblical faith, fideism became a common means of weaning Europeans and mainline Christians away from the Bible and to accepting the authority of modern science.

[27] 'New Christian' was the name given to recent converts from Judaism.

to synthesize the religion of his ancestors with his Calvinist faith, he challenged the Christological understanding of the Zionist prophecies that Christians had believed since the days of the Apostles. La Peyrere managed to escape prosecution by converting to Roman Catholicism, blaming his errors on his Calvinist training. His excuse was not without merit. Reformed theologians were also learning from rabbinical teachers of Hebrew how to interpret the Scriptures in a way that would profoundly determine the modern understanding of the Bible – from secular skeptics to Protestant Fundamentalists.

Most infamously, La Peyrere taught that since the Bible gave only the history of the Jews, Gentiles had to be descended from men who lived before Adam. He denied their common ancestry in Noah's family by claiming that Adam and Noah were Jews and the Flood an event limited to the land of Israel. This began the modern way of seeing the Flood as limited to one locality. To explain why numerous Scriptures conflicted with his teachings, La Peyrere suggested an answer from Islamic and Jewish apologetics: the text of the Christian Bible had been corrupted. He believed this was also true of the Hebrew text. Taking up his dim view of the Scriptures, the English royalist Thomas Hobbes (1588-1679), the excommunicated Jew Benedict Spinoza (1632-1677), and the Catholic scholar Richard Simon (1638-1712) began the modern criticism of the Bible.

Protestants responded to Catholic skepticism by ever more championing the Bible and reason against Catholic apostasy and superstition. Increasingly, Protestant 'reason' came to mean the characteristic Reformed way of understanding the Scriptures as the preordained laws and decrees by which God governs his Creation. By 'superstition' they meant the spiritual powers claimed by the Catholics. They denied that Catholics had the power to admit or to refuse admittance to Heaven. Such powers were unnecessary since, according to the doctrine of Predestination, those who will be saved or lost had been decided from the foundation of the earth.

In the hands of Reformed Protestants, Predestination developed into the broad doctrine of *Providence*, more similar to Stoic fatalism than to a God who provides for his free creatures, but judges what they do.[28] According to the Calvinists, not only had God established firm laws through his General Providence for making the world hospitable for mankind, he long ago determined all that will ever happen. Calvin explained miracles as instances of God's Special Providence. Following Philo and Augustine, he envisioned the Lord God of Genesis more in line with the fully transcendent God of the philosophers. Like them, he disparaged literalists who accepted at face the "anthropomorphic" depictions

---

[28] The Stoic doctrine of *Providence* was also an important religious teaching among the pagan Romans of late antiquity.

of the Lord God in the Scriptures. For Calvin, God's sovereignty required that he determine all the actions and choices of his creatures.

Though intended to assert the sovereignty of God against Catholic claims, the doctrine of Providence undermined biblical faith in subtle ways. The doctrine of General Providence encouraged Protestants to champion natural philosophy against the darkness of Catholic and pagan superstitions. Insisting that the Scriptures be read in the light of scientific theory is but a development of the notion that the words of the Bible must be read in the light of theology. Early scientists were theologians. Their theology gradually transformed into modern science.

The Reformed doctrine of Providence helpfully informed the mechanical understanding of the world which Isaac Newton (1643-1727) put forth in his mathematical and physical principles of natural philosophy. This great transitional thinker between the biblical and Enlightenment views understood a Creator God to be responsible for whatever happens – including ongoing history as foretold in the prophecies of Daniel and Revelation. Newton saw the Bible as coding the specific events of history much as the physical laws he discovered governed the motion of matter. Building on the interpretations of Joseph Mede but following La Peyrere, Newton understood the biblical prophesies as requiring that Jews be restored to the ancient land of Israel where they would rebuild Solomon's Temple. He invented the popular biblical prophecy that dominates today – the kind of Zionism embraced by many evangelicals, which revises its predictions to accord with the latest current events. Newton understood prophecy the same as he did his physics: an empirical science in need of verification.

Newton's uncompromising defense of a Creator, his writings on biblical prophecy, his fervent anti-Catholicism, and his scientific accomplishments that banished the magic, astrology, and sorcery found among the pagans, Jews, and apostate Catholics caused many to see the great scientist as the unsurpassed champion of the Bible and the Protestant faith. His orthodox fans were unaware of or chose not to believe rumors that Newton secretly taught and wrote things detrimental to the Bible and Christian faith. Newton was much influenced by the rationalist interpretation of the Scriptures of Rabbi Moses Maimonides. He used the Trinitarian gloss found in the Latin copies of the first epistle of John[29] not only as an excuse for taking up La Peyerre's skepticism concerning the Bible's present text but also to deny the divinity of Jesus. He was far more influential than La Peyrere, Hobbes, and Spinoza in convincing men that the Bible had long been subject to Jewish and Catholic corruptions.

Newton was the great champion of a philosophical religion that saw Christianity less in the exceptionalist terms of sacred Scriptures than as the highest and

---

[29] Also found in 1 John 5:7 in the text of the King James Bible.

best version of ancient truth taught, however vaguely, in heathen records and myths. The Renaissance scholar Ficino (1433-1499) had translated the magical *Hermitica* writings that glorified the wisdom of ancient Egypt. By Newton's time, many were coming to believe that the ancients possessed superior wisdom. These Gnostic-inspired *Hermitica* may have influenced Newton, himself an assiduous student of the magical arts. If so, it is an interesting connection between ancient Gnosticism and the modern Enlightenment. Both rejected the Scriptures for philosophical truth that could only be comprehended by a spiritual or intellectual elite.

New acquaintance with the peoples of Asia influenced scholars to challenge the biblical chronology. They pointed to the great antiquity claimed by the Chinese and Hindus. The myth that the *Hermitica* originated in a far more ancient Egypt led most skeptics to guess Egypt as the oldest civilization. In his published *Chronology of the Ancient Nations,* Newton maintained the general course of ancient history found in the Bible. Secretly, he favored the ancient Egyptians as owning the most excellent wisdom, believing them to have understood the mathematical principles of natural philosophy that he had only rediscovered. He reckoned Noah to have passed this knowledge to his grandson Egypt, and believed that the Egyptians taught Moses the Genesis account of Creation. Newton's views as revealed in the recent publication of his private writings resemble the secrets of the ancient rites of Freemasonry far too much for the genius of Newton not to have been their source. Sharing Newton's proclivity to secrecy and gaining membership from politicians and scholars of the highest rank, the movement more than rivaled the influence of their enemies, the Jesuit Confessors. Empowered by its opposition to Catholicism and shielded by its infamous secrecy, Freemasonry spread the notion of an enlightened elite throughout Europe and America.

More than anything marking the transition from pre-modern to modern thought is the rejection of unseen spirits, whether of divine or demonic source, supposed able to influence the present world. The Cambridge Platonists, Henry Moore (1614-1687) and Ralph Cudworth (1617-1688), lamented that nothing undermines belief in the Bible so much as ceasing to believe in spirits. Doing so meant seeing the Bible as filled with, if not the product of the superstitious beliefs of a primitive age. These benighted "pre-moderns" included Newton's most learned contemporaries. Robert Boyle (1627-1691), father of modern chemistry and influential advocate of the New Science of mechanics, defended the existence of the spiritual world by empirical evidence he put forth in his scientific lectures before the Royal Society. Another Fellow, the influential Latitudinarian and champion of religious toleration, Sir Joseph Glanville (1636-1680) advocated deciding by the evidence, strongly witnessing to the supernatural including the preternatural powers of witches. Cotton Mather (1663-1728) referred to these scientific publications in his defense of the Salem witch trials.

Again, the Calvinist teaching of Providence prepared the way for the rejection of spirits. In a world completely understood in terms of general laws and immutable decrees there is no room for any kind of free will, independently acting agent, or spirit. Rene Descartes (1596-1650) had shown how to explain the world by the principles of mechanics, making the soul more passive observer than actor. According to Spinoza's monism, the soul was an unnecessary proposition. Newton's contribution was not so much his science as his reduction of what the pre-modern world understood as supernatural or spiritual agency to ordinary mental activities and physical causes.

Isaac Newton developed the modern way of explaining away the spiritual world by rationalizing passages in the Bible. The Devil that tempted Eve was but her own fleshly lust. The angels depicted in Scripture were but human messengers. Demon possession is insanity of various types. Witchcraft is only the conjuring of substances.[30] The spiritual entities described in the books of Daniel and Revelation are symbols for historical kingdoms and flesh-and-blood humans, and the spiritual activities in these books are historical events. Newton interpreted the locusts from the Abyss in the seventh chapter of Revelation as the coming of Mohammed's armies. The angels blowing the trumpets to pronounce God's judgment were great Protestant theologians. Instead of seeing spiritual powers influencing earthly events, Newton supposed these events to be influenced by the prophecies in the Bible. These prophecies, which did not so much foretell as determine what they foretold, functioned much as the laws he had discovered that governed the motion of matter. Newton had the spiritual experiences of man including those of the prophets of the Bible existing solely within the mind. Also reducing spiritual experiences to ordinary mental processes, Newton's fellow millenarian David Hartley (1705-1757) founded scientific psychology. Modern psychology and psychiatry share the intellectual roots of popular biblical prophecy. Popular biblical prophecy is indeed a product of the Enlightenment.

The historian Edward Gibbon (1737-1794) was cynical of Christianity, but found it difficult to disbelieve so many well-attested miracles. By contrast, Newton was uncompromising in his rejection of the phenomena and powers of the spiritual world recorded in the Scriptures, witnessed by the natives of all nations, and until modern times taken for granted by Christians. He was singularly responsible for persuading moderns to systematically reject testimony and arguments for the existence of spirits, angels, demons, and witches, anything supernatural or miraculous – even the spiritual nature of the human soul. New-

---

[30] Newton's unpublished papers reveal his extraordinary interest in alchemy.

ton's Epicurean view of the soul denied consciousness in the afterlife, at least until some distant resurrection of the body. Luther had emptied Purgatory, but Newton emptied Heaven. He banished from scientific understanding and serious modern discourse not only unpleasant demons and witches, but also angels and saints in Heaven. He led moderns to attribute evidence of supernatural or preternatural powers to superstition, hysteria, fraud, or pre-scientific beliefs. Systematically rejecting whatever evidence does not accord with their materialist dogma, they would hereafter proclaim that no evidence for miracles and spirits exists.

Newton's great reputation among Protestants led to the banishment of spirits even from their theological explanations. Not only were the Reformers skeptical of the spiritual claims of the Catholics, but increasingly Protestant theologians limited encounters with God, the healing of the sick, and all manner of miracles to the times of the Bible. Protestants would change from claiming that Catholic miracles were owing to preternatural sources such as the Devil to denying that they even occurred. The disenchanted world now blamed on modern science in fact stems from Protestant theology, but these Protestant theologians were building on the views of earlier Christian theologians.

Pagans had accused the earliest Christians of atheism for denying the gods, a charge previously leveled against their rationalist and skeptical philosophers. Defending their rejection of the pagan gods, Christians pointed to the Roman historian Plutarch's account of an incident that occurred during the reign of Tiberius Caesar: "On his way to Italy by way of the island of Paxi, a sailor named Thamus heard a great voice upon the waters calling him by name and telling him upon reaching shore to proclaim to all, 'The great Pan is dead!' This Thamus duly obeyed, terrifying all who heard him." Those Christians desiring a more philosophical faith contended that upon the death of Christ, the pagan oracles fell silent.[31]

While new acquaintance with pagans and infidels resulting from the Crusades generated a revival of interest in spirits and spiritual phenomena during the Renaissance, Protestant theologians holding an even more transcendent view of God would come to believe the Lord himself was muted at the death of the Apostles. If the Reformers had viewed "enthusiasts" who claimed to hear from God as dangerously deceived, Protestant theologians began regarding all post-biblical experiences of God as likely products of confused or unenlightened imaginations. Though aimed at Catholics, contemporary prophets, and Protestant revivalists, the skeptic David Hume (1711-1776) would turn the

---

[31] This argument was important in disputes over the revival of images: the demonic spirits now banished or defeated, images could be safely revived as Christian art.

same arguments against the miracles, revelations, prophecies, and divine encounters of the Bible.[32]

With a long Augustinian tradition behind them, Calvinists believed that in denying the existence of the spirits they were only better explaining the Scriptures. Few understand the consequences hidden in their well-intended theology. The doctrine that history had been fully determined from the beginning leads not only to Newton's physics, but also to Deism. If Calvin allowed that some Scriptures should not be literally believed, Newton regarded them as a vulgar account of what was better explained by his physics. He showed orthodox theologians of the Protestant Enlightenment how to explain the Bible's miracles to accord with a rationalist understanding, without denying the Bible's general account of the past. But if Protestant theologians of the Enlightenment believed Scripture and reason complementary, the Deists declared that reason alone should discover the natural truths of religion. They despised the Bible because they acknowledged its clear witness to miraculous powers that contradict Nature's laws.

Newton's reputation as defender and champion of the faith not only licensed his probabilistic estimate of the Bible's account of history but also his relativistic view of Christianity. Newton discovered in rabbinic anti-Christian apologetics the modernist way of understanding the Scriptures. Until modern scholars began to question the Bible's version of history, the modernist view of the Old Testament belonging to Newton and the Enlightenment hardly differed from the view of Jewish rabbis from whom they borrowed it. Likewise, they borrowed from the rabbis a ready-made skeptical view of the New Testament.[33] Though Newton saw the Bible interpreted along the lines of rationalist Judaism as the highest and best source of ancient wisdom, by relegating the Holy Bible to profane history he breached its sacred demarcation, leading to its relativization. Following Newton, liberal Christians would demand that the Bible be studied as if it were but another book.

The excessive rationalism of the Enlightenment led to seeing religion as something natural rather than as resulting from the supernatural and imparted by special revelation. Their naturalistic outlook caused members of the worldly establishment to envision the Christian religion along the pattern of the official religions of pagan Greece and Rome. They admired the pagan Cicero (106-43BC) who defended a civilized form of religion – on the one hand, against the materialists and skeptics, and on the other hand, against superstition – that

---

[32] cf Robert Bruce Mullin, *Miracles and the Modern Religious Imagination* (Yale University Press, 1996).

[33] cf Richard H. Popkin, *Disputing Christianity: The 400-Year-Old Debate over Rabbi Isaac Ben Abraham of Troki's Classic Arguments* (Humanity Books, 2007).

is, religion which they could not or did not control. Like Cicero, they believed religion to be important for keeping order among the masses even if the ruling classes no longer believed its myths. Popular during the Enlightenment were the views of the classical pagans that nothing is new in human history, challenging the exceptional history in the Bible. For these ancient authors, history is useful only for teaching lessons about the vanity of unchanging human nature. Enlightenment historians David Hume and Edward Gibbon wrote history the same way. The pagans they so admired persuaded them to see the eternal truths of philosophy as superior to the contingent truths of history. While Augustine, Aquinas, Calvin, and Newton had tried to accommodate the Scriptures to their theological philosophies, the Deists sought to extract philosophy and natural religion from its biblical dress.

As the Age of Reason advanced, Protestants and Catholics associated with the secular courts of Europe turned from a historical and biblical to a philosophical and earthly understanding of man. Creation was increasingly seen as eternalist Nature. They found a philosophical answer to human origins by seeing the varieties of mankind as different kinds of creatures eternally proceeding from a Great Chain of Being. This Great Chain of Being developed from the hierarchical world of Aquinas, but the seventeenth century rationalist philosophers extracted it from the biblical clothing in which medieval theologians had wrapped it. The Enlightenment version was chiefly a hierarchy of various organisms and forms found in visible Nature.[34] It had no more place for history than did the great hierarchy of the medieval Neo-Platonists.

The new scientific discoveries, on the other hand, were seen as a powerful argument for the existence of a Creator of great intelligence. Newton taught them to call him the Supreme Creator so as to distinguish him from Jesus. The timeless Great Chain of Being allowed Deists to distinguish the Supreme Creator from history-creating Jehovah. As biblical theology declined, *physico-theology*[35] based on the revelation of God in Creation replaced it. Growing confidence in the perfection of Nature and its complete governance by divine law caused Deists to reject and Enlightenment-era Christians to overlook the Bible's teachings about the effects of sin: man's alienation from God, the existence of evil spirits, and the struggle of saints as pilgrims in a fallen world. This set the stage for Darwin to argue the imperfections of Nature and the existence of natural evil as evidence of the Creator's complete absence from earthly processes.

Neither the theory nor the fashionable passion for evolution began with Darwin. The modern view of evolution developed from a shifting of the gradations in the hierarchy of the Great Chain of Being from a philosophical to a temporal

---

[34] cf A. O. Lovejoy, *The Great Chain of Being* (Harvard University Press, 1936).

[35] *Physico-theology* was an Enlightenment version of Intelligent Design.

Chapter 5   The Enlightenment's rejection of biblical history

basis.[36] That began with Descartes' speculations about the origin of the earth entirely through mechanical processes. More important was Gottfried Leibniz's (1646-1716) rejection of Newton's interpretation of history in terms of Special Providence, something that allowed Newton to see the Bible as encoding God's special design of the solar system and plan for history. Supposing that God must always have a sufficient philosophical reason for whatever he does, Leibniz saw history as the unfolding of a plan by which God aimed to create the best of all possible worlds. From this developed the view that the special revelation found in the Bible could be understood as the evolutionary development of morality, ever more improving as civilization advances. In Chapter 10, I will explain how the geological and biological details of the temporal shift in the Great Chain of Being arose from studying the earth in the light of the Bible. The Great Chain of Being thus served as a non-historical philosophical interlude between history based on the Bible and modern naturalistic history based on evolution.

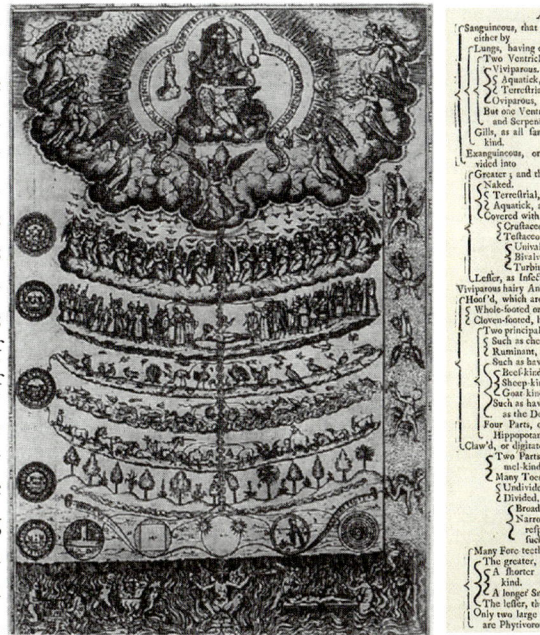

Figure 6   The Enlightenment's Great Chain of Being

Despising the great separation of man from the animals and the specialness of man that characterizes the "anthropomorphic" God of the Bible, the Enlightenment saw man more as a product of mother Nature than as a child of the distant and uninvolved Supreme Creator. Instead of specialness and separateness, in accordance with Leibniz's principle of plenitude they looked for continuity of man with the rest of Nature. Discoveries of the vastness of the heavens, of fossils from the deep abyss of time, and of new species of manlike apes pushed man's position in the Chain of Being even lower. The Scottish Primitivist, Lord

---

[36] Ibid., Chapter IX.

Monboddo (1714-1799), believed that humans were born with tails that midwives discreetly removed before showing the babies.

Enlightenment philosophers understood some kinds of men to be lower in the order of Nature than others. Their new science of anthropology imagined a progression of the varieties of mankind according to their innate abilities and character. These ranged from primitive savages to civilized Europeans. Northern Europeans knew that until the coming of Christianity their barbarian ancestors were less advanced than the great civilizations of the ancient Orient, but they saw those belonging to the older civilizations as having already reached their pinnacle of development. Regarding Oriental civilizations as more connected to the world of the Bible, they preferred seeing them as exotic and distant from the civilization of enlightened Europe, an attitude persisting into the twentieth century.[37] Identifying more with the pagan Greeks and Romans, the men of the Enlightenment began regarding the Bible as the product of strange orientals and superstitious barbarians.

Their attitude to the Bible was the opposite of what arose in the Protestant Reformation. This time Europeans were seeking to be liberated less from a corrupt and apostate church, than from the Bible itself, now coming to seem an inconvenient guide. Not surprisingly, the new philosophical and scientific laws accorded with the economic interests of Europe's establishment, not only the *ancien regime,* but even more the new class of planters, merchants, and bankers. Beginning with the Commercial Revolution, Europe's establishment, together with their colonialists, aimed to extract maximum wealth from overseas colonies and trading missions. These governments sponsored or chartered enterprises to pirate the silver and gold of American natives and to exploit mines and plantations worked by chattel slaves. To increase taxes and tariffs, these colonial governments promoted profitable trade in which trinkets, firearms, alcohol, tobacco, and opium were exchanged for slaves, ivory, fur, spices, silk, and china.

Those are not Christian aims or enterprises. They are not things Christians do to those in need of the light of the gospel. This explains why most of the merchants, plantation owners, and colonial governors did not like missionaries preaching to natives and slaves. They did not want the Bible or religion meddling in commerce, science, or government any more than they expected business, science, or the affairs of the state to dictate the terms of religion. Like many today, they wanted religion restricted to private belief or religious ceremony, which is just the way their established Christianity was developing. The slave owners preferred the established churches. As it became increasingly difficult to justify these overseas enterprises as bringing Christianity to the natives, Enlightenment thinkers shifted to justifying their activities as offering

---

[37] cf Edward W. Said, *Orientalism* (Penguin Books, 1978).

Chapter 5 The Enlightenment's rejection of biblical history

civilization to benighted peoples. Pagan Greeks and Romans used similar arguments to explain their exploitation of barbarians. Reason, as used to defend such practices, together with the manners of the European courts replaced the teachings of Christianity as the new ideals of the Enlightenment.

> **The Enlightenment solved the issues of Christian obligation by replacing the traditional Christian/heathen division of mankind with less troubling white/colored racial distinctions.**

The Bible's monogenesis teaching – the common origin of all mankind from a single family, and more recently from Noah's family – was a severe problem for those who wanted to see non-Europeans as innately different creatures. Even worse was the difficulty of selling a spiritual sibling in one's own Christian family. Not surprisingly, the Great Chain of Being envisioned polygenesis or separate origins for different races. The Enlightenment solved the issues of Christian obligation by replacing the traditional Christian/heathen division of mankind with less troubling white/colored racial distinctions. Selling members of a species specifically designed for slavery, whether by the Supreme Creator of Nature or through the natural processes of evolution, is a business decision.

Not all the men of the Enlightenment favored slavery. Some understood the practice to be degrading to European morals or the presence of slaves as endangering the purity of race. Such scruples notwithstanding, those who rejected the biblical vision of mankind were racist to the man. The more enlightened they were, the deeper their racism. Voltaire (1694-1778) thought Negroes more closely related to the orangutan. Thomas Jefferson introduced these enlightened ideas to the American South in the only book he published. *Notes on the State of Virginia* (1787) marked the beginning of Southern racist teachings. It is not anachronistic to judge the men of the Enlightenment on this matter, nor can we excuse them as a product of their age. They shifted to their racist anthropology as Quakers were taking the lead in abolishing the slave trade and as revivalist Christians were seeking to end various kinds of human exploitation. As missionaries and revivalists reached out to include natives and slaves in the family of God, scientific anthropology – essentially the invention of modern racism – became increasingly popular with the commercial classes. The colonial patrons of the Enlightenment were owners of slave plantations, wealthy merchants, colonial officials, or those who owed their livings to the same. Not only did the teaching of the Bible oppose their chauvinist culture, it threatened their economic interests. Enlightened "Christians" learned how to revise their interpretation of the Bible to accord with reason, but Deists wanted religion to be based on reason alone. Their "reason" was more that of the pagan Romans who despised Christianity as a religion of the weaker classes, women and slaves.

The scientific anthropologists saw racial differences and privileged social classes just as did the classical pagans: the proper order of Nature.

Africans, Asians, and the natives of the New World were not the only ones whom the men of the secular Enlightenment regarded as inferior, mysterious and strange. The Hebrew scholar J. D. Michaelis (1717-1791) applied Enlightenment notions to the Bible by supposing its message to be shrouded in an ancient and foreign culture and language. The message of God in the Bible would have to be extracted from its captivity to the customs of an ancient barbarian tribe. Under the direction of Michaelis, the King of Denmark sponsored an expedition to study the roots of the Bible among the tribes and geography of southern Arabia. Michaelis excluded missionaries from this international team because he did not want evangelistic activities interfering with the scientific study of exotic tribesmen and natives. These investigators wanted to study the natives in an objective, detached, and scientific fashion, creating or emphasizing distance and strangeness rather than closeness and familiarity (family) of the earth's people. The scientific findings of this adventure as published by Carsten Niebuhr (1733-1815) would deeply influence biblical studies.

So would the new scientific history of Rome written by Niebuhr's son, Barthold Georg Niebuhr (1776-1831), the first of the modern secular histories of the ancient nations. Young Niebuhr sought to discern the true history of Rome by discarding whatever traditions and myths were unacceptable to the latest scientific thinking. There is no doubt that the pagan histories were enshrouded in myth and that Niebuhr's insights into the development of ancient Rome are still to be highly regarded, but many supposed that the Bible had the same character and could and should be viewed in the same way.

— 6 —

Developing the modern historiography of ancient and world history

Accoording to the modern version of history, the origins of man are prehistorical. They can only be known by science, the new science of anthropology created by Prussia's Immanuel Kant (1724-1804). Modernists seem unfamiliar with Kant's contribution to anthropology, but they do credit him with defining the autonomous man of the Enlightenment and putting forth the critical principles by which scholars now study history and the Bible. Kant taught modernists to reject authority and replace their pre-critical beliefs with the truths established by reason alone. The professor dutifully submitted his teachings to the Prussian State, but for him rejecting authority and possessing an autonomous mind meant rejecting the "pre-critical" teachings of the Bible for the pure truths of philosophy.

The critical thinking of Kant's autonomous mind determined that the copper-colored savages of the cold, dry North American climate were the lowest of the human species. He based this on the "fact" that they were incapable of education or enlightenment. The nomadic Americans were inferior to the agrarian Negroes produced from the soil of warm, wet climates who could be trained for service by the split-bamboo cane. Kant explained the details of making this instrument inflict maximum pain. He learned from reading the enlightened David Hume that "Not one of them is talented in the arts, sciences, or anything praiseworthy." According to Hume and Kant, Negroes are natural slaves because "they lack manliness." As did the classical pagans they so admired, and as have brigands and gangs from all ages, the men of the Enlightenment much esteemed machismo. In their view, slights to a man's honor must be settled by the duel.

However objective he supposed it to be, Kant's science was not the empirical kind used to develop practical technology, nor did it advance by testing and correcting predictions. He agreed with Hume's radical skepticism of knowledge that comes from experience, but explained that the truths of pure reason are innate to certain minds. Though history's first professional philosopher never left his home in Eastern Prussia, he was assured of what he knew about those he had never met owing to *a priori* reason that belonged exclusively to the mind he shared with other blond members of cold, damp northern Europe. While white brunettes were marginally inferior, it was only necessary that European minds shed pre-critical beliefs. By the latter, Kant had in mind miracles, legends, and the many accounts in the Bible that did not accord with the principles of pure reason discovered by Isaac Newton.

Kant's contributions to modern thinking have been remembered more for his defense of freedom and equality and for how he allowed a place for moral truths that spring from within. Aside from his desire to be freed from traditional religious and political restrictions, none of these ideals belonged to the Enlightenment, nor were they the creation of professors and professional philosophers, especially those of the conservative Prussian State. The humanitarian ideals of equality and freedom are in fact rooted in the brotherhood of the family of God as taught by Jesus. Though suppressed by the ancient Roman class system that controlled Christendom in the Middle Ages, the Reformation revived these biblical ideals, giving rise to the priesthood of believers. The latter was actually practiced by some Anabaptists, Separatists, Quakers, and other dissenters willing to pay the price for religious freedom even if it meant persecution or the hardship of re-settling to the American wilderness. It was this kind of voluntarism that pioneered grassroots democracy and self-government in America.

These Christian sources of freedom and equality should not be confused with libertarian insistence on one's right to pursue his self interest without constraint by governing authority, ambitions that early Christians and early American Christians universally opposed. Libertarian ideals derive from the aristocratic Greeks who did not want to be constrained by Greek democracy: a demagogue appealing to ordinary citizens' resentment of the privileges and abuses of the aristocracy. These libertarian ideals did indeed motivate Kant and the men of the Enlightenment.

Both sources of freedom and democracy existed in early America, but in truth it is sin that keeps mankind in chains of darkness, and only the truth will set them free. Evangelists such as George Whitefield (1714-1770), who birthed the Great Awakening, opposed the cold rationalism, flowery moralizing, and unbelief stemming from the Enlightenment. Unlike the Reformers, the revivalists preached against personal sin, calling all to repentance. They also spoke against "the dangers of an unconverted ministry." But in contrast to the nationalist character of the churches of the Reformation, the Great Awakening was international. Reaching all classes and races, it was more egalitarian and inclusive than these cosmopolitan but elitist and racist men of the Enlightenment. Revivalist Christianity was responsible for the grass-roots character, the growing enfranchisement, and the widespread success of democracy in early America.

A generation before the Founding Fathers, the fires of the Great Awakening melted different ethnicities, languages, and separate and competing colonies and sects, each with their own governments and leaders, into a peaceful Christian nation, the Bible their founding document of this new nation. Disliking its leveling tendency, those opposing the Awakening tended to become Loyalists. The revivalists and Deists such as Benjamin Franklin and Thomas Jefferson who sympathized with their cause against the established churches were Patriots, almost to the man. The American War for Independence was fought not to win but to preserve this faith-rooted freedom. In Europe the American success was wrongly viewed in political and revolutionary terms. Following the American War for Independence, fervent hopes for political freedom and determined resistance to the inherited inequalities of Europe's Old Order swept through Europe, inspiring the French Revolution. Instead of peace, these ideals of freedom and equality sought through revolution and political change only created violence within and wars between the nations of Europe, continuing until the sponsored democracies of the twentieth century pax Americana.

Also looking to the Bible and to the inward response of the heart rather than to outward profession, Continental Pietists were in many ways of similar spirit to the British and American revivalists. By focusing on the Bible rather than the theology of the Protestant Confessions, Pietists were better able to bridge the sectarian divide between Reformed Prussians, Orthodox Lutherans, and Roman Catholics. The nominally Reformed Prussian despots saw the Pietists as less divisive and more pliable to their aims of training their subjects in the ways of a non-sectarian secular Enlightenment. They sponsored Pietist universities to be used for educating their subjects. If less egalitarian than the Americans and more willing to submit to the established orders, the Pietists were cosmopolitan in their missions. They also taught Kant, the son of a Pietist mother, to give attention to the heart.

However much some may wish to separate his racism from his philosophy, Kant saw philosophy as an aspect of anthropology, something inherent to the minds of men. As a man of the Enlightenment, he did not see the need for extending human rights beyond an enlightened elite. Though elitist and racist, the Enlightenment aimed to be cosmopolitan, and its ideals did spread beyond national and ethnic boundaries and into the European colonies. The owners of small slave plantations and privileged mulatto slaves in the French colony of Saint Dominque (Haiti) embraced them.

Part III   The Roots of Modern Historiography

The Romantic movement, beginning in France and spreading to Germany, recoiled from the cosmopolitan and philosophical Enlightenment. Jean-Jacques Rousseau (1712-1778), father of the new movement, could not find in France's enlightened civilization the kind of happiness he knew as a young man in the household of his pious and kindly patroness. It seemed to him that France was losing the better life enjoyed by peasants who were still clinging to their instinctive ways and feelings. Like Rousseau, Kant believed that religious and moral truths spring from within. But Kant claimed that in order to become a basis for moral actions, these truths, regardless of their source, had first to be justified by reason. He separated the truths of *practical reason* that inform morals and religion from the truths of *pure reason* that pertain to science. However universal either of these kinds of truths might be for cosmopolitan Europeans, Kant saw them neither in the manner of revivalist missionaries, as being like the Holy Spirit which could be possessed by all who believe, nor in the manner of Quakers, as an inner light possessed by all mankind. Kant was a racist of climate-and-geography stripe.

The violence unleashed by the French Revolution caused Europeans everywhere to recoil from the new Age of Reason and look back to the stability of the older Age of Faith. But concerned that the *ancien regime* would unite Europe's armies to take away their new liberties, the French solidified their identity as a nation directed by the will of its people. Opposing the cosmopolitanism of the Enlightenment and the *ancien regime* with a newly discovered nationalism, the Romantics shifted from philosophy to imagined history, and from the universal principles of philosophy to national and ethnic specifics. This only shifted the racism and elitism of the Enlightenment into national and ethnic boundaries. This shift in understanding the science of man occurred between Kant and one of his students J. G. Herder (1744-1803), cofounder with him of anthropology.

The Pietist focus on the Bible created a need for the study of languages. Unlike philosophically inclined Kant, Herder appreciated the Pietist trait of placing philology and language above theology and philosophy. Herder and the notable poet of the German Enlightenment Johann Wolfgang von Goethe (1749-1832), came under the influence of the *Sturm und Drang* of their mutual friend, the Neo-Pietist, J. G. Hamann (1730-1788). These Neo-Pietists failed to try the spirits to see whether they be from God.[38] As did Rousseau and Hamann, Herder favored peasants and their ethnic traditions and languages, which were scorned by the cosmopolitan Enlightenment. He agreed with Kant that the character of a people is determined by the climate and geography of their homeland, but he defined nations by language and by the culture that belongs to each language. Following Herder, German scholars would rewrite

---

[38] 1John 4:1

the history of mankind and nations as the spread of languages. To this day, the historiography of the world, especially of ancient times, broadly follows their revisionist histories.

Culture was formerly an agricultural term. The modern idea of 'high culture' or 'becoming cultured' comes from Herder's application of the term to humans: the special soil where a particular species of the man plant is grown determines the culture expressed through one's language. Herder also invented the idea of *volk* or folk: people sharing a common language, culture, and homeland. Herder's was a collectivist vision in which individuals obtain their identity from their nation. Not only did he redefine nations as all who speak the same language, but according to him, one's language determines the very thoughts he is capable of thinking. These special thoughts could not be translated into another language. While his teacher Kant saw minds as immutably fixed to the color of one's skin, Herder understood human souls as forever divided by tongue, which includes the culture found in the oral and written literature belonging to their language.

According to Herder, it is impossible to understand the thoughts and intentions of those of a foreign language and culture. That would include the languages and the people of the Bible. While J.D. Michaelis had seen the Hebrew Scriptures as addressing the issues and concerns of their authors' times and their truths needing to be extracted from the primitive language and culture in which they were enveloped, Herder declared this program impossible. This meant that nations needed to seek their religious and spiritual truths in pagan ancestors who spoke their language. The spiritual truths that the Enlightenment denied of the teachings of the Bible Herder affirmed as existing in pagan darkness. His teachings would lead to Hitler's neo-paganism and eventually to multicultural pluralism.

Trained in Germany, the modern critics of the Bible turned Herder's linguistic theory into the dictum of distance that *historicizes* the Scriptures by supposing that the God of the Bible is unable to speak through other tongues. Herder even refused to acknowledge, as supposed by the Enlightenment's Michaelis, that universal and timeless truths could be extracted from these ancient oracles. But whether following the Enlightenment or Herder, modern scholars would deny that the ancient Scriptures of the Jews could possibly speak truth to modern man.

Though Herder rejected the possibility of understanding foreign peoples and cultures through language, he retained the Enlightenment view that they could be studied by means of *intuition*. That meant looking inside them, as looking through a window. Rather than communicating with peoples of other cultures and languages and trying to understand their thoughts, anthropologists must

Part III   The Roots of Modern Historiography

| Imannuel Kant | The Brothers Grimm | J. G. Herder |

FIGURE 7   FOUNDERS OF ANTHROPOLOGY AND FOLK HISTORY

study them with scientific "objectivity." Whatever they might grunt or babble or whatever their eyes might plead is a matter for detached scientific study. Here is the logic of Carsten Niebuhr's expedition to the tribes of Arabia and the rationality of Hitler's scientists.

At the beginning of the nineteenth century, Central Europe remained a rural and undeveloped land of hundreds of small states. Government professionals and ambitious businessmen in these states wanted to see them united to form a large commonwealth that could sponsor the same kind of Industrial Revolution then occurring in England and France. Standing in the way of these efforts to unite the German states were the princes, the hereditary heads of the small states. The princes did not want to lose power to a centralized government whether headed by Catholic Austria or by the growing power of Protestant Prussia. In any event, sectarian Christianity had lost its power to inspire political or military causes. The need for a large state became clearer when Napoleon invaded Central Europe. The great military genius had just lost France's Western Empire due to his defeat by black Haitian slaves, the first successful slave revolt in history. Napoleon avenged his loss by humiliating the famous Prussian Army in the battles of a single day. The terrors unleashed by the French Revolution had marked the end of the Enlightenment in England, but Napoleon's invasion of Central Europe marked its end in Prussia and Austria.

Still faithful to the cosmopolitan principle of the Enlightenment, Herder had made no special case for the superiority of German or any other language. But during Napoleon's occupation of Central Europe, another of Kant's disciples, J.G. Fichte, (1762-1814) electrified German-speaking people by advocating the formation of a new nation based on the German language. According to Fichte, being German was the same as having character and nobility. He explained how this new nation must come about through the suffering German-speaking people projecting their superior moral will to become the "Savior" of the world. Fichte rejected the vestiges of objective truth stemming from Kant's external world (which Kant called the "thing in itself") for completely subjective "truths," identified as the feeling and will of the German people. According to Fichte, the will and spirit of the German people was the will of God. Before the end of the century, a new country defined by and named for the German language appeared in Central Europe.

No matter how radical Fichte's teachings now appear, following Rousseau, he merely shifted the Divine Will formerly expressed through the divine right of kings and the absolute despots of the Enlightenment to the collective will of the people. Many saw Fichte's rejection of an objective external God and truth as amounting to atheism, but deifying man is more than mere atheism. Atheists are not inclined to play God or to own the authority once attributed to him. Fichte's collective will manifested through the power of the State not only denies God and truth, it replaces them. Fichte's disciple Arthur Schopenhauer (1788-1860) generalized this philosophy of will and power into a frankly atheist philosophy. The latter's notable disciples included Richard Wagner (1813-1883) and Friedrich Nietzsche (1844-1900). If there is no God or objective truth, the government, the people, or the individual can choose to become God. Fichte's philosophy turns man into God and exhorts him to fulfill his destiny as superman or super race.

A Romantic invention, nationalism is rooted in historiography: what is widely taught and believed as history. The new nation of Germany needed a glorious history that could inspire a German nationalism, a history that could appeal to Orthodox Lutherans, Reformed Germans, Pietists, Roman Catholics, and the many who were no longer inspired by religion. Though these groups did not share the same translation of the Bible, Herder pointed to the debt that the German language and culture owed to Luther's Bible. He taught moderns to accept the Bible as culture rather than as sacred Scripture, and to see Luther more as a nationalist hero than as a religious Reformer.[39]

Unfortunately, the Bible had no specific mention of Germany aside from the obscure ancestor Gomer, son of Japheth, son of Noah. This slight mention of Germany in the Old Testament only made the Bible a problem for German nationalism, but neither was there history elsewhere in the German language to compete with the ancient and glorious national histories of England, France,

---

[39] For a more extensive study of the shift from seeing the Bible as revelation to seeing it as culture, see Jonathan Sheehan, *The Enlightenment: Bible Translation, Scholarship, Culture* (Princeton University Press, 2003).

Italy, or Greece. Linguists such as the Brothers Grimm (1785-1863, 1786-1859) sought to resolve the problem by discovering a German history in orally preserved folk tales. They culled Charles Perrault's (1628-1703) new genre of fairy tales for stories they believed might come from Germany's pagan past. Inspired by Rousseau, Romantic Germans saw their ancestors as innocent and noble peasants. They had no thought of regarding their ancestors as savages or, despite their romanticism, of regarding foreign savages as noble.

Other linguists sought an origin for the noble German race in Sir William Jones's discovery of Sanskrit's relation to the European languages. The romantic poet Friedrich Schlegel (1772-1829) supposed the ancestral religion of the Germans to originate among the Aryans or the nobles of India who spoke Sanskrit. German linguists turned Japheth's family into Aryans, or what some then called the Indo-German family of languages,[40] and would seek their origins in central Asia, northern Europe, or someplace other than the family of Noah.[41]

The feudal-rooted Great Chain of Being had divided men into three classes: the first estate consisting of the clergy, the second estate composed of the nobility, and the third estate that included everyone else. In the German states, professors worked for the state rather the Church. These professors regarded their leaders who fought wars as superior to the provincial churchmen to whom they gave orders. The Romantic Germans understood society's first order as warriors, the second as priests, and the third and lowest as serfs or slaves.[42] Their historians and philosophers determined that the ancient Aryan warriors of Asia were a nobler race than the supposedly priest-led Semitic races. Ignoring the Bible in favor of the opinions of the ancient Greeks, they re-envisioned the Jews of the Bible as one of "the minor peoples of the Levant," still the way they are reckoned in modern histories of the ancient world These Germans were aspiring to a world empire on the order of the ancient Assyrians, Greeks, or Romans. They refused to suppose that such glory ever belonged to the Jews who they despised.

Though emphasizing reason instead of feeling, the influential German philosopher G. W. F. Hegel (1770-1831) followed Fichte's path when he explained history as the development of the mind of God. God first expressed his will in

---

[40] After the defeat of the Nazis, scholars would revert to calling this family *Indo-European*.

[41] For an overview of these linguistic developments in Germany, see Tuska Barnes, *In Babel's Shadow; Language, Philology, and the Nation in Nineteenth-Century Germany* (Wayne State University Press, 2008).

[42] Meanwhile, those wanting to apply Noah's curse on Canaan to all the children of Ham found their views supported by the latest scholarship and science. Their linguistic logic identified the languages of Africa, presumed to be the Hamitic languages, as belonging to a race of slaves. Affluent Americans of the nineteenth century who obtained their education in Germany would incorporate these views into their science and theology, and teach them in America's most influential colleges and churches.

the hierarchical society and in the will of statist Asian kings who dominated and totally defined the lives of their people.[43] Hegel saw the divine mind developing to a second stage in which God expressed his thoughts through the aristocracies of the city-states of Greece and the Republic of Rome, where only a few men were free. Ultimately God would recognize himself in the Absolute, the free people governed by the modern German State. That meant that Hegel's own thoughts were the same as God's thoughts. Though with widely varying details, Hegel's historicism became the essential framework upon which the modern versions of ancient and world history would be taught.

The romantic nationalist histories of nineteenth century poets and philosophers created a reaction among historians who looked to the example of empirical science. The scientific school of history made famous by Leopold von Ranke (1795-1886) insisted on writing history from the records of government archives. That is indeed the way to give a more accurate account of things from the perspective of the powerful. This bias towards the records of institutional governments favored the accounts of the Ancient Near Eastern empires over histories of families and ordinary people as found in the Bible. Ranke's influential school served to legitimize the dialectical and poetic history that the professors of the German state would discover for the ancient world of the Bible.

In recent times, social histories that include the histories of ordinary people are challenging the notion that history should be the exclusive province of the powerful establishment. Unfortunately, few documents are available from the period covered by the Bible, and with that notable exception almost all that did survive were written from the perspective of the rich or powerful. As I delightedly discovered from my first reading, the Bible is concerned for ordinary people, for the powerless, for the poor, for the stranger, for orphans, and for widows.[44]

The modernist revision of ancient history originally inspired by the needs of German nationalism has been modified by more recent archaeological discoveries of the far older histories in the Ancient Near East. Nonetheless, the chauvinistic way that the Enlightenment and German Romantics looked down on the world of the Bible still colors the writing of ancient, biblical, and world history, only today mythical noble savages and pagans replace mythical noble German peasants.

---

[43] In truth, the ancient kings and emperors of the Orient were too occupied with their responsibilities, ambitions, and harems to be bothered by the ordinary concerns of their subjects. Hegel's anachronistic view of these ancient rulers was but his projection of the German princes and the absolute despots of Prussia who ruled over their subjects as fathers over children.

[44] cf Norbert Lohfink, "Poverty in the Laws of the Ancient Near East and the Bible," *Theological Studies* 52 (1991).

Despite these problems, Ranke's insistence on the use of sources has improved the writing of history where sources are available. History, more interesting because better understood, is being uncovered by those able to read the primary sources in their original languages. Without their work, I could not have not have uncovered what I have written about the history of ideas and values since the time of Christ. Unfortunately, such important work has not been applied to ancient and world histories. The subject of our origins and our history should be more interesting than the stale and muddled accounts being written today, updated only by trendy spins which reflect our own times more than they do the ancient world. A thick fog of human vanity has settled upon modern man's understanding of the past.

— 7 —

Revising biblical history

THE OLD TESTAMENT was a big problem for German nationalism. Though the German language and culture depended on Luther's Bible and on Christianity, the ancient history it contained conflicted with the new version of German and world history. German nationalism had to somehow sever the umbilical cord that attached Germans to the Bible. Friedrich Schleiermacher (1768-1834), father of liberal Christianity, took the first step by separating Christianity from the Old Testament. Using Kant's philosophy of practical reason, he redefined Christianity in terms of religious feeling. This was not so different from Fichte's teachings, which inspired German nationalism. Their Neo-Pietist and Romantic roots may have suggested to Schleiermacher and Fichte that what feels right must somehow be right. Regarding the Christian faith to be securely grounded in internal religious experience, Schleiermacher declared faith to be independent of the contingent truths of history. The Bible might now be studied by pure reason or science without harm to Christianity – even if it found the Bible to be full of historical errors and outmoded or immoral teachings. This is liberal Christianity.

Schleiermacher agreed with those whom he called "Christianity's cultural despisers" that the Old Testament belonged to an obsolete and foreign culture unworthy to be embraced by modern Germans. Just as did the ancient Gnostics, by severing Christianity from the Old Testament, he opened the door for German nationalists to attack and freed liberal Christians to say bad things about the Old Testament.

A more troublesome issue in the attempt to remove the Old Testament and its history from the minds of Germans was the mere existence of Jews in the German-speaking states. The problem was not the Jews unwillingness to accept the new nationalist history. Germany's oldest and most prominent Jewish communities had enthusiastically embraced the Enlightenment. As did liberal Christians, these Reformed Jews had little problem seeing the Old Testament as false or outmoded history. Jews were becoming secularized at a faster rate than non-Jews and made ideal candidates for the new nationalism. Jewish enthusiasm for non-religious nationalism and secular history easily followed from their position as a minority religion in Christian and Muslim worlds.[45]

No matter that Germany's Hasidic Jews spoke a dialect of High German. No matter that Jews thought of their religion more in terms of the Talmud and were less guilty than Protestants of actually reading and seeing faith and history in line with the Old Testament. No matter that they might wish in every way to embrace German nationalism. Unfortunately for the Jews, Luther had followed their rabbis in teaching Germans to think of the Old Testament they wanted to reject in terms of Rabbinic Judaism and in seeing Rabbinic Judaism in terms of the Old Testament. This explains a virulent new strand of anti-Judaism that appeared as soon as Napoleon's occupation ended. *Anti-Semitism,* first mentioned at this time, reveals that the nationalists understood that the very existence of *Jews* pointed to the historicity of the Old Testament and to the absurdity of their new nationalist history.[46]

Though Jews would suffer for their mute testimony to the Bible's historicity, the Bible was the real threat to the mythical world history that German scholars had created from racist anthropology using the "laws of history" discovered by Hegel. The ancient and venerable account of history found in the Bible had somehow to be explained – in fact, to be explained away. It should surprise no one that those who invented a history to suit their nationalist and religious agenda would "discover" a similar propaganda-driven, mythical history for ancient Israel. Nor should it surprise us that they would employ the same Hegelian logic by which they developed their own history.

When conducted as historical criticism, higher criticism helps scholars better understand literature and history. As pioneered by the Renaissance humanist Lorenzo Valla (1406-1457), it requires understanding the history and times – the people, the events, the concerns, the culture, the language and scripts – in which the documents under review were written. For instance, Valla demonstrated that the fourth century Emperor Constantine did not deed the oversight of Western Europe to the Bishop of Rome as recorded in the *Donation of Constantine*. The great scholar used medieval documents and his knowledge of medieval history and language to show how this spurious document was composed for the political needs of the eighth century.

---

[45] The same impulse causes members of minority religions and beliefs in America to champion secular patriotism and religious pluralism rather than seeing the roots of the nation in America's Christian past.

[46] In contrast, where the Old Testament is believed, as in America's Bible Belt, Christians tend to be more philo-Judaic than anti-Semitic.

Without pertinent documents, or perhaps archaeological remains, historical criticism is impossible. In truth, there are excellent source documents for the history of ancient Israel. Collectively, they are known as the Old Testament. The Israelites did not write them on baked clay, hence there are no copies dating from the times of the Old Testament. The oldest then known dated only to the tenth century, but scholars had no earlier relevant documents that could have caused them to question their antiquity. Those who pioneered the "historical criticism" of ancient Israel would explain away rather than constrain their history by the sources most connected to the time, the customs, the events, the peoples, and the concerns of the people of the Bible. German scholars rejected these primary sources in favor of imagined sources they discovered within these primary documents by using the light of racist anthropology based on modern tribespeople, and by using Hegel's dialectical logic for the development of history. Hegel's logic of history could prove that these source documents came from the latest period of Israel's history. Again, they were projecting into the Bible their own experience: the new history of the German people was indeed a late creation. The requirement that the history of the Bible's composition must be as late as can be plausibly asserted is known as biblical minimalism. It is the chief constraint used in modern historical criticism of the Bible. It may be contrasted to the historical maximalism by which they date the documents and compositions of the Oriental religions used in the development of the Aryan history of Germany.

The pioneers of revisionist Old Testament history, J. K. W. Vatke (1806-1882) and Julius Wellhausen (1844-1918), each proposed a three-fold Hegelian development of Israel's history. For the first stage, they took their information from anthropological studies of contemporary peoples that were primitive according to their evolutionary logic. Vatke suggested that Israel's religion developed from the animist and polytheistic beliefs of Abraham, Isaac, and Jacob. Wellhausen modeled the patriarchs on the happy-go-lucky Arab and Bedouin sheiks that Carsten Niebuhr observed in Southern Arabia. Wellhausen's second stage of Israelite history had the ancient Hebrews advancing to serve only one of many competing gods. At this stage, he sees the Hebrew prophets developing an ethical dimension to the Jewish religion. Wellhausen reckoned the third state to have evolved to ritualistic and priestly religion based on an elaborate system of laws, which he supposed to be as legalistic as Rabbinic Judaism. As he reckoned, the early Christians and more recently the Protestants continued the evolution of morality stemming from the Hebrew Prophets. He followed the German historians in believing that the backward Jews could have become acquainted with a system of administrative law only from one of the great civilizations of the Ancient Near East. They supposed this happened to the Jews during their

Babylonian captivity, and claimed that the Jews of the captivity composed the Pentateuch, projecting an elaborate sacrificial system back to the time of Moses. This development from simple beginnings to an advanced civilization based on laws was much the way that German scholars had imagined their own history, only in this history priestly Semites replace virile warriors, the conquering Aryans.

The French doctor Jean Astruc (1684-1766) had proposed that different names of God, Jahweh (J) and Elohim (E), might indicate different sources used in the composition of the book of Genesis. According to the anti-Semite activist William de Witte (1780-1849), Deuteronomy was the lost Book of the Law that the priests of King Josiah's day found in the Temple.[47] Wellhausen agreed that a Deuteronomist (D) historian composed the version of Israel's history found in the books of Joshua, Judges, Samuel, and Kings to rationalize Josiah's reforms. He distinguished these primary sources from what was added by the priestly (P) editors of the books of Moses during the Babylonian exile. These four speculative sources came to be known as the JPED theory of the composition of the Old Testament.

Believing the tribal Jews had to have learned about systems of law from the Babylonians, Wellhausen claimed that the priestly editor created the system of law found in the Torah. Because Old Testament books of prophecy seemingly written before the captivity did not accord with this revisionist history, they proposed late compositions, multiple unknown authors, and anonymous redactors. They had no historical evidence for any of their proposed source documents or editors, but Kant's *a priori* type of reasoning did not require them. This summarizes how critical modern scholars explain the composition of the Old Testament.

Because literary theory based on the "laws" of logic and history needs no verification, Wellhausen despised the mention of inscriptions and texts from archaeological remains with direct connections to the Bible being made even as he was writing his highly influential compositional theory of the Bible's history. These discoveries resulted from neocolonial expansions of the European empires into lands formerly ruled by the Ottoman Empire from which Europeans had long been excluded. The first discoveries related to the Bible were inscriptions mentioning Assyrian kings previously known only from the Bible. These texts also alluded to kings of Israel and Judah, and even to some of the same battles mentioned in the Bible. These widely acclaimed discoveries explain why most critical scholars retreat from challenging the existence of the divided kingdoms of Israel and Judah.

---

[47] 2 Kings 22:8; 2 Chronicles 34:15

Chapter 7   Revisiing biblical history

A worker for the British Museum made an even more remarkable discovery. Among texts written on baked clay sent by archaeologists to the museum, George Smith (1840-1876) deciphered an Assyrian account of the Flood. Though couched in polytheistic terms, the Assyrian account had several details in common with Noah's Flood. This similarity could be explained in three different ways. Initially, most assumed that this account was an independent version of the same historical event recorded in the Bible. Though the Assyrian account had obviously mythical accretions, they saw it as important confirmation of a Bible that German scholars were declaring a late composition.

Some proposed a second theory: that the Assyrian account had been taken from the Bible. That is not an unreasonable suggestion. Israelite charioteers served the Assyrian kings; perhaps their scribes did as well. Whether or not Israelite scribes assisted with the Assyrian library, some Assyrians did understand the Hebrew language.[48] The Assyrian kings were obsessed with proclaiming their greatness, and how they conquered the people of other gods. It seems reasonable that these kings would expect the same scribes who memorialized their victories to create a more glorious library than those belonging to kings of the nations they had conquered. Why would the great Assyrian king who sponsored the library allow the founder of the Israelite nation whom he had just defeated a more miraculous history than the ancient King Sargon, for whom he himself had been named? Thus, we find in the library from these very times an account of the ancient Sargon as a baby being drawn from a floating basket. Instead of an Egyptian Princess, the goddess Ishtar adopts baby Sargon. Sargon's name however does not mean "drawn out of [water]." He was in fact no Moses.

Some of the Assyrian accounts do indeed seem to have come about in the same way that the Germans created their own mythical history. In addition to the manifest mythical elements to these Assyrian chronicles, their nationalistic agenda, and the fact that there could be no acts of God outside what German professors know as the normal course of Nature disposed them to categorize the biblical account as mythical. This meant rather than a shared history, these writings derive from a common literary source. According to the Assyriologist Friedrich Delitzsch (1850-1922) in his "Bibel vs Babel" lecture series, the original account had to have come from the "greater" civilization of Assyria. As he explained in these lectures in honor of the German Kaiser, not only is this superiority proven by the fact that the Assyrians left more magnificent monuments and ruins, but pictures of the Assyrian kings and their blonde-haired wives found in the ruins show them as being of the greater Aryan race.[49]

---

[48] 2 Kings 18:26; Isaiah 36:11

[49] Following Germany's defeat in WWI, the Kaiser sent a memorandum from his exile in the Netherlands to the leaders of Germany's churches. He recommended reform of Germany's

Part III   The Roots of Modern Historiography

Max Muller (1823-1900), who founded comparative religion and the history of religions school of biblical scholarship, spread to the English-speaking world the idea that Oriental religions influenced the Bible. Muller had studied India's Sanskrit while language searching for the roots of his German language. Though a linguist, he was more interested in the religious and cultural aspects of Aryan history. According to the Hindu scriptures, the chariot-driving Aryans conquered the dark-skinned Dravidians as they invaded the lands of India from the north. In Muller's history, Aryans were light bearers who spread their superior religion and culture as they migrated through Asia and Europe. Though he did regret it, Muller gave Europeans a rationale for their brutal neo-colonial expansions into Africa and Asia. Indeed, did not the elite Brahmans hold India's Untouchables in utter contempt? His teachings influenced the racial theories of the French aristocrat Joseph Arthur Comte de Gobineau (1816-1882) and the Old Testament criticism of Wellhausen and Delitzsch.

Likewise, Muller's 'history of religions' school supposed the New Testament to be rooted in Persian religion and Hellenistic cult. The earliest writings of Zoroastrianism and the Hellenistic cult of Mithraism date well after the latest writings from the Bible, but Aryan myth required their greater antiquity. Oral traditions were suddenly invested with great antiquity and respect. When the dates of written evidence are considered, Mithraism develops from Gnosticism while the Avesta Scriptures attributed to the ancient sage Zoroaster derive from Mithraism. Porphyry (234-305) tells us that the Hellenistic cult claimed that Zoroaster was their founder. The source of dualism in "ancient" Persian religion is more likely rooted in the Gnostic heresy. When scholars are free to ignore the dates of their sources, anything and everything from sources as ancient as one pleases can be found in the rich literature of Oriental religions. These can then be used for a composition of the Bible as late as one pleases. Notwithstanding these loose rules, what American students dutifully learn as the assured results of two centuries of biblical scholarship is the creation of German nationalism.

With the advent of form criticism pioneered by Delitzsch's friend and colleague Hermann Gunkel (1862-1932) the arsenal of techniques for constructing an imaginative history of the biblical documents increased immensely. In his influential *Legends of Genesis,* Gunkel explains why the Bible contradicts the ancient and biblical history taught by German professors. To begin, proper history requires a great institutional government like that of Imperial Germany and is not interested in the accounts of ordinary families, as one finds in the

---

churches based on the formula, "Out with Jewry and its Yahweh!" [From Morgens Trolle Larsen, "The 'Bible/Babel' Controversy and Its Aftermath" in Jack M. Sasson, *Civilizations of the Ancient Near East* (Hendrickson, 1995).]

Bible. True history is routine and mundane, but also contains sordid affairs such as the palace intrigues of King David, which Gunkel regarded as the earliest portion of the Bible that could possibly be regarded as history. Certainly, the remarkable events of early Hebrew "poetry" cannot be history because:

> Uncivilized races do not write history; they are incapable of reproducing their experiences objectively, and have no interest in leaving to posterity an authentic account of the events of their time. Experiences fade before they are fairly cold, and fact and fancy mingle; only in poetical form, in song or saga, are unlettered tribes able to report historical occurrences. Only at a certain stage of civilization has objectivity so grown and the interest in transmitting national experiences to posterity so increased that the writing of history becomes possible....The objection is raised that Jesus and the Apostles clearly considered these accounts to be fact and not poetry. Suppose they did; the men of the New Testament are not presumed to have been exceptional men in such matters, but shared the point of view of their time. ...How is it conceivable that a people should preserve a great quantity of the very minutest details from the history of its primitive ancestors and at the same time forget its own national history for a long period following? It is not possible for oral tradition to preserve an authentic record of such details so vividly and for so long a time. And then, consider these narratives in detail. The question how the reporter could know of the things which he relates cannot be raised in most cases without exciting laughter. How does the reporter of the Deluge pretend to know the depth of the water? Are we to suppose that Noah took soundings? How is anyone supposed to know what God said or thought alone in the councils of Heaven? [Gunkel, *The Legends of Genesis*. Translated by W.H. Carruth. (Wipf & Stock, 1901) 1-7.]

The prophet asked: "Who has been the Lord's Counselor?" It was perhaps Gunkel, one of the servants of the German State who thought God's own thoughts. He knew what the Creator and Living God could or could not, would or would not reveal to his chosen prophets and servants. He knew the history of the Israelites better than the ancient Israelites. He is certain that he knew more than Jesus. He knew everything – except what he might have learned from the Ancient Near Eastern texts that he rejected in favor of his theory of the necessity of oral tradition for early Hebrew records: that writing and detailed records existed not only in the Sinai desert at the time of Moses but even before the biblical date of the Flood.

German criticism of the New Testament and Old Testament worked along the same paths. Gunkel's friend Rudolph Bultman borrowed his form criticism to "demythologize" the New Testament. They did all this in the name of Christianity – the Christianity of the Protestant states and the now united Germany. Luther had backed away from his earlier view of the priesthood of believers and his championship of the authority of the Bible alone, declaring that the Word of God did not come from the individual's private reading of the Bible but what the professors and ministers of the German states determined should be preached from the pulpit. In the end, these learned professors and divines determined the Bible to be chiefly myth.

Julius Wellhausen   Hermann Gunkel

FIGURE 8   LEADING EXPOUNDER OF THE DOCUMENTARY CRITICISM OF THE BIBLE (LEFT) AND FOUNDER OF FORM CRITICISM OF THE BIBLE (RIGHT)

— 8 —

The archaeological recovery of biblical history

In contrast to the subjective creations proclaimed as fact by chauvinist pronouncement that has informed the "critical" study of the Bible, the discoveries of archaeology and the recovery of texts and inscriptions – the objective and empirical evidence of history – are returning the Bible to the center of the study of ancient Near Eastern history. In recent years, a bumper crop of names previously known only from the Bible, including that of King David, have been uncovered in Israel. Archaeologists have returned to what an earlier generation of scholars derided as working with the Bible in one hand, and a spade in the other. But without this light, they were working in the dark.

The Bible enlightens the entire Ancient Near East, telling of ancient nations that would otherwise be lost to history. It is a far better light on ancient times than the Greek histories critical scholars have used to understand the history of the ancient world since the Enlightenment. The British critical scholar S. R. Driver (1846-1914) claimed that the biblical writers obtained their knowledge of the ancient nations from the Greeks. One nation of significance in the Bible that the earliest explorations in the Near East failed to find was the Hittites. Since the Greeks seem never to have heard of the Hittites, the higher critics viewed this as evidence of made-up Old Testament history. By 1906, evidence of these people previously known only from the Bible was being found in places ranging from Egypt to their homeland in Turkey. Just as the Bible suggests, the Hittes owned a great empire before the rise of the ancient Kingdom of Israel around 1000 BC. The Hittites were closer neighbors to the Greeks than any of the kingdoms of the Ancient Near East. Their great empire existed only a few centuries before the first Greek historians, and in fact they carried on trade with the Greeks, the "fathers of history." If Greek historians seem never to have heard of Solomon's glory, neither had they heard of their Hittite neighbors with whom their ancestors had traded and to whom Solomon exported horses.

Part III   The Roots of Modern Historiography

The discovery of more massive ruins from Egypt, Assyria, and Babylon than from Israel should provide no surprise for readers of the Bible. Israel was prominent only in brief periods, reaching its greatest glory during the reigns of David and Solomon. Based on the relative egalitarian and free society of Israel and on God's instructions that kings should not seek wealth and glory, what archaeology discovers for Israel's history is about what we should expect.

J. G. Herder's anthropology, which equates nations with languages, still shackles the study of Ancient Near Eastern history. Each time a new language is discovered, scholars attribute it to some previously unknown people sweeping down from the mountains or riding in from the desert, seemingly birthed by the cold rocks or the dry sands. Were they to use the history of those times as found in the Bible, they would see that the ancient nations mentioned in the Bible changed their languages, though not so much their character as Herder would also require.

Contrary to what arrogant scholars and ideological, political, or scientific archaeologists claim, the Bible sheds a great deal of light upon archaeology and ancient history. The light is badly needed to understand what would otherwise be meaningless or confusing remains. Due to their docile and fearful captivity to modern orthodoxy, not only "critical" scholars but also anxious or fawning conservative scholars have been more reluctant to use this light than were the Aristotelians to look through Galileo's telescope.

Discoveries of archaeological remains and ancient texts also help us understand the context and the meaning of formerly obscure matters found in the Old Testament. As those in the field of biblical archaeology know, the Bible is making an exciting comeback. The text itself is becoming clearer owing to the very historical criticism once used to attack the Bible: only this time there are actual source documents and external evidence to be used as the basis for such a history.

The most famous of the new texts are the collection of scrolls and fragments discovered in the caves of the Dead Sea, which date to just before the time of Christ. Some of these documents tell of the warfare between the children of light and the children of darkness, an understandable reading of the Old Testament prophecies composed centuries before the oldest writings containing the dualistic views of the Gnostics, Hellenistic cults, and "ancient" Persian religions. The most important documents found in these caves are fragments and scrolls of the Old Testament, pushing back our oldest copies of these documents more than one thousand years. Though more closely related to the text from the Old Testament quoted in the New Testament, they are essentially the same texts found in the Bibles we presently use. Other writings among these Dead Sea Scrolls show a form of Judaism close to what we see in the New Testament. That should not be surprising. The New Testament is by far the best document and light for the last years of Second Temple Judaism. At least for the New Testament, discoveries from the Dead Sea Scrolls are sweeping away the kind of biblical criticism discussed in the last chapter.

In response to these challenges, those who do not want to believe the Bible have retreated to purely literary criticism. All history is literature and all history is written as narrative, but in modern terms 'literature' and 'narrative' have become code words for legends or fiction. Ignoring the new evidence for the historicity of the Bible, they dogmatically proclaim that the Bible is narrative or literature rather than an account of history. Many of these claims are associated with political positions and ideologies, with numerous traditional theologies, and with many new fashions in literary criticism. Evangelicals who do not want to be confronted by the plain words of the Scriptures also favor this type of biblical understanding, which allows them to twist the Scriptures however they please.

FIGURE 9   **AWARDS DAY**

Whatever those scholars who study the Bible as literature discover, their findings do not agree about what they "discover." Some level of consensus is crucial to progress in the fields of science and scholarship. But instead of developing consensus, these literary theories of the Bible are only becoming more fragmented. The lack of consensus is the scandal of literary criticism of the Bible. Many years ago, Albert Schweitzer (1875-1965) pointed out that what critical scholars "discover" concerning Jesus reflects the scholars more than it does Jesus. Literary criticism is an art, and a most fanciful art. As the Germans saw the Bible, it is poetry. Art and poetry do not need consensus because beauty lies in the eye of the beholder, and meaning lies in the reader's response. In this *Alice in Wonderland* world of modern biblical criticism, all have won and all must have prizes.

Recently attacks on the text and canon of the Bible have gotten a lot of attention, but these attacks are irrelevant if it turns out the history that we have learned from these allegedly imperfect and selective documents is proving true. History is about truth. That is why the message of truth in the Bible is conveyed as history. Truth threatens those – whether traditionalist or modernist – who have some agenda other than the truth. And indeed those who created the modern version of ancient history and the critical history of the Bible did have an agenda other than the discovery of truth.

It is unreasonable to expect archaeology to confirm every detail of the Bible, or for extra-biblical texts to mirror the perspective found in the Bible. It is enough that eras and cultures revealed in the background of the Old Testament history match the corresponding archaeological and social patterns of the lands of the Bible. The latter serve as fingerprints to test the historical details found in the biblical writings pertaining to the places and eras that can be identified in the extra-biblical evidence. Astonishingly, it seems that most of the places and numerous people mentioned in the Bible can be identified in archaeological inscriptions and ancient texts, pointing not only to the historicity of the Bible but also to the literacy of the people of the Bible from earliest times. Hardly from the margins of civilization, the history recorded in the Bible was in fact in the center of the core developments in human history. Although there is controversy between conservative scholars and biblical minimalists concerning specific issues, the general culture of the land of the Bible revealed by archaeology matches the Bible wonderfully, at least back to the time of Abraham. In contrast to our fathers who believed the truth of the Scriptures by faith, we have powerful evidence of their historical truth.

Unfortunately, in one vitally important area confirmation of the Bible by archaeology is still lacking. As I noted in my introduction, earlier than the time of Abraham the correlation between the Bible and ancient history breaks down. It is not only the presence of the massive ruins of ancient civilizations, such as those of the Pyramids, which are unnamed in the Bible. It is also the early history of man that science has discovered in the light of geology. Those developing this geology were working in Britain and France and operated from scientific presuppositions largely independent of the German-derived revisionist history of the Bible. I found the conflict between these oldest remains of man and the earliest history of man as recounted in the earliest chapters of Genesis deeply perplexing.

Part IV

Scientific Prehistory and the Problem of Noah's Flood

— 9 —

Jesus and Noah's Flood

THE FIRST ELEVEN chapters of the Bible record in exact chronological order the history of the world from its beginnings to the time of Abraham. Contrary to scientistic myth, the logical and orderly account of Creation in the first chapter of Genesis has more in common with the natural history taught by modern science than either view shares with strange creation myths taught by pagans such as the ancient Greeks. Though similar because the framework of natural history preserves vestiges of its biblical roots, the scientific version has manifest deficiencies. Not only does it ignore the source and inadequately explain the remarkable origins of the universe, of living things, and of conscious awareness, but it blissfully ignores the miraculous preservation of ongoing life.

The naturalistic fallacy is to suppose that an *ought* can be derived from an *is*. Hence, naturalistic accounts can never explain the purpose or meaning of life or why there should be something rather than nothing. Rejecting the self-existing personal God of unsurpassable love, power, and wisdom, the materialist scientist conveniently discovers the Creator in mindless matter. Rather than perpetually pretending to be on the verge of answering the deeper questions by spinning the latest scientific fashions, it becomes scientists to acknowledge the limits inherent in naturalistic methods, and instead of boorish dismissal, to acknowledge the plentiful evidence that contradicts their naturalistic account.

The offenses of the Bible are not these philosophical issues, where the Bible has answers that neither philosophy nor science can provide. Nor are they in the account of Creation in the first chapter of Genesis, which Christian apologists prefer to address. While the scientific account of origins disagrees that God directed the world's creation and with details of the biblical explanation, there is little in the first chapter of Genesis to offend the scientific mind. To a naturalist trained to eschew anthropocentric explanations this chapter seems more rational because it focuses on Nature rather than on man. But very different are

Part IV   Scientific Prehistory and the Problem of Noah's Flood

the chapters that follow. The Bible's record from the Garden of Eden to the era following the Flood is a type of history that modern science disdains even to consider. Far from the detached, fully transcendent Creator that philosophers prefer, in these passages the Lord God is an actor in his Creation. In distressingly "anthropomorphic" fashion he focuses his attention on man – even worse, on particular but ordinary men. As he does elsewhere in the Bible, God acts in an unscientific way as he responds to the actions of men and changes the world over the course of history.

Our current science refuses to acknowledge the extraordinary acts of a God *within* history, including the possibility of special revelation from the Creator. It is these special, personal, and extraordinary acts of the God of the Bible that truly offend the rule of science. Hence, the science that dominates our world today recognizes neither mankind's ancestry in that first couple, nor the curses on mankind and the earth due to their sin in the Garden of Eden, the long life spans of our most ancient ancestors, the wicked ancient civilization that perished in the Flood, the miraculous preservation of a single family together with the seed stock of land animals in the Ark of Noah, the ancestry of all mankind in Noah's family, nor the scattering of the nations from the Tower of Babel.

Notwithstanding scientific antipathy, because the Bible gives specific information about these events, they should enlighten the evidence from early man that archaeologists and scholars discover. These events belong to what our conventional scientific history understands as the comparatively recent history of man: from the Neolithic to the Bronze Age. Though the modern scientific history of mankind developed from anthropology rather than from historical memory and records, what it tells us about the general history and conditions of ancient times ought at the least to line up with what we read in the Bible. But instead of harmonizing, they conflict.

Still, the main thing making these chapters difficult for moderns is the strangeness of this world to the one that science knows. It is different from the kind that most Christians know. In those days, men walked and talked with the Creator of the universe. It was a world in which the serpent is wise but people behave as children, chiefly as disobedient children. Answering questions about our beginnings that every child wants to know, no wonder these accounts are popular with children. But nothing can fill a child with so much wonder as envisioning a line of all kinds of animals marching up a ramp into Noah's Ark and behaving themselves for the space of a year.

Even curious children see the challenges presented by the account of Noah's Ark and the Flood. A family of eight, three of them centenarians at the time of the Flood, must build a seaworthy ship, the size of a short aircraft carrier. The same family must grow and gather the proper food to feed for the most of a year

Chapter 9 Jesus and Noah's Flood

FIGURE 10   FROM ATHANASIUS KIRCHER'S *ARCA NOE* (1675)

the widely varying needs of every kind of animal that lives on the earth. During their stay on the Ark they must water and feed the animals and deal with all their waste. After that ordeal, they must restart life on earth in a world just devastated by the Flood.

The animals faced obstacles of their own migrating to the Ark from their native ecological niches in the most distant parts of the earth. Some had to find their way across large deserts, high mountains, great rivers, and wide oceans. Only God and his angels know what they might have eaten and how they managed not to get eaten as they made their way to the Ark. Finally, there is the issue of the source and destination of water sufficient to cover the earth more than twenty feet above Mount Everest. Were all the water in the deep oceans raised to just above sea level, it would not cover all the earth's mountains as it did during the Flood. These things puzzled me. It seems they have puzzled everyone but children, or perhaps those who think like children.

Nonetheless what we perceive as childlike or ridiculous can be culturally conditioned. It may be owing to the deceptive view of ancient times possessed by our current culture, and a mistaken estimate of our sophistication. I will never forget my painful grin when the Lord suddenly opened my eyes. What

Part IV   Scientific Prehistory and the Problem of Noah's Flood

we think scientific sense or nonsense is also relative. Once, the most learned philosophers and scientists did not believe Galileo's impossible claim that the earth was spinning and flying through the heavens at great speeds. Thomas Jefferson thought it easier to believe that two honorable men from New England should lie than to accept their testimony that rocks [meteorites] had fallen from the heavens. Many, including the great scientist Albert Einstein, had trouble accepting the empirical "absurdities" discovered by quantum physicists. Others could not accept the absurdities that Einstein himself taught about time and space. Formerly, no one but a few Greek philosophers guessed that the world that we know could have resulted by pure chance. Eminent men of science now believe that we are the product of a long streak of winnings in the cosmic Las Vegas. That we keep surviving all those scientifically predicted disasters like Forest Gump is even more amazing when we consider that these scientists believe neither in guardian angels nor in Providence.

It is understandable that scientists should see many things that might threaten our existence. Life on earth is fragile and complex. There are countless things to go wrong. Murphy's Law predicts that everything that can go wrong will go wrong at the most inopportune time. Because I am a systems engineer I know from experience that everything that has not been carefully planned and tested will fail. The Second Law of Thermodynamics derives from the truth that disorder is just what we should expect from unintelligent Nature. Chaos does not need to be explained. It naturally exists unless some capable intelligence gives it order. A good outcome requires careful planning by some favorable intelligence and sufficient power. To ask why God is involved in miracles of salvation, but not in disasters or tragedies is to fail to comprehend this fundamental truth. God does not save everyone for reasons perhaps known only to him, but if anyone is miraculously spared, she or he might reasonably attribute it to God – to the great mercy and patience that God showers on all mankind, even to those who do not acknowledge him.

What is true does not have to accord with what seems sophisticated. Jesus rejoiced that God hides himself from the wise and prudent, but reveals himself to babes. He declares that we cannot enter the Kingdom of Heaven except we humble ourselves as little children. Their humility and wonder would be appropriate even for a mind capable of the finest human accomplishments when the time comes for him to appear before the one who created, sustains, and ultimately governs our inhabitable world. Blinded by conceit, our modern world attributes to its accomplishment what is chiefly due to God's grace.

Yet when it comes to determining the truth it ought to be the evidence, and only the evidence, that counts. This includes whatever confirms or contradicts the various accounts and miracles of the Bible. If the Bible is true, what

Chapter 9 Jesus and Noah's Flood

is recorded there ought to enlighten the extra-biblical evidence pertaining to the times, places, and peoples of the things it mentions more than should the scientific history of man.

Miracles should leave evidence, in fact more evidence than ordinary events. Science will not be able to explain them if they are truly miracles, but evidence should exist that is in accordance with biblical miracles, as it should also accord with any true testimony or history – that is, if these miracles really occurred and if we can correlate them with history and place. To conduct such an investigation we must precisely identify the time, place, and nature of the miracle. Most of the numerous miracles of the Bible involved only a few people at some one place and at some one time in ancient history. It is remarkable enough that we should have even a single record of particular events from ancient times, though miracles that powerfully impress contemporaries are better preserved than ordinary matters in the memory of history. The resurrection of Jesus is perhaps the greatest example.

It is not reasonable that we should expect to find evidence of specific events that immediately affected so few people, so long ago, and in one small part of the earth's large surface, but the Creation of the world and Noah's Flood are great exceptions. We should have plenty of evidence of both great singularities. Indeed, in the twentieth century physicists and astronomers realized that the universe did indeed have a beginning and scientists cannot explain why. The Bible has triumphed over the timeless views of the world long championed by science, philosophy, and Eastern religions. Likewise the Flood, an event involving every man, woman, child, animal and plant living on earth, should have left plenty of evidence. After covering the earth for most of a year, the biblical Flood must have deeply transformed not only all mankind, but also the entire earth together with all its vegetation and wildlife. We should expect to find plenty of evidence of this great miracle. That does not seem to be the case!

Perhaps I could accept this matter as some kind of parable by which the ancients understood God had it not been for the pointed references that Jesus himself made to the Flood He referred to Noah's Flood as a historical and worldwide event, comparing the decadence and complacency of the world caught by the Flood to the conditions that would ensue just before his return. Lest there be any doubt, references to the Flood are part of the Q sayings that even the most liberal scholars recognize as the authentic words of Jesus.[50]

Contemporary Christian teachings – that the Flood was a geographically local affair, or that it was an edifying story developed from the legends and myths of the Ancient Near East – do not square with the recorded words of Jesus when he compared the days of the Flood to his Second Coming. The distant past

---
[50] My appreciation to Professor James Tabor for this information.

is certainly difficult for any mortal to know or understand. How much more uncertain the inscrutable future! Had Jesus himself, or even his Apostles, been captive to the understanding of his contemporaries, as Hermann Gunkel led many to believe,[51] might not his wonderful and comforting words concerning the impossible-to-know future be similar to the way they imagined his preexisting past?

Some have claimed that because of a "will to believe" Christians are inescapably biased in the investigation of the Bible or any matter of history or truth.[52] This is certainly the case of those who will *not* to believe the Bible, while those who are indifferent to the Bible's truth have been most careless in investigations pertaining to the Bible. But like the soundness of an airplane or parachute, the matter most concerns those who plan to use the vehicle. They are the most concerned with its truth, and are the least willing to overlook any sound reason that it is not. But this may illuminate why so many explain away the challenging words of Jesus, accepting instead the cheap grace of theologians. The latter claim it is impossible to follow Jesus at his words.

In truth, it is easy to follow Jesus at his words if it is costly, but impossible to do so if it is not. For the very reason that it is so costly no one would do so unless they believed it to be based on truth. A good reason to believe Jesus and his Prophets and Apostles is that they themselves refused to be rewarded by conforming to the world, instead undergoing great deprivations and suffering to stay faithful to their message. The Apostle Paul acknowledged that those who follow Jesus in the costly way that he calls his chosen must of all people be most miserable were it based on deception.[53] Paul was not afraid to state the truth. Someone has indeed been greatly and sadly deceived: either those who believe in the Jesus of the Bible, or our entire modern world that does not. May we discover who refuses to face the truth by their will to believe!

---

[51] "Jesus and the Apostles clearly considered these accounts to be fact and not poetry. Suppose they did; the men of the New Testament are not presumed to have been exceptional men in such matters, but shared the point of view of their time." [See Chapter 7, page 67 of this book]

[52] Van Austin Harvey, *The Historian and the Believer: The Morality of Historical Knowledge and Christian Belief* (Macmillan, 1966).

[53] 1 Corinthians 15:19

— 10 —

How theologians and geologists have understood the Flood

WIDESPREAD DISBELIEF IN the Flood is unique to modern times. Though now associated with those whose faith is based on the Bible, it seems that all the great civilizations in the Ancient Near East, the Mediterranean, and Asia knew of the Flood. While some of their philosophers became the first skeptics, most Greeks believed in both Creation and the Flood.[54] Knowledge of the Flood was likewise widespread in the islands of the Pacific and among the peoples of the New World. To the extent that peoples concerned themselves with history, versions of the Creation and the Flood were the most universally remembered events.

In no case was the matter of the Flood so important as to Christianity where the truth of the Flood is tied to the truth of salvation: the testimony of Jesus and the Apostles. This explains why Christians have been among those most concerned with denials of the historicity of the event. Until modern times this was hardly a matter of concern. In contrast to their arguments for the Flood of recent centuries, some Jews and Christians in earlier times chauvinistically denied that pagan nations retained any truth concerning the Flood. Their arguments concerning the Flood were aimed at defending the biblical account against the varying stories of the nations.

From the earliest days of faith, Christians knew of extra-biblical reports concerning the Flood, Noah's Ark, and the place where the Ark landed. The Flood once seemed the best explanation for seashells found on land and upon the mountains. In ancient times, as today, rumors of remains or relics from the ark were quoted as evidence of the Flood's historicity. The ancients offered evidence because they knew how extraordinary was the matter of the Flood. They asked

---

[54] For an examination of Creationism among the Greek philosophers, see David Sedley, *Creationism and Its Critics in Antiquity* (University of California Press, 2007).

Part IV   Scientific Prehistory and the Problem of Noah's Flood

the same questions that we do today. How large did the Ark need to be to hold a pair of all the kinds of animals? Where are the sources of the water that covered the high mountains of the earth? How did the animals manage to migrate to and from the Ark?

These difficult questions caused the philosophers Plato and Aristotle to contend that the Flood was confined to the plains, allowing men and animals to escape by going to the mountains. These were the two philosophers who most influenced Christian theologians. Their impact was not so much their denial of the Flood's universality as their provision of a philosophical alternative to the Bible's historical view of the earth. Plato turned the attention of Christians from the visible earth, while Aristotle caused them to study the world as an eternal system, viewing the earth in an unhistorical way. Because the history-creating Flood could not be easily fitted into views of an unchanging world, philosophers preferred to see the Flood as a geographically local event that did not impact the earth's general features. But aside from the notorious Isaac La Peyrere, Christians who contended for a local Flood believed it occurred at a time when the earth's population was confined to one locality. Still, through the ages the great majority of Christians have believed that the Flood covered the entire earth.

For most of Christian history, the scientific issue concerning believers was neither the Flood nor the age of the earth, but whether the world was created. Teaching that the earth had existed from eternity, Islamic Aristotelians proposed cycles of the earth's history lasting for 36,000 years. Influenced by them, but noticing that the earth had not changed since the time of Adam, the French priest Jean Buridan (1300-1358) reckoned that the development of the earth might have taken a billion years. His purpose was to show that the stars could not be the cause of the earth's cycles of development, thereby refuting the astrology and cosmology of Islamic science. Until modern times, the age of the earth was hardly an issue in the Christian defense of the Bible.

One effect of the Creation account in Genesis and the Bible's larger focus on the history of man was to separate the history of the earth from that of man, something that the pagan myths and Greek philosophers tended not to do. Because the first chapter of Genesis makes no mention of man until God had almost completed Creation, a natural history absent the presence of man was easy to conceive. Geologists working in the light of Scripture had little difficulty understanding what the Bible calls the "age old mountains"[55] as far older than man. They could explain this by epochal days of Creation. Does not the Bible itself say that a day of the Lord is as a thousand years?[56] Some saw an initial

---
[55] Habakkuk 3:6
[56] Psalm 90:4; 2 Peter 3:8

Chapter 10   How theologians and geologists have understood the Flood

Creation in the first verse of Genesis, separate from the six Creation days. To the age of the earth in distinction from the age of man most gave no thought at all.

The return to the Bible due to the Reformation and new accounts of the Deluge brought to light by European explorers revived interest in the Flood. Athanasius Kircher (1602-1680) made a detailed scientific study both of Noah's Ark and the Flood. His explanation of the Flood's waters reveals the difficulty of fitting the Flood into an Aristotelian worldview. He proposed that the waters came from great caverns inside the earth to which the waters of the Flood also returned. As knowledge of the earth increased, these underground streams and passages proved difficult to find.

The rise of modern science occasioned a shift in the study of the Flood from history, biology, and geography to the new science of historical geology. The Copernican Revolution explained the earth as a planet suspended in the fixed heavens. Separating the earth from the greater cosmos gave rise to explanations of the earth's development apart from that of the cosmos. Descartes was the first to develop such a theory. Though he ignored the matter of the Flood, his diagram of the earth showed a deep ocean below the earth's surface in line with what Kircher had suggested as a source for the waters of the Flood.

Thomas Burnet (1635-1715) refined Descartes' geological history to include the breaking forth of the waters to create the Flood. His *Sacred History of the Earth* extended the view of the earth's history into the future according to the arrow of history found in the Bible. According to Burnet, the smooth surface of the earth at the time of the Garden of Eden gradually decayed from the time of Adam's Fall. Eventually the surface collapsed, giving rise to the Flood. The Flood created the mountains and uneven surfaces that we see today. At some future era, the drama of earth's history will end in a conflagration. After the burning, it must return to the smooth surface with which the earth's history began, an era he associated with the Millennium.

Though he followed the course of history given in the Bible, Burnet explained the Flood and everything else in his "sacred" history by what was then called General Providence: God acting through secondary causes, what we would now call scientific laws. He explained that what appeared to the vulgar as sacred history was only the necessary progression of general laws the Creator had established. Using the ordinary mechanical laws discovered by Isaac Newton, Burnet had difficulty showing how the creation of the earth could occur in the short six days of the Bible. To the delight of the Deists, he declared the account of Creation in Genesis to be an edifying story, no more to believe than Aesop's Fables.

William Whiston (1667-1752), Isaac Newton's chosen successor to his chair of mathematics, showed how God added Special Providence to his General

Providence so as to order history both according to Newton's laws of mechanics and the biblical account. Whiston proposed that the waters of Creation came from a comet that was trapped by the sun's gravity and peeled away matter from the sun, giving rise to the creation of the earth. On the second day of Creation, God divided the waters of the comet to form the earth's atmosphere. This blocked the view from the earth of the sun, moon, and stars, which became visible only on the fourth day.

Whiston explained that immediately following Creation the earth did not yet rotate daily. This meant that days were then one year long, night and day coming as the earth circled the sun. One-year days confirmed the day-year formula found in Ezekiel, popular among millenarians for interpreting prophecies – as are the seventy weeks of days [years] in the book of Daniel and the 1260 days [years] in the book of Revelation.[57] Whiston agreed with Edmond Halley [1656-1742] that Noah's Flood was caused by a comet. Not only did Halley's comet provide the floodgates of heaven, its impact spun the earth into its present 24-hour daily rotation.

However speculative and however much these ideas have been modified by later developments, Newton and Whiston set the course for the scholarly versions of ancient history, for the modern understanding of the biblical account of Creation, and for the scientific explanations of the earth's origins. Newton and Whiston used ancient writers' observations of the constellations in the sky as a way of anchoring pagan histories both to our modern calendars and to the Bible, allowing for a precise correlation of the history in the Bible with the records of the gentile nations. Viewing the "creation" of the sun, moon, planets, and stars as merely their appearance in the clearing sky on the fourth day of Creation and their contention that the six day Creation in the Bible pertains only to the earth rather than the cosmos still teaches many Fundamentalist Christians how to read these accounts.

The French geologist Comte de Buffon (1707-1788) used Whiston's idea that the days of Genesis are not the same duration as present solar days to defend his computations of an ancient age for the earth. Buffon suggested that the days of Creation be understood as extended epochs in the earth's early history. He based his estimate of the time since Creation on the rate of sinking of the waters from the initial Creation and upon how long it took for the earth to cool from its initial creation when a comet separated the earth from the hot sun. In the next century, Lord Kelvin (1824-1907) would use the same reasoning to hamstring Darwin's theory of evolution by limiting the age of the earth. That stymied Darwin's version of evolution for a generation, until equally speculative ideas could be found to refute Kelvin's estimate. By combining the Enlighten-

---

[57] Ezekiel 4:6; Daniel 9:24; Revelation 12:6

Chapter 10 How theologians and geologists have understood the Flood

ment's Great Chain of Being with the arrow of history from the Bible, Buffon created a framework of natural history from which the modern theory of evolution developed. Buffon himself considered that evolution may have resulted from interbreeding between species, but rejected the idea because he noticed that hybrids were infertile.

Voltaire accused Buffon of creating the world "by the stroke of a pen." The Deist Voltaire did not like the fact that Buffon accommodated advanced science to the light of the Bible. In fact Buffon constrained his theories by empirical observations and calculations. Voltaire's accusation is better applied to the new worlds systems created by Bruno, Descartes, Burnet, and Leibniz whose views Voltaire preferred. But indeed the Copernican Revolution and the New Science of mechanics hatched a multitude of new world systems not seen since the ancient pagan mythmakers and Greek philosophers.

Because the Bible gives a historical rather than a philosophical account of the world, it accommodates various scientific views more easily than Aristotle's system. Because of this, and because the intelligence and power of the Creator in the Bible is so much greater than the human mind can conceive, the Bible encourages empiricism. Roger Bacon (1214-1294) had championed empiricism against the system of Aristotle, but it was the cacophony of new theories of the earth birthed by the rise of science that caused leading eighteenth century scientists to reject the speculative theories of the earth like those of Descartes, Burnet, and Leibniz and insist that geology be determined by empirical data gathered by naturalists. Biblicists and empiricists preferred Francis Bacon's (1561-1626) inductive method of determining theory from patterns seen in careful observation.

John Woodward (1655-1722) irritated his fellow geologists by pointing out how their systems conflicted with what was observed in the earth. He noticed that geological phenomena were distributed in various strata, some of which included fossils. Interpreting the Bible according to the most up-to-date scientific thinking, Woodward proposed that sometime during the Flood, God suspended the laws of gravity that bound the earth's crust. He explained the distribution of strata as coming from the end of the Flood as God gradually re-introduced gravity. Differences in specific gravity and density would have caused various rocks, fossils, and other materials to settle at different levels. Of course, regardless of his criticisms of other theories for failing to conform to the empirical facts, Woodward added speculations of his own. However, these would help geologists develop a framework for fitting the empirical data into a history of the earth.

Following Woodward, geologists determined that primary rocks in the earth such as granite or basalt – rock formations that show no signs of strata – were formed during the earth's initial creation. Secondary rocks like sandstone and formations that included regularly occurring strata were from natural deposits accumulating from the time of Creation until the Flood. Those strata containing fossils of animals that roamed the earth belonged to the Tertiary level, were understood as having been deposited by the Flood. Later, they added the Quaternary level. This topmost level was presumed created from deposits since the time of the Flood. Most geologists, including Nicolas Steno (1638-1686) who pioneered the understanding of fossils and geological strata, found no problem with the six thousand years then accepted for the entire history of the earth.

It was the lack of human fossils and artifacts in the Tertiary level (which contained the remains of ancient mammals) that caused biblical geologists to reckon it as unlikely to have come from the Flood and thus to question the six thousand years of earth history. Evidence of humans was lacking in all but the last or the Quaternary period. This meant either that humans were confined to some locality before the Flood or more reasonably, since God destroyed mankind through a *worldwide* Flood, the Flood itself occurred during the Quaternary period. Placing the Flood in the Quaternary period brought widespread acceptance among biblical geologists that the earth had a long history prior to the creation of man.

One must not, as many have done, confuse these geological issues with a controversy during this era that concerned biblical chronology: the antiquity of man given in the Bible versus the age claimed for Egyptian and Asian civilizations. This controversy, which did not concern geology, was not the same as the one today that is defended by young earth geology and chiefly concerns the duration of the days of Genesis before the creation of man. The chief *geological* controversy pertaining to the Bible in those days did not concern the age of the earth but whether the earth had a beginning and whether any evidence of the earth's history could be explained in the light of the Bible.

Aristotelians denied that the earth was created. To explain why the mountains were not eventually worn away by erosion, they taught that the mountains were growing as fast as they were being eroded. In Aristotle's science the earth had processes, but no history of development. Likewise, *Telliamed,* a book published anonymously in 1748 that proposed an ancient evolutionary history of the earth from the subsiding oceans, was really aimed at proving that the earth had no beginning. Studying the earth in the Bible's light was essential for developing the geological *history* of the earth.[58] What is presently known as the geological column, or the evidence of earth's history, is a refinement of the four basic geological divisions developed from the history of the earth given in the Bible.

---

[58] cf Martin J. S. Rudwick, *Bursting the Limits of Time* (University of Chicago Press, 2007).

Chapter 10   How theologians and geologists have understood the Flood

As they were expanding the traditional timeframe for the history of the earth, biblical geologists had to contend not only with Aristotelians but also with Deist geologists who believed that the world was created, but likewise denied that the earth developed over history. James Hutton (1726-1797), regarded as the father of modern geology, taught that the earth "showed no vestiges of a beginning and no prospects of an end." He modeled his theory of the earth on the steam engine invented by his friend James Watt (1736-1819). As a good Deist, Hutton envisioned the earth as a system perfectly designed for man's habitation. Hutton and the Deists were nominal Christians who agreed with the Bible when it came to seeing man as an exception to the rest of Nature. Where Deists and those studying the earth in the light of the Bible divided was the matter of whether the earth itself, considered by both to be God's Creation, showed evidence of history.

Evidence of either Creation or the Flood would reveal a history within the earth. Denying that seashells in the mountains were evidence of Noah's Flood, Voltaire claimed that pilgrims had left them, but few could accept his view. Seeing fossils as coming from living things suggested that the earth revealed a history of development. Challenging this, some denied that fossils could ever derive their appearance from formerly living things and thus could never have been in the sea. Aristotelians and Deists could imagine fossils as sports of Nature or as substantial forms along the continuous plenitude of the Great Chain of Being. Unlike the Aristotelians and Deists, believers felt the geological record confirmed the fact of the earth's Creation and the biblical account of man as the last thing that God created.

The new geological discoveries did impact the matter of the Flood since it could no longer be easily maintained that the majority of the earth's fossils, completely absent of any evidence of man, were from the Flood. Nonetheless, there was still plenty of geological evidence apart from fossils that attested to a worldwide Flood. The most eminent defender of the Flood during this period was the Swiss geologist Jean-Andre Deluc (1727-1817). Deluc challenged Hutton's teaching that the processes forming the earth in the past were of the same kind and order as those that occur today. He pointed to the V-shaped banks of rivers, which clearly seemed to derive from the actions of presently existing rivers and familiar floods. These rivers however flowed through wide U-shaped valleys that could more easily be explained as caused by a great Flood.

Moreover, closer studies of the rock formations and fossils in the earth's strata were finding evidence of sudden changes that appeared to date from ancient times. The French naturalist Georges Cuvier (1769-1832), who pointed this out, towered above his colleagues in the new field of paleontology. Contesting Jean-Baptiste Lamarck's (1744-1829) contention that ancient animals were

Part IV   Scientific Prehistory and the Problem of Noah's Flood

transformed through evolution, Cuvier established that some kinds of animals that once lived have since become extinct. The father of vertebrate paleontology, Cuvier discovered how to reconstruct the way extinct animals may have looked – often based on a single bone or even a piece of bone. Most importantly, he identified the sudden end of various earlier epochs of the earth's history when numerous kinds of prehistoric animals became extinct and new kinds of animals suddenly appeared. He pointed out what paleontologists now call the Cambrian explosion, the mass extinctions, and the sudden appearance of mammals.

Opposing Hutton's view that the processes that formed the earth in the past are the same as those that occur today, Cuvier established the catastrophic school of geology. He taught that revolutionary changes in the earth created new epochs in the earth's history. These epochs triggered a further refinement of the divisions of the earth's history. According to Cuvier each of these epochs ended with some kind of catastrophe. Oxford's eminent geologist William Buckland (1784-1856), who wrote the first full description of a fossil dinosaur, proposed the biblical Flood as the best explanation for Cuvier's last catastrophe. Though regarding the Bible as only one of many witnesses to this ancient catastrophe, Cuvier did not disagree.

The *diluvial* layer (named for the great deluge) marking Cuvier's last catastrophe consisted of a deep but chaotic assemblage of sediments, ranging from muds, silts, sands, and gravels to the bones of extinct animals. In river valleys, this diluvial layer lay just below the *alluvial* (post-Flood) level on the top of the earth's surface. The latter was marked by finer silts and by the bones of animals that still roam the earth. This topmost level was found along the V-shaped banks of rivers, and could be seen as clearly deriving from the presently observed actions of rivers and their floods.

The chaotic diluvial layer just below the better-organized topmost alluvial series of soil also contained the bones of animals similar to those still roaming the earth. Below it, fossils and rocks again appear in regular strata. The deeper layers below the diluvial layer contained only minerals, rocks, and the fossilized bones and shells of extinct animals.[59] Clearly, some great catastrophe of recent times was responsible for the intermediate-lying diluvial phenomena and deposits. Moreover, this level was found throughout the wide U-shaped valleys into which the rivers cut their V-shaped banks.

More evidences of this recent catastrophe were huge scratched boulders at great distances from and at higher elevations than the point of their geological origin. Also lying in this stratum, scattered as far south as southern Europe, were the bones of reindeer and arctic birds while mammoths or elephants, now

---

[59] A. Hallam, *Great Geological Controversies* (Oxford University Press, 1989), 87-88.

Chapter 10   How theologians and geologists have understood the Flood

Georges Cuvier (catastrophism)   William Buckland (diluvialism)

FIGURE 11   **DISCOVERERS OF THE GEOLOGICAL FLOOD**

understood as tropical animals, were found in these levels near the arctic. The Flood perfectly explained all these exceptional deposits. Though geologically recent, the diluvial level was well within the time-frame of the biblical Flood.

Neither Buckland nor Cuvier aimed to "prove the Bible." In their day it was more fashionable to discover some sort of naturalistic or scientific explanation for various geological phenomena. Nonetheless, everyone agreed that some kind of worldwide flood was the best explanation for this set of distinct worldwide deposits. Aiming desperately to put their field on a scientific basis, many geologists spent a great deal of time looking for natural causes for the diluvial phenomena. They proposed that giant tidal waves had shot arctic animals far to the south of Europe. They also suggested that ice had formed around the giant boulders. The tidal waves would grab and carry the icebergs along with the great stones thousands of feet up the mountains. The geologists needed the Flood, but they did not want the Bible.

Over the course of the nineteenth century, catastrophism itself went out of fashion as an accepted mode of geological explanation. This can be attributed to Charles Lyell (1797-1875), Darwin's mentor and regarded alongside Hutton as the founder of modern geology. Championing the view of Hutton, Lyell forbade the use of both "cosmology" and catastrophes. By cosmology Lyell meant

Part IV   Scientific Prehistory and the Problem of Noah's Flood

theories of how the earth came to be. Such a proscription was useful for challenging Lamarck's theory of evolution that was gaining popularity in Lyell's day but which neither Creationists, Aristotelians, nor Deists liked; but what this Deist seemed to have more in mind was a firm and systematic way of prohibiting the use of the Bible in the service of geology. He strenuously attacked those who were beginning to call themselves *Scriptural geologists*.

Lyell explained what appeared as geological evidence of the earth's creation or of sudden changes, as might have been caused by a great Flood, as being caused instead by ordinary processes that are still observed today. He did this by stretching out periods of geological time into immense ages – into what geologists now call 'Deep Time.' If sufficiently extended, one can imagine ordinary processes explaining anything and everything that might be found in the earth. Darwin learned from his mentor how to imagine ordinary processes to cause what appears to be sudden changes by stretching out time. There is no way to test this since such stretches of time are far beyond what humans can actually observe. His theoretical claim that only actual processes should be used for geological data seem to have given Lyell's geological way of thinking, what the philosopher William Whewell (1794-1866) would call *uniformitarianism* the veneer of being empirical, when in fact it is deeply theoretical. This way of thinking turns "Who knows?" into a scientific principle for explaining the evidence. When people become accustomed to the new fashion of explanation, its advocates proclaim what is actually theory as "scientific fact." Similar mysterious principles can of course be used to defend theology, or even some theory of the Flood. All of these equate imagination with demonstration.

Like Aristotle and Hutton, Lyell did not believe the earth had a history of progressive development. Challenging Cuvier, he denied that any animal, including the dinosaurs, could ever become permanently extinct. Holding firmly to the Great Chain of Being, Lyell was determined to put geology on a firm scientific basis, though one that was more theoretical than empirical, which accorded with the fashionable mechanical principles that were in fact responsible for the Industrial Revolution. Lyell reckoned that what were being supposed as diluvial remains were in fact from the accumulation over a vast Pleistocene era in which the slowly sinking continents were flooded by the slow rising of the oceans, after which the land would again rise above sea level. As Buckland and others were finding ever more evidence for the diluvial geological era, a new theory arose to explain some of the associated phenomena. This was the idea that glaciers far larger than any now seen were responsible for moving the rocks and depositing the diluvial remains. The man responsible for popularizing the notion of a great Ice Age was Louis Agassiz (1807-1873), who moved from Switzerland to Massachusetts to become Harvard and America's foremost

Chapter 10   How theologians and geologists have understood the Flood

geological authority. Buckland quickly accepted Agassiz's theory of the Ice Age for explaining the surficial geological deposits he and other scientists had been attributing to the Flood, despite the fact that Buckland himself found diluvial evidence in such far-flung and unlikely places as the Himalayan Mountains. Aggasiz found the same kind of evidence of the Ice Age in the tropics of Brazil!

Ice covering the warm tropics was too much for Lyell to attribute to an Ice Age. Though initially supporting Aggasiz's Ice Age theory, he was stung by the criticism of Whewell and other geologists concerning its violation of his principle of uniformitarianism. With his disciple Charles Darwin, Lyell insisted until his death that these remains came from icebergs in rivers of water deriving from a tsunami that swept across the earth's mountain ranges, in the process creating broad valleys and inland lakes. As more geologists were converted to the Ice Age, Lyell agreed to accept the new explanation, providing its domain be limited to the northern regions and to specific localities where glaciers may be seen as normally forming. The Ice Age was scarcely less catastrophic than the Flood, and it was even more difficult to imagine a naturalistic cause for one-time reshaping of the earth. Still, it allowed scientists to avoid all reference to the Bible.

Notwithstanding the issues that concerned learned geologists, the notion of an approximately six thousand year history of the world was becoming increasingly popular due to the growing influence of the New Science of mechanics in conjunction with mathematical chronologies of the nations such as those of James Ussher and Isaac Newton. From the eighteenth century, Ussher's dates were printed in the margins of the King James Bible. Interest in the Millennium, very prevalent during the nineteenth century, added to its popularity. A shortly-to-appear Millennium would give a neat seven thousand years to biblical history. Many asserted the dates of Ussher against those who contended for a more ancient date for the civilizations in Egypt or Asia.

It is important to note that those who are against a literal understanding of the Scriptures may defend the same scientific views as those who claim to be studying the earth in the light of Scripture, and vice versa. As I will explain in Chapter 12, we may perceive something to be the "light of Scripture" because we have become accustomed to reading Scripture in a certain *scientific* light. The arch-Deist Voltaire had no problem with a world created in 4004 BC. Early Deists and today's literalists subscribe to young earth views. Interestingly, those Scriptural geologists with young earth views were reading Scripture through mathematics and mechanical science while they were opposing not only Deist geologists like Lyell, but also those who created modern historical geology by studying the earth in the light of Creation and the Flood – the light of Scripture. It was a matter of confusing theology with Scripture. This does explain

Part IV   *Scientific Prehistory and the Problem of Noah's Flood*

Charles Lyell (uniformitarianism)   Louis Agassiz (The Ice Age)

FIGURE 12 OPPONENTS OF THE FLOOD AND CREATORS OF MODERN GEOLOGY

why thoughtful Christians easily accepted the notion that the earth had an ancient history before God created man.[60]

It is thus anachronistic to project the present controversy concerning the age of the earth on these Scriptural geologists, even if most of the latter contended for a young earth. What they were chiefly opposing were the demands of Deists – and others going back at least to the Aristotelians in the medieval universities – to separate the study of Nature from the Bible. Today, those who demand that faith and science be regarded as separate realms also insist that the findings of science determine the basis of the harmony. While rejecting the light of Scripture on Creation, they insist that the Scripture be re-interpreted in the light of science, even if it means understanding Scripture as an edifying but outmoded allegory or myth.

One must also distinguish controversies concerning the age of the earth from the related but separate issue of the length of the Creation days in Genesis.

---

[60] One might compare this situation to the recent astronomical discovery confirming the Scripture's teaching that the universe had a beginning. While some Christians rejoice in this empirical confirmation of biblical Creation, others see the "Big Bang" as threatening the theology by which they have been taught to read the Bible.

Chapter 10   How theologians and geologists have understood the Flood

Martin Luther was perhaps the first to address this subject as he also addressed the age of the earth. Writing in the sixteenth century, Luther reckoned the age of the world at about 6,000 years. Regarding the Creation days, he preferred ordinary days, famously insisting on calling a spade a spade. We may be tempted to read the present controversy into Luther's concern. In fact, Luther's concern was Augustine's philosophical creation where the latter had supposed Creation to have been instantaneous. Augustine explained the Creation days as different aspects of a philosophical framework, the Creation of the different days in Genesis 1 depicting various aspects of God's instantaneous Creation. Luther's concern is that the days be seen as historical and literal rather than as philosophical. Though Luther declares for ordinary days, the length of the Creation days was not a subject that Christians then debated. Concern over the exact length of the Creation Days began with Isaac Newton.

Aside from prohibiting its use in geology, Lyell did not attack the Bible. He simply wanted to separate all history from geological science. Ascribing to philosophical idealism, Lyell had no way of integrating his understanding of man with the study of Nature. Had Lyell not rejected studying the earth in the light of the Bible, the Creation described in Genesis would have given him a rational means of distinguishing a time in the earth's history when humans did not exist. Lyell was most responsible for promoting the notion that the Flood was a recent historical event confined to some local region of the Ancient Near East or Asia, having no significance for the earth's greater geological history. As the nineteenth century drew to a close, a popular scientific explanation attributed the widespread ancient reports of a Flood to the melting of glaciers at the end of the Ice Age. The discoveries of the Mesopotamian accounts of the Flood caused even conservative Christians to embrace the notion of a local Flood, believing that humans had not spread beyond the locality where the Flood occurred.

In the early twentieth century when Fundamentalists were fighting evolution and modernism in the churches, most of them believed in an ancient earth and most of them were willing to embrace the notion of a local Flood. Those who did not, such as George McCready Price (1870-1963), were coming to seem an embarrassment to some Christians. The anti-evolutionist crusader William Jennings Bryan (1860-1925), himself a Day Age Creationist, championed Price as a believing scientist at the famous Scopes trial. Many conservative Christians sought to be known as "Evangelicals" rather than as Fundamentalists because they did not want to be seen as opposing science. The issue of the Flood was important because a worldwide Flood was no longer understood to be supported by science. In the early fifties, the prominent evangelical scholar Bernard Ramm (1916-1992) wrote an influential book defending scientific views of the earth and man's early history and attacking the notion of a worldwide Flood.[61] Billy Graham and the new evangelical establishment supported Ramm, but not everyone agreed.

---

[61] Bernard Ramm, *The Christian View of Science and Scripture* (Eerdmans, 1954).

—11—

Young Earth Creationism, its contributions and its problems

TODAY, MOST WHO believe there exists physical evidence of a worldwide Flood have in mind either the various claims concerning the remains of Noah's Ark or the theories and theology of an increasingly popular school of evangelical apologetics pertaining to the early chapters of Genesis. The latter is called Young Earth Creationism. Since their theory has become the most influential and currently almost the only well-known explanation of a Flood that covered the earth, I looked first to them for answers.

Young earth interpretations of the days of Creation and the age of the earth are ancient, but the Young Earth Creationist explanation of the earth's history is recent. Evangelicals began embracing Young Earth Creationism only in the sixties after John Whitcomb and Henry Morris wrote the book *The Genesis Flood*.[62] Responding to Ramm's book declaring a local Flood, it put forth a scientific theory supporting a worldwide Flood. It is easy to understand why sincere believers might want to oppose Ramm. Rather than advocating an uncompromising biblical faith in the clear teachings of the Bible, Ramm's influential book was more a celebration of modern science. This attitude flourished in middle twentieth-century America, the time of the splitting of the atom, the beginning of the race to space, and a drug culture that promised a pill for every human sickness or longing. Even Christians were expressing almost unlimited confidence in the potential of science. Some thought that the discoveries of science might allow people to live forever!

This era was also a high point in the development of the field of systems science; but as a systems engineer, I know that technological success is a triumph of human organization, specialization, management, and economic power –

---

[62] John C. Whitcomb and Henry M. Morris, *The Genesis Flood: The Biblical Record and its Scientific Implications* (Presbyterian & Reformed, 1961).

things that have been available in the earth since ancient Babel. God knows how much men can accomplish when they work together. Notwithstanding such potential, not only to be a faithful Christian but also to be a good scientist, we should be skeptical of broad scientific claims. We also need to be skeptical of scientific theories and theological systems that claim to be based on the Bible.

Young Earth Creationists effectively criticize theories that interpret the biblical Flood as a merely local affair. They point out that a Flood covering the tops of local mountains will cover the earth within forty days. They also explain that an Ark would not have been the best solution for surviving a geographically local Flood. I must agree. The "God" of a local Flood is either not serious, or not bright. Young Earth Creationists helped me understand that the Bible clearly teaches a worldwide Flood: one that covered "all the high mountains under the entire heavens." Here their exegesis is outstanding, while the readings of those who advocate a local Flood are contrived.

The Young Earth Creationists point out that Jesus taught in the context of a worldwide Flood. I have explained that Jesus' words drove me to seek the evidence of a Flood that must have occurred, regardless of the most esteemed opinions of our present age. Whatever my criticism of their science and theology, I am indebted to these Creationists. Their frank acknowledgement that the Scriptures teach a worldwide Flood explains why Young Earth Creationists have won the allegiance of so many believing Christians. In the latter years of the twentieth century, it seems that most evangelicals as well as many orthodox Jews and Muslims have adopted their understanding of the early chapters of Genesis. In the eyes of many, especially themselves, they are *the* Creationists.[63]

As the views of Creation and the Flood listed in the accompanying table demonstrate, this has not always been the case. The table is not exhaustive of views concerning the early chapters of Genesis, and a minority of those who hold views going by the names of the listed schools have positions that are slightly different from what I have summarized. Young Earth Creationists do not necessarily hold the most literalist view of the Bible, even concerning the earliest chapters of Genesis. Still, since the time it became clear that mankind long ago spread throughout the earth, making a local Flood impossible to square with the Scriptures, Young Earth Creationists seem to have stood alone in advocacy of a worldwide Flood. That has given this school a reputation of uncompromising fidelity to the Scriptures.

A frequent practice of Young Earth Creationists is to lump opposing views, including Darwinists and evolutionists who do not believe in God, under what they suppose to be an "Old Earth" school. The effect is to obscure the bib-

---

[63] Ronald Numbers, *The Creationists: The Evolution of Scientific Creationism* (University of California Press, 1993).

Chapter 11   Young Earth Creationism: its contributions and its problems

Views of Creation and the Flood

School	Creator	Age of Earth	Genesis Days	Age of Man	Flood
Darwinist	No God, or Deist God	~4.5 billion years	Myth	1 million plus years	Myth
Framework	God of Bible	~4.5 billion years	Days of Revelation	1 million plus years	Myth, or Local
Theistic Evolutionist	Deist God or God of Bible	~4.5 billion years	Day Age	100,000 years plus	Myth, or Local
Progressive Creationist	God of Bible	~4.5 billion years	Day Age	~6,000 years	Local
Young Earth Creationist	God of Bible	~6,000-10,000 years	24 hours	~6,000-10,000 years	Worldwide
Gap (Ruin & Restorationist)	God of Bible	Ancient	24 hours	~6,000 years	Local or Worldwide
Author's View	God of Bible	~13.7 billion years	God's workdays	~6,000 years	Worldwide

Correct view

lical commitments of conservatives who believe in an old earth but do not believe in evolution. They have succeeded in convincing many evangelicals – and many who are hostile to the Bible – that the days of Genesis can only be read in the sense of twenty-four-hour days, that the Bible teaches that not only man but the earth itself is no more than six to ten thousand years old, and that such a reading and dating has always been held by faithful Christians. Young Earth Creationist views have triumphed like this since my childhood. Nonetheless, I can remember when the majority of conservative Christians – including the most conservative Fundamentalists and the biblicist Pentecostalists – taught and believed in an old earth. Though believing in an old earth, the older generation of conservative Christians believed more strictly than the Young Earth Creationists that Adam and Eve, from whom all mankind descend, lived only about six thousand years ago. They were far less concerned that their view be regarded as scientific than are the Young Earth Creationists.

Young Earth Creationists are best at criticizing Darwinian evolution and the existing science pertaining to the ancient history of the earth. They were also the first to apply postmodernism to geology. These Creation Scientists agree that geology and ancient history can and should be studied in the light of the ordinary events and processes that the Bible itself recognizes and which science can study. Against the uniformitarian dogma of Charles Lyell that became the basis for modern geology, Young Earth Creationists point out that the ordinary

If God's workday is not 24 hours, Jesus could have been in the tomb for 3,000 years

processes we now see cannot explain *everything* that we know about the history of the earth. The world of the past may have been different from the world of today. There are also unique and sudden events that cannot be explained by the normal processes that we observe and study.

Owing to discovery of evidence for the "Big Bang," believers – and now modern scientists – recognize the initial Creation as one such event. But because of its association with a universe that is billions of years old, Young Earth Creationists do not believe in the Big Bang. They believe that both the earth and the universe were essentially created at once, in 144 consecutive hours, and that almost all the evidence of geological history since Creation was created by one catastrophic event: the Flood. Opposing Lyell's uniformitarianism, they reintroduced a form of catastrophism into geology, though not the scientifically prestigious geological catastrophism of Cuvier, which assumed that the earth revealed an ancient history punctuated with sudden changes.

Catastrophes are again in scientific fashion for explaining the disappearance of the dinosaurs some sixty million years ago and the far more recent disappearance of megafauna – mammoths, giant sloths, giant bears, and saber-tooth tigers – at the end of the last Ice Age when humans were present. Young Earth Creationists don't believe that dinosaurs became extinct before the Flood. Interestingly, they accept the Ice Age as the explanation of what was once attributed to Noah's Flood: the diluvial deposits near the surface of the earth wherein are found the last remains of the megafauna! The Young Earth Creationists need the Flood to explain the presence of so many fossils and so much coal, oil, and gas – all remains from former living things – found deep within an earth so young. They see the Flood as entirely destroying the surface of the earth, transforming its geology and creating gas, oil, coal, and fossils. They strenuously oppose views of the Flood that see the earth's interior undisturbed to thousands of feet below the present surface. This means that the pre-Flood surface of the earth, which would have contained the remains of antediluvian man, is no longer recognizable.

Young Earth Creationists explain that the layers of massive shells found deep under the earth were already present in great oceans when the Flood covered them. Vertebrates such as dinosaurs appear above them. Fossils of the mammals appear at the upmost levels because they were the most intelligent and agile, allowing them to climb higher as the waters of the Flood rose. Regardless of this explanation for the ordering of fossil remains, they deny that there is any particular order to the geological column. They use their version of the Genesis Flood to explain almost everything or anything that might be found in the earth's geological history pertaining to living things.

Chapter 11 Young Earth Creationism: its contributions and its problems

Whatever the Flood cannot explain about the earth's history, they attribute to God creating things with the appearance of age. This does not just mean mature or fully developed things: the first man Adam, created as a physically mature adult so as to name the animals in a single day before the creation of Eve; or the mature trees bearing fruit in the Garden of Eden that God had prepared within the same week. It also refers to changes due to "apparent" aging such as the slow buildup of strata and evidence of "apparently" long periods of radioactive decay. This allows them to see a young and rapidly created earth, one that is only a few days older than man.

Young Earth Creationist science provides plentiful mysteries. Why would God create things with the appearance of age? If God created whatever we happen to find, perhaps he also created what Young Earth Creationists now attribute to the Flood. In fact, such an initial creation would better explain the strata and the sand in the sandstone of the Grand Canyon that Young Earth Creationists attribute to the Flood. A flood mixes things, sorting them by currents and specific gravity. One can see this by examining the stratum created by known floods. Repeated floods may create strata, but single floods – whether local and small, or covering the entire earth – should not. The lack of strata within the diluvian (now called Pleistocene) deposits caused earlier geologists to identify this level with the Flood. The problem of the Grand Canyon is far more difficult than appears. Had the Flood somehow created the deep strata, how in the same year did it carve the deep canyon through the same strata?

A bigger problem is that there are fossils of living organisms in the massive sandstone forming the canyon walls, but sandstone comes from the erosion of the same type of rock as found in the sand. Because these scientists understand that the less than two thousand years between Creation and the Flood is too short for ordinary erosion to create the needed sand, they claim the Flood ground the sand from the primary stones of the earth's initial creation at places where this type of stone is found, then transported and deposited this sand together with living organisms in the canyon, formed the rocks, and eroded the canyon.

I can see how the Flood may have carved or widened this great gully and deposited some remains, but I could never understand how the Flood might have created its deep fossil-laden strata as the Young Earth Creationists claim. Neither could I understand how they suppose that mammals are better swimmers than fish. In light of the biblical account, I could not understand how most of the victims of the Flood were creatures that lived in the sea.

As part of his solution to the mystery of the Flood's water source, Henry Morris proposed a vapor canopy that covered the earth before the Flood, suggesting that this vapor canopy gave rise to a more tropical environment before the Flood. This contrasts with what they see as a great Ice Age after the Flood when dinosaurs saved by the Ark roamed the earth. But Morris's vapor canopy cannot hold water. A cloud is essentially a vapor canopy, though one that holds only several inches or feet of water. When it does have a few feet of water, the sun does not get through. Water vapor is lighter than air, but not if it somehow contains enough water for it to have substantially contributed to the Flood, in which case it would have displaced the lighter atmosphere below. It is perhaps not surprising that a professor of hydraulic engineering rather than a practicing engineer proposed this theory.

The Young Earth Creationists tell us that men walked the earth during the era of the great dinosaurs. They believe that dinosaurs roamed the earth *after* the Flood. In fact, no human remains have ever been found even remotely associated with the places where we find dinosaurs. Nor are dinosaur bones found alongside the remains of early humans. Despite Young Earth Creationist illustrations, there are no dinosaur remains in the diluvial deposits now attributed to the Ice Age. (Perhaps someone confused mammoth remains with dinosaurs). In any case, the presence of large animals suggests a frigid rather than a tropical climate. The more responsible Young Earth Creationists admit that there is no evidence of men associated with dinosaurs, but if they found such things they would not attribute it to the Flood. As I will explain, they don't want to find evidence for the remains of human beings who drowned in the Flood!

Darwinists love having proponents of a young earth, with their artificial interpretation of the "Flood" and of an earth with only the appearance of age, represent Creationists and those who believe the Bible. Young Earth Creationists are happy to own this calling, joyfully enduring the scoffing world. For this, I admire them. It also brings them valuable attention from the media and from those who find their claims an easy way to discredit those who believe in Creation, especially those who claim to literally believe the Bible. This explains how Young Earth Creationists managed to appropriate 'Intelligent Design' from the learned and sophisticated opponents of Darwinism who created the new science and introduced the term in the early nineties.

By now it should be clear: whether coming from Young Earth Creationists or mainstream scientists, geology is highly speculative. Regardless of the problems with their particular views, because I needed to believe in the Flood I might have been satisfied with their contention that mainstream geology had made some great mistakes. Since I knew that geology is in fact very subjective, I could have left the matter there, were it not for the facts I mentioned in the first chapter of this book: Young Earth Creationists are uncomfortable discussing evidence from ancient man prior to the time of Abraham, or relating what

Chapter 11 Young Earth Creationism: its contributions and its problems

the Bible says about these things to what they agree we know from archaeology and ancient history.

For them and for me, the Pyramids are a troubling problem. We know these predate Abraham. Israel borders Egypt, and the Israelites lived there four hundred years. Young Earth Creationists claim that all human remains date from after the Flood, but why doesn't the Bible mention these extensive civilizations of the Ancient Near East? In the less than five hundred years that separate Abraham from the Flood, how do we account for so much evidence of early man: the remains of the Paleolithic and Neolithic throughout the earth and those of the extensive Early Bronze civilizations throughout the Ancient Near East? What caused me to reject Young Earth Creationism is their inability to shed light on the massive remains that exists for early man in the era prior to Abraham.

Because it is the Bible, we cannot say that such things don't matter. That would put the Bible on the level of myth. The Bible is about truth. Moreover, the Scriptures tell us that we should test things for their accordance with the truth. Escapist myth does not and cannot shine revealing light on the simple truth of history. If the early chapters of the Bible are truth rather than myth they ought to help us make sense of the evidence of early man. Young Earth Creationists cannot explain the remains from mankind's earliest history, which is to conclude that the Bible gives little light!

Neither are the Young Earth Creationists consistent in their claims to interpret the Bible literally. While rigid about the duration of the days of Creation, they stretch out the biblical time-scale from the creation of Adam and from the time of Noah in order to account for an Ice Age and for so much evidence of ancient man. They have no trouble expanding the genealogies found in the Bible, and seeing the Creation of Adam as early as ten thousand years ago. Despite their claims and reputation, they explain parts of the early chapters of Genesis in a rationalistic and non-literal manner.

Astonishingly, Young Earth Creationists teach that there is little or no evidence of the violent human civilization that God sent the Flood to destroy. That would contradict their young-earth geology. They need a Flood of evidence-destroying capacity in order to explain the lack of human remains among the dinosaurs and deeper fossils, though human artifacts of metal and stone, even human bones, are harder than soft dinosaur bones. In any case, the Bible says nothing about God intending mainly to drown or destroy dinosaurs, giant elephants, ferns, and forests, all for the seeming purposes of creating coal, gas, and oil for use by our modern world. For this, they are not using the light of the Bible.

Neither are they fully consistent with regard to the Flood destroying all the evidence of antediluvian man. They point to the considerable evidence of the

Part IV   Scientific Prehistory and the Problem of Noah's Flood

worldwide spread of ancient man as contradicting the notion of an anthropologically universal but geographically local Flood. The Flood seems to have obliterated all the evidence of the wicked generation that lived at the time of the Flood, yet somehow plenty of remains from those who had lived and died before that great event were preserved. How were the Tigris and Euphrates Rivers that watered the Garden of Eden preserved from a Flood that entirely destroyed the surface of the earth as it rearranged geology thousands of feet below?

One eventually discovers that the chief concern of the Young Earth Creationists (the scientific school, though not all who believe in a young earth) is not the matter of the Flood, but as their name suggest, using the Flood to defend a young earth and 24-hour Creation days. This is because from its very beginnings, Young Earth Creation science has been deeply influenced by Seventh Day Adventist theology concerning twenty-four-hour creation days, and denying even animal death before the fall of Adam. These and related ideas concerning Creation are rooted in the visions, dreams, study, and religious beliefs of Seventh Day Adventist founder, Ellen G. White (1827-1915).

Ellen G. White   George McGready Price

FIGURE 13   FOUNDERS OF MODERN YOUNG EARTH CREATIONISM

Mrs. White explains that she was carried back in a vision to the Creation where she was showed that God created the earth in six consecutive twenty-four hour days. She was also shown how forests buried by the Flood created deposits of coal and oil. She endorsed the view that the Flood was responsible for the earth's fossils. More to the point, the literal days of Genesis showed that Christians were wrong not to observe a literal Sabbath (Saturday). One can see how Seventh Day Adventists were delighted with a vision confirming a neo-Judaizing theology that most Christians opposed. The now unheralded Adventist founder of Young Earth Creationism, George McCready Price, acknowl-

Chapter 11   Young Earth Creationism: its contributions and its problems

edged her theology and teachings as his motivation and guide. Whitcomb and Morris expropriated the system of the Adventist geologist as the basis of their influential book. Though mentioning Price as a geologist, they did not explain just how much their book and theory owed to his science. That Price did not complain does not justify such neglect.

However much suspicion it may cast, the motivation behind a system of ideas does not entail its falsehood. That must be independently determined, but suppressing these roots does not speak well of the transparency of those who borrowed Adventist theology and geological theory. It does explain why the majority of Young Earth Creationists do not know the roots or much understand the theory that has gained their allegiance. One indication of Adventist influence upon Young Earth Creationists is the tendency to defend this interpretation of the first chapter of Genesis by accusing Old Earth and Day-Age Creationists of "compromise." Christians ought to separate themselves from those who compromise righteousness or truth, but that seems an odd and severe charge to make concerning the exegesis of scripture pertaining to chronology — that is, until one realizes the importance this matter holds for key tenets of the Seventh Day Adventist sect. I cannot understand why a non-Adventist would make such a charge unless he believed the teaching so indefensible that his students and supporters need to be shielded from criticism and from other views.

This attitude does not represent the majority of young earth Creationists who only want to believe the Bible with integrity, in accordance with their commitment to truth. They are my brother and sister believers, and my brother and sister pilgrims along the journey toward greater light. In truth, Whitcomb and Morris convinced me that the Bible teaches a worldwide Flood. There was in fact a time when old earth Creationist William Jennings Bryan and young earth Creationist George McCready Price could work on far more serious issues *together*.

Like everyone else, Young Earth Creationists work mainly with the various data obtained from modern geology and archaeology that have been developed from an understanding of an ancient earth. They must explain away the appearance of age seen in the deep strata of the Grand Canyon and in the fossils of strange animals that no longer roam the earth. Their geology mainly consists of rearranging the pre-interpreted facts of modern geology to fit a young earth theology.

> Creationist use the Bible as their basis for a young earth God created everything in 6 days. Anyone teaching otherwise is a false teacher.

— 12 —

The light by which we see

ONE CANNOT BLAME Young Earth Creationists for creating geology in their young-earth light by revising conventional geology. They point out, as did Alfred North Whitehead and Albert Einstein, that there are no un-interpreted facts. Bare data impacting our instruments and eyes is meaningless. Without some kind of interpretive light we see and remember nothing at all, hence everything we know has to be seen, described, discussed, and remembered in some kind of light. And for the last three hundred years, almost everything known about geology has been gathered under the light of an ancient earth. Practically everything known about the earliest history has been gathered in the light of a historiography of man that extends to hundreds of thousands or even to millions of years ago. All this information has been analyzed in the light of strictly natural causes because as a matter of dogma modern scientists refuse to consider divinely caused miracles, the purposes or intent of God, or revelation from a God who acts within the course of man's history. The history of the earth is no longer studied in the light of the Bible or in the light of the Flood.

Whether skeptic or believer, scientist or theologian, the intellectually sophisticated understand that this has more to do with philosophical commitments than with the evidence. Our choice is not whether we use some kind of light to view the evidence, but what kind of light we choose. More than we consciously choose, we absorb the light we use from our parents, culture, training, and personal experiences. Our postmodern generation understands this better than the older modern era when science was naively understood as innately objective, giving what they supposed to be a realist view of the world.

Scientific theories are a form of light. The fashionable word for the big theories such as Darwinian evolution or Young Earth Creationist science by which we view many and various things is *paradigm*. Thomas Kuhn (1922-1996), who introduced the term to the philosophy of science, explained that science normally proceeds by working within some unquestioned paradigm that scientists accept as the premise of their understanding.[64] Kuhn explained how a shift to a new paradigm occurs as its proponents gain attention, new students, and political and institutional support and as the influence and numbers of proponents of the old paradigm fades. A new paradigm creates a scientific revolution as everything previously known comes to be explained in the new light, but this doesn't mean that all paradigms are equal. We know that successful practical application is important. Unfortunately, in the case of the all-encompassing theories concerning the big issues of our world, of life, and of man, I have observed that political and social fashions are even more influential. Religious views function in much the same way.

Scientific paradigms are lights by which the observations of our physical senses are explained. The Aristotelian earth-centered universe was once the paradigm used by medieval astronomers to study the skies. With the Copernican revolution, they shifted to a sun-centered cosmos. Paradigms may be embedded within still larger paradigms, more commonly called philosophies, though nowadays called worldviews. The earth-centered cosmos embedded in Aristotelian philosophy was adapted to Christian theology in the late Middle Ages. The Copernican view was likewise compatible with both biblical and naturalistic views. World-encompassing philosophies or views function the same way as Kuhn explained scientific paradigms. This is to say none of them can be established by logic because they themselves determine how one reasons. They are just accepted (on faith), whether for good or bad, personal or practical reasons.

As an example, those wedded to scientism systematically reject reports that cannot be physically explained, assigning them to hallucinations, untrained imaginations, or wishful dreams. Their light shows spiritual sources as darkness. Those using the Bible as their light might test whether they come from either holy or unclean spiritual sources, or whether they are indeed from a more ordinary source whether of the imagination or some drug. Trusting the spiritual world of the Bible allows one to live in a richer, more interesting world, one full of significance from the smallest details to the cosmic dimension. The light of the Bible functions well in ordering observations and experiences because, as do systems of science, it also recognizes a definite order to the world. The Psalms and the books of wisdom, Job, Ecclesiastes, and Proverbs, notably extol the firm order and beauty of Creation. The faith of the Bible differs from strange myths, philosophies, religions, and even scientific claims that ignore the created order.

No one should suppose that a scientific paradigm or scientistic philosophy deriving from the hard sciences is more objective than the biblical view. Despite the supposed impersonal objectivity of empirical data, all evidence – even the

---

[64] Thomas Kuhn, *The Structure of Scientific Revolutions* (University of Chicago Press, 1962).

empirical observations that we associate with science – eventually becomes human testimony because someone must record and preserve the observations, and someone must evaluate their meaning. Owing to social and political factors at work in the selection of paradigms, scientific observations and theories do not escape human bias and subjectivity as often supposed. Notwithstanding earlier pronouncements that the worldview of the Bible is soon to die, and despite the recent dominance of the modernist worldview, the Bible has crossed into more nations and cultures and has better stood the test of time than any philosophy or system of science. That includes modern science and the modernist view that, ironically, defines itself through its opposition to the Bible.

Just as scientific paradigms are different kinds of light, so are various theologies or systems of theology, whether they are rooted in the Bible, some sect, some teacher, or some philosophy or science. Scripture itself is light. So are the luminaries or the people in whom we believe. Whatever books, or whatever Scripture, or in whatever or in whomever we truly believe is the light by which we see. Our most important light comes from the things that we deeply and implicitly believe. These are the "truths" we assume that everyone believes. It may never have occurred to us to question certain things. We may be so convinced of inherited truths that we are unaware that we have at some point learned, absorbed, or chosen to believe them. Usually, we discover this only when we encounter those who do not believe things that we have never doubted.

A. Consideration   **B. Conversion**   **C. Conviction**
FIGURE 14   STAGES OF BELIEF

A light of which we are hardly conscious has become part of our very soul or being. We can compare a paradigm to a lamp that has been turned on and taken for granted. If we are conscious of some new idea or teaching and are considering whether to believe it, it is like a light-bulb that we are evaluating to determine whether it is a good or bad bulb, though we have neither turned it on nor used it. [Fig 14A] We turn on the lamp the moment we believe it. [Fig 14B]

If we really believe it, we will use it until we become unconscious of doing so. [Fig 14C].

Taking up a new paradigm, even a scientific paradigm, can also be compared to conversion to some religion or sect of belief. Karl Popper (1902–1994), another important philosopher of science, writes about various ideas that were in the air in Vienna in 1919, immediately following the collapse of the Austrian Empire:

> **Whatever books, or whatever Scripture, or in whatever or in whomever we truly believe is the light by which we see.**

> I found that those of my friends who were admirers of Marx, Freud, and Adler, were impressed by a number of points common to these theories, especially by their apparent *explanatory* power. These theories appear to be able to explain practically everything that happened within the fields to which they referred. The study of any of them seemed to have the effect of an intellectual conversion or revelation, opening your eyes to a new truth hidden from those not yet initiated. Once your eyes were thus opened you saw confirmed instances everywhere: the world was full of verifications of the theory. Whatever happened always confirmed it. Thus its truth appeared manifest; and unbelievers were clearly people who did not want to see the manifest truth; who refuse to see it, either because it was against their class interest, or because of their repressions which were still "un-analyzed" and crying aloud for treatment.

> The most characteristic element in this situation seemed to me the incessant stream of confirmations, of observations which "verified" the theories in question. A Marxist could not open a newspaper without finding on every page confirming evidence for his interpretation of history; not only in the news, but also in its presentation – which revealed the class bias of the paper – and especially in what the paper did *not* say. The Freudian analysts emphasized that their theories were constantly verified by their "clinical observations." As for Adler, I was much impressed by a personal experience. Once, in 1919, I reported to him a case which to me did not seem particularly Adlerian, but which he found no difficulty in analyzing in terms of his theory of inferiority feelings, although he had not even seen the child. Slightly shocked, I asked him how he could be so sure. "Because of my thousandfold experience," he replied; whereupon I could not help saying: "And with this new case, I suppose, your experience has become a thousand-and-one fold."

> What I had in mind was that his previous observations may not have been much sounder than this new one; that each in its turn had been interpreted in the light of "previous experience", and at the same time counted as additional confirmation. What, I asked, myself, did it confirm? No more than that a case could be interpreted in the light of a theory. But this meant very little. I reflected, since every conceivable case could be interpreted in the light of Adler's theory, or equally Freud's. I may illustrate this by two very different examples of human behavior: that of a man who pushes a child into the water with the intention of drowning it; and that of a man who sacrifices his life in an attempt to save the child. Each of these cases can be ex-

plained with equal ease in Freudian and Adlerian terms. According to Freud, the first man suffered from repression (say, of some component of his Oedipus complex), while the second man had achieved sublimation. According to Adler the first man suffered from feelings of inferiority (producing perhaps the need to prove to himself that he dared to commit some crime), and so did the second man (whose need was to prove to himself that he dared to rescue the child). I could not think of any human behavior which could not be interpreted in terms of either theory. [Karl R. Popper, *Conjectures and Refutations* (Routledge and Kegan Paul, 1963).]

In the next chapter I will return to Popper's important insight, which challenged 'verifiable observation' as the basis of scientific knowledge. Here I want to mention one important paradigm or light that is not so much thought of in terms of a scientific, social, political, or theological hero or genius – though Isaac Newton was the most important contributor – as centuries of cultural development. This paradigm that transcends scientific and religious parties is vital to the way that modern man reads the Bible, to Young Earth Creationists' interpretation of the days of Genesis, and to the way we all envision the age of the universe.

FIGURE 15   INFLUENTIAL PHILOSOPHERS OF SCIENCE

I refer to the common sense framework of absolute and physically measurable time and space underlying Newton's science of mechanics that, however outdated it has become in the science of physics, still defines the way our modern Western minds interpret the world, history, and the Bible. When Newton called absolute space and time "the sensorium of God," the way that God perceives things, he projected the physical way that man perceives things onto God, as if God had a physical body. The Scriptures tell us that God is a spirit, or Spirit. He is also absolute and remembers things that men have forgotten. He can and does erase things from his time and from our time, something that would not be possible in the kind of absolute time that Newton imagined. God can erase things from the physical world and from the memories of men as if they had never happened. Only God is absolute and

Chapter 12   The light by which we see

unchanging. Time has no independent existence. It is God's creation, subject to what he wills it to do.

Some philosophers have noted that there are different kinds of time. One is the quantitative or *measured* time, used in the absolute time of Newton's science of mechanics. We can also call it clock time because markers such as the successive ticks, pendulum swings, or movement across the markings on a clock face are used to measure this time. Various kinds of time-markers are provided by the daily appearance of the sun, the monthly changes in the phases of the moon, and by the annual rotation of the stars in the heavens. Days can be divided into hours by clocks, and endlessly sub-divided by our many ways of envisioning time. Quantitative time is used in industry, business, social and institutional affairs. As we would measure a space by a rod or length of standard measure, some measure of time is externally imposed on whatever span of time whose duration we wish to determine.

Another kind is qualitative or *genetic* time, which is created when subsequent events follow previous things upon which they depend. Logicians would explain it as time based upon internal rather than external relationships, as is the case when we use an external measure. The arrow of history belonging to the Bible is genetic time. The stages of the growth of an organism and the personal history of each of us also concern genetic time. We experience things organically and genetically as well as mechanically and quantitatively. Though these quantitative and qualitative kinds of time may be combined, they are distinct. All of us experience genetic time in our undivided moments of experience, when we are fully involved in what we are doing without self-consciousness or analysis. Genetic time may seem to have a certain measure because we are aware of living and experiencing through our physical body and senses that are subject to measure. Whatever the measure, the duration may be of no great significance to those who experience the event being measured. The inhabitants of Heaven, one might suppose, live in genetic time, while those in the earth tend to see things through measured time. Seen though the eyes of God, genetic time is an aspect of eternity though the man who is made in the image of God can also experience this kind of time.

The Creation days of Genesis must also be genetic time because they are presented to us, we presume, through the experience of the Creator who is not subject to our measure of time. God specifically uses "evening and morning" to describe the Creation days, but these directional and boundary markers are aspects of genetic rather than measured time. One might reckon that God described his days of Creation like this specifically because they were not ordinary solar days. The account in Genesis does not mention "evening and morning" for the seventh day because God remains in his seventh day rest.[65] The seventh day of the Creation week has lasted far more than twenty-four hours, but in truth when we observe the Sabbath, we are off the clock.

The sun did not exist for the first days of the Creation week, but we can project them as solar days or imagine them divided into twenty-four hours, which is a measure of clock time. We can project such time infinitely into the past, or as beginning at some point in an absolute frame of reference. Most of us have done this because it is the kind of time that belongs to the world of man, especially the world of the businessman and the modern West. We can also imagine the days of Genesis to be measured like this, but we must keep in mind that we only imagine this.

It is not just the days of Genesis that cannot be comprehended by measured time. The prophecies in the Bible have the same independence from measured time. Their fulfillment may not depend on some measure of time, but on the occurrence of certain conditions according to God's measure of mercy and grace. The great Day of the Lord appears like this. Nor is it just the Bible where the two kinds of time are used and where discriminating between these two kinds of time is necessary for a proper understanding. Modern physics has discovered that Newton's laws break down at the limits – whether at the beginnings of the cosmos, at great speeds, or at the smallest levels of matter. Quantum states cannot be divided. This deeper and more sophisticated understanding of physics – what is labeled in the narrow sense as modern physics – dates only to the twentieth century with the rise of relativity and quantum physics. This suggests that genetic time is more fundamental than measured time, and that the beginnings recounted in Genesis should be understood in the same way.

The more meaningful human experiences occur in genetic time. We can reflect on them in measured time but fail to comprehend either the measure or the meaning. The purpose of the Sabbath was for man to forget his time-driven activities for a day by trusting in God. God is not "on the clock." The clock does not govern him. He governs the clock. Such an ignoring of temporal or visible significance by the God of the Bible does not just pertain to the measure of time. The Old Testament Scriptures make it clear that God does not judge or evaluate by the same measure as man. Even more do Jesus and the Apostles emphasize this point. On the other hand, the things of God may have little significance in the eyes of the world that measures according to the visible or physical world. The great periods of prehistoric time or the great expanse of our universe as understood in terms of our physical observations and measures which so impresses man may have little significance to the Creator who does not himself dwell in physical space and time. Regardless of their great extent

---

[65] Hebrews 4

by physical measurement, God is sovereign over both the visible and invisible worlds.

Because of the successful application to astronomy of Newton's laws of physics, we know that Newton's way of looking at aspects of the world has a measure of truth. That such a physical understanding works so well for non-living things such as rocks, planets, and missiles, for the physical properties of our living bodies, and to plan our human affairs – even for liturgical calendars and biblical chronology, history, and geography – does not mean that it applies to life itself or to the spiritual dimensions of our existence. Nor does it mean that the spiritual dimensions of this world such as our souls must depend on the physical world. This framework fails completely to comprehend spirits, or spiritual understanding. This was the great mistake made by Isaac Newton, his predecessors at Cambridge University, and those who have followed them in interpreting the sacred Bible in this profane and materialist way. As were many American biblical teachers, the Seventh Day Adventists were particularly influenced by Newton's materialist, date-calculating way of interpreting biblical prophecy.[66]

Nor is it only the Young Earth Creationists and Fundamentalists who use this reductionist framework to interpret the Bible. Modernists share this same reductionist scientific framework for understanding the world. It developed from the Scientific Revolution, when the assumption that reality is fundamentally physical acquired scientific support. Young Earth Creationists point out how modernist biblical scholars, though they view these Scriptures as pious myth, claim that the days of Genesis should be literally read as 24-hour days. They point to the example of the late James Barr (1924-2006).

If one prefers these Scriptures to be myth, I understand why one would want to believe such things. I can see why our contemporary world that doesn't want to believe the teachings of the Scriptures would be especially fond of reading the words of the Bible in such a fashion. Barr however is complaining, though he is writing as late as the seventies, that the literal way Fundamentalists were reading the Bible – that is, the Creation days as eras – was not the way his modernist mind demands.[67] His literalist view demands that the ancient prophets, like other primitives, were materialists in their understanding, and that what they wrote must have only concerned themselves. Barr did not believe an ancient text like the Bible could possibly be intended for modern folks, nor would he be inclined to believe that it contained truth that would together with modern physics challenge his primitive version of scientific truth. In truth, both Fundamentalist and liberal views of the world are modern. This explains why controversies over the length

---

[66] cf Adventist scholar Leroy Edwin Froom's magisterial 4-volume *The Faith of Our Fathers* (Review and Herald, 1954).
[67] James Barr, *Fundamentalism* (SCM Press, 1977), 40-55.

of the days of Genesis post-date Isaac Newton. Many of us read the entire Bible and every other book, document, or human communication pertaining to the world or history in the light of the same kind of mechanical time. We do this as unconsciously as ancient folks saw things in terms of an earth that did not move and in terms of a sky that did.

We may even believe that the God who inspired these Scriptures intended for us to read his words this way. Having believed what Young Earth Creationists and anti-biblical modernists were teaching, I once made the mistake of claiming that before the rise of modern science no one would have taught that there was a gap between the first and second verses of Genesis. I had the embarrassing misfortune to write this to some who were actually familiar with early and medieval Christian and Jewish interpretations of the first chapter of Genesis.[68] After better instruction, I learned that most of today's explanations of the first chapter of Genesis have a long history. We modernist are not so sophisticated as we suppose.

Some ancient readers of the Bible also noted that the sun that marks the days was only created on the fourth day. Others saw how, in distinction from so many pagan creationists, Genesis shows God creating everything in Nature before he created man. Still others reckoned that there was some long era before the beginning of the six days of creation. What about all the activities of God with the angels before some of them rebelled? That must have occurred before Satan tempted Eve. What of the other activities of Adam, such as the naming of all the animals before the creation of Eve, which we suppose happened on the sixth day? Everything created has to follow the beginning of Creation, but six short solar days of Creation did not fit much of what the Bible related pertaining to God, man, and the angels.

I have explained that before recent times few regarded the age of the earth or the length of the Creation days as a matter pertaining to faith. The great skeptic Voltaire accepted Ussher's teaching that the world was created in 4004 BC as a matter of acceding to the most advanced learning and philosophy. If believers in Ussher's day may have been more skeptical at such a scholarly attempt at dating Creation, some who rejected the God of the Bible for the God of the Deists believed in a young earth. The earliest concerns with the Bible's chronology came more from the greater antiquity claimed for Egypt and for Asian nations such as China and India. Far more important than the age of the earth or the duration of the days of Genesis was the great antiquity being claimed for man, and the fact that man was coming to be seen as evolved from apes or monkeys. These are the concerns that caused Bryan and Price to work together. The matter is different today because the only current defense of a worldwide Flood is linked to

---

[68] My special appreciation here to William ("Bearded Bill") Thurman.

Chapter 12 The light by which we see

the Young Earth Creationists' interpretation of the first chapter of Genesis, and because an unbelieving world has delighted to see such an artificial and what now seems outdated interpretation fastened to the Bible.

> His teaching is incorrect on creation. If we believe God created the earth and all that is in it in thousands of years, it destroys all confidence in any biblical teaching that references time. Was Jesus in the tomb for 3 days or 3 thousand years? What is the Day of the Lord? It is clearly the Rapture and beginning of God's judgment, but is it one day or 1,000 years? and what of the 1,000 year reign of Christ on earth, is it 1,000 years or 1,000,000 years? We must believe that God spoke to us clearly and believe His word. 1,000 years as a day and a day as thousands years, simply reveal that God does not operate in our time.

— 13 —

How light can be tested

MANY HAVE COME to understand that the wildly different kinds of light that have been advocated for various fields of science or for explaining the workings of society, human minds, and human history are less objective than once thought. Others have noticed the same lack of objectivity in the conflicting theologies by which different sects and schools teach the Scriptures and the history of the Church. Careful historians have studied the political and social circumstances and the cultural and religious fashions in which these scientific paradigms and religious traditions are rooted. All this explains the recent move to postmodernism and to championing pluralistic beliefs against truth. But however understandable their skepticism, postmodernists, who admit to being in darkness, have no business lecturing anyone about light.

Instead of humbly acknowledging their lack of light, many today seem intent on privileging *their* view that truth is unknowable, unimportant, or does not exist. In truth, when choosing our light we need not be captive to skepticism as some demand. Jesus warns us to be careful that the light within us is not darkness. Bad light shows things in a dim or distorted fashion. In poor light mere shadows may appear real, while real entities such as the Lord God may be hidden in what appears to the world as darkness. At the dedication of the Temple, Solomon declared, "The LORD has said that he would dwell in a dark cloud." [1Kings 8:12] As I discovered in my encounter with God, he is just where the best wisdom of this world is absolutely certain that he isn't. That is what makes the darkness thick. God hides himself in darkness or what the world believes to be darkness because they have chosen darkness as their light.

Fortunately, there is a way to discern light from darkness, good light from bad light. Jesus recommended that we judge a tree by its fruit. Along these lines, a light can and should be judged by how poorly or how well it helps us see and by how much we can practically accomplish with it. Francis Bacon, illustrious champion of inductive reasoning, described ways of thinking based on tradi-

Chapter 13   How light can be tested

tion, commerce, or idle speculation as *idols* of the tribe, marketplace, or cave. Bad light believed infallible is indeed the same as an idol, a false god, or cult. False teachings give some explanation or interpretation of the world and of the Scriptures but, like idols, depend entirely on the support and labor of their devotees. Not only do false beliefs fail to show us what is truly important, their defects must be constantly explained away. By contrast, a true light should be like the true God: not dependent on us, but able and faithful to help, heal, prosper, liberate, and bring life and peace to those who believe and obey. The true God does not depend on devotees; everyone requires his help both to live and to see. His truth sets us free from the darkness chaining our minds and hearts.

Even if a light is inadequate for many things, certain kinds of light can still be useful for putting light on special things. Figure 16 illustrates three kinds of lights that one might use in searching for the evidence of Noah's Flood. Though in different ways, all three should assist this search if genuine light is coming from them.

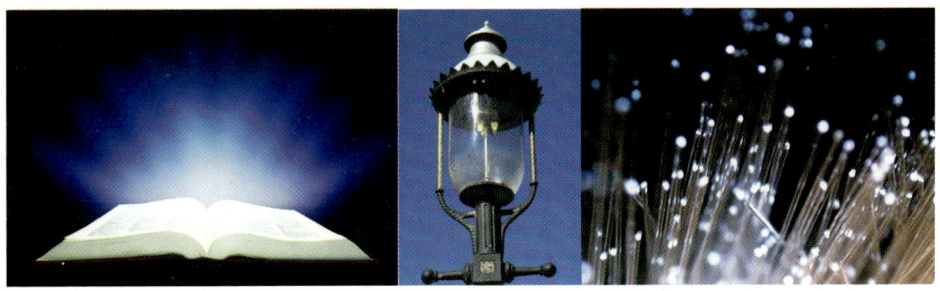

| The Light of the Word | Young Earth Theology | Modern Science |

Figure 16   **Three kinds of light for understanding ancient history**

The first light is from the Scriptures. If the Scriptures truly are communication to us from the Creator and Supreme Ruler, they certainly ought to illuminate the evidence both of Creation and the early history of man. It may be that our modern world sees no light from the Scriptures because it refuses to turn on this lamp. We keep it as an old lantern in the museum of science and history, as an outmoded light that men used before modern, scientific lighting. Since my conversion, when this "outmoded" lantern turned on inside my heart, I determined to use its straightforward words to investigate our world and history.

The second and third pictures depict light from two kinds of science. If imperfect, each should give light in certain areas because both originated from studying the earth in the light of the Bible. Keep in mind that modern scientific theory has its roots in theology developed from the Bible. Many today equate

115

or ~~conflate~~ Young Earth Creationist theology with the light coming from the Bible. As I explained, it is Adventist theology indebted to science, though some outdated versions of science, and to areas of science developed specifically to oppose the Bible and the Flood. Using the lens of Adventist theology, it builds on the science of Copernicus, Descartes, Newton, Burnet, Whiston, Woodward, Agassiz, and even their geological nemesis Charles Lyell more than it builds on the plain words of the Bible. Its light also deflects us from the central teachings of the Scripture. *[margin: not true]*

Young Earth Creationism seems to be more concerned with showing us how we should read Scripture than helping us understand Creation and the history of man, in fact the same as in the case of the modern literary criticism of the Bible! As is modern critical scholarship – and as were the theologies of Augustine, Aquinas, and Calvin – Young Earth Creationism is a light used not just to enlighten the scientific or historical evidence, but also the Bible. The difficulties I find with this light are not owing to its fidelity to the Bible – certainly not its teaching of a worldwide Flood – but to its scientific interpretation not only of Creation, but also of Scripture. Young Earth Creationists promoted their theology as science rather than as teachings of the Bible in order to get it accepted in America's public schools. That effort failed, but this school of Creation theology loves referring to and seeing their work as scientific. As have many evangelical schools of higher learning, Young Earth Creationists are increasingly concerned with scientific credentialism. Their aim seems to be winning respect from science and from the world! Those with demonstrably good light will be giving rather than seeking credentials. *[margin: Because their view is both Biblical and correct]*

Despite the claims of secularists, the roots of modern science and especially modern geology are rooted in the Bible. Thanks to belief in the monotheistic Creator of the Bible, the notion of common laws for both the heavens and the earth triumphed over Aristotelian science. Likewise, our modern sense of linear history derived from the Bible triumphed over the eternalist world of the same Aristotelian science. I have explained how the basic divisions of geological strata and the understanding of a long prehistoric era prior to man developed from studying the earth in the light of the Flood. Ironically, modern science is based more carefully on studying the earth in the light of the biblical teachings of the Creation and Flood than are the theories and theology of the Young Earth Creationists!

Young Earth Creationist science suffers by repudiating the understanding of the earth in the light of Genesis and the light of the biblical Flood that modern geology partially retains. Moreover, their science is out of date. That is why I represent this particular theory or light by the gas lamp. It does however have greater integration and unity than the highly fragmented condition of modern

[margin: The Author is more focused on secular geologist time table rather than Genesis time table which creationist use. He consistently falsifies their beliefs.]

science since the latter cut its moorings from the Bible. This explains why I use unbundled fiber strands to represent the light of modern science. In the next chapter, I will discuss the problem caused by modern science's fragmented nature. The strands of fiber optics also reveal the excellence of modern science in its narrow and specialized applications such as telecommunications, genetics, and medicine. Scientific light is useful for understanding only the physical things of this world, and the narrower or more specialized, the better it serves as a light. A theory that makes specific predictions about the behavior of specific things so as to be practically useful is the same kind of theory that can be tested and possibly proven false.

Karl Popper, who wrote the passages I quoted in the last chapter, put forth testability or falsifiability as the proper criterion for determining whether a theory is scientific. Marx, Freud, and Adler had all declared their theories to be scientific. Popper compared their theories with Einstein's theory of relativity, which was coming into prominence at the same time. Unlike them, Einstein had no need to assert that his theory of relativity was scientific because even though many then doubted whether his theory of relativity was true, everyone regarded it as scientific. Popper attempted to explain what gave Einstein's theory scientific status and how it differed from the pseudo-scientific theories of Marx, Freud, Adler, as well as various kinds of astrology and magic. He pointed to the famous test of Einstein's theory that occurred when Sir Arthur Eddington traveled to the coast of West Africa to measure the deflection of starlight by the sun during the solar eclipse of 1919. Einstein's theory of general relativity predicted that the sun's gravity would bend the light from stars by a specific and measurable amount. Those gathered in London for a meeting of the Royal Society anxiously awaited Eddington's telegram from Africa to be read by Alfred North Whitehead, then President of the Royal Society. Would Einstein's theory be confirmed – or refuted, as most thought? Had the results been greatly different from what Whitehead read to the Royal Society, Einstein would not have become the scientific hero that we know today.

As Popper explained, philosophers were then claiming that what made a particular theory scientific was its *verifiability*. The disciples of Marx, Freud, and Adler explained that numerous observations verified their theories, but nothing had ever refuted them. The difference between Einstein's theory and those of Marx, Freud, and Adler was not this instance of verification, but the great possibility in most minds that the theory of general relativity would prove false. Thus Popper put forth *falsifiability* or testability rather than verifiability as marking the difference between science and non-science.

Popper explained how bad theories (or lights) consist mainly of abstractions.[69] They make only general predictions that are insufficiently specific to be tested. Because Freudian psychoanalysis applies to all behavior, it predicts no specific behavior. Similarly, Marx's theory of dialectical materialism did not predict *when* the world will enter communist paradise or specifically *how* proletariat revolutions will occur. Whatever Marx may seem to have predicted – without fulfillment – the Marxists easily explain away.

The proponents of these theories pride themselves on their ability to explain everything that is already known, as well as anything that might be found later. The defenders of various kinds of rationalist science, philosophy, and theology favor unfalsifiable theory. Like the Aristotelians, or German philosophers such as Kant and Hegel, they meet any challenge by *ad hoc* elaboration of *a priori* theory or theology. This causes these know-it-all theories to become ever more complicated and elaborate.

We see that these non-falsifiable theories function as paradigms or philosophies rather than as an empirical description of facts. By contrast, empirically-based theories make specific predictions that allow them to be tested. These are more useful, not so much because of what they explain, but because of what they forbid. Because the information they do give is specific, it is more surprising and more simply arranged. They simplify by forbidding all outcomes but the specific ones predicted. They constrain what outcomes might occur under specified conditions. Good scientific light is focused and pointed. It is like laser light directed through fiber-optic strands.

Simplicity is a principle of good philosophical and scientific explanation, known to logicians as Ockham's Razor. Bad light gets complicated and confusing as it tries to explain away things that one might otherwise accept aside from its special light. The unnecessary complexity that comes from defending a theory must be distinguished from the richness and elegance that belongs to a theory that is specific and useful.

Bad light can be compared to the web of stories one hears from someone who has an agenda or is afraid to tell the truth. They always have an explanation. Those who want to believe them may assist them by entering into a state of denial, ignoring numerous signs pointing to problems. The same is true whenever the learned population wants to believe some fashionable truth that accords with their desires or prejudices. Those doing so may include most of the learned population, as was once the case with Aristotle's philosophy and has now become so regarding Darwinian evolution and so much else.

Popper could have included Aristotle's philosophy and Darwin's evolution in his criticism of pseudoscience. According to the late Stephen J. Gould, Darwin-

---

[69] Karl Popper, *The Logic of Scientific Discovery* (Springer, 1934).

ism doesn't even predict a progressive direction to evolution. In other words, Darwinian evolution predicts everything we shall ever see. Because it predicts everything, it effectively predicts nothing. Popper did note that Darwinism is not a testable scientific theory, but he refused to allow it to fail his own test of restricting science to testable theory.

Sometimes various systems seem to predict things that do not occur, but their proponents refuse to allow them to fail, developing ad hoc explanations to address the contradictions. For example, Darwin predicted that missing links between species will be found among the fossils once the fossil record was sufficiently explored. More than one hundred and fifty years later, every fossil found belongs to some identifiable species, or is reckoned to belong to a new species. Many Darwinists do not appear to understand what this means, but Stephen Gould was a paleontologist. A fossil record that shows one species developing into another species is still missing. Gould put forth his theory of 'punctuated equilibrium' to explain the lack of evidence for evolution. His new theory suggested that evolution happens only in spurts. These spurts always happen too fast for us to see the evidence, or else they always take place where we are not looking. Amazing!

Like the Marxists and the Freudians, Darwinists tell us how much confirmation the theory of evolution has received. "It is no longer a theory!" They create countless documentaries for public television showing how some speculative evolutionary process allowed animals to marvelously adapt to their environments. We never see evidence of the transitional forms that time has now erased, but it must have happened because "evolution is true." Darwin's theory of evolution will never be refuted because its proponents have discovered how to use it to explain anything that we shall ever see.

Price's Young Earth Creationism had the same potential for predicting something that we would ordinarily not expect: that human remains would be found among dinosaurs, because the theory claims that man and dinosaurs lived at the same time. Henry Morris's *Genesis Flood*, which spread Price's theory to the evangelicals, did make the claim that such evidence had been found near Glen Rose, Texas. After further investigation, Morris retracted these claims. Young Earth Creationists properly criticize Darwinists for not being empirical, but when faced with such difficulties in the evidence they make a pious retreat to the authority of the Scriptures – in fact, their interpretation of the Scriptures. Aiming to settle the matter by theological dogma suggests that Creation Science is in fact just a game.

But aren't we to believe what God has said? There is a great difference between what the Scriptures plainly say and the theology or light by which Young Earth Creationists interpret the Scriptures. An increasingly favorite dogma concerns their assertion of no animal death before Adam sinned, a new spin on Romans 5:12.[70] Young Earth Creationists suppose this is sufficient to settle the matter of whether the fossil record is older than Adam, supposedly settling the matter of a young versus old earth. Of course you will search the Scriptures in vain to discover this dogma. You will also fail to find it in any of the historical creeds or confessions, though you might find it the writings of Ellen G. White. In fact, it is a dogma with a modern or naturalistic ring in that it levels the great distinction between man and the animals that is found everywhere in the Scriptures. It is an interesting proposition when we consider that even before Adam sinned, the Lord God commanded the animals to multiply after their own kind. Perhaps Adam sinned before the rabbits overran the Garden, but I am eager to learn how Creation might have proceeded had Adam not sinned. I doubt that the Lord God intended the Tree of Life as animal feed, but this may give us some insight as to why there is no marriage in Heaven.

In truth, we cannot hide our light under a bushel of dogma, because the Scriptures were given to us as a light for understanding the world. The Scriptures also concern Creation and history; hence we cannot dismiss its evidence from the historical record. That would be turning the Scriptures into something like myth: something to be believed by devotees though it has no application to history or to the world. The Scriptures ought to shine a clear light on the earliest remains of man. We don't need to test the Scriptures, but obviously we ought to test theology.

It is not just Karl Popper, but the Scriptures themselves that tell us we are to test teachings to see whether they are true. This is especially the case for teachings that claim to be based on the Bible. Not only should we test science that claims to be based on the Bible, but we should also test various interpretations of Scripture to see how much they owe to *light coming from* Scripture versus a *light that is put on* Scripture. As I explained in the case of Augustine and Calvin, as is true of all theologies not explicitly taught in the Scriptures, and as Young Earth Creationists themselves point out in the case of the proponents of a local Flood, a certain theological light might be shining on the Scriptures to make them accord with certain philosophies, theologies, or teachings that are not clearly taught by the Scriptures. These function as theological paradigms. Their teachings might even be contradicted if the words of Scripture are taken at face value and allowed to judge the theological system. What Popper explained as distinguishing science from pseudoscience also distinguishes the truth of Scripture from speculative theology. Is not Scripture prophecy, and is it not one of the purposes of prophecy to actually predict? In addition, it should illuminate what has taken place in the past.

---

[70] In fact this Scripture declares death as coming specifically to man.

Chapter 13   How light can be tested

Though it has not been part of the discussion within the philosophy of science, one should note that historical texts referring to specific events, people, places, and times in history have the same character as the most excellent and useful scientific theories. History, if true, is an empirical record of the past. Using these texts, we may be able to predict both general and specific things that we should expect to find in the archaeological remains or in the memories from ancient times. They should function in the same way that truthful testimony assists an investigation.

This is why the Bible is so essential for the archaeology of the Holy Land and the Ancient Near East as it should also be for the early history of the whole world. Though fearful modern Christians do not want to admit it, archaeology has the potential either to refute or to confirm the Bible. We should not forget the contest on Mount Carmel between the prophet of the Lord and the prophets of Baal. The God of the Bible is the God of Elijah. That is why biblical archaeology remains popular with serious believers, and with all others who love truth.

> Though fearful modern Christians do want to admit it, archaeology has the potential either to refute or to confirm the Bible.

Archaeological remains studied in the light of the Bible, in turn, enlighten the text in the sense that we may be able to better understand certain obscure matters in the ancient Scriptures. Putting the Bible to work always helps in understanding the Scriptures. Keep in mind that using what we see in the Bible's light to better understand the Bible's words is not the same as putting the light of science (or theology) on the Bible. It is comparable to a believer who studies the original languages in order to better translate the Bible.

We should not refuse help from whatever light may be available, whether from archaeological excavations or from ancient texts pertaining to various times and places connected to the Bible. Neither should archaeologists, scholars, or historians refuse help from the light of the Bible. Any text or material remains from such ancient times will be superior to our unguided imagination and theories. If we actually have good light, it is going to make things clear for those who are willing to use it.

If what we find concerning ancient times and places does not make sense in the light of the historical text – or if it requires numerous *ad hoc* hypotheses and assumptions in order to harmonize it with the text – the account might reasonably be regarded as false or misapplied. On the other hand, if the account enlightens or simplifies the relevant archaeological or historical data, it becomes a powerful tool for understanding ancient history. That is how the writings from the Dead Sea Scrolls and archaeology from the same era show what a powerful light the New Testament is for understanding the period of biblical history pertaining to the time of Christ. Against those who have been reading Hellenized Christianity or later Rabbinic Judaism back to the time of Jesus, they depict late Second Temple Judaism very much as does the New Testament. Similarly, the Dead Sea Scrolls and other ancient texts from these times help us better understand otherwise obscure details in the New Testament.

Trusting that the Bible is true seems the riskiest of beliefs because it makes so many amazing claims that might actually be tested, claims that the world believes should prove false. The Bible is replete with references to specific individuals, peoples, and events. It usually gives a clear picture of the time in history when such people lived or when such events occurred, and its narratives of the do not hide their simple historical truths in the form of vague abstractions or philosophical theology. This is how the Bible differs from philosophy and from myths. Philosophies have almost nothing to say about the concrete facts and contingent truths that concern history. As I explained in Chapter 3, all history is grounded in the Bible – that is to say, in the God, the people, and in the great events that are recorded in the Bible.

Many myths seem disconnected from the physical and historical realities with which we are familiar. One hardly knows what part of a myth should be regarded as a miracle, and what is simply a normal part of the mythical world. It is difficult to know how these stories might relate to the world that we actually know, let alone to historic people, places, or events. Even if myths are rooted in some historical event, they have since lost their historical connection. The miracles of the Bible, on the other hand, are notable for the very reason that they violate what the Bible's readers understand to be the ordinary order of the world. Their exceptional nature is an important reason for their appearance in the Bible. Most importantly for investigating their truth, the Bible usually gives some idea as to the times, places, and circumstances in which such things occurred. Because of this the Bible has great potential for being a better or more powerful light than might be obtained from any mere human theory or paradigm. That should indeed be the case if the Bible is the truth of history rather than something from the imagination of men. But if the Bible is true, why do we not see the evidence of the Flood?

— 14 —

The challenge due to the fragmentation of knowledge

A GOOD LIGHT SHOULD not be difficult to use. Unfortunately this is not the case with modern scientific teachings about the past. Though that which is based on truth should be integrated and simple, as modern knowledge "advances" it becomes ever more fragmented. Because of this fragmentation, it is difficult for anyone to learn what science collectively believes about ancient times. Thus the greatest challenge I faced in my search for the Flood was untangling the muddled understanding of the origins of the earth and the history of early man being taught today. No one book, one institution, or even one library can give us this modern light. It is spread among all the many experts, specialties, books, journals, universities, and institutions in dozens of languages and in more than a hundred nations. This modern light contains many contradictory theories with one common denominator: they do not believe in the Bible, in miracles, or in an invisible world of spirits, angels, and divine beings.

To discover the modern understanding of the ancient world, one must investigate numerous scientific and scholarly specialties. He must understand Ancient Near Eastern history, ancient American history, and ancient European, African, and Asian history. He must also know the archaeology and the prehistory of all these separate continents, each the province of specialists. He must understand the archaeological and historical chronologies, the systems of dating for each region of the world. To investigate the past, one must know a

FIGURE 17
BRISTLECONE PINE, OLDEST
LIVING SPECIES OF TREE

123

Part IV   *Scientific Prehistory and the Problem of Noah's Flood*

great deal about astronomy, geology, climatology, paleontology, biology, genetics, and DNA. He must understand the principles, the developments, and the latest findings of scholarly fields such as linguistics, philology (ancient texts),

Paleontology   Anthropology

FIGURE 18   SPECIAL FIELDS IN THE HISTORICAL SCIENCES

and paleography (ancient scripts used for writing).

One who would do this must also be skilled in demography, ancient economies, ancient ecology, religious and cultural history, ancient religion, and the history of science, technology and industry. He must know how to evaluate scientific dating derived from paleography, dendrochronology (tree rings), radiocarbon, pollen analysis, ocean and ice-core bores, and lake varves. He must know the history of our present understanding of natural history, comprehend and keep up with the development of all the various specialties related to natural history. The list goes on.

Early in my days as a scientist and inventor, I learned how important it is to understand how the currently received scientific theories, processes, and historical conclusions arose. Most of them depend on conditions and limitations that no longer exist and on theories and "facts" that are no longer believed. Typically, students and technicians who learn how to apply, maintain, and operate technology, as well as those who use these inventions do not want to know the history of their fields. They may view them as unimportant historical trivia. Such students can become technicians, but they will require new training or programming for every new stage of technology.[71] But a good scientist has also to be a good scholar and historian. I learned what Isaac Newton and Albert Einstein confessed: no one makes any important contribution to science without standing on the shoulders of those who preceded them in their field of study.

---

[71] The same is true in the various fields of scholarship such as biblical studies. The more one esteems his formal training the more likely he is to be filled with myth and nonsense.

Chapter 14   The challenge due to the fragmentation of knowledge

It is obvious that if all or even some of this scientific understanding of history or knowledge of the Bible has been developed under false assumptions or even partially defective paradigms, it is certain to contain numerous errors and systematic distortions. Because men are fallible, everyone should know that it must. This being the case, the received knowledge is certain to present the various kinds of data or facts from the ancient world in a muddled and misleading light. This well describes Western man's present understanding of the ancient eras of our earth.

Why then have modern folks, especially Christians, been so uncritical of and confident in mankind's scientific knowledge of the past? Why do Christian professors direct their skepticism at the inspired words of the Bible but uncritically swallow the latest scientific and scholarly theories? The simplest believers in the Bible are more logically sound, may also be wiser, and certainly have displayed more dignity than those groveling theologians in the seminaries and "Christian spokesmen" in the media that are so impressed by science: these who giddily parade their shallow understanding of the same.

As a systems engineer, I am accustomed to assimilating expert knowledge from dozens of related specialties concerning the most complex systems that man has ever created: the world-wide telecommunications network that I was instrumental in helping develop. My last project in the company I founded was to design the network management system for the Department of Defense's communications and control network and to keep it working in case of nuclear war. I also worked as an infrastructure scientist, requiring me to assimilate broad knowledge concerning the development of human economies that would be capable of supporting growing populations.

All such work requires systematic questioning of expert knowledge in every related area so as to develop practical and effective solutions. Most of these specialists will return to their offices, laboratories, and drawing boards to

FIGURE 19   SYSTEMS SCIENCE, TELECOMMUNICATIONS

125

consider obvious issues they have overlooked or ignored. Few specialties survive being transformed and the science rewritten in the process of the development of workable systems solutions. Consider what happened to our knowledge of the solar system and the universe as a result of the NASA space program. Why should it be different concerning our travel to the past with scientifically guided archaeology and ancient history? Our present understanding of the ancient world may be as outmoded as the dinosaurs that currently loom so large in our histories of the earth.

As I entered the study of the science and scholarship pertaining to the ancient world, I was appalled by the comparatively sad and sloppy state of these fields. Many of these fields were pioneered by wealthy explorers, by art historians, and especially by theologians and social theorists who did not build on practical experience or a base of well-tested knowledge. Professors that teach these fields in universities and command the scientific organizations pertaining to these fields are insulated by tenure from real-world accountability. Many owe their allegiance to the politics or commercial concerns of their various academic and research institutions, while those without passion operate as domesticated functionaries with little curiosity for thinking outside their "institutionally correct" boxes. All function more as the sectarian theologians that formerly commanded these fields than as adventurous scientists. Most are reluctant to question or to seek out the basis upon which the received knowledge is based, activities that should be the earmark of a good scientist. This explains why career-focused scientists are so unproductive in creating useful knowledge, despite these drones absorbing almost all the public funds for scientific research. In academic science pertaining to our knowledge of the past, I find little of the rigor, the sound methodology, the requirement of testing assumptions, and the demonstration of practical development that I remember from my days in applied science and technology. Because we could not afford failure, we questioned *everything*. We saw problems as opportunities to make things better – not to defend the status quo!

There are notable exceptions, but most scholars and scientists working in the more settled fields would wither from the kind of examination, challenge, and review that is systematic in applied science. Peer review can be a frightening experience for anyone, but the only ones who need to fear examination are those who love their opinions and ambitions more than they love truth. As technological entrepreneurs know, such rigor is the only way to create things that actually work. Greater discipline is required in industry because in the proper function of these systems corporate destinies and even human lives are often at stake. How unlike the idolatrous reverence of scientific knowledge displayed in the media and in Christian seminaries!

Chapter 14   The challenge due to the fragmentation of knowledge

As long as it is not too greatly revered, science does not have to be a bad word. To describe such understanding as we now ascribe to scientists, we could perhaps return to a more ancient term such as *sage* or *wise man*. According to Socrates, a truly wise man is one who understands his need of wisdom. Those who have ready answers for everything are not interested in questions. Unfortunately, the word *science* too often suggests too great a reverence for the latest theories and a lack of respect for the wisdom of the past. The word *wisdom* implies the opposite. We can err in either direction – respect for ancient or for modern knowledge – but as Jesus explained regarding the treasures of the Kingdom of God, we should be open to both old and new things.[72]

A scientist ought to respect knowledge that has stood the test of time, but a scientist that does not investigate and test the basis of the received knowledge in his field will not advance his science. The worst things a scientist can do are to revere the received opinions of science and to be too impressed with his own. Though not everyone has been pleased with his great insight, Popper was profoundly right: practical scientific knowledge advances only by challenging what we formerly believed to be true. When we arrive at the truth, we will know because it will work, and because it will easily withstand our most effective challenges to disprove it.

---

[72] Matthew 13:52

— 15 —

My methodology for searching for the Flood

I BEGAN MY search for the Flood by looking closely at the scientific and scholarly challenges and at the explanations provided by believers. Eventually, I was done with the arrogance by which science first obscured, then refused to look again at the Flood. I was disgusted by the vain theories of biblical composition. But I was disappointed by the explanations of the Young Earth Creationists and discouraged by the fact that other believers seem to have abandoned efforts to explain a worldwide Flood. Instead of dogma, either from religion or science, I wanted to consider only the evidence, whether it favored or weighed against a historical Flood.

Many say there is no evidence, but of course we do have some evidence: the numerous accounts found among the scattered nations of the earth.[73] The Egyptians, the Assyrians, the Babylonians, the Chinese, and even the Greeks believed in the Flood. Skeptics speculate that such accounts are due to the influence of Christian missionaries. Are we also to attribute the accounts of the ancient pagans to Jewish missionaries? In any case, scholars automatically reject influences from that direction because they follow the pagan Greek and modern German assumption that ancient Israel was a small and provincial nation with no impact on the wider ancient world. Others believe these Flood accounts are embellishments of commonly occurring floods. But there are other kinds of natural disasters. Why don't the nations share a common myth of the world once being destroyed by famine, disease, earthquake, or fire?

As I noted in an earlier chapter, scholars now propose that the Old Testament account of the Flood derives from Ancient Near Eastern accounts. They have in mind epics like the one of Gilgamesh, of which archaeologists have recovered copies at several sites in the Ancient Near East. Gilgamesh's and other accounts

---

[73] Sir James Fraser, *Folklore in the Old Testament*, Vol. 1 (Macmillan, 1918).

Chapter 15 My methodology for searching for the Flood

from the Ancient Near East have more similarities with that of the Bible than do accounts reported by the peoples of Asia and the New World, at least in the form that Europeans encountered them during their Age of Discovery. Should we not expect the accounts to become more vague, varied, and embellished as mankind becomes more dispersed through the distant and less literate parts of the earth, and as the ages roll on? Biblical scholars would do well to expand their horizon beyond their blinkered focus on ancient Israel. After all, this portion of the Bible does not claim to be the history of Israel, or even the history of the Ancient Near East. Are not scholars to consider how the text reads? The prophets inspired by the God of all mankind are giving the history of the entire world and of *all* mankind.

Would Old Testament scholars have us believe that the disciples of Gilgamesh traveled to India, China, the Pacific islands, and the New World on a mission to evangelize the world through proclaiming a myth of the Flood? Would any *myth* have impressed them to embark on such a remarkable and difficult mission? Even if we are to accept that the accounts gathered by early European explorers from so many numerous and various natives stemmed from an ancient myth, there must have been some kind of dispersion in the recent history of mankind. So much for the confident proclamations that there is no evidence of a recent dispersion of all mankind!

Yet if we are to believe that the Flood actually occurred, where is the material evidence? I have explained why I could not believe what the Young Earth Creationists propose as evidence of the Flood. But what would serve as genuine evidence? We have in the Bible some picture of what happened, but how do we translate that into the picture of the world that we understand today? Making a study of an event so unique as the Flood of the Bible is no simple matter. We need some way to model the Flood in order to predict its material effects, and so we can test evidence against that. Science studies regularly occurring processes: for example, the kind of floods and storms that we normally observe. How could I model the Flood when neither I nor anyone else knew the processes begun by the command of a powerful and invisible God? According to the Bible, his decision created a worldwide event on an order that no one now living on earth has witnessed, or will ever see. As I explained in Chapter 9, no matter how exceptional, we could study the Flood from the material evidence as we now study the impact of the ancient comet that many believe destroyed the dinosaurs. But the evidence of the Flood itself seems to be missing.

Owing to my study of the history of the science, I understood the great subjectivity inherent in geology. I refer not only to the theologically determined geology of the Young Earth Creationists, but also to the undisciplined theories recently put forth in the science of plate tectonics. Historians of this science

Part IV   Scientific Prehistory and the Problem of Noah's Flood

note that plate tectonics is a move away from empirically-driven geology and a return to the speculative geological theories of the early eighteenth century.[74] The difficulty of proving such speculation wrong is easy to understand: no one was around at the time and places (long ago and deep inside the earth) where most of these geological processes occurred. Thus, there are few objective methods and ways of controlling geological speculations. This is why I became suspicious of all kinds of geological interpretation.

Our most useful and reliable modern knowledge comes from the practical sciences pertaining to various technologies. By contrast, the historical natural sciences have yielded only a few items of practical usefulness – for such pursuits as oil and gas exploration, earthquake, and climate prediction – and even here, our knowledge is anything but reliable. Contrary to the opinions of most theologians and philosophers, and notwithstanding what I explained in Part III, I have more confidence in our modern knowledge pertaining to human history – at least in that part that is based on pertinent sources – than I do in speculative science. Scientific knowledge pertaining to ancient times is much like its speculation about futuristic societies. The latter projects *present* scientific knowledge into the future, while the former projects current fashions into the world of the past. Speculative science is the modern world's special form of myth making. It is all science fiction!

Leaving the field of geology, I decided instead to search for the Flood in the record of archaeology and human history. Unlike geology, the pertinent data of archaeology lies near or at the surface of the earth where investigators can more easily access it. In comparison to the greater part of the geological record, the events pertaining to humans occurred only a short while back. The record should accordingly be far better preserved. According to the Bible, the Flood took place more recently than five thousand years ago. It is no older than the Pyramids of Egypt! We have human observations or records pertaining to events in that period of ancient history, including some texts that date to the third millennium before Christ. We have data from paleography, linguistics and genetics. Thus, in the more recent human era there are enough correlations and connections to be able to constrain and test, support or refute various interpretations of the Flood, or claims that it did not occur.

I began my methodological search by deciding what I reckoned would necessarily be sure historical and archaeological evidence of the worldwide Flood described in the Bible. Fortunately for my quest, the teachings of Genesis are sufficiently specific with regard to the extent, time, and results of this exceptional event to be able to make these predictions. Here is a case where the Bible

---

[74] Naomi Oreskes, *The Rejection of Continental Drift: Theory and Method in American Earth Science* (Oxford University Press, 1999).

Chapter 15   My methodology for searching for the Flood

should exonerate itself, or fail the test. It is a test of the light of a literal reading of the Bible. If the Bible is true and if Jesus was speaking the truth, we should be able to find evidence of the Flood in the record of human history. Rather than speculating on what might have been the case, I considered only what had to have been the certain result of the Flood of the Bible.

As I first determined, clear and certain evidence of the Flood would be (1) a sudden disappearance of the earth's population sometime earlier than the second millennium before Christ, (2) a new dispersion of people from the Ancient Near East following this sudden depopulation, and (3) a clear worldwide discontinuity of archaeological culture that would necessarily mark the depopulation and new dispersion. It did not occur to me to look for the remains of those human beings and their civilizations that might have perished in the Flood. In any case, the Flood may have destroyed their remains as the Young Earth Creationists claim.

For years, I searched diligently for evidence of these three things in books and journals of ancient history and prehistory. Unfortunately – due, as I later learned, to the muddled state of our present knowledge of the ancient world – I found it difficult to detect any point in ancient history where such a clear and dramatic loss of population and new dispersion of people from the Ancient Near East might have occurred. Skeptics of the Flood claim that if such evidence could be found, the prehistorians or the historians of ancient time would have noted it. Presuming they were competent archaeologists and some of them had actually searched for the Flood, there was no evidence of the Flood to be found; but I had to search this important matter for myself.

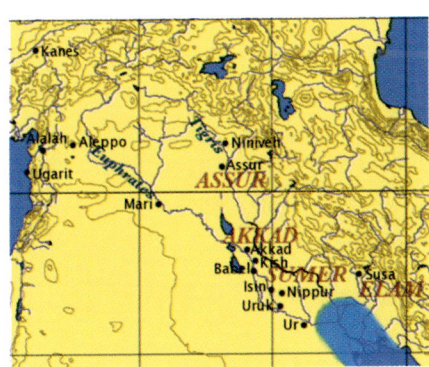

Figure 20
The Early Bronze Age in the Ancient Near East

The issue is easiest solved by my third criterion: evidence of culture continuity. One or two instances of such continuity of human culture are all that is needed to disprove the Flood. Historians of the Ancient Near East currently employ a fairly precise dating of ancient events, assigning the reigns of ancient kings and kingdoms as early as the late third millennium to decades and actual years. The civilizations of Egypt, Sumer, and China seem continuous with those of the same culture and place a millennia or so earlier. If this dating is even nearly correct, there was no Flood.

Part IV   Scientific Prehistory and the Problem of Noah's Flood

Alarmingly, the sacred book seemed to be failing the tests that I had proposed based on the most literal reading of its narrative of ancient human history. Just as the Darwinists have failed to find their missing links, and just as the Young Earth Creationists have failed to find human footprints among the dinosaurs, I was failing to find evidence of the disappearance of the earth's population and the repopulation of the earth. What I did find refuted the discontinuity in the pattern of human culture that must exist if the Bible is telling the truth

I so despaired of these results that I gave up searching for the Flood. My heart could never give up faith in the living Jesus I had encountered, but my mind was confused. I even began to look favorably at that new fashion in skepticism then coming to be known as postmodernism. To be truthful, this matter of Noah's Flood hung over me as the shadow of a dark and depressing cloud.

Part V

Finding the Flood

— 16 —

Discovery

Having given up on the Flood, my biblical and historical interests turned to other areas. One of these developed from reading passages in the book of Isaiah[75] concerning sacred oaks and human sacrifices. The Lord had forbidden his people to imitate the idolatrous and evil practices of the surrounding nations. They did not obey him; thus he sent them into exile. As I read those words, I was reminded of the Druid religion of the ancient Celts, the name by which the Greeks knew the same ancient people that the Romans called Gauls. Druids, the priests of the ancient Celts, were named for their sacred oaks. The Celts lived in ancient Europe and finally settled in Britain and Ireland. I wondered how Israelites or Canaanites might have possessed similar religious practices as those who lived in far off northwestern Europe.

As I pondered this, I realized that these words of Isaiah were composed in the eighth century BC, but the tribal and migrant Celts first appear in accounts of the Greeks and Romans only a few centuries before Christ. The archaeological site La Tene in Switzerland, location of the earliest distinctive Celtic culture, dates to the fourth or fifth century BC, but archaeologists see some of their art and their distinctive Iron-Age chariots as having connections to the ancient Near East. Wondering if this explains the common religious practices, I purchased a book on biblical archaeology: Amihai Mazar's newly published *Archaeology in the Land of the Bible: 10,000-586 BCE.*[76]

I soon learned that the land of Israel – Canaan, as it was known in the first six books of the Bible; Palestine or the Holy Land, as it was known through most of the Christian centuries – is the epicenter of world archaeology. The land of the Bible lies along the roads connecting Egypt to the other great civilizations of the ancient world. This means its inhabitants were frequently involved in the larger history of the Ancient Near East. Because it is the land of the Bible, Israel

---

[75] Isaiah 1:29; 57:5
[76] Published by Doubleday in 1992.

Part V   Finding the Flood

is by far the most archaeologically investigated part of the earth's surface, but not all of the discoveries here pertain to the Israelites. Some of the oldest human remains and some of the oldest settlements and cities of mankind have also been found here. If one desires to understand the archaeology of early mankind, Israel is the place to begin.

As I read this book of archaeology pertaining to the land of the Bible, my interest shifted to learning more about mankind's rise from his earliest and simplest settlements to his point of highest civilization. I was fascinated to learn how humans discovered agriculture and where they first domesticated animals. As I read these things, I thought of Cain and Abel, the sons of Adam and Eve and their connection to the rise of agriculture. Every stage of man's material development seems deeply connected to the Bible. Otherwise, there would not exist the possibility of conflict between the Bible and what is believed to be history. Myth does not generate such heated arguments.

Each chapter of the book chronicled a major step in the growth of civilization – from the first agriculture, to the oldest human settlements, to the first use of pottery, to the first manufacture of items in copper and bronze. These precocious workers of metals made me think of Tubal-Cain, a descendent of Adam and Eve's eldest son, Cain. Tubal-Cain forged all kinds of tools from bronze and iron. [Gen 4:22] Next comes the climax of mankind's rise to civilization – the first walled cities of the highly populated and materially refined urban world of the Early Bronze Age.

Then comes something unexpected.

In March 1994, I made a surprising but happy discovery. As I was reading Mazar's book, I learned that Israeli, Palestinian, and biblical archaeologists have already discovered the sudden depopulation for which I was searching. In the second half of the third millennium, the land of the Bible suddenly turns from a thickly populated urban culture of the Early Bronze to one that is sparsely populated with migrating pastoralists.[77] This is around the same time (ca. 2300 BC) as Noah's Flood can be calculated from the Bible!

As might be expected following the Flood, during this new era new settlers were moving into the land of the Bible. The famous biblical archaeologist William Foxwell Albright (1891-1971) also identified it as the time when Abraham moved from the land of the Chaldeans to this land of Canaan. Following the small population of the Patriarchal period occurs a second era of walled cities. Archaeologists identify these as the Canaanite cities we know from Joshua's conquest recounted in the Bible. Note how precisely, beginning with the time of Abraham, the archaeological periods match the biblical history of this land.

---

[77] Ibid., p. 151.

Until now, the Middle Bronze Age has been the earliest anchor of archaeological periods to biblical history. The Middle Bronze Age is the time of Abraham and the Patriarchs and extends through the time of the walled Canaanite cities. But my discovery concerned the first era of walled cities, the portion of the Early Bronze Age that precedes the Patriarch era – the time when the population and cultural pattern in the land of the Bible suddenly disappears. It exquisitely matches what we should expect from the biblical account of Noah's Flood. To quote one Israeli archaeologist:

> A phenomenon so central in Palestinian history as that of the formation of urban society, with all its consequences for the material and spiritual culture of the country, dissolves before our very eyes. [Amnon Ben-Tor, *The Archaeology of Ancient Israel* (Yale University Press, 1994), 123.]

Could the solvent have been water? As the quote indicates, archaeologists have seen the sudden loss of population as a great mystery and have searched for an explanation. Because many of the Early Bronze cities were walled for security and show signs of burning, Albright attributed the population loss to destructive invasions. But many Early Bronze cities were simply abandoned and left to decay. Moreover, the new inhabitants seem peaceful. Archaeologists eventually abandoned the assumption that the destruction and loss of population were due to widespread invasions. Interestingly, they now attribute this sudden depopulation to a sudden and important "climate change." They reached this conclusion long before the era of when "global warming" became popular. If it removed the inhabitants of the land of Israel, this climate change was indeed serious.

Whatever the cause of the loss of population, does the phenomenon exist throughout the greater Ancient Near East? Some see continuity between the new inhabitants and earlier sites in Syria, but entry from the north is just the direction of settlement we should expect from new settlers streaming from the vicinity of the mountains of Ararat, where Noah's ark settled. Archaeologists do in fact suggest that discontinuities occurred around the same time in Egypt, Mesopotamia,[78] and Europe.[79] One calls this the first "Dark Age" of history.[80] Around this same time in India, a great civilization along the Indus River collapsed. That destruction, attributed by some archaeologists to a devastating flood, had to have been sudden because bodies lie in the streets.[81] Searching the

---

[78] Ibid., p. 151.
[79] Stuart Piggott, *Ancient Europe* (Aldine, 1965),106, 113-123.
[80] Barbara Bell, "The Dark Ages in Ancient History," *The American Journal of Archaeology* 75, no. 1, (Jan, 1971): 1-26.
[81] George F. Dales, "The Decline of the Harappans," *Scientific American* 214 (May, 1966): 93-100. Reprinted in C. C. Lamberg-Karlovsky, *Old World Archaeology: Foundations of Civilization*

matter further, I discovered similar discontinuities in the archaeology of this era on every continent: in Asia, America, and even Australia. The time marks the end of the Neolithic Age in China and the Archaic Era in North and South America.

When my skeptical brother-in-law, a learned minister, heard that I may have discovered evidence of the Flood, he asked why the Flood that I now supposed discovered does not appear in archaeological strata of Jericho. The presence of the deep strata at Jericho, long regarded the world's oldest city, has caused many learned believers to suppose that civilization is far older than seems possible according to the Bible. The ancient city's deep strata, suggesting long and continuous occupation, seemed proof the Flood did not occur. Having the same troubling thoughts, I had already rechecked Kathlyn Kenyon's (1906-1978) archaeological report, nervously anticipating a refutation of my new thesis. [See Jericho strata in Figure 21.]

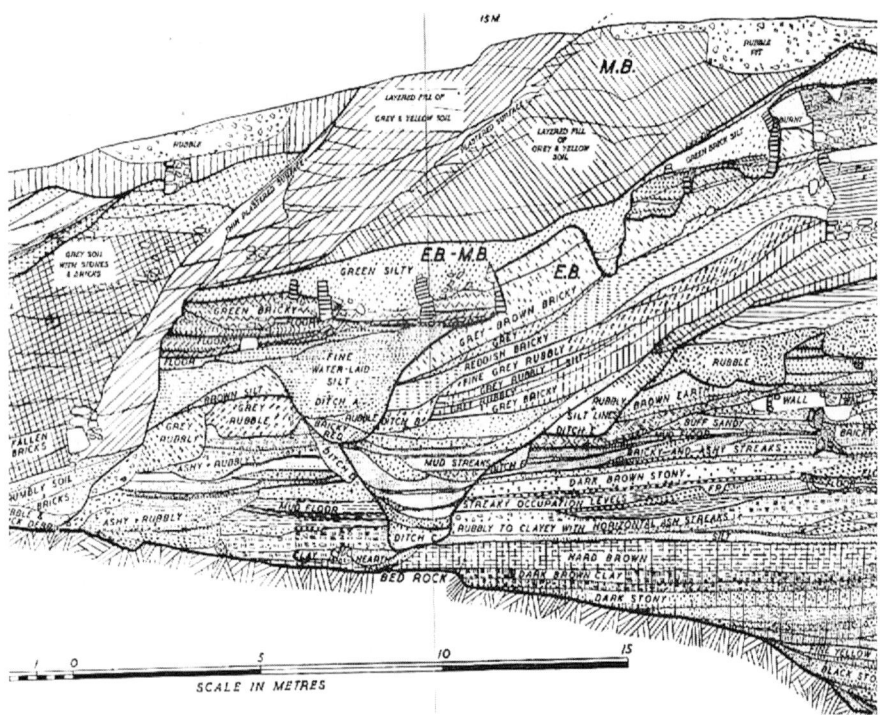

FIGURE 21   KATHLYN KENYON'S SKETCH OF JERICHO

(Freeman, 1972), 157-164.

Chapter 16   Discovery

Eureka! Dame Kenyon's excavation report for Jericho shows Flood silt and erosion precisely between the Early and Middle Bronze layers. [Figure 20] Her pioneering prehistory of the Holy Land offers extensive discussion of severe erosion occurring throughout Palestine at just this era in ancient history.[82] My brother-in-law and I missed this because we were inclined to think the presence of strata as indicating continuity of settlement; but in fact strata is evidence of discontinuity, and often calamity. Note that the Middle Bronze level walls that belonged to the Canaanite city in the level above the Early Bronze level, around which the Israelites marched, are fallen, just as described in the book of Joshua.[83]

Biblical scholars have long known about the sudden loss of population at the end of the Early Bronze Age. Are we moderns so convinced that Noah's Flood is myth that no one has even ventured to look at the archaeology of the earliest ages of the land of the Bible in the light of the early chapters of Genesis? Before giving up the historicity of the Flood, should not *Christian* scholars and scientists have insisted on a detailed explanation of how the archaeology of this period *does* look in the light of the biblical account of the Flood? Perhaps the whole world has been deceived by too much confidence in scientific opinions, which are always in need of more study and revision.

There is also another reason why, for the past fifty years, archaeologist have been unwilling to consider even interregional or intercontinental influences, much less migrations of people and populations from civilizations in the Ancient Near East to such places as northern Europe, Asia, and America. This is a dogma known in the field of archaeology as anti-diffusion.[84] There are numerous nationalistic, ethnic, institutional, and professional reasons for this prejudice, but it is often justified as a reaction to the Aryan invasion theories of Nazi Germany. As a result, coordinated study of the archaeological patterns in the various parts of the ancient world has been given little attention. Mainstream archaeology has practically abandoned the study of intercontinental diffusion of material culture, much less migration occurring after the time of the earth's first settlements.

This is one important reason why the archaeology and history of the ancient world is so confusing. The resulting poor archaeological coordination between regions was also the reason I had difficulty in finding evidence of a similar

---

[82] Kathleen Kenyon, *Archaeology in the Holy Land* (Ernest Benn, 1979), 130-134 and *Digging Up Jericho* (Ernest Benn, 1957), 45, 93, 171, 259-60, 263.
[83] Hershel Shanks, et al, *The Rise of Ancient Israel: Symposium at the Smithsonian Institution October 26, 1991* (Biblical Archaeology Society, 1992), 15-17.
[84] cf Colin Renfrew, *Before Civilization: The Radiocarbon Revolution and Prehistoric Europe* (Penguin Books, 1990).

Part V   *Finding the Flood*

population drop during the Middle Bronze Age in Iraq (ancient Mesopotamia), only five hundred miles from Israel. That led me to study Sir Leonard Woolley's excavations of Ur, the city many believe to have been the ancient home of Abraham.[85]

FIGURE 22   SIR LEONARD WOOLLEY (R)
WITH ASSISTANT LAWRENCE OF ARABIA (L)

---

[85] Sir Leonard Woolley, *Excavations of Ur: The First Full Account of Twelve Years Work* (Ernest Benn, 1954), Chapter III.

— 17 —

Light from Sir Leonard Woolley's Excavations at Ur

IRONICALLY, WHILE HE was digging at Ur in 1929, Woolley himself announced to the world that *he* had discovered the Flood. When he made his discovery, Woolley wasn't so much searching for the Flood mentioned in the Bible as the one described by writings from the Ancient Near East. As in the Bible, king lists found in these ancient texts tell of ancestors who lived long life spans both before and after the Flood. Woolley had found an archaeological inscription in the ruins of Ur containing the name of one of these kings who lived shortly after the Flood. He was digging into the archaeological layers below the level containing that king's name when his workmen came upon a ten-foot layer of clean, water-laid mud. Below this mud they found another archaeological culture that archaeologists had assigned to the earliest period of Mesopotamian civilization. Woolley guessed that the ten feet of mud was likely the result of the famous Flood that had ended the earlier culture at Ur, the world's oldest civilization.

Woolley telegrammed the papers in London: "We have found the Flood!" Major newspapers throughout the world picked up the story. This remarkable confirmation of the Bible caused a great stir. Not long after, other archaeologists working in Mesopotamia found similar evidence in nearby cities: at ancient Kish, to the north; and at ancient Susa, to the south. There was more excitement. At last, archaeological evidence of the famous Flood had been found.

Disappointingly, further investigation dampened the hopes of the archaeologists and the public. The floods announced for the discoveries at Kish and Susa seem to have occurred at different times than the one at Ur. Moreover, the layer of mud discovered by Woolley did not even cover the complete city of Ur.[86]

---

[86] I was prompted to develop criteria that would serve as clear and certain evidence of a worldwide Flood when I read the disappointing analysis of Woolley's discovery of the Flood in Chapter 3 of Werner Keller's *The Bible as History* (William Morrow, 1981).

Part V   *Finding the Flood*

Excitement over Woolley's flood rapidly abated. Keep in mind that these were the days when most people believed in a local Flood. Woolley assumed that the Flood would have covered only the low-lying areas of the Mesopotamian plain. Moreover he was looking for a flood that dated more than a thousand years earlier than the biblical Flood. For such things, he trusted calculations based on the king lists of the Ancient Near East more than he trusted the Bible.

I was interested in Woolley's excavation because he and his colleagues had defined the conventional archaeological periods of Mesopotamia. Because I needed to match them with corresponding periods in Palestine to determine whether the Flood that I hoped I had found extended as far as Mesopotamia, I carefully read Woolley's own account of his excavations of the royal tombs of Ur. Here, Woolley dug up such famous and beautiful treasures as have seldom been found at any archaeological dig. They include the golden helmet of Prince Mes•kalam•dug, sculptured with the detail of hair; an elaborately-designed gaming board; the golden headdress of Queen Shuba; and a ram-shaped harp that was held by one of the dancing girls whom Woolley claimed was put to death at the burial of the king. [Figure 23] Woolley believed that not only the Queen and dancing girls, but soldiers, the oxen who pulled the Queen's sled, and even the grooms that attended the oxen had accompanied the king at his death. [See his sketches of the tombs, Figure 24] Woolley acknowledged that there was no historical evidence of the practice of suttee (attendants being sacrificed at a king's death) in the entire literature of the Ancient Near East, but how else to explain these burials!

Figure 23   Treasures found in the royal tombs of Ur

Woolley gives in considerable detail his re-creation of what he explained as a grisly death ritual. Some things about his interpretation seemed odd. The location of the royal graves in the garbage dump area of Ur was a mere detail that Woolley glibly and condescendingly attributed to "oriental insouciance." It just didn't make sense to me that so much effort, and so many beautiful and expen-

Chapter 17   Light from Sir Leonard Woolley's Excavations at Ur

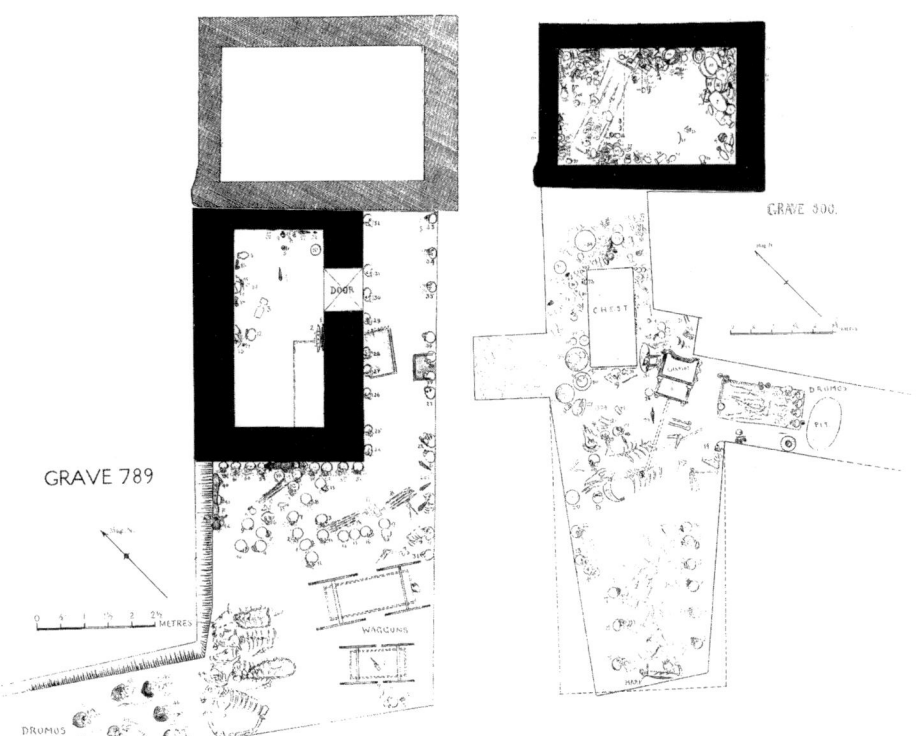

FIGURE 24 **WOOLLEY'S DRAWINGS DEPICTING THE ROYAL TOMBS OF UR**

sive treasures would go into this funeral – and then for all these magnificent preparations to be so unceremoniously covered with dirt and trash?

What got my attention was not only Woolley's macabre and jarring reconstruction of the gruesome funeral but his complaint that most of the treasures in these graves had been robbed in ancient times. The most puzzling question of all was not why so many of these treasures had been robbed in ancient times, but why there was any gold or silver left there for Woolley to find! Those who bury people do not ordinarily leave so much treasures for the dead – or rather, for the grave robbers.

As I pondered this, the answer dawned. It was as if a light had switched on in the darkness that had long covered these ancient remains. The reason those treasures were there is that no one who witnessed this unplanned burial survived to tell what was buried there. Nor was this an elaborately planned funeral. There was a party going on at ancient Ur when the waters from Noah's Flood suddenly swept into these ancient chambers.

143

Part V   Finding the Flood

As would happen to every low-lying city and dwelling in the ancient world, the Flood would eventually have swept the topsoil and vegetation covering the mountains down into the valleys and plains, burying these graves and cities. As also happened in first century Pompeii, the residents, their personal effects, and the building's furnishings might lie undisturbed – for millennia.

> There was a party going on at ancient Ur when the waters from Noah's Flood suddenly swept into these ancient chambers.

At length I would understand the true reason for the great *tels* marking the Early Bronze cities of

Figure 25   Diagram of Tel Megiddo strata

the Ancient Near East. After centuries of decay and the growth of new vegetation, well-built homes would appear as mounds. Ancient towns and cities such as Ur would appear as low-lying hills or *tels*. It is also true that some, such as Tel Megiddo (pictured on the cover) were built on hills as a measure of defense. [See strata structure, Figure 25] Still, the height of all these *tels* was not just owing to the deposits from centuries of repeated building, as archaeologists now suppose. The Flood gave them a substantial start. Part of the deeply buried and heavily fortified Early Bronze city underlying Tel Megiddo was uncovered in an excavation earlier in the twentieth century. Fortunately excavators photographed the Early Bronze city before reburying its ruins. [Figure 26]

Likewise, I would come to understand how the "Indian" burial mounds of America, the kurgans of Central Asia, the barrows and passage graves of Great Britain, and the millions of similar structures found in almost every country

Chapter 17   Light from Sir Leonard Woolley's Excavations at Ur

FIGURE 26
PHOTO OF EARLY BRONZE TEL MEGIDDO

and nation of the earth were created in a single year of ancient history. The cities of the Early Bronze Age, along with their fortified walls and well-built houses and "temples" – though of course I now understood that these elaborate buildings were not really built as temples for burying the dead with the elaborate provisions that are found with them – would have held in place much of the soil and debris of the receding waters. No wonder that in the low-lying valleys and especially in the river deltas, Early Bronze cities lie too deeply under the earth for inexpensive excavation. Such ruins as those known to be lying under the delta of the Nile have never been excavated. But also found on the higher plains of most continents are numerous examples dating to this era of strange semi-subterrain dwellings. These are places where the Flood only partially covered the antediluvian houses.

Exceptions to this kind of burial would occur in the rocky highlands and

FIGURE 27   NAWAMIS OF THE SINAI
(NEOLITHIC STRUCTURES IN THE HIGHLANDS)

mountain areas where the Flood washed away the topsoil once covering these areas, leaving Neolithic or Early Bronze stone structures exposed to sight. [Figures 27 and 28] The remains of the former occupants lie on dirt-covered floors of many of these houses, just as we find in houses of the valleys. The phenomenon of these Flood-exposed highland ruins is by no means limited to the Near East. It exists on every continent. As can be determined by tree rings, the earliest settlements on the Mesa Verde cliffs in the American Southwest [Figure 29] date to the first millennium after Christ. But these settlements overlie ruins of a completely different culture in which the dead are found lying in soil covering the floors of their houses.

145

Part V   Finding the Flood

FIGURE 28

NEOLITHIC OR EARLY
BRONZE REMAINS FROM
ISRAEL'S GOLAN HIGHLANDS

FIGURE 29   CLIFF DWELLINGS AT MESA VERDE, COLORADO

There was no valley deep enough, nor was there any mountain high enough to contain the waters which then covered the entire earth.

— 18 —

Flood forensics

AT UR, IN the very ruins where Woolley searched for the Mesopotamian "Flood," is massive evidence of the civilization that perished in the biblical Flood. In fact the evidence includes the entire Early Bronze civilization of the Ancient Near East, the same era of civilization that had disappeared at that same time in ancient Israel. To see this evidence one had to look at "the forest," the bigger picture. Woolley and others who examined the evidence were unable to see the true dimensions of the Flood because they were expecting a mere local Flood and because they were studying "the trees" of individual tombs or houses and cemeteries or cities. The historical Flood was an event too great in magnitude for one to discover in the details of the individual sites that archaeologists spend a great portion of their lives excavating.

I learned from my mother, who has cleaned flooded basements, that the red clay of our Piedmont region of North Carolina is the first thing that settles from the waters of a flood. The heaviest particles in muddy water are those from iron-laden clay. Before the waters of the Flood had receded, a great stream of mud was flowing through the streets of Ur into the lower floors of these ancient palaces. Ironically, as Woolley's workmen began digging into this stream of mud, they were already standing in the ruins created by the great biblical Flood.

The massive evidence of the antediluvian civilization was something for which I had not been searching because in all the vast literature pertaining to the Flood there is little discussion of the remains of humans and their civilizations that must have perished. Taking a cue from Plato's Atlantis, New Age and alternative archaeologists have been speculating on what is indeed massive evidence of advanced ancient civilizations throughout the world that collapsed without written record of their existence. They have certainly been right in recognizing the evidence of advanced ancient civilizations that were unknown to later historical peoples who inhabited the same lands.

Part V   Finding the Flood

This explains why no one knew how or why were built the Pyramids and the Sphinx in Egypt, Stonehenge in England, the megalithic "tombs" of Europe, the "Indian" burial mounds in Eastern America, the advanced prehistoric civilizations of the American Southwest, the pre-Ceramic civilization of Peru and South America, the Harappa civilization of India, the pre-dynastic burials of China, and other ancient sites too numerous to mention here. The archaeological sites created by the Flood are a sizable percentage of archaeological sites from all over the world. In fact the Flood created the vast majority of the truly elaborate sites. Though this does not suit the kind of sparse and primitive pre-Flood civilization suggested by current defenders of the Flood, it does well suit the picture of the antediluvian world that one might obtain from the Bible.

Ironically, perhaps none have misled or obscured the truth of the Flood more than the Young Earth Creationists, who have assured us that the world of that era was primitive, scantly populated, or otherwise "archaeologically insignificant!" They tell us it is unlikely that any human skeletons from before the Flood will ever be found.[87] *[handwritten: Not true, they believe the population could have been 1 billion]*

All these graves, cemeteries, or entire cities of the dead are as varied as their different cultures and geographies, but they also have numerous common traits. Archaeologists find buried together family members and servants of every age. Most appear to have died young or in the prime years of life. Infants are often found in baskets. There are a lot of jar burials that may have been due to infants being bathed at the time of the Flood. Some jar burials may have simply been due to so many jars being available for those after the Flood to collect and bury the bones. It is likely that the phenomena of urn burials and cremations derived from this practice. Accompanying everyone are far more personal effects than is the case of planned burials, but substantial numbers of these burials include *all* the things required for living including beds, kitchen furnishings, domestic animals and carts, as in the ancient cities of Ur, Kish, and Susa. In some cases, gardens and fences surround the tombs![88]

Whereas planned burials are formal and usually confined to a small area to reduce the expense of digging, the artifacts found at these sites are in the patterns and spacing that one might expect from the ordinary conditions of living. Many of the artifacts are strewn and broken as might be expected owing to the currents of the Flood, though confined within these structures that suddenly became tombs. Unlike stone and brick dwellings, wooden or thatched struc-

---

[87] cf Answers in Genesis website, "Where are all the human fossils?"
[88] cf John Manley, *Atlas of Prehistoric Britain* (Oxford University Press, 1989), 96; Walter B. Emery, "The Tombs of the First Pharaohs," *Scientific American* 197 (July, 1957), 112. Reprinted in C. C. Lamberg-Karlovsky, *Old World Archaeology: Foundations of Civilizations* (Freeman, 1972), 189.

[handwritten: The author ignores the fact that all of those civilizations are dated after the flood.]

tures covered with earth soon rot. They now appear to archaeologists as ancient shafts or ditches. Thus, archaeologists interpret what was once buildings housing as graves.

Due to the presence of numerous dead within these buildings archaeologists have identified them as tombs or temples and have assumed that they were actually built into the depths in which most of them are found. If there were no human remains, they would have regarded them as ordinary houses, palaces, or shops. Similarly, the wooden or thatched buildings that have rotted together with their inhabitants appear to archaeologists as "shafts" or "ditches" and are interpreted as having been dug to serve as elaborate graves. The organic remains in all these dwellings would have dried and rotted, and would have burst into flames whenever some forest fire swept over the land. I suspect there were a lot of these fires in the centuries soon after the Flood. That explains all the burned cities that caused Albright and other archaeologists to reckon that the Early Bronze civilization was destroyed by invading attackers. As the oxygen was consumed in these underground chambers, the fires would have self-extinguished, explaining the "ritual of half-cremation" by which archaeologists presently explain these partially burned skeletons and remains.

Unlike the worn and broken artifacts that one expects to find in the garbage and ruins of ordinary settlements and despite the damage owing to the currents of the Flood, many of these artifacts are unbroken and show little wear and tear. In other cases, artifacts are in practically new condition or are found still in the early stages of manufacture. [See Figures 30 and 31] I would guess that archaeologists find more than ninety percent of the unbroken pottery they recover in graves dating to just this time. Archaeologists properly see these as graves, but they ignore the plentiful and manifest evidence that these are not ordinary graves. The Flood not only created these graves but probably buried the majority of gold and silver artifacts now on display at museums throughout the world, including the treasures from Ur, the "King Midas" jewelry found by Schliemann at Troy, and the Maikop tombs from ancient Turkey.

FIGURE 30
METAL FROM EUROPEAN SHOP BURIED BY THE FLOOD

Part V   Finding the Flood

Most pre-Flood houses and buildings were of round construction, as we can tell from the remains of buildings not swept away or completely destroyed by the Flood. But there were also long, rectangular log cabins from those days found all over Europe. Many of these buildings, even ones in North America, were constructed with impressive precision, suggesting a technical capability far beyond that known by the natives of the same areas in historical times.

All over the world, vast numbers of these kinds of burials are found, most dated to the third millennium before Christ. In every case there is almost no evidence for settlements where lived the people who were buried in these massive and elaborate graves.

Figure 31
Metal Hoard found in Israel

One example is the mastabas or cities of the dead lying beside the great Pyramids in Egypt. [Figure 32] These contain numerous burials with "the provisions

Figure 32   Mastabas beside the Pyramids

for living" for everyone. But where did the people who constructed these tombs live? Archaeologists have no clue. Where did those live that built the Pyramids? That is a problem in Egyptian archaeology. These questions can now be an-

Chapter 18   Flood forensics

swered. Those who constructed the Pyramids lived at the same place in which we find them buried. These mastabas are actually the foundation structures for huge wooden palaces that accompanied the ancient Pyramids.[89] Some were then connected by waterways and harbors, where were moored a fleet of boats, such as those recently excavated at Saqqara and Abydos. I suspect that the historical burial cults of Egypt were inspired by these graves, so well preserved in those dry desert sands.

Another place, long subject to endless speculation, is Stonehenge in southwestern England. In fact, megalithic structures exist all over Great Britain, Europe, Asia, and the Ancient Near East. We can now understand that these standing stones do not mark a cemetery as has recently been concluded. They are the pillars of a great antediluvian palace, built upon a slight elevation. The so-called burial "ditches" that surround these pillars [See Figure 34] were once wooden structures, perhaps the walls of a wooden fort where lived and worked

Figure 33   Stonehenge

the attendants and soldiers of this palace.

---

[89] Walter B. Emery, *Scientific American* 197 (July, 1957). Reprinted in C. C. Lamberg-Karlovsky, *Old World Archaeology: Foundations of Civilizations* (Freeman, 1972), 184-190.

151

Part V *Finding the Flood*

FIGURE 34 BURIAL "DITCHES" SURROUNDING STONEHENGE

Interestingly, many of those found in the graves at Ur and other places lay in a flexed position, with arms and legs curved forward and outward. [See Woolley's diagrams of the skeletons at Ur, Figure 23] Forensics experts tell us that the arms and legs of floating bodies tend to extend forward with the torso bending at the waist. That is evidence of drowning![90] The skulls are often found elongated, deformed, or more often, crushed. That does not indicate a strange ancient race, as has been often supposed, but simply the fact that these bodies and skulls have been under a great deal of pressure as would be encountered under very deep water.

We might actually have some idea of how the people from this era dressed and looked. This is due to cold storage or to mummification in some of the driest places on earth, and especially to the combination of cold and dryness. Some of the Tarim mummies from central Asia [1st and 2nd pictures of Figure 35] do not look like Asians.[91] The reason for this may be the same as the reason why the skeletons of earliest Americans do not resemble native Americans.[92] Both belong to people who lived in the lands of these natives before the Flood.

---

[90] Dix, Graham, and Hanzlick, *Asphyxia and Drowning: An Atlas* (CRC Press ,2000), 20.
[91] J. P. Mallory and Victor H. Mair, *The Tarim Mummies* (Thames and Hudson, 2008).
[92] James C. Chatters, *Ancient Encounters: Kenniwick Man and the First Americans* (Simon and Schuster, 2001).

Chapter 18   Flood forensics

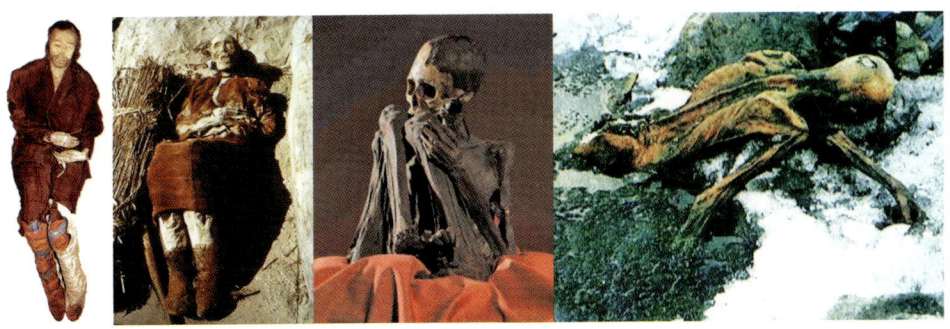

        Western China   **Chile**   **the Alps**

    Figure 35   **Mummies of some who may have perished in the Flood**

Some of the Chinchorro mummies found in the highland deserts of southern Peru [3rd picture] date to this time. Another example is "Ötzi the Ice Man" [4th picture] recently found in the Alps. Archaeologists date him to about five thousand years ago, the era of Noah's Flood.

153

— 19 —

The world before the Flood

From Europe to the Ancient Near East, from Asia to North and South America, archaeologists studying the sites that I have linked to the Flood frequently point to evidence of excessive violence. Many skeletons from this time such as that of Ötzi the Ice Man or those of the same era only recently uncovered beside Germany's Soule River[93] show signs of injury from weapons. Archaeologists find arrowheads and spear points embedded in the bones of many of the human remains. Vast numbers of the skeletons of males that date to this period are accompanied by weapons such as battle axes, sabers, slings, spears, and daggers. These man-killing weapons differ from the metallurgy found in sites belonging to the relatively peaceful Middle Bronze period that follows, in which are found knives and tools appropriate for controlling and butchering animals.

The remains from the Lung Shan Neolithic period of China,[94] the Windmiller and Consumnes cultures of California,[95] and the Hardaway culture of the American East betray evidence of particularly gruesome scenes. It was the discovery of numerous weapons, fortifications, and signs of violence inside the "Indian" burial mounds that caused early Americans to regard them as a noble

---

[93] Wolfgang Haak, Guido Brandt, et al, "Ancient DNA, Strontium isotopes, and T analysis shed light on social and kinship organization of the Late Stone Age," *Proceedings of the National Academy of Science of the USA* 105, no. 46.

[94] Kwang-chih Chang, *The Archaeology of Ancient China* (Yale University Press, 1986), 248-250, 270-271, 287.

[95] Stuart J. Fiedel, *Prehistory of the Americas* (Cambridge University Press, 1992), 137-139.

Chapter 19   The world before the Flood

> Now the earth was corrupt in God's sight, and the earth was filled with violence. And God saw the earth, and behold, it was corrupt, for all flesh had corrupted their way on the earth. And God said to Noah, "I have determined to make an end of all flesh, for the earth is filled with violence through them. Behold, I will destroy them with the earth. [Gen. 6:11-13]

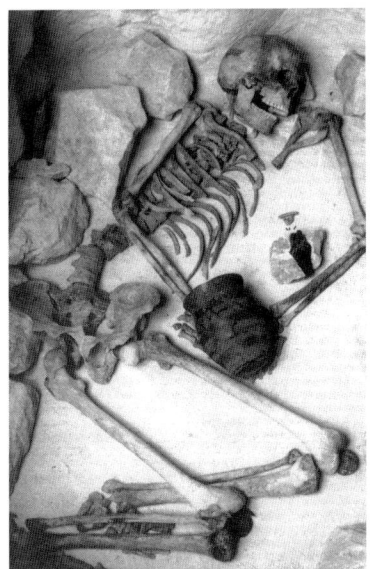

FIGURE 36
DAGGER WIELDING BEER DRINKER

race that had been entirely wiped out by bloodshed. These conclusions inspired Joseph Smith's *Book of Mormon*.[96]

Almost every house, settlement, or city dating to these times is fortified, and the fortifications are remarkably robust. Note the thickness of the walls belonging to the Early Bronze City under Tel Megiddo. [Figure 26] A great defensive tower was incorporated into the thick wall of the ancient city of Jericho. Arrowheads and spear points are found in abundance around settlements and cities of this era. The hilltops of Europe are replete with ancient fortresses, which the Romans called *oppida*. Though the Romans and their enemies made use of these ready-made fortifications, the original structures date from before the Flood.

Though later remodeled as tombs for kings, the Pyramids may have been originally constructed as fortresses for securing treasures from frequent raiders. The antediluvian world must have had plenty of pirates. That better explains massive and expensive enclosures equipped with disguised doors and secret passages.[97] Could they have also been deposit banks serving clients from the antediluvian world?

There is considerable evidence in these pre-Flood dwellings and cities of the excessive use of alcohol and drugs. The remains of numerous males are accompanied by giant beakers. Some of these beakers are coated with a residue of hops from the evaporation of beer. [Figure 36] Other vessels from this era show residue pointing to the consumption of large amounts of wine. With some burials are found tiny vessels and pipes, useful only for the partaking of medicine or drugs. Archaeologists surmise that large amounts of hemp found at other site

---

[96] Robert Silverberg, *The Mound Builders* (Ohio University Press, 1968), 29-73.
[97] The disguised doors inside the Pyramids should not be confused with the fake funerary doors in decorated mastabas, which likely date to after the Flood.

Part V   Finding the Flood

> The Nephilim were on the earth in those days—and also afterward—when the sons of God went to the daughters of men and had children by them. They were the heroes of old, men of renown.
> [Gen. 6:4 NIV]

are more than might be expected for manufacturing ropes.

By the standards of most eras of history, many skeletons found in these graves are big and tall. Their size and health points to a time of great prosperity. Inscriptions that Sir Leonard Woolley found on vessels accompanying Prince Mes•kalam•dug of Ur cite the prince as "hero of the good land."

Indeed, the world just before the Flood was thickly populated and highly advanced with regard to technology and refinement. These "heroes of old" and "men of renown" were capable of building the Pyramids, the fine furnishings at Ur, the palace at Stonehenge, and the many other astonishing things found in these ancient archaeological sites.

Detractors of the historicity of Noah's Flood have declared the Ark to be too great an undertaking for primitive man. An era capable of building the Pyramids should be presumed capable of building a vessel as sophisticated as Noah's Ark. I am inclined to imagine Noah as a prosperous farmer and ship-builder who traded the produce from his fields and vineyards to obtain provisions for the Ark.

The culture of this antediluvian or Early Bronze period differs greatly from the unwalled and seemingly peaceful settlements belonging to the early Middle Bronze of the Ancient Near East that immediately follows. The wealth and refinement in the arts and buildings of the earlier period can be attributed to the extensive population and to the specialization in manufacture and production that affords. It seems to have been a time ominously similar to our own. As today, the population of the ancient world had reached a peak at the time of the Flood. So numerous are these burials relative to those that can be seen as the ordinary formal burials from ages past, it is conceivable that by the time of the Flood more people were living than had yet died.

I have yet to make a careful study using the light of these discoveries of the evidence of mankind's history earlier than this most decadent period of ancient history. Among other things, it would provide a picture of the settlement in the antediluvian world. When someone does make this study, we should expect no less surprising results. It may also answer perplexing questions – such as the location of the city that Cain built and marriages between the sons of God and the daughters of men – that accompany our understanding of the early chapters of the Bible.[98] Two things should greatly assist such a study. The first is having a more exact location of the Garden of Eden. That task may have already been ac-

---

[98] Genesis 4:17; 6:2, 4

complished in the recent discovery of a dry riverbed crossing Saudi Arabia. Harvard geological archaeologist James Saur notes that the course of this river precisely matches the Genesis description of the Pishon River.[99]

This river seems to have flowed into or perhaps from the congress of the Tigris and Euphrates rivers at a point within the boundaries of present-day Kuwait. I would guess that the Gihon, the fourth river issuing from the Garden of Eden, which the text mentions as flowing through the land of Cush, has now widened into the Persian Gulf. As I will explain in Chapter 23, descendents of Cush settled southern India and northeastern Africa from Mesopotamia via the Persian Gulf.

We should withhold our judgment concerning how these rivers flowed in the earliest history of mankind until we have more carefully studied the historical topography. As I will discuss in Chapter 26, we know that the great deserts in this part of the earth were tropical and well watered only five thousand years ago. We also know that the Tigris and Euphrates Rivers did change their course at just this time. As with numerous other changes to topography and terrain that resulted from the Flood, this needs more investigation.

I will return to the subject of ancient climate in Chapter 26. In the next chapter I will explain the second tool to help our study of mankind's earliest history: a worldwide chronological marker dating to sometime in the third millennium BC. This will be of inestimable value in helping archaeologists clarify what many archaeologists already know to be a perplexing picture of prehistory.

---

[99] James Saur, "The River Runs Dry – Biblical Story Preserves Historical Memory," *Biblical Archaeological Review* 22 (July/August 1996), 52.

— 20 —

Dating the ancient world and the Flood

No wonder our scientific history of ancient times is such a muddle. Archaeologists have been operating under the assumption that mankind's dwellings in the era before the Flood together with their furnishings and inhabitants are *deliberate* burials. But there appears to be a problem: these graves belong to cultures and periods ranging from the Paleolithic to after the time of Christ!

The Paleolithic is the Old Stone Age. That men used tools made of stone before the era of bronze and that they used bronze before they had tools of iron is found both in the Bible and in ancient Greek texts. Early in the nineteenth century, Scandinavians invented scientific archaeology by using the criterion of stone, bronze, or iron artifacts to date archaeological sites. They refined their system of relative dating by examining changes over time in the manufacture and styles of stone and metal artifacts. With the stone age still in man's memory, few supposed that any of these human remains were more ancient than about six thousand years.

That changed in 1859 when human tools and bones were officially recognized as being in the unstratified deposits of the diluvium, formerly regarded as the evidence of the Flood.[100] Ignoring the lack of strata that defined the diluvium and renaming it the Pleistocene, Charles Lyell wanted to see it deposited over a very long time. Basing his estimate on the depth of a deposit containing mammoth remains, he judged its age as not less than 100,000 years. Soon, geologists would reckon the Pleistocene as resulting from an Ice Age lasting from 220,000 to 240,000 years. The Pleistocene would eventually be extended to about ten times that duration, but as I will explain in Chapter 26, there are in fact no radiometric or other reliable chronometers for dating these remains. No wonder: it all pertains to the antediluvian world that perished in the Flood.

---

[100] These were discussed in Chapter 10. In truth, with or without human remains, geologists were no longer willing to see the diluvium as evidence of the Flood.

Lyell's estimate of the duration of the Ice Age was a pure guess, but to calculate the time elapsed since the Ice Age ended, he modified the rate of erosion of Niagara Falls as measured by an American geologist who had used it to compute the time elapsed since the Flood! Evidence of rivers and settlements once abundant in the Sahara convinced anthropologists that these could only have come from the melting of Ice Age glaciers. So, they supposed, did mankind's memories of the great Flood. The 35,000 years that Lyell computed since the Ice Age was too long for those who wanted to see the rise of civilization in the Ancient Near East follow the end of the Ice Age. In Chapter 26, I will explain how the time since the Ice Age was set to 12,000 years. Of course, all this meant that man is far more ancient than is taught in the Bible.

The notion of prehistory, the time that men had forgotten, had arrived. With it came the problem, still with us today, of dating things beyond the time scale of men as given in the Bible. As I explained in Chapter 3, history and with that the chronicling of history stems from the Bible. Non-biblical cultures are hardly concerned with history and the problem of dating, whether concerning relative or absolute time. For absolute dates, our Western world and much of the East have long dated things according to an ancient calculation of the birth of Christ. Long ago, Christians correlated the calendars of the ancient Romans, Greeks, and Jews to the BC/AD calendar we use today. Eventually, they would correlate the chronicles of all the nations to this calendar.

As may be learned from the Bible, ancient dates were referenced to the beginning of the reigns of kings, to the beginnings of cities, to great events, or to offices held by priests or recorders. The Olympiads, held every four years, served as a common system of dating for the competing Greek city-states. Mention of the same event or persons in the records of different nations allow their calendars to be synchronized. The recording of an identifiable astronomical event in an ancient text may allow us to calculate the date of the sighting, improving the precision of already synchronized ancient calendars or anchoring some unsynchronized ancient system of dating to our own. Using these things, scholars have long been able to compute historical records going back to the time of the Assyrian Empire. Ancient Near Eastern texts found in recent centuries have pushed these back to the latter years of the second millennium before Christ.[101]

In 1865, the banker Sir John Lubbock (1834-1913) published his *Pre-historic Times*,[102] introducing the recently coined idea that a time existed before any human records or memory. He divided the Stone Age into the Paleolithic, the Old Stone Age when stone tools were roughly chipped, and the Neolithic, the New

---

[101] When I began my search for the Flood, I did not know that is still the limit of reliable historical dating.

[102] The hyphen in his title indicates the word was not in common usage.

Part V   *Finding the Flood*

Stone Age when they were smoothly polished. Lubbock linked his Paleolithic era to the Ice Age, now called the Pleistocene. Soon pictures of rough looking cavemen clad in fur, making fire, and carrying clubs or spears while pursing or being chased by mammoths over ice-covered plains began appearing in books and magazines. His Neolithic would define what would be supposed post-Ice Age deposits, marking what is now called the Holocene, the most recent era of prehistory.

How did Lubbock explain the fact that savages discovered only in the nineteenth century were still using rough-hewn stone tools? He solved the problem by bringing into archaeology the racist version of evolution introduced by his childhood friend, Charles Darwin. Unlike these men's European ancestors, present-day savages were *incapable* of advancing to the higher stages of herding, farming, and civilization; but as Darwin had noted, they would soon be eliminated in the struggle for existence. These racist views would become the metric for dating man's prehistory. So far as the accuracy of the dating, it hardly mattered that man was dated with this metric rather than from the equally speculative glacial phases.

In the neocolonial nineteenth century, the highest levels of society and learning, particularly successful businessmen and professionals, embraced evolution. They saw history the same way they saw the future: through eyes for "progress." Though many contended for a more romantic version of evolution, seeing it as guided by the better instincts, or in a more Christian version, as guided by God, evolutionary views began replacing the traditional views of Creation. Many adopting these views may have preferred the biblical account, but Darwin's explanation of evolution by unsupervised natural selection gave his theory a seemingly objective and inevitable aura. As the ways of industry and science were determining man's future, the principles employed there must have always been the key for progress. That would be the judgment of so many young men aiming to ride the wave of the future.

As still happens, most accept more than closely examine these latest teachings of science, where evidence is regularly manufactured more unconsciously than deliberately in order to defend fashionable theories. It is because those doing so are amply rewarded in fund raising and bureaucracy, while those resisting are being refused or punished. More than any facts, the needs of evolution were driving the growing antiquity of animal and human remains. Lubbock followed Darwin who added evolutionary progress to Lyell's uniformitarian geology in directing as well as stretching the hand of time.

Following the path of Lyell, Edouard Lartet (1801-1871) had already established the archaeological dates for the periods of human occupation found within the Ice Age according to the remains of bison, reindeer, mammoths, and cave bears, which he believed to have dominated different periods of the Ice Age. The hippopotamus age was soon to precede all these. Though rarely questioned, it is a fantastic assumption. Combining the insights of Lartet and Lubbock, Gabriel de Mortillet (1821-1898) established the familiar archaeological periods: Acheulean, Chellean, Aurignacian, Mousterian, etc. If named for archaeological assemblages rather than animals, they are essentially the same periods that Lyell and Lartet populated by pulling dates for the remains of elephants, bears, reindeer, and hippos from their zoological hats.

According to Darwin's theory, evidence of evolution should be best preserved in the remains of man, the most recent of creatures. It should be observed not just in their artifacts but also in the way they looked and thought. The beautiful drawings in the rock shelter of Cro-Magnon in southwest France proved these inhabitant essentially modern men. Contrast this with a specimen found in Germany's Neanderthal Valley. In the eyes of the eminent pathologist and anthropologist Rudolph Virchow (1821-1902), here was a victim of rickets, but to Darwin's bulldog Thomas Huxley (1825-1895) it was the most ape-looking man he had ever seen and similar to the present inhabitants of Australia. "Neanderthals" were soon to be found inhabiting caves from Spain to Palestine.

Dorothy Garrod (1892-1968) found Neanderthals among other skeletons in the caves of Mount Carmel on the coast of what was then called Palestine. Following Lyell's logic of 'depth of deposit equates to age,' its 25 meters of sea sand, clay, and silt pointed to the caves habitation by man for more than one hundred thousand years. The large cave bears, reindeer, and mammoths were not to be found in these warm climates, but smaller animals were. These were being hunted with microliths, smaller arrowheads appropriate to the smaller size of the game. Anthropologists used this opportunity to add a middle age, the Mesolithic, as being the time when men switched from hunting big animals like mammoths and cave bears in cold northern Europe to hunting small animals like deer and rabbits in the warmer Ancient Near East where civilization would begin.

In truth, most of these rather ordinary humans found in caves and graves were living at the same time, all buried at once in the year of the Flood. The correlation of rickets (curvature of bones) to caves was likely from the poverty of those reduced to living in caves. This explains the extraordinary fact that, aside from the differences one should expect from latitude and geography, the same changes in each step of man's prehistory are occurring simultaneously throughout Eurasia, Africa, and the Americas. That once bothered anthropologists, who tried to explain it by such things as the psychic unity of man, the diffusion of styles and inventions, or migrations of people, all now frowned upon in archaeology. The tools these pioneering archaeologists discovered are appropriate to the different game, but the supposed advances in manufacture of stone tools and weapons create the passage of time in this new evolutionary history of man's past.

The new scientific prehistory had to be linked to history, first recorded in the Ancient Near East. For these scholars the Bible was the least satisfactory record. Due to the writings of Plato, to the *Hermetica* from late antiquity, but especially to Isaac Newton and freemasonry, most Europeans regarded Egypt as the most ancient civilization. From the time Napoleon's troops opened Egypt to European exploration, Egyptologists had been busy proving them right.

The modern controversy over the antiquity of Egypt had not abated since Joseph Scaliger revived the writings of Manetho, a Hellenistic Egyptian historian who lived in Alexandria about two centuries before the birth of Christ. Though the details of his Egyptian kings and dynasties differ from those preserved by Josephus and various Christian scholars, Manetho dated a continuous reign of Egyptian kings back to 35,000 years. Writing at a time when historians competed to claim greatest antiquity for their own nation, Manetho stretched out Egypt's history. Likely, the same fashion is responsible for the longer life spans found in the Adam-Abraham genealogies that appear in the Greek versions of the Bible. Manetho and the first Greek translation of the Torah are from the exact place and time. Because historians adapted Joseph Scaliger's dating of Egypt based on the Greek versions of the Scripture while sticking with the Hebrew dates for the chronology of the Bible, Egypt seemed the more ancient.

King lists go back to Ancient Near Eastern recorders and historians, some of whom did their own surveying of documents and monuments and making guesses of their own. These dynasties and reigns may be overlapping or contemporary due to different domains or to co-regencies. In addition, breaks between dynasties are subject to elasticity. These are only some of the many guesses necessary when using king lists. Based on fragmentary texts, modern recreations of king lists are hardly more reliable than the ancient recreations, especially for combining dynasties recorded in different lists. Something so basic to our understanding of Egyptian history as the Old Kingdom, Middle Kingdom, New Kingdom and the intermediate periods between may be more a nineteenth century invention than an ancient reality. It is likely that instead of following, the first "Intermediate Period" in Egypt's history precedes and parallels the Old Kingdom, Egypt's first civilization following the Flood.

In the early years of the twentieth century, the German Egyptologist Eduard Meyer (1855-1930) gave what appeared to be scientific precision to the history of ancient Egypt using calendar assumptions and astronomical calculations based on Sothic dating. Sothic sightings occur on the first day of the year that Sirius, the brightest star appearing in the southern skies, could be seen from

Chapter 20   Dating the ancient world and the Flood

some supposed official sighting location in Egypt. The Sothic sighting advances one day every 4 years through a 365-day Egyptian solar calendar, and it shifts through the year every 1460 years because the Egyptian calendar has no leap year. A sighting was found in a text dating to the 12th Dynasty, and another from the 18th Dynasty.

Censorinus, a Roman era writer, tells us that in the year we now equate to 139 AD, Sirius was first sighted on New Year's Day of the Egyptian calendar. Guessing the location in Egypt where these observations were made, Egyptologists reckoned that the 12th Dynasty sighting occurred about 1870 BC, and the one in the 18th Dynasty, about 1540 BC. Supposing that New Year's Day must have marked the beginning of Egyptian civilization, it took three Sothic cycles to satisfy what Egyptologists could accept as encompassing the extent of Egypt's past. That is a long chain of reasoning, no better than its weakest link, for which there are plentiful candidates. The ancient Egyptians including Manetho had different notions of Egypt's beginnings, while the notable Egyptian astronomer Claudius Ptolemy (90-168) failed to mention that Egypt used two calendars, but when America's eminent archaeologist, historian, Egyptologist, and head of the University of Chicago's prestigious Oriental Institute James Breasted (1865-1935) confidently proclaimed 4228 BC as the first recorded date in human history, who are ordinary historians to disagree?

There remained the problems of connecting what was believed to be the oldest human history to archaeology, connecting Egypt to the other civilizations of the Ancient Near East, then connecting this historical archaeology to the prehistory that anthropologists were finding in the glacier remains. The man who would do much of this was Sir Flinders Petrie (1853-1942) who first went to Egypt to measure the Great Pyramid so as to determine the mystical pyramid inch. Discovering that to be based on nonsense, he opted with the devotion of a convert to become a priest in the new religion of science – not so different from what once happened to me. Of a family of the Plymouth Brethren, a sect deeply interested in historical prophecy, Petrie was well acquainted with the history of the nations of the Ancient Near East. His most valuable contribution to archaeology was to tie various archaeological sites in Egypt to the king lists and to connect artifacts from those sites in Egypt to the Minoan civilization, which John Evans (1823-1908) had discovered in Crete. Petrie also connected his Egyptian pottery to what he found in Palestine, beginning the linking together of Old World archaeology. He also developed an archaeological prehistory leading to Egypt's recorded past.

A potential problem was the fact that the archaeology of the Ancient Near East would depend on the previous recreation of Egyptian history. This suspect history could not be tested by archaeology because the archaeology was itself tied to the history it needed to test. Petrie's problem was that he had no stratified sites in Egypt such as could be found all over the Ancient East. That might have suggested that Egypt was not as ancient or as continuously occupied as other places in the Ancient Near East, including nearby Palestine. Petrie was eager to investigate archaeology there, and did find stratified sites in Palestine, but his new religion of science allowed for no chronology from the records of those who lived there in ancient times. Instead, he imposed his Egyptian chronology on the land of the Bible. This led Kathleen Kenyon to raise John Garstang's (1876-1956) dating for the fall of the walls of Jericho to 1550 BC, proving this destruction of the city could have been from the invasion led by Joshua in 1400 BC. Presuming the Pharaoh of the Exodus a Ramses and using the same system of Egyptian chronology, she declared Israel's entry into the Promised Land could not have occurred earlier than the thirteenth century BC.

In a study even more suspect than Egypt's archaeological history, Petrie filled the spaces of what he supposed to be Egypt's pre-dynastic history with sequences of slightly different shapes of pottery that he found in graves and cemeteries. In fact, all these graves date to the year of the Flood. How then did he assign them to different centuries and millennia? Petrie introduced what is now called *seriation* to determine archaeological chronology, but he did not find his "later" pottery in archaeological levels above his "earlier" pottery. Like Lyell and Lartet, Petrie had no stratified sites by which to check the relative dating of his completely subjective phases of prehistory. That did not stop archaeologists from creating seriations of their own to create whatever eras they needed to fill the blank centuries of archaeological prehistory

Following Lyell, anthropologists and archaeologists established numerous archaeological periods to fill the 25,000 centuries of the Paleolithic Ice Age and the 75 centuries from the end of the Ice Age to the end of the Early Bronze, the time of Noah's Flood. The plentiful remains from that event became the basis not only for perhaps every imagined period from before the Flood but also for plentiful archaeological periods dated to numerous centuries following that event. These numerous periods and sub-periods – most divided further as early, middle, and late – were named after types and styles of artifacts, wild game, and sites belonging to those who perished in the Flood. Their metric of advancing time was their judgment of improvements in skeletons, weapons, industry, and commerce: a true mirror of neo-colonial values.

This artificially created time explains several mysteries surely noticed by anyone who has studied the archaeology of early humans: why idiosyncratic types of arrowheads or pottery have been the style for centuries, even millennia! When new ones appear, they cross the surface of the earth in a flash. More or less arbitrarily defined levels have been created to fill the intervening years in

Chapter 20   Dating the ancient world and the Flood

archeologically defined periods. This sometimes makes for a strange mixture of cultures that define mankind's earliest settlements and civilizations. According to the current view of ancient Near Eastern prehistory, occupied sites hop around the geography of the region, but get stuck at a few sites for centuries or millennia. Once occupied places spend the vast remainder of human history in deserted quiet. This also explains why Egypt has appeared to be a static civilization. Civilizations do not last for centuries without changing. As is the case at Herculaneum and Pompeii, plentiful remains point to the suddenness of destruction – not to long passages of time. This points to the problem of following the path of Lyell by using the depth of unstratified deposits to estimate the duration of occupation.

Egypt was not the only place other than the Bible where records existed from ancient times. Archaeologists working in Iraq, Iran, Turkey, Syria, and elsewhere were finding texts written on baked clay that not only recorded stories of the Flood, but the lists of ancient kings that guided Leonard Woolley's investigations of Ur. Correlating the archaeology there with that of Egypt revealed the much older civilization of Sumer in ancient Mesopotamia. I have found a few cases, such as in Syria where the Egyptian chronology clashes with the one from Mesopotamia, where archaeological periods from later times are currently seen as occurring before periods that in fact precede them. Even so, this history could only be tied to archaeology no earlier than the invention of writing. Whether that was in the third or fourth millennium before Christ, it would not be useful for the period of Ancient Near Eastern history more than twice as long since the end of the Ice Age as supposed in recorded history.

The now historical archaeology of the Ancient Near East had still to be connected to the prehistory of the man from the Ice Age and to prehistorical archaeology in the greater part of the world from which historical records date to much later times. Already Mortillet had connected the La Tene ruins to the historically known Celtic invasions of northern Italy. The German nationalists wanted to see light spreading from the Aryans of southern Asia, but after studying artifacts being uncovered by archaeologists, Oscar Montelius (1843-1921) saw the beginnings of agriculture and the earliest settlements of Europe as spreading from the Ancient Near East. Following her discoveries of the Neanderthal caves on Mount Carmel, Dorothy Garrod discovered at nearby Wadi an-Natuf evidence of the first invention of agriculture, allowing the hunter-gatherers of the Ice Age to settle down as Neolithic farmers who had not yet learned the art of pottery. Using Montelius's concept of the spreading of light from the Ancient Near East, V. Gordon Childe (1892-1957) developed a detailed analysis of the spread of agriculture and civilization from the Ancient Near East into the most western and northern regions of Europe.

Part V   Finding the Flood

After the Second World War, the growing opposition to colonialism, the rise of independent nations, and numerous new nationalisms brought archaeological studies based on diffusion of light from the Ancient Near East almost to a standstill. Each newly independent nation took control of its antiquities from the colonial Europeans, making it more difficult to correlate archaeology between nations. Some have attributed the cessation of archaeological studies based on diffusion and historical migration to opposition to Hitler's Aryan archaeologists, but in the same manner as Hitler's archaeologists, nations from Europe to America and Asia would assume their ancestors or natives owed little if anything to any foreign culture or land. This led to a revival of evolutionary views of the development of mankind, replacing studies of the historical spread of agriculture and metal with the use of technologies. Archaeologists would be assisted in their seemingly impossible task by a new method of dating: the discovery in 1949 of radiocarbon dating.

Radiocarbon dating is based on the fact that carbon dioxide ingested by plants in the process of photosynthesis consists of both Carbon 12 and Carbon 13, the stable isotopes of the carbon atom, and Carbon 14, half of which decays after about 5730 years. Carbon 14 is created by cosmic radiation impacting the carbon atoms of carbon dioxide high in the earth's atmosphere, but which eventually mixes with the air below. This dating method assumes that the ratio of Carbon 14/Carbon 12 atoms is about the same from place to place over the earth's surface and remains stable through time. After plants die they no longer ingest carbon dioxide, thus the proportion of Carbon 14 to Carbon 12 in the plant decreases over time, thereby indicating its age. This also works to date human and animal remains because they ingest living plants and the meat of animals that do the same.

All systems of dating have their problems. Aside from historical chronicles and reference to astronomical sightings found in ancient texts, radiocarbon dating is the most useful and accurate method of dating ancient history yet discovered. As demonstrated in the test of historically known items, radiocarbon dating can be very reliable. It has also been tested by dating tree rings, and shown to be reliable back to about 1500 BC. Based on the dating of tree rings, it seems to begin underestimating dates, presumably due to slightly higher levels of Carbon 14 in the atmosphere in earlier times. The measured dates however can be calibrated from the dating of tree rings to compensate for that.

Tree-ring calibration has its limits. Despite what is claimed, I could find no evidence in the scientific journals of a continuous tree-ring sequence from historical times beyond about 5000 years. I suppose the Flood explains this upper limit. The oldest tree may be less than 5000 years because in some years trees may experience two or more growing cycles. Published corrections for

Chapter 20   Dating the ancient world and the Flood

radiocarbon dating older than this are not from matching tree ring patterns but from matching wiggle-patterns of calibrated radiocarbon dates.[103] Scientists are developing sequences using the very radiocarbon dating they are supposed to be calibrating! Matching sequences of tree ring patterns is not the simple task depicted in popular illustrations. Though giving the non-expert an appearance of precision and accuracy, computer-determined matches masks helpful human assumptions. With the advent of the world wide web, the technology to publish micro-images of tree-ring sequences together with wiggle-matching patterns is now available. Should laboratories do this, it would improve my confidence in radiocarbon calibrations.

Aside from the problem of calibration, radiocarbon dating is useful back to about 50,000 years or so long as enough Carbon 14 remains to be tested. There is a problem using radiocarbon to date the remains of animals and humans that consume their food from rivers, lakes, or sea, because the waters of the earth absorb far more carbon dioxide than exists in the air. Carbon dioxide long absorbed in water is less radiated than what is found in the atmosphere, causing the radiocarbon dates to seem far too old. Though affecting only a minority of things dated, it has probably had a dramatic but little recognized effect on the dating of ancient human populations.

A more familiar problem is that of contamination, the undesired presence of organic remains from periods other than that being studied. This contamination may have entered the site at any time from the most ancient to most recent. Coal fires have been around for centuries. So have oil lights and gas lamps. Whale oil used for so many centuries brings the too-old readings of the sea. Bitumen has been used at least since the time of Noah. Things covered with that also last the longest, but are never so old as the bitumen. The topsoil found near most sites contains the compost of vegetation dating far back in time.

A far greater problem is not so much contamination as simply identifying what is being dated. Among organic remains, it is mainly charcoal, bones, teeth, shells, antlers, and hard seeds that survive from times as old as the Flood. The very things most often used for dating look the same in every period of history. To have significance for an archaeological dating, an artifact must have been made of these materials, or else they must be clearly associated with some artifact that has a clear relative dating in archaeological history. Dating large numbers of organic remains at different locations from the same identifiable periods, and large numbers from the same level of particular sites make for the best radiocarbon archaeological dating.

---

[103] cf Minze Stuiver, et al, *Radiocarbon Calibration Issues* 28, no. 2B (1986); 35, no. 1 (1993); 40, no. 3 (1998).

Part V   *Finding the Flood*

This points to the rarely discussed but in truth greatest problem of radiocarbon dating: there is no way of separating radiocarbon dating from archaeological interpretation. It is one more human judgment whether a datable sample of non-human remains belongs to some particular period of human occupation, or whether it gets defined as an entirely new period of occupation. Because every archaeological site is as old as the earth's surface or as recent as your own back yard, when a sufficient number of archaeological sites are sorted by date, they will range from the present into the increasingly distant past. This stretches out periods of occupancy and pushes the earliest dates as far back or as recent as needed to suit the needs of the archaeologists. The earliest-dated sites tended to be those with active excavations and study. This explains why archaeological dates keep getting pushed back, and will keep getting pushed back towards infinity until someone calls this game.

The seeming objectivity of radiocarbon dating masks the great subjectivity of archaeological judgment, making radiocarbon dating of ancient sites all the more deceptive. Archaeologists complain that favored radiocarbon dates are published, tolerable ones are footnoted, and unacceptable ones ignored. Published dates will tend to conform to the established archaeological periods, but however one may accomplish it, those able to get others to use their claims to the earliest dating write the scientific history of the human race.

The same problems ensue with other types of dating for periods earlier than the historical era. Absent a reliable clock and calendar, we cannot date things. Judgments of earliest datings should be made only with regard to samples from assemblages that are archaeologically clear, that are independently dated, and in sufficient number to be statistically significant. Dates mean nothing unless these criteria are met, and unless they are tied to some meaningful human history. Dates not accompanied by a clear and archaeological description of what is being dated ought to be ignored, but this information is rarely available in the archaeological publications easily available to the public. All tests made at a particular site should be recorded with the explanation of all those rejected, just as testing laboratories should not be provided with archaeological information. The problem in archaeology and paleontology is that the media and public are chiefly interested in the oldest of whatever is being studied. Archaeologists are hardly exempt from marketing pressures.

Due to the scientism that has long characterized American science and education, one can understand why archaeologists need attention. Inspired by radiocarbon dating, the use of computers, and precise methods of testing, a movement back in the sixties called the New Archaeology seemed to bring with it the notion that subjectivity would be removed from archaeology. Flow charts would replace narratives, statistics would replace conclusions, systems would replace nations, and the new evolutionary science would replace the soft science of history. The result was the replacement of archaeologists by technicians and consultants complying with government requirements for archaeological preservation. It worked. Few cared and fewer still understood what was being measured, tested, and published. Most universities would soon close their departments of archaeology or merge them into some other discipline. They might have learned from Einstein: not everything that counts can be measured; not everything that is measured counts.

What is important for the present discussion is how this scientific archaeology looks in the light of the Bible. At the beginning of the radiocarbon revolution, the beginning of agricultural settlement was traced to the Ancient Near East in the late sixth millennium before Christ. The beginning of cities and civilization came from the same place, about a millennium later. That is not far out of line with the places and dates of the Bible, especially if one uses the Greek text. This dramatically changed with a single radiocarbon date from Kenyon's Jericho that pushed back these dates for the beginnings of agriculture a few thousand years. But what did Kenyon really measure? What is more likely: that archaeologically identifiable organic material survived for eight thousand years at a site that does occasionally get flooded or soaked by rain, or that some form of old carbon was present in the sample used for dating an unclear assemblage? The point here is not so much to criticize Kenyon or her dates, but how uncritically the worldwide archaeological community functioned for something of such great importance.

This is not to say that those with the most archaeological expertise in the oldest remains were not the most critical. As happens with sensational news – and finding or determining the oldest example of something is sensational – media attention eclipses more expert and cautious voices. Robert Braidwood (1907-2003), who was working on the beginnings of agriculture in the Ancient Near East at Jarmo, then the world's first human settlement, found his extensive analysis being ignored due to Kenyon's good fortune of replacing him as being the one investigating the beginnings of agriculture and excavating the world's first city. Prominent archaeologists in Europe such as Professors Vladimir Milojcic (1918-1978) and Stuart Piggot (1910-1996) found that the new patterns coming from radiocarbon dating conflicted with their careful reconstruction of European prehistory. Piggot called some of the new dates "archaeologically unacceptable." If the archaeological dates do not make sense, what are we dating?

Naturally, Kenyon was pleased that her star rose with the scientifically determined dating. Similarly delighted were those involved with the Cro-Magnon caves in southwest France. They would soon "discover" that their cave men had developed such advanced and beautiful art more than 30,000 years ago. Remarkable indeed, even if more recent studies have dated them to 17,000 years. Whatever were those cave men doing for tens of millennia? How do we know that the smoke covering the beautiful Cave Man paintings in southern France came from the wooden torches of those who painted these drawings rather than from the oil lamps of recent times? To determine the age of the inhabitants of these Cro-Magnon caves, what were the laboratories dating: ancient wood, whale oil, kerosene, or coal? An archaeological judgment would date them to similar drawings in Germany that date to about 5,000 BC. Problems of radiocarbon dating surfaced in the controversies over the Shroud of Turin, vastly younger and far better preserved than the decaying ruins of far more ancient times.

Australian aborigines discovered that their ancestors had crossed the difficult currents separating them from Asia more than 55,000 years ago. Where is the evidence of such a long and sustained occupation? Isn't it more likely that these earlier inhabitants, as did the later aborigines, obtained a substantial portion of their diet from the sea, in which case radiocarbon dating will be too old? The same would explain why Early Jomon pottery from Japan has been given an older date than the earliest pottery from the Ancient Near East.

Understanding the processes discussed above, it should surprise no one that a great pushing back of dates accompanied the radiocarbon revolution. Another pushing back stemmed from the change to calibrated radiocarbon dates. These latter changes encouraged archaeologists working in Europe to challenge the long-presumed dependence of these cultures on earlier cultures in the Mediterranean and the Ancient Near East.[104] Their claims to greater antiquity can be explained by the simple fact that archaeologists in the Ancient Near East resisted the challenge of the radiocarbon measurements to their historical dates. The European archaeologists didn't seem bothered by the fact that they were comparing Europe with the Ancient Near East using different systems of dating, rationalizing this by declaring a "fault line" that isolated European prehistory from that of the Ancient Near East. Archaeologically determined dates and the earliest migrations of mankind were becoming obscured as radiocarbon dating, anti-diffusion dogma, and archaeology controlled by national antiquities authorities and prehistory promoted by nationalists and indigenous peoples were coming to control archaeology throughout the world.

Radiocarbon dating is improving the dating of archaeological remains in the historical period, where radiocarbon dates are more reliable. One example is the Egyptian chronology that depended on so many questionable assumptions.

---

[104] Colin Renfrew, "Carbon 14 and the Prehistory of Europe," *Scientific American* 225 (October, 1971), 69. Reprinted in C. C. Lamberg-Karlovsky, *Old World Archaeology: Foundations for Civilizations* (Freeman, 1972), 201-209.

Chapter 20   Dating the ancient world and the Flood

Due to radiocarbon dating, Egyptologists now agree that the current chronology is in much need of revision, but a new consensus has been slow to develop.[105] This means that historically determined dates earlier than the Neo-Assyrian Kingdom of the late second millennium cannot be trusted. It is in these earlier areas that important conflicts with the Bible occur. This may change due to a recently published radiocarbon dating of samples from Egypt found in museums throughout the world.[106] These push back the date of the building of the Pyramids to a time that better matches the era just before the Flood. Though they are presumed to have been built in the Old Kingdom, in fact the Old Kingdom was when they were remodeled as tombs for the Pharaohs. These new dates seem most compatible with the biblical date of the Exodus and the traditional dating of the fallen walls of Jericho

Since 1859, hypothetical cultures based on burials from the era of the Flood have been assigned to periods from the beginning of the Ice Age to the first millennium after Christ. Assignments of these burials to times after the Flood are due to the vast number of burials versus the sparse and worn out evidence from garbage piles and destruction levels, the chief evidence available for archaeologists to recognize ordinary human settlements. Not recognizing Flood cemeteries as settlements of the living, archaeologists have associated many with nearby dated sites that were settled after the Flood. We can know that the graves do not belong to these settlements because the artifacts found in the graves are completely different from those found in the remains of the settlements. Some archaeologists explain this difference by positing the manufacture of special mortuary pottery. They should also posit a special mortuary civilization, and a special mortuary race: those who perished in the Flood!

Examples of graves without settlements are those of the "migrating pastoralists" that populated the land of the Bible soon after the Flood. Kathleen Kenyon assumed that those buried in shafts in the hills around Jericho were migrating pastoralists because no settlements were found where those buried might have lived. Most probably, they lived in the same places where she found them buried. The loss of population following the Early Bronze Age, which led to my discovery of the Flood, was far greater than the archaeology currently reveals.

A notable example of wrongly associating these burials with actual settlements occurs in the archaeology of America. The Paleolithic and the Archaic remains from all over the New World are clearly from before the Flood. So are

---

[105] Ian M. E. Shaw, "Egyptian Chronology and the Irish Oak Calibration," *Journal of Near Eastern Studies* 44 (October, 19850 295-317. William A. Ward, "The Present Status of Egyptian Chronology," *Bulletin of the American Schools for Oriental Research* 288 (1992), 53-66.
[106] Christopher Bronk Ramsey, et al, "Radiocarbon-Based Chronology for Dynastic Egypt," *Science* 328 (June 18, 2010).

the impressive burials of the widespread Hopewell and Adena cultures. Newcomers from cultures that follow the Flood, bringing with them sand-tempered pottery and the bow and arrow, used some of these same advantageous sites for new settlements and for their own simple burials. Because the impressive burial cultures of the erstwhile inhabitants have also been assigned to the newcomers, Woodland sites are currently dated to around the time of Christ. The extensive and informal contents of these burials mark them as created by the Flood more than two millennia earlier. What makes them elaborate is that they are ordinary homes filled with all the things of the living.

The first scientific investigation ever sponsored by the U.S. Government and the first supervised by the Smithsonian Institution concluded that the Hopewell and Adena cultures were not those of Native Americans.[107] While the investigators distinguished these burial mounds from the temple mounds built by Native Americans, they had no way of properly dating the two kinds of mounds. The latter mounds contain ceremonial burials, but simpler than the far more elaborate unplanned burials created by the Flood. Often found on the same mounds as those created by the Flood, these burials do in fact belong to Native Americans, but the subsequent Smithsonian report attributing all these mounds and everything in them to the present natives of America became the definitive opinion.[108]

Most of these earliest dates for human beings from all over the world pertain to burials and artifacts that I have identified as once covered and perhaps partially or completely buried by rivers of soil and debris washed over them by the swift waters of the Flood. The population explosion of the world in the years just prior to the Flood points to some ancient version of an agricultural and industrial revolution. I doubt that many human settlements were abandoned before the Flood. I would guess that the largest part of them date from several hundred years before until the time that they were buried together in a single year.

More often than not, the graves from the Flood are the only evidence of pre-Flood cultures and periods. At some point, archaeologists should have wondered where lived all the people who built the most elaborate graves of all history. We find that most of these burials have been assigned to different periods based on arbitrarily dated sequences of various artifact types. More rural and rustic artifacts are defined as Paleolithic. It is likely that many were hunting camps or the butchering sites of "Neolithic" or Early Bronze peoples. Neolithic settlements

---

[107] Ephraim G. Squier and Edwin H. Davis, *Ancient Monuments of the Mississippi Valley* (Bartlett and Welford, 1848).

[108] Cyrus Thomas, "Report on the Mound Explorations of the Bureau of Ethnology," *Bureau of Ethnology for 1891*(1894).

Chapter 20   Dating the ancient world and the Flood

lack the wealth and metals of those assigned to the Early Bronze, though they are contemporaneous with the same.[109] The most urban and refined artifacts are classified as late Early Bronze. The larger the site and more refined the artifacts, the further they are assigned along the timescale of unilinear evolution.

There is no question that worldwide archaeology is currently a confused muddle. Prehistorians can scarcely draw a clear picture of the history of the ancient world. The best they can do is to offer a millennium-by-millennium summary of the archaeology of various regions, mostly unconnected with the archaeology of other regions.[110] Even these are grossly in error. The fragmentation is so great that no one can make sense of the mess now called prehistory. Like other natural scientists, archaeologists and prehistorians are reluctant to publicize the sad state of their discipline. Only the most competent and secure will do that, if only because they must explain prehistory. Because of these difficulties, curiosity concerning the many mysteries has probably been more punished than rewarded. The best defense of the status quo is reasonable: why keep bringing up the problems if no one can offer a solution? Fortunately, the Flood has given us the chronological marker we need to remove the confusion in ancient archaeology. It should be interesting to examine archaeology throughout the world with the understanding that all these graves date to precisely one year of the third millennium before Christ.

But what is the date of the Flood? Why not use the best in scientific dating – calibrated radiocarbon dating? Can we trust it? Since great climatic changes did occur at the time of the Flood, one might suppose that they would somehow affect radiocarbon dating. The destruction of all the earth's vegetation would have added new carbon dioxide to the atmosphere. On the other hand, the addition of new waters to the oceans would have increased the capacity of the oceans to absorb carbon dioxide. Something like this may explain the known discrepancy in radiocarbon dating earlier than 1500 BC, necessitating the calibrations from tree-ring dating. Figure 37 from Harappa in India, Figure 38 from Jomon sites in Japan and Figure 39 from a study of Stonehenge in Britain are examples of systematically calibrated radiocarbon dates of the remains of this era that meet all these criteria. If we can trust these dates, we have our date for the Flood. It is

---

[109] The same argument was made by McGill University's Sir John William Dawson (1820-1899) to his mentor Charles Lyell. Trigger notes that Lyell found it easier to ignore than to refute Dawson's arguments. [Bruce G. Trigger, *The History of Archaeological Thought* (Cambridge University Press, 1989),102-103.

[110] cf Jacquetta Hawkes, *The Atlas of Early Man* (St. Martin's Griffin, 1976); Grahame Clark, *World Prehistory* (Cambridge University Press, 1977); Robert J. Wenke and Deborah I. Olszewski, *Patterns in Prehistory* (Oxford University Press, 1990); *The Times Atlas of Archaeology: Past Worlds* (Crescent, 1995), Robert W. Ehrich, editor, *Chronologies in Old World Archaeology* (University of Chicago Press, 1992).

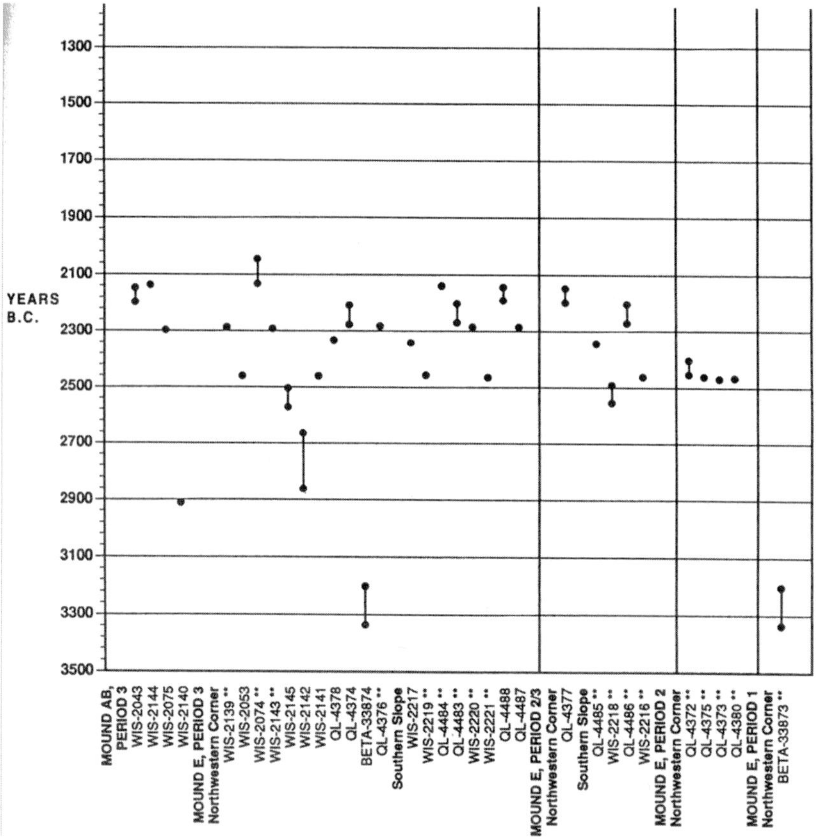

Part V   Finding the Flood

FIGURE 37   CALIBRATED RADIOCARBON DATES FROM HARAPPA BURIALS, NEAR THE INDUS RIVER

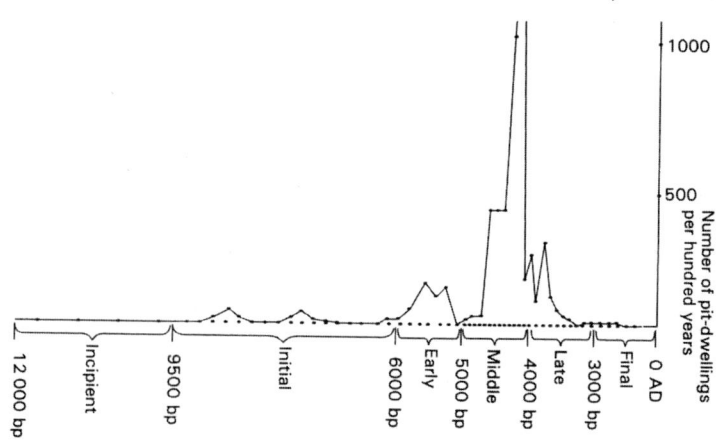

FIGURE 38   CALIBRATED RADIOCARBON DATES FROM JOMON BURIALS (Japan)

Chapter 20   Dating the ancient world and the Flood

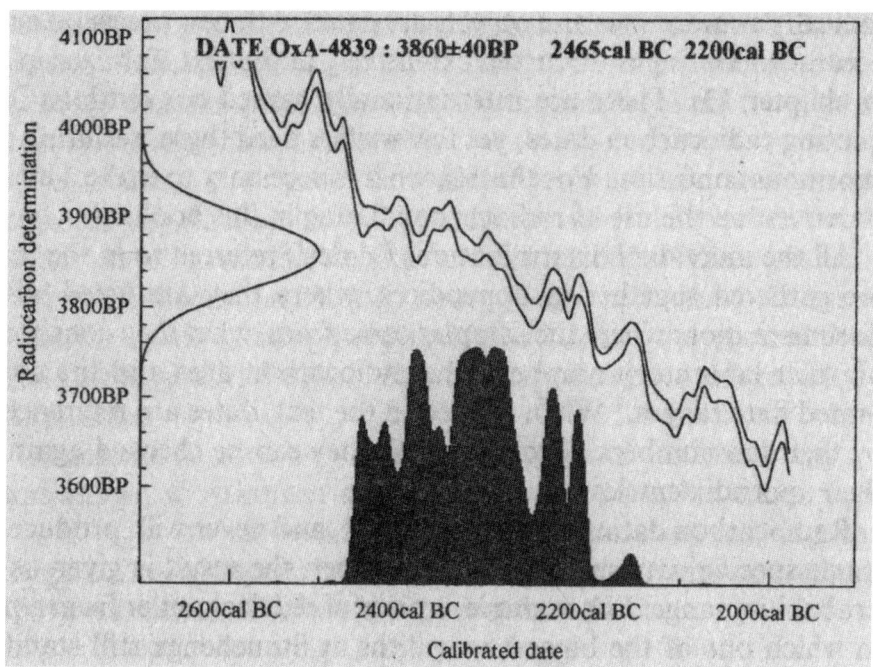

FIGURE 39   CALIBRATED RADIOCARBON DATES FROM STONEHENGE

close to the date of the Flood calculated by James Ussher and printed in the margins of some older versions of the King James Bible.

— 21 —

Tracing the Middle Bronze cultures back to their source

From the very beginnings of my discovery, it occurred to me that it should be a simple thing to study the archaeology of the period following the Flood. At the beginning of this period we should have what I determined to be the clear evidence of the Flood: a complete break in archaeological culture. In fact, we see such a break at every archaeological site in the world that spans the burials of the Flood. In the Americas it distinguishes the Archaic era from the Formative states of the historic cultures. In China it distinguishes the Neolithic period from the earliest historical sites belonging to Hsia, Shang, and Chou. In much of Europe the break distinguishes the Early Bronze Age from the urnfield sites of the Late Bronze Age. The latter are continuous with the earliest historical cultures of Europe. In the Ancient Near East the break distinguishes the Early Bronze from the Middle Bronze period.

We discover that even in the Ancient Near East, where the survivors of the Flood first settled, the archaeology pertaining to the Middle Bronze period is sparse. This is what one would expect if the world had been so recently and dramatically depopulated. When we subtract all the cemeteries inappropriately assigned to the Middle Bronze the remains will be seen to be even sparser. Interestingly, most of what we know from cuneiform texts of the ancient world pertains to the sparse remains dating from the Middle Bronze Age.

If my theory is correct, no matter where on the surface of the earth we start we should be able to trace the Middle Bronze culture back to its origins: to the very source of the new dispersion of mankind from the Ancient Near East. This task turned out to be far easier than I imagined. The first culture overlying the Early Bronze period in the land of the Bible is inappropriately named Early Bronze III. It belongs to the beginnings of the Middle Bronze. This culture, called Khirbet Kerak (or Beth Yerah) from the site near the Sea of Galilee where it was first defined, is a sparse pastoral culture. It belongs to the earliest

Chapter 21   Tracing the Middle Bronze cultures back to their source

Figure 40   Tracing the source of the culture from Israel's sparsely populated interlude

part of the pastoral interlude from which I first identified the Flood. Archaeologists find this culture scattered throughout the Ancient Near East, but as Figure 40 indicates, they have traced it to its origins in the upper river terraces of the Kura and Araxes Rivers.

Archaeologists of the Caucasian regions tell us that "Kura-Araxes traditions apparently emerge during a rapid burst of cultural evolution, the early stages of which remain undocumented or unrecognized." [Peter Glumac in *Chronologies in Old World Archaeology* (University of Chicago Press, 1992), 203.]

The truth is, it may have been documented. The upper terraces of the Kura and Araxes Rivers begin in the mountains of Ararat! Those responsible for this highland culture are members of a single family who had just disembarked from the ark. It was not the Mayflower, but your ancestors did arrive on this boat.

Figure 41   Settling down in the mountains of Ararat

Part V   Finding the Flood

> "And in the seventh month, on the seventeenth day of the month, the ark came to rest on the mountains of Ararat. And the waters continued to abate until the tenth month; in the tenth month, on the first day of the month, the tops of the mountains were seen." [Genesis 8:4-5]

And as one would expect, they were expert agriculturalists. Those Transcaucasians making the Khirbet Kerak pottery built granaries as if they had long experience collecting agriculture surpluses for a time of need. They were expert at growing food and tending herds and flocks. This Armenian plateau and surrounding areas, which sit at the apex of the famous Fertile Crescent, are the homeland for many plant and animal species of Old World domesticates.

Not surprisingly, the survivors made extensive use of tents. They pitched their tents above round platforms, the foundations of which have been im-

FIGURE 42   POTTERY (LEFT) AND TENT PLATFORMS (ABOVE) FROM THE EARLIEST SETTLEMENTS AFTER THE FLOOD

properly described as *tholos* or keyhole-shaped structures. [Figure 42 (right)] Such structures do seem to have evolved, however, from the earlier hide-covered dwellings.

Animal figurines and horseshoe-shaped andirons are found in the remains of their camps and fires. The survivors of the Flood have temporarily lost the knowledge of the fast pottery wheel, but their campfire pottery is burnished and beautiful.[111]

---

[111] cf Stephen J. Pfann, "Khirbet Kerak." In *Anchor Bible Dictionary*, edited by Noel David Freedman (Yale University Press, 1992); Charles Burney and David Marshall Lang, "From Caucasus to Euphrates – The Early Trans-Caucasian Culture." In *The People of the Hills: Ancient Ararat and Caucasus* (Littlehampton Book Service, 1971).

Chapter 21   Tracing the Middle Bronze cultures back to their source

[Figure 42 (left)] Appropriate to such a great loss in population – compare early Europeans settling in small colonies in the wilderness of the New World – the culture of the Ancient Near East suddenly turns from one that is urban and refined to one that is rural and rustic. This happens whenever people find themselves alone in a new land and have to become economically self-sufficient.

"May God enlarge Japheth, and let him dwell in the tents of Shem, and let Canaan be his servant." [Gen. 9:27]

— 22 —

The first international economy on the plains of Shinar

In ancient Israel, the widely-spread Khirbet Kerak or Beth Yerah (also called Trans-Caucasian or Kura-Araxes) culture ends suddenly around 2200 BC. It is replaced by the conventional Middle Bronze culture, marked by the distinctive calciform pottery. The fast wheel has returned for making this thin-walled pottery, whose design seems to imitate metallic vessels. Many other refinements and new inventions suddenly appear. Though the chronology of the Ancient Near East is deeply confused during this era, it appears that Late Uruk markers such as bevel-rimmed bowls and cylinder seals are joining the Khirbet Kerak culture and spreading outward from the spring waters of the Tigris and Euphrates Rivers. The new settlers also seem to be spreading some of the pottery from earlier eras: the beautiful Halaf and Nineveh V pottery. The treasures from the civilizations from before the Flood must have been mined and reused or traded.

The Middle Bronze culture probably derives from the city of ancient Uruk in southern Mesopotamia. The Sumerians who settled Uruk trace their ancestors to a mountainous place in a land called Arrata. One had to cross seven mountains to return to the original homeland. That fits perfectly the geography lying between the land of Sumer and the mountains of Ararat. We also know that the Sumerians and many other peoples had an account of the Flood. As it now appears, all these accounts came from the same ancestors, the family of Noah.

Skeptics have declared that the writers of the Bible knew nothing of the far more ancient civilization of Sumer, ancestors of the Babylonians, but the great Sumerian scholars Arno Poebel (1881-1958) and Samuel Noah Kramer (1897-1990) saw in the root of Sumer (or Shumer) the name of Shem, son of Noah.[112] The writer of Genesis needed to learn nothing at all from the Babylonians. The

---

[112] Samuel Noah Kramer, *The Sumerians* (University of Chicago Press, 1963), 297-299.

Chapter 22   *The first international economy on the plains of Shinar*

Hebrews own ancestors were Sumerians, from the Ur of the Chaldeans. In fact, the name *Chaldean* derives from Arphaxad, or Arpaachshad: Shem's son and Abraham's ancestor.[113] The Chaldeans lived along the Zagros mountain range and in southern Mesopotamia to the borders of Elam.

Perhaps owing to the confusion caused by the mixing of the sparse remains of the post-Flood culture among the extensive ruins of the civilization that perished in the Flood, archaeologists date Late Uruk culture earlier than late Early Bronze archaeological cultures. In fact, Late Uruk should follow the Early Bronze. Several published radiocarbon dates confirm that the Late Uruk era was dated about one thousand years too early.[114] This is not the only region where the mixing of pre- and post-Flood remains has led to chronological confusion, but the problem here is compounded by the temporary residence of most of the world's inhabitants in that great and famous city. Before the end of the third millennium, Uruk becomes the largest city in the ancient world. Some believe that no other ancient city excelled its size until the era of the Roman Empire. Certainly no other city of that size would appear before Jonah's Nineveh or Nebuchadnezzar's Babylon, more than one thousand years after this city. Called Erech in the Bible it was one of the sites established by Nimrod on the plain of Shinar soon after the Flood.

> Cush fathered Nimrod; he was the first on earth to be a mighty man. He was a mighty hunter before the LORD. Therefore it is said, "Like Nimrod a mighty hunter before the LORD." The beginning of his kingdom was Babel, Erech, Accad, and Calneh, in the land of Shinar. [Gen. 10: 8-10]

Theologians have followed ancient legends concerning Nimrod, but according to the Bible this famous man was a hunter of animals rather than of men. During a time when dangerous wild animals roamed these parts and when new settlers had to live off the land, a skilled hunter would have been a valuable explorer and pioneer. Nimrod seems to have been the Daniel Boone of Mesopotamia. In relatively peaceful times, he led settlers from the mountains of Ararat to new areas he found by following tributaries to the main course of the Tigris and Euphrates Rivers.

The biblical name Shinar refers to the land of Sumer and Akkad.[115] Most likely, Akkadians are those speaking the language of the later descendents

---

[113] Richard S. Hess, "Chaldea." In *Anchor Bible Dictionary*, edited by Noel David Freedman (Yale University Press, 1992).

[114] I found that radiocarbon dates for Late Uruk are hard to obtain, but dates for Yanik E. B. II are 2640-2305 BC, 2180-1925 BC [Robert Schacht, "Early Historic Cultures." In *The Archaeology of Western Iran* (1987), 191; dates for Late Uruk at Tel Brak are 2195-1960 BC, 2225-1985 BC [D. Oates, *Chronologies of Old World Archaeology*, Vol. 1 (1992), 189.

[115] Op. cit., Kramer, 297.

Part V   Finding the Flood

of Nimrod, son of Cush, son of Ham, son of Noah. For the era of Israel's Judges, Ancient Near Eastern scholars know those from this region as the Kassites (Cushites). In the Late Uruk period we find in the city of Uruk a huge unfinished platform built of brick, along with a great workshop of molds fired by burning bitumen.[116] The city is surrounded by a 10-kilometer wall built of plano-convex mud bricks. For the scant population of the earth of this era that is a gigantic undertaking.

> Now the whole earth had one language and the same words. And as people migrated from the east, they found a plain in the land of Shinar and settled there. And they said to one another, "Come, let us make bricks, and burn them thoroughly." And they had brick for stone, and bitumen for mortar. Then they said, "Come, let us build ourselves a city and a tower with its top in the heavens, and let us make a name for ourselves, lest we be dispersed over the face of the whole earth." [Gen. 11:1-4]

FIGURE 43 RUINS OF URUK (SITE OF THE TOWER OF BABEL)

Gilgamesh, widely known from the Flood story that is so similar to that of the Bible, claims credit for building this famous city. This famous ruler may indeed have been the chief architect. Some have identified him with Nimrod, but the book of Genesis explains the project as a community decision. One does not need to explain the attraction of a large city for those accustomed to the hard work of the self-sufficient economies that existed on frontiers before the Industrial Revolution allowed regular trade with distant places. Cities are necessary for prosperity because they allow workers to specialize, thereby become more productive in their separate vocations. That is why rural people migrate to large cities. Prosperity also allows leisure. What is inexplicable by natural causes is why this great city was suddenly, if perhaps not completely, abandoned not long after it was built. Absent some calamity, or some act of the gods, how does one explain this?

And the LORD came down to see the city and the tower, which the children of man

---

[116] Hans J. Nissen, *The Early History of the Ancient Near East* (University of Chicago Press, 1988), 95, 80-83.

Chapter 22   The first international economy on the plains of Shinar

had built. And the LORD said, "Behold, they are one people, and they have all one language, and this is only the beginning of what they will do. And nothing that they propose to do will now be impossible for them. Come, let us go down and there confuse their language, so that they may not understand one another's speech." So the LORD dispersed them from there over the face of all the earth, and they left off building the city. Therefore its name was called Babel, because there the LORD confused the language of all the earth. And from there the LORD dispersed them over the face of all the earth. [Gen. 11:5-9]

Conflicts occur when communication breaks down, explaining why people prefer to separate themselves from those whom they do not understand. The citizens of this city might have followed emigrants speaking their own language to newly found fertile ground, hunting lands, or fishing sources. The Bible may suggest that invisible angels, sons of God, led the nations to their assigned destination.[117] This explanation accords neither with popular teachings about ancient Babel nor descriptions of the Tower of Babel [Figure 41], but it accords with the account in the Bible.

FIGURE 44   THE TOWER OF BABEL BY PIETER BRUEGHEL THE ELDER (1563)

Immediately following this era, we find the first archaeological evidence of the widespread Indo-European and Semitic languages. The evidence dates to just the time and place that we should expect from the Bible: the later centuries of the third millennium before Christ. Appropriately, the evidence is found in the Ancient Near East, the place of the next dispersion.

When peoples speaking the same language split into isolated populations, the languages of the separate groups form dialects, and when the separated peoples can no longer understand the other dialects, they have come to speak separate languages. What happens to languages is similar to what happens to the genes of isolated populations. As in the case of DNA tests where similarities in genes reveal the closeness of ancestry, the similarities in words and structure of different languages reveal the closeness of their ancestry. But importantly, this cannot be the case of language groups with such great structural differ-

---

[117] Genesis 11:7-9; Deuteronomy 32:8 (Septuagint, Dead Sea Scrolls); Acts 17:26

ences as exist between the Indo-European (in fact, *Japhetic*), the "Semitic" (in fact, *Hamitic*), and the Sumerian families. The sudden appearance of the Indo-European and Hamitic language groups with such great structural differences cannot be explained apart from such a singularity as the Bible claims for the origin of mankind's languages.

As I explained in Chapter 8, the history of the Ancient Near East has been developed on the assumptions of German scholars that ancient nations arose like their own Germany, created in the nineteenth century from those parts of Europe speaking the German language. Following Herder, these scholars assumed what is manifestly not the case: that nations are identical with languages and that nations never change their language by adopting new tongues. In fact such changes often occur due to the advantages of trade or schooling or to the privileges accorded those able to communicate with some new foreign ruler, while a people's culture and their deeper identity with their ancestors may still be preserved. In some cases the scholars have mistaken the language used by scribes or scholars as the language of the people, but no more in ancient times than today does the language of literacy necessarily reflect what the local peoples may be speaking.

An important example of the errors this has introduced into scholarly biblical history concerns the language of the ancient Hebrews. It is reasonable to assume that when Abraham entered the land of Canaan, the patriarchs or their children would learn to speak and eventually adopt what the Bible calls "the language of Canaan."[118] Though the German linguist A.L. Schlozer (1735-1809) may have only been following Rabbinic and Catholic myth when in 1804 he named the "Semitic" family of languages for the German form of "Shem," he nonetheless made a colossal blunder. The language of Canaan, a version of which became biblical Hebrew, is clearly the language of Ham.

The original language of the Hebrews was probably closer to that of their relatives the Hurrians. I am guessing that the name *Hurrian* probably refers to the Assyrians (also descendents of Shem) before they began writing, and then for commercial reasons, adopting an Akkadian or Cushite tongue as happened by the era of the Old Assyrians. The militant culture of the Assyrians is very much like that of the ancient Hurrians,[119] but some of those using what is now called the Hurrian language may have been ancient Hebrews, including Abraham and his family. There are in fact "Hurrian" names among the "Semites" who lived in Egypt as well as among the early Hebrews.

---

[118] Isaiah 19:18
[119] See Figure 22, depicting a Hurrian chariot warrior.

… — 23 —

The new dispersion

DERIVING FROM THE Ancient Near East, the Middle Bronze culture belongs to us all. It is the ancestral culture of Europeans, Asians, Africans, native Americans, the aborigines of Australia, and the inhabitants of the most isolated islands of the Pacific. This rich culture varies widely, but we find such general traits as the heddle loom; wattle-and-daub construction; multi-generational megaron houses; the lost-wax form of bronze working; the bow and arrow; hieroglyphic scripts; bark paper; spoke-wheel wagons; advanced agriculture and animal husbandry; chevron patterns on pottery as well as patterns created by various incisions and stamping; gray, sand-tempered, and egg-shell pottery, some styles appearing to have developed from metallic predecessors; side lugs for tying and carrying pottery; giant urns for storing grain, cremations and urn burials. It is also characterized by the seven-day week, animal sacrifices, a God or Great Spirit who lived in the heavens or sky, and accounts of the great Flood.

This culture spread from the Ancient Near East to Europe, Africa, Asia, the Pacific, and eventually to the Americas. Unoccupied land, much of it fertile or rich in valuable minerals, was available in every direction. At the same time, the move away from the ancient population center would also have entailed the loss of specialized skills. Those who believe in the progressive evolution of human culture, seemingly supported by the experience of the Industrial and Scientific Revolutions, have a hard time accepting that material culture ever degenerates. The settlers in ancient times faced the same problems as the Europeans who first came to the American wilderness. Material progress and refinement depends on the specialization of skills, possible only with large populations and an economically integrated civilization. Rusticity, a return to a more primitive material culture, *always* happens when people travel into unsettled and distant lands, the more so as small groups of people become increasingly isolated.

Part V   Finding the Flood

We can trace the spread of migrating people by shining the light of the Bible on the data from archaeology, historical philology, linguistics, and genetics. What we discover in the case of the earliest settlements following the Flood closely matches the patterns of archaeological settlement by Noah's family given in the tenth chapter of Genesis, the so-called "table of nations."[120] The Genesis table of nations in turn helps us understand the archaeological and linguistic trail left by these migrations. Families speaking different languages but carrying various aspects of this same culture spread from their homelands in the Ancient Near East to the most remote areas of the world. In following the dispersions discussed in this chapter, it will be useful to refer to the earliest homelands depicted in Figure 45, and the dispersions depicted in the map on the inside cover of this book.

The Japhetic or Indo-European group has been the longest studied and best researched by archaeologists and linguists. Some of the best authorities see it spreading from a homeland in eastern Turkey.[121] This dispersion corresponds closely to the time and locations of Japheth's family as noted in Genesis. The linguistic evidence agrees with the dispersion associated with the spread of Minyan pottery through the upper Mediterranean that begins in the late third millennium. This is the root of the Mycenaean civilization in Greece, and the proto-Villanovan culture in Italy. Archaeologists have connected this culture with the urn-burials of central Europe, the first evidence of new people in Europe following the Flood.

The archaeological remains pertaining to these new migrations overlie or are imposed upon those of the previous civilizations that perished in the Flood. In the intervening centuries, the organic remains in those earlier civilizations have thoroughly dried and burned, giving some archaeologists evidence to claim that the new migrations are from violent invaders. Such evidence suggested to the German nationalists that virile Aryan invaders were spreading out from southern Asia and conquering inferior peoples. Though sympathies have since inverted in today's feminist age, it is still supposed that Indo-Europeans conquered agriculturalists, reckoned as peaceful and matriarchical by the widespread presence of mother goddess dolls. In reality, the evidence we discussed in an earlier chapter points to these first agriculturalists (the pre-Flood inhabitants) as far

---

[120] For connections of the family of Noah with historical peoples, I recommend Victor P. Hamilton, "The Book of Genesis Chapter 1-17" in *The New International Commentary on the Old Testament* (1990), 330-348 and various entries in the *Anchor Bible Dictionary* (Yale University Press, 1992).

[121] c.f. discussion of the various views in J. P. Mallory, *In Search of the Indo-Europeans* (Thames and Hudson, 1989).

Chapter 23   The new dispersion

FIGURE 45   GEOGRAPHICAL DISPERSIONS FROM THE TABLE OF NATIONS IN GENESIS 10

Part V   Finding the Flood

more violent than the first "Aryans." In fact the violence of these "vegetarians" led God to send the Flood.

As the Genesis account relates, the descendents of Japheth spread along the coasts to the northern countries of the Mediterranean. Japheth's name seems to have been appropriated for Indo-European words for god (Jupiter, Iapetus, Zeus, Deus, etc.), and father (or *pather*). Named *Greeks* by the Romans, the Hellenes, as the Greeks called themselves, remember their father Javan as the son of their god Iapetus.

Those who study the history of the Ancient Near East might wonder how Noah's family could so soon have departed from trust in the God who had saved them. Abraham's own father served idols, as often did his children, the Israelites. The tendency then, as also observed in later times, was for ancestors and heroes to turn into gods (or saints). Thus the pagan gods were mainly local. The ancestral households became temples. Likewise, the material possessions of our ancestors became sacred objects. Then as today heirlooms became the object of possessiveness, the sources of our entitlement. They become idols! The same phenomena happens both with local and sectarian Christian traditions, which tend to be held more dear than our common faith. Idolatry does not need to be explained. It occurs naturally as the result of ordinary selfishness, possessiveness, and greed.[122]

The Japhetic peoples also spread north into central Europe. In the sixth century before Christ, Medes (or Persians speaking the language of the Medes) spread eastward into India. Despite their current designation as *Indo*-European these languages would not have gotten to India before the invasion of the Persians at the time of King Cyrus. The ancient oral epics of Aryan India were first written down in Sanskrit, a dialect of the Old Persian language, when, as it appears, literacy first reached India. Their content points to a greater antiquity, suggesting their composition in a more indigenous language in India, likely one related to Dravidian. The Aryans, of course, have long been regarded as the original Europeans, and descendents of Japheth. But I will have more to say below about these Aryans and other descendents of *Shem!*

Some scholars believe that the ancient city of Hamath in Syria may have gotten its name as being the home of Ham. Hamitic groups spread from a homeland in Syria to the ancient land of Canaan and by way of the port of Byblos to Upper and Middle Egypt, and Crete. They established the Minoan civilization of Crete. The Etruscans who founded Tuscany may been related to this same group of settlers. Another Hamitic group spread from Nubia in Upper Egypt into central Africa.

---

[122] Ephesians 5:5, Colossians 3:5

The ancient city of Kish and the Kassites, as the peoples of Babylonia were called in the days of Israel's judges, may have both obtained their names from Cush, son of Ham. The Cushites spread from a homeland in Mesopotamia around the Persian Gulf to the coasts of East Africa and South Asia. That explains why Genesis describes the River Gihon as flowing through the land of Cush. From South Asia, Cushites spread to Indonesia and Australia.

The descendents of Shem spread from homelands in Armenia, northeastern Iraq, and southwestern Iran. These included the chariot driving Aryan conquerors of the dark-skinned Cushites of southern India. Contrary to the myths of the German nationalists, it is unlikely that these real Aryans spoke the "superior" Indo-European languages until the era of the Persians, when Sanskrit would come into use. The language of the Aryans would have been nearer that of the ancient Sumerian, modern Chinese, and other agglutinative languages such as those of the Native Americans. I suggest the name *Shemitic* for all the agglutinative languages.

Some Shemites spread into Europe, becoming the ancestors of the Finns, the Estonians, the Hungarians, and perhaps the original Basque people of northeastern Spain. Other descendents of Shem traveled what would become the Silk Road, spreading their Middle Bronze pottery to the Kansu region of China.[123] From there, some sailed down the Yellow River to establish the Chinese civilization. The beginnings of the first Chinese dynasty, the Xia or Hsia, correlates with the time of scattering from the Tower of Babel, and the beginning of Chinese history dates from before the Flood but correlates closely with the life of Noah, who was born 500 years before the Flood. The Chinese preserve historical records including an account of the Flood and our Heavenly Father, as traditional Chinese know God, perhaps better than any records outside the Bible.[124] Other groups followed the Yellow River to the Yellow Sea and southern Japan. By following the rising sun, some arrived at Ecuador and the upper portions of South America. To my eye, Native Americans most resemble the Japanese, but there was more than one crossing and some may have departed from other parts of the Far East.

Of all the early dispersions of mankind, none were so long as those who travelled by way of the steppes of Asia to the Far East, and then to the Pacific islands and to America. The danger and requirements of ancient travel are sufficient to explain the harsh hierarchical cultures of Asia and of those that early European

---

[123] Pottery and culture having these traits are described as Hsin-tien, phase B, in Kwang-chih Chang, *The Archaeology of Ancient China* (Yale University Press,1986), 380-384.

[124] From Natalie, Erika, and Aaron Chou, then in their early years of home school, I learned the Chinese character for a large ship. It consists of the sign for a boat, combined with signs for eight mouths (number to be fed).

explorers observed among the Pacific and American natives. There can only be one leader of a caravan, captain of a ship, or admiral of an armada. Orders must be quickly and firmly obeyed. Severe discipline is required to maintain such order, while class distinctions are useful for the perpetuation of hierarchies.

Why should prehistorians have supposed that America's earliest settlers or re-settlers would have taken the difficult land route from Asia through Siberia, the Bering Strait, Alaska, and the mountainous ranges of Canada and Western America when they could have conveniently traveled and fished along the coasts and rivers? On top of this, according to the current beliefs, one must also explain how they managed that journey when deep ice from the last Ice Age blocked the way. In any case, archaeological evidence for such a proposed journey is completely lacking, but it is not lacking along the Pacific coast, indicating that the pioneering journeys most likely came by the convenient path of this great ocean.

Long before the European explorations, ships or boats were the chief means by which early man traveled. As is still the case in Far East, folks can actually learn to live on boats or ships, preparing them for the skills needed for long periods of life at sea. Conveniently for their dispersion, these descendents of Noah had not lost their excellent skills at building and traveling by boat. Like books and other organic materials, the remains of boats rarely survive from these times. This does not mean that early man was primitive in the way that modern anthropologists and archaeologists have supposed. Boat building is no more difficult than other universal skills such as speaking and farming. Likely, every forested area of the earth was first settled by families carrying their possessions in canoes, rafts, or ships navigating up rivers and along seacoasts.

Inventors of the fast-sailing catamaran, the ancient fishermen of the Pacific were among the best sailors of history. Many centuries before Europeans visited remote Pacific spots, settlers from Asia had managed to find their way to the Easter and Hawaiian islands. This is not to say that they did not also experience hardship. Widespread cannibalism in the Pacific and the New World point to the great hardship and horror the earliest settlers of America must have experienced on these long journeys.

Before anti-diffusion dogmatism had become fully entrenched archaeologists had traced the roots of the Formative cultures of the natives of America to Ecuador.[125] The archaeological situation is understandably confusing because there are also definite similarities between pre-Flood Valdivia culture in Ecuador and the pre-Flood Jomon culture of Japan. It appears that Ecuador was the main port to America for the eras both before and after the Flood.

---

[125] James A. Ford, editor, *A Comparison of Formative Cultures in America* (Smithsonian Institution Press, 1969).

Chapter 23   The new dispersion

Why was Ecuador the main port to America, before and after the Flood? Experienced sailors know the terrible danger of sailing in circles. The most reliable primitive navigation on the ocean is based on observing the sun, the place of its rising or setting. No matter where one begins along the Asian coast of the Pacific, if one follows the rising sun he will eventually arrive on the coast of Ecuador, named for the Equator. (This may also explain why sun worship is found among the New World natives.)

From Ecuador there are archaeological links to the initial settlements of the Chavin culture of pre-Inca Peru and to the Olmec and Mayan cultures of Central America and southern Mexico. The Olmec culture flourished on the Gulf Coast, but it is continuous with earlier settlements near Ocos on the Pacific coast where are also found links to Ecuador.[126]

The links of these cultures to later and more widespread cultures of North, South, and Central America have also been established.[127] The earliest settlers to North America spread by means of canoe from the Gulf Coast, up the Mississippi, Ohio, and Tennessee Rivers into the heartland of America. Others spread eastward around the Gulf and Atlantic coasts. Traits common to the North American natives, including the bow and arrow, maize and squash agriculture, ceremonial temple mounds, and American ball games like lacrosse are rooted in the Formative cultures of Meso-America. These cultures spread very early into the Caribbean and around the Atlantic coast to northeastern South America. A branch from these spread from the Greater Antilles into Florida.

From the Negroid appearances in the statuary of ancient Olmecs, some may have crossed from America to West Africa establishing colonies on the Niger and Benue Rivers. Most would probably reckon the reverse, but the era and direction of migration and the seafaring capability suggests a direction from West to East. Negroid features are also found among peoples of Asia. Whether this explains the origins of Bantu-speaking Africans needs more study. In any case, members of Shem's family certainly did come from the Far East to settle in the southern part of East Africa. Considering this, together with the Hamitic Nubians, Egyptians, and Cushites from East Africa and the Japhetic or Indo-European settlements in North Africa, it is no wonder that Africa is such a genetic and linguistic puzzle.

Links in the other direction – between the Formative cultures of America and similar cultures in Japan and China – have also been well established.[128] A millennia or so later, even newer settlers from the Orient, those related to the

---

[126] op. cit., Fiedel, 314-315.

[127] op. cit., Ford.

[128] Michael D. Coe, *The Maya* (Thames and Hudson, 1993), 55-57; Betty J. Meggers, "Contacts from Asia." In *The Quest for America* (Praeger, 1971), 234-259.

Part V   Finding the Flood

totemic Polynesians, spread into and from the northwestern coasts of North America as far down as the American Southwest. The Apaches appear to represent the most southern advance of this more recent family of American natives. The Eskimos of North America seem to have spread from Siberia as a distinct third group of first Americans.

All these new inhabitants brought with them such innovations as wattle-and-daub huts, sand-tempered pottery, the bow and arrow, some knowledge of the Great Spirit, and reports of an ancient Flood from which their ancestors were spared.

Captain James Cook Discovers Tahiti

FIGURE 46   REUNION OF NOAH'S FAMILY

— 24 —

Summing up my search for the Flood

THE NEW DISPERSION was the third of the three items that I had been seeking as hard and certain evidence of the Flood. These three criteria were to discover clear evidence of:

1. A SUDDEN AND dramatic depopulation of the earth before the beginning of the second millennium before Christ;
2. IMMEDIATELY FOLLOWING THIS, a new dispersion to the most remote parts of the earth; and
3. AT EVERY REGION in the earth, an absolute discontinuity in the culture of the remains of man from just this time in history.

What I discovered matched the account of the Bible even more precisely than the criteria for which I was searching. I also found:

4. THE RUINS OF the antediluvian civilization with a character that perfectly matches the violence and decadence pictured in the Bible for the period just before the Flood.

What I found in the era following the Flood also matches what we learn from this same small section of the Bible:

5. NEW BEGINNINGS IN the mountains of Ararat;
6. A SECOND NEW beginning on the plains of Shinar;
7. EVIDENCE OF THE sudden appearance a great city, then evidence of sudden abandonment, both corresponding to the biblical events on these plains;
8. A CLOSE MATCH of the new scattering with the table of nations in Genesis springing from Noah's family, and at the same time the first evidence of the modern Indo-European (Japhetic) and Semitic (Hamitic) families of languages.

Part V   Finding the Flood

What I found conformed to the Genesis account far more precisely than I ever imagined or hoped. What might not seem in perfect accord is perhaps due to reading these chapters more in line either with unsound tradition or scholarly theory than from shining the light of Genesis on the remains from the era it describes. As I will show in the next section, scientific evidence that seems to deny these archaeological and historical facts is more likely due to defects in our scientific knowledge than to defects in the Bible.

I will end this section of the book on the archaeological evidence of the Flood by noting that I pursued this quest with little of the understanding and insights into the history of archaeology, language, and geology by which I have prepared the reader. In contrast to my present great confidence, increasing every year, I pursued my quest with much fear and trembling. I was particularly concerned that I had not connected my archaeological search with what seemed to be powerful evidence against the Flood from the science of geology.

My first clue as to the true nature of the "Ice Age" occurred as I was reading about the Glacial Kame culture in the upper Midwest. There Adena-style burials are found under glacial burins from "the last Ice Age." As is now the custom, such burials were attributed to elaborate religious ceremonies. In this case, it would have required digging under glacial burins, constructing the elaborate graves, then ceremoniously re-covering the elaborate graves with soil from the glacial mounds.

I suppose the first and last steps had to be repeated many times as each member of the family died. According to the eminent American archaeologist Dean Snow, it was an attempt by country cousins to duplicate the practices of their more sophisticated Adena relatives.[129] Snow is an excellent archaeologist. He may no longer hold this view. His profession however has become so accustomed to religious interpretations of these burials that it only seems normal to think in this fashion.

Such interpretations are not from any particular prejudice against the Flood. Even early archaeologists who believed in the Flood supposed that these burials belonged to the *descendents* of Noah's family. For some reason even those who believe the Bible seem unable to imagine that the world only recently discovered by the Europeans had been highly populated prior to the Flood. They haven't seemed able to believe that the supernatural author of the Bible knew of the existence of the New World.

A glance through the bibliography in the back of this book will give the reader some idea of how many archaeological books, and how many various archaeological regions and sites I examined for this quest. Based on that and on my present knowledge of the cause of these graves, I dread reading one more

---

[129] Dean Snow, *The Archaeology of North America* (Viking Press, 1976), 39.

194   Author's relentless attack on Christins is appalling. Everyone that believes in the Bible believes people lived before the flood it is the whole point of the flood to destroy them

Chapter 24 Summing up my search for the Flood

account of the religious meaning of such burials. I refer to explanations such as the widespread ritual of partial cremation, the re-entry of graves to paint the bones of the dead with the color of life-giving ochre, the reburial of disarticulated bones following exposure to the elements and wild animals, the immense energy that goes into carrying by hand the millions of baskets of soil necessary for covering the remains of elaborate tombs and temples, and – most distasteful of all – the religious explanations of numerous other odd burial practices that once occupied, or preoccupied, the ancient world. The confidently expressed scientific descriptions of the religious ceremonies associated with these burials have given rise to new mythologies that – as is the case with scholarly influence upon all religious traditions, including those of Christians – are subject to being embraced by natives wishing to "preserve their ancient culture."

I have a simpler explanation for each of these so-called mortuary phenomena. As an example, consider the often-described practice of re-opening these underground tombs after flesh has decayed in order to paint the bones and artifacts the color of "living-giving" ochre. What I learned about floods from my mother must certainly have helped these ancient morticians. Water from later floods would have turned the powdery red clay from the original Flood now lying on the floors of these tombs into a container of paint. When these later floods subsided, the delicate task of these morticians would have been completed. Some archaeologists note that this mortuary practice seems limited to areas where the iron-oxide clay prevails.

These morticians needed all the help they could get – from the gods or from God's Creation. I cannot believe that any society, then or now, so completely consumed by elaborate funeral practices as archaeologists and prehistorians currently presume could possibly survive. The morticians and funeral home directors must then have been the ancient world's foremost tycoons. Of course the only ones so obsessed, so possessed, and so consumed with religious madness are the scientific anthropologists, archaeologists, and sociologists who offer these explanations. How ironic that modern science should have supposed it was those following the light of the Bible whose understanding has been darkened by religion.

Q.E.D.

Part VI

The Flood's Implications for Science and Scholarship

— 25 —

The Bible and Science

AN EVENT AS significant as the biblical Flood had necessarily to impact not only the history of mankind but the whole of natural history. Indeed, we may wonder how all the leaders and workers in fields from climatology, geology, biology, and genetics to anthropology, ancient languages, and biblical studies could have missed what must have profoundly shaped their subjects. But in no field should the manifest fact of the Flood have been more difficult to miss than in archaeology. Yet, I have shown how workers in this field misinterpreted the massive evidence of this world-shaping event. Failing to understand the great changes from this sudden purging of the earth more than five thousand years ago cannot but be detrimental to what is now being taught.

The best minds in numerous fields do recognize profound problems of which laymen and ordinary workers are unaware, but even scientists and scholars have only a lay knowledge of subjects outside their specialties. Thus few are aware of the larger problem in the state of mankind's knowledge of the greater issues pertaining to mankind and the world. As in the case of archaeology, a great problem is the fragmentation, the conflicting schools, and the slight understanding of the foundations of the sciences and humanities even among those who work and publish in these fields. In Chapter 1, I explained how Christians have become accustomed to overlooking the serious implications that the problem of Noah's Flood poses to our faith. In truth the members and supporters of any enterprise do not like to be informed or reminded of problems in the foundations of their activities. It is no different in the case of scientific schools, let alone the institutions, the media, and the general public who have become accustomed to trusting the authority of science.

When I began my search, I had no intention of pursing the implications of the Flood beyond archaeology. Examining the many related fields seemed beyond my expertise and resources. However, as I became firmly convinced of the Flood's historicity, my interest in the other sciences related to ancient times

Part VI   *The Flood's Implications for Science and Scholarship*

soared. I could not wait to discover how the facts in other fields would appear when seriously examined in the light of Genesis. It was much easier than I had imagined because the more I discovered, the more I was able to discover. The more I learned, the easier it became to understand the past. I realized that the very chapters of the Bible most widely regarded as fable were not only a powerful light for studying the past, but also for major fields of science.

When we reject the light from the Creator, we substitute some human invention. This points to the root of the modern world's failure to see what is in fact powerful and manifest evidence of the Flood: supposing scientific methodology without benefit of revelation from the Creator to be a reliable authority for the big truths about the world and supposing the Bible but another example of the darkness that enveloped pre-scientific man.

But it is important to note that those who are openly hostile or uninterested in the Bible have been far less influential in turning the world from the Bible to science than those who teach within the folds of "the faith." It has become commonplace for Christian teachers, even conservative and evangelical expositors of the Bible, to remind their auditors and readers: "The Bible is not a book about science." As I explained in Chapter 3, the Bible is indeed far more a book of history and revelation than of science, but these Christian teachers imply something else: that what the Bible has to say about origins and the most ancient history cannot be literally believed because they are only parables expressing "spiritual truths." The implicit assumption is that science without benefit of revelation is capable of independently discovering and confirming whatever vestiges of truth about ancient times might be found in the Bible. The sad truth is that Christian theologians and teachers have been more impressed and less critical of science's claims than practicing scientists. But supposing that the truth about the world and mankind can be discovered without help of revelation reduces the mind of the Creator to the same order as man's. It is to be underwhelmed by the manifest glory of Creation and unimpressed by its Creator.

In the remaining chapters of this section I will show how the evidence from specific sciences appears in the straightforward light of Genesis, contrasting it with the confusing ways these facts are presently explained. I will point out that what is now taken to be myth is in fact the powerful truth, while what is currently supposed to be the scientific truth about our world's past is in fact but science fiction.

When scientists explain the history of their fields they usually begin in the Enlightenment, occasionally mentioning concepts held by the ancient Greeks that they regard as anticipating modern views. As they understand the Enlightenment, it was the point when scientists and scholars deliberately rejected the light of the Bible.[130] Since then, rejecting the history of mankind found in the Bible has been regarded as prerequisite for establishing the scientific authority of some plausible alternative. For the rest of the present chapter, I will explain the unsound foundational principles underlying the Enlightenment and modern science: their rationalism, materialism, naturalism, and their unreasonable restriction of empiricism to physicalist boundaries. Bear in mind that words applying to philosophical abstractions are vague and variously defined. It is not my aim here to dispute definitions, thus I will note the specific ways in which I use and criticize these terms.

I address first the claims of rationalism, by which I mean: supposing truth to be accessible and recognizable absent any external authority, something that a sufficiently clever and supposedly informed human mind is capable of independently determining. This type of rationalism should be distinguished from the critical use of reason: determining whether there are contradictions within claims or whether various claims contradict the evidence. In truth, those calling themselves rationalists more often use reason to rationalize away whatever evidence conflicts with their particular rationalist understanding. Because the mind of man is not the mind of God, all rationalist views of the world are necessarily no more than but products of the imagination.

> **Because the mind of man is not the mind of God, all rationalist views of the world are necessarily no more than but products of the imagination.**

While rationalism may not be irrational in the sense of being self-contradictory or unsupported by arguments from reason, it is in fact unreasonable.[131] For it is but reasonable to believe that the world was created by some intelligence and power far beyond what man has seen or can comprehend. It is but reasonable to believe the Creator would have concern for his Creation, would reveal this truth to man, and would have reminded us by additional revelation what mankind had forgotten. Reason would seriously consider the inspiration and authority of the Scriptures. Indeed, the Bible itself commends the proper use of reason. Unfortunately, rationalism is not the best, but the worst use of reason. Not only does it unreasonably reject divine revelation and the way of faith for man's limited understanding, it rejects whatever empirical knowledge does not conform to its particular version of rationalist understanding. There is no

---

[130] Note that all along, the Bible has been responsible for the modern views, albeit due to a reactive rather than submissive use of revelation.

[131] In *Orthodoxy* (1908), G.K. Chesterton pointed to the obsessive rationality of madmen, as one will not fail to observe in a visit to an asylum for the insane. Their problems stem not from too little, but from too much rationality.

"rationalist understanding" because rationalists hold a multitude of conflicting versions of a rational world.

Rationalism tends to concern itself with general principles instead of with individuals and particular truths – what rationalist philosophers have disparaged as the "contingent truths" of history. Thus rationalists prefer the truths of science and philosophy to those of history. Those we love are special, but the importance given to individuals and to the special people of the Bible, the so-called scandal of particularity, offends the rationalist way of thinking.

Because the exceptional things recorded in the early chapters of Genesis do not conform to a scientific understanding, rationalists charge those who believe these chapters with anti-intellectualism. Certainly there is plenty of anti-intellectualism among those who champion the Bible, some stemming from spiritual pride and some from an understandable dislike of sciolism, but believing what is written there does not mean that one is opposed to the best use of the intellect. Few are wise enough both to value intellect and also to recognize its limits. C.S. Peirce (1847-1914), perhaps the greatest logician in that field's history, declared reason an unreliable guide for vitally important topics. Indeed, while recognizing and commending reason and wisdom, the Scriptures declare the fear of God to be the beginning of wisdom. Because an unseen God of unfathomable power and wisdom created the world and ourselves, our un-aided understanding cannot comprehend how he did it. Thus, man's reasoning is not the place to begin our understanding, however important and valuable reasoning can be. Though many great intellectuals have been theists or deists, a rare few, like the Apostle Paul, have trusted the simple truth of the Scriptures. So far as acknowledging this fact, defenders of the faith have rarely been so candid as Jesus and Paul.[132] God is not impressed by rational men.

The issue is the rationalist's desire to judge in a completely autonomous manner, but is it even reasonable to suppose that man's understanding does not need assistance from his Creator? Moreover, what valid authority granted any man the inalienable right to reject God's authority? Should one protest that he needs first to know what *is* God's authority, he should perhaps use the reason that he so commends. As the account in the Garden of Eden illustrates, this desire is rebellion that ultimately leads to death. On the other hand, though contrary to what rationalists claim, neither the rejection of rationalist demands nor the act of humbling one's inmost heart to the true and living God should be supposed an irrational perspective. It is in truth a most reasonable thing to do. Rationalists should understand that neither non-rational nor anti-rational attitudes are irrational, nor are they unreasonable.

---

[132] 1 Corinthians 1:20, 26; Matthew 11:25; Luke 10:21

Chapter 25   The Bible and science

Faith is not in fact irrational. Because of our limited knowledge and understanding, what we presently see or hear may seem to contradict faith, but there must be no actual contradictions between what we believe and what is true. Fideism is indeed irrational because it accepts contradictions between faith and facts, but biblical faith is not Catholic fideism. Faith cannot be rightly separated from the object in which it rests. To be worthy of trust the object of our faith must be based on righteousness and truth. Fideists blindly trust some earthly religious authority while others blindly trust scientists and secular authorities for issues they do not understand. Rationalists trust their own understanding, the least reliable of authorities. This may explain why some of the greatest of the intellectuals – the Apostle Paul, Tertullian, and Pascal – have themselves been anti-intellectuals.

Perhaps the chief reasons for the success of science's deceptive claims are the great prosperity and technological advances in modern times. This problem stemming from the deception of materialism is not limited to the defense of science; it is the justification of any status quo. Many suppose the scientific worldview itself to be responsible for the recent increases in knowledge and prosperity, though this is not the case. Genuine scientific advances, those pertaining to useful advances in technology or medicine, have little or nothing to do with worldviews. Contrary to modernist conceit, pre-modern worldviews are not incompatible with technological advancement. To the contrary, the biblical worldview has always been fertile ground for technical and social progress.

Neither is the modern era the first time the eyes of the world have been profoundly blinded by prosperity and marvels. The world that perished in the Flood was also prosperous and technically advanced, as were the ancient pagan empires just prior to their decline. According to the Bible, prosperity leads not only to apostasy but also to a deceptive understanding of the source of man's benefits.[133] In truth, the records of all the great civilizations from the impressive antediluvian world to those of Greece and Rome demonstrate that prosperity and technical achievements guarantee neither security nor the continuance of these benefits.

Though by the time of Christ, the ancients had accumulated a considerable store of practical knowledge in agriculture, metallurgy, textiles, transportation, geography, architecture, writing, astronomy, music, mathematics, and government, most of the world had drifted into great darkness about God and Creation. The prosperity was simply owing to specialization in industry made possible by an increase in population and worldwide trade, the same cause leading to today's prosperity. No one was then in greater darkness than the powerful Romans, who obtained their wealth through exploiting great masses who lived

---

[133] Deuteronomy 8, Daniel 4

in slavery and heavily taxing the nations whom they ruled by torture. Still, their famous roads and aqueducts, their terrible war machine, and their highly effective system of government did not keep the Empire from collapsing into the Dark Ages as a result of the very exploitation and corruption upon which the prosperity depended. The disruption of the pagan world left only the despised Christians as a force capable of promoting cooperation within and among the nations, which would eventually lead to the rise of the West.

Biblical faith, then found chiefly in Europe, was certainly the cause of the rise of Western Europe. Contrasting with the cacophony of pagan myths and the competing dogmas of Greek philosophy were the Scriptures' brief but authoritative account of the past. However rich in meaning, the nature and origin of the world and of mankind are taught in a straightforward narrative in the first few chapters of the Bible. The relative brevity of the account was essential for its preservation and for widespread teaching of these important truths. Though the Scriptures do not explain all mysteries or the details of Creation, they do teach what is essential for survival and prosperity. Moreover, the firm order God gave to Creation supported a scientific understanding of aspects of Creation useful for arts and industry.

Because the Bible gives descriptive and historical rather than philosophical or scientific explanations of the world and of man, an empirical and progressive study of Creation can proceed unhindered either by philosophy or religiously-defined scientific dogma. This is not to say that those claiming the Bible have not frequently read philosophical, theological, or scientific dogma into the Scriptures, but the descriptive and historical account of Creation found in the Bible is always there to challenge any theory. Aside from important ethical concerns, believers may employ whatever scientific principles may be useful. Indeed biblical societies have always excelled in the practical arts and sciences.

Notwithstanding what some have falsely claimed, faith in the living God of the Bible is far from the kind of traditionalism that hinders progress in understanding and human betterment. In truth, biblical societies are and have always been dynamic, not static. In fact it is the *naturalism* to which many wrongly attribute the success of modern science that has hindered its progress. The Aristotelians and Stoics are examples of naturalists who held back progress in science, faith, and human betterment. These conservative philosophers taught men to accept what they supposed to be "the proper nature of world." But the "natural" order of the world changes with beliefs and traditions.

Following in their footsteps, the history of science contains many examples of opposition to new knowledge and methods that contradict what were once supposed "laws of nature' – meaning not what is actually observed in Creation, but what we would now call science. Naturalism is in fact a form of traditionalism, no less rigid than religious beliefs. We do not see science as traditionalism only because modernists trumpet the fact that what we understand as natural or scientific today is different from what was once believed, while the religious assert the antiquity of their traditions. Although the scientific paradigms have changed, most religious traditions are likewise far more recent than supposed. Indeed, many cherished beliefs of the "old time" religion are no older than our parents or grandparents, the first generation to champion them. In any case, as I pointed out in Chapter 12, scientific paradigms are in truth no less difficult to overcome than are religious traditions.

Many philosophers and scientists agree that naturalism is dogma, but defend it as necessary methodology. They argue that science must remain committed to a naturalistic worldview because a natural cause might someday be discovered for things for which no such cause is presently known. They point to the discoveries of natural causes for phenomena formerly explained as divine design or attributed to unseen spirits. In truth, "divine design" was but an earlier form of science, while rather than explaining, scientism merely blinds its eyes to the manifest existence of spiritual realities. Naturalism is in fact nothing more than the dogmatic refusal to acknowledge exceptional experiences or events, no matter the evidence. Anything truly exceptional, including the fact of Creation, refutes naturalism.

So far as the numerous false claims that are found in religion, naturalistic philosophers should not suppose they are the most concerned with their presence, or that they are best suited to dispute them. A jeweler who claims that all precious stones are counterfeit hardly possesses expertise for testing jewelry. In fact, no one dislikes the false claims of religion more than those committed to the truth of the Bible, which has a great deal to say about false religions, false signs and wonders, and the mass appeal of both.

Because of their rationalism and naturalism, the Greeks have been credited as the authors of the best scientific knowledge in the ancient world, but in fact they borrowed it from the Ancient Near East. The competitive Greeks were not inclined to reveal their sources, but their touted contributions to mathematics, astronomy, physics, medicine, biology, and geometry arose during the Hellenistic era when they came into contact with the nations of the Ancient Near East. If the Greeks had themselves obtained empirical knowledge they would not admit it because they viewed it as the kind of knowledge possessed by slaves. Their dogmatic attachment to rationalism and naturalism did more than anything to limit rather than expand what men through the ages have been able to see and understand. Contrary to popular belief, it was not the Bible but the spread of Greek philosophy that was responsible for the impoverishment of science from late antiquity to modern times.

This brings us to the misunderstood and too little discussed subject of empiricism: the discovery of knowledge through experience and exploration. If Greek success in the sciences was severely limited by rationalism, modern science owes its success to its rejection of rationalism in favor of empiricism. The Bible also favors the method of empirical or practical knowledge; thus it is not surprising that modern science arose immediately following the back-to-the-Bible Reformation. Following the biblical and humanist focus of the Reformed Puritans, Enlightenment theologians rejected the science of Aristotle that had been the basis of Thomas Aquinas' natural theology, but embraced what was then called the New Science of mechanics, more in harmony with the mathematical understanding of the world deriving from Plato. But however important mathematics were to the rise of modern science, empiricism is even more fundamental.

Contrary to popular belief, it was not the Bible but the spread of Greek philosophy that was responsible for the impoverishment of science from late antiquity to modern times.

Because the Reformers championed Scripture alone as the basis of faith one might suppose that Protestants would reject rationalism and return to studying science through the lens of the Bible and focusing on practical affairs rather than theory, as has always characterized those who literally believe the Bible. Indeed, in seeking to return to a more literal understanding of the Scripture, the Reformers preached against scholastic philosophy. The Sovereign God as taught by Calvin could be understood as beyond human reason and judgment, favoring empiricism and leading certain radicals among the Calvinists to embrace an antinomian form of the faith. Nonetheless, official Protestantism would not take the direction either of anti-rationalism or religious experience because the Reformers also embraced reason as a means of countering the authority and spiritual powers claimed by the Roman Catholic Church. And they were no less keen to reject the revelations claimed by Protestant radicals. The Protestants of the official churches soon developed their own form of scholasticism in which the Bible was to be read through the particular theological systems of their confessions. I explained in Chapter 5 how mechanistic science developed from a theology of Providence that had more in common with the natural theology of the Stoics than the historical explanation of Creation put forth in the Bible. It is difficult to note the exact point in which the dogmatic theology of the Protestants became dogmatic mechanistic science, but it surrounds the time of Isaac Newton.

Most types of rationalism have been opposed not only to the Bible, but also to empiricism. Even those rationalist sciences that claim to be based on empiricism systematically reject whatever evidence fails to conform to their rationalist principles. From before Socrates, the rationalist philosophers were explaining away the facts of experience. Aristotle is often claimed as an empiricist because, in contrast to Plato's philosophy, he recognized the reality of the world revealed by the five senses. But Aristotle is only an "empiricist" in the sense of his *a priori* commitment to dogmatic materialism. The same can be said of modern scientism. As philosophers from the ancient Epicureans and medieval Aristotelians to modern scientism understand it, materialism is not in fact empiricism but philosophical dogma about the nature of reality. Rather than opening minds to all manner of evidence and experience, both the old and new science filter evidence.

In contrast to its condemnation of rationalism, the Bible hardly opposes empiricism. Far from ignoring the facts of experience, the Bible is itself the record of the experience of ancient Israel and of the Apostles' experience of Jesus. Because the Bible does not provide a philosophical or rationalist account of Creation, it is more accommodating to empirical science and to a progressive or self-correcting understanding of theories used to explain the natural world. From the time of Roger Bacon, the same biblical tradition in the British Isles that opposed Aristotle defended observation and experience as the way of the sciences. Not surprisingly, a move towards empiricism accelerated with the Reformation. Seeing knowledge possessed by the Catholic church as corrupt, British millenarians rejected the dogmatic science of Aristotle for the empirical and inductive science taught by Francis Bacon. Pioneers of the New Science, Isaac Newton and Robert Boyle not only championed the Bible against the Deists, but they also championed empiricism against the authority of Aristotle and against the mathematical-logical rationalist systems put forth by the Continental philosophers, Descartes, Spinoza, and Leibniz. The Puritan expectation of increasing light to accompany the return of Jesus recommended a self-corrective way of advancing knowledge that led to the falsifiable and testable science that would be put forth by C. S. Peirce and Karl Popper.

John Locke, himself the son of Puritan parents, became the great champion of empiricism as the source of all forms of human knowledge. Opposing the views of the rationalist philosophers that ideas were innate to the mind, Locke declared that the mind began as a blank slate. Disturbed by the crisis of skepticism developing from the Reformation, Locke embraced the probable and evidential form of truth concerning science as put forth by the Royal Society, and concerning religion as taught by Anglican Latitudinarians. The Latitudinarians, many of whom were themselves members of the Royal Society, assumed that the conclusions of reason are always tentative because new evidence may later come to light. According to them, Christianity was likely true unless someone could demonstrate a general conspiracy behind the rise and dominance of the faith. Not only did Locke reject this idea, he regarded the truth of Christianity as having been established by the miracles of Jesus and the Apostles. Locke declared the reasonableness of Christianity, acknowledging its contribution to the ethics required for a just society.

Regardless of how conservative Locke may seem today, by making reason the ultimate judge, he led the way for modern science and rationalism to replace the authority of the Bible. Locke was chiefly concerned with refuting the divine right of kings and the religious authority claimed by the Pope. It is unlikely that he supposed that reason would eventually reject the gospel. But Deists understood that by proclaiming reason the judge, Locke was placing reason as the judge of the Bible. Unlike him, they found miracles repugnant to reason. Unfortunately, Locke himself regarded the Bible as more important for the masses who were unable to follow the arguments of reason. As a matter of method, Locke's teachings led to the systematic ignoring of the Bible even as a light for the study of Creation, a trend that would eventually remove the Bible from science. It turned scientists into experts, not just about physical things, but even concerning religion! Enlightenment philosophers supposed that true religion could be discovered without the assistance of divine revelation. In effect, scientists became the new priests and science the new religion, replacing the Bible as the modern world's authority for truth.

Were Locke's methods valid, religious experience might be expected to have led to similar improvements in religion. Revelation is certainly from religious experience rather than reasoning. The Jews looked for signs rather than wisdom.[134] Jesus advised us to judge a tree by its fruit, a definite recommendation of careful empiricism. Though the Holy Spirit cannot be seen, it can be experienced in one's soul. The Holy Spirit is also the divine spirit of truth that both teaches and leads the born-again people of God.[135] But the Holy Spirit, the presence of God, is also extraordinary, manifesting the power of God with extraordinary signs and wonders.[136] Despite his advocacy of empiricism as the way to truth, Locke rejected anything new or extraordinary in the way of religious experience. Locke's rejection was due to his dislike of Enthusiasm, which he supposed to be opposed to reason. *Enthusiasm* has two meanings, though the opponents of Enthusiasm have always preferred to link rather than distinguish them. One refers to radical religious commitments in politics, which led to religious wars. The second refers to private revelation or to any extraordinary experience or communication from God.

---

[134] 1 Corinthians 1:22
[135] John 3:8, 14:17, 16:13
[136] Acts 1:8, Romans 15:19

Chapter 25 The Bible and science

In the wake of the Reformation, a few leaders of peasant revolts and those who wanted to bring in the millennial kingdom of God by armed conflict also claimed the authority of private revelation. Others claimed spiritual authority for questionable or immoral behavior. Certainly, claims of private revelation must be tested, but from earliest days the established churches wanted no competition either from those quoting the authority of Scripture or from the presumed authority of religious experience, whether their claims were bad or good. This remained the case long after the Reformation, even though religious experience and biblicism more often result in a notable positive and productive change in behavior. This was because biblicists had a tendency to separate from the established churches: an implied if not explicit challenge to the religious authority of the state. In truth, the charges from the orthodox religious establishment notwithstanding, most religious separatists were pacifists and more than willing to recognize the secular authority of the state.

Despite his bigotry concerning Enthusiasm, Locke was prepared to tolerate all religions except those, like Roman Catholicism, which required loyalty to a foreign prince. His challenge of the divine right of kings in favor of a government chosen by the people, and his support of freedom of religion made Locke's writings popular in Europe and America. The Enlightenment, understood as the authority of reason, together with the empirical method of science, spread with Locke and Newton's teachings. Though today the Enlightenment is thought of in terms of irreligion, it was in fact a broad movement ranging from the Puritan Cotton Mather and American revivalist leader Jonathan Edwards, to the leaders of the established churches in Scotland and England, to the most radical Deists of France. Jonathan Edwards was a rare member of the Enlightenment who defended religious experience, though he believed that all such claims had to accord to the teachings of the Scriptures.

Many of America's first settlers migrated to the New World in order to separate from the churches and worldly society of the Old World. Modeling themselves as a New Israel, some sought to establish a Godly commonwealth. Others, modeling themselves on the separated communities of early Christianity, accepted that worldly matters should be handled by whatever government God might assign. While recognizing the need of governments to rule a larger world that does not fear God, they could not have had better rulers than those who provided general security and protection of property without interfering with religion. Because these spiritual fathers of America believed that scientific progress would accompany the dawning light of the Millennium, helping dispel the Catholic darkness long enveloping Christianity, from the nation's beginnings all parties in America held science in high regard.

Part VI   The Flood's Implications for Science and Scholarship

At the same time, though never without opposition even within churches that nourish it, from the experiential religious callings of America's first Puritans, to the Great Awakenings, all the way to the most recent Charismatic revivals, America's most characteristic Christianity has in fact been both biblical and experiential. Experiential religion has also been the chief force driving America's social progress, from effective and robust democracy to labor reform and the abolishment of slavery.[137] One might reasonably conclude that science has failed to make the improvements in the psychological and social arenas that it has enjoyed in the physical sciences because its concept of experience has been too narrow.

Though concerns about the direction that science was taking would eventually be expressed in many churches, causing some of America's European-educated elite to fear the eventual rejection of science (current scientific dogma), the churches and secular state existed in harmonious separation for as long as education, health, and social affairs remained the province of the churches. Whoever controls education effectively controls religion.

---

[137] For a discussion of Latin America's social progress deriving from Pentecostalism, see Harvey Cox, *Fire From Heaven* (Da Capo Press, 1995).

— 26 —

Climate change and dating the earth's history

As I was investigating my subject, 'climate change' acquired a meaning other than the great changes in the earth's climate due to the Flood. Politicians, the media, and prestigious scientific agencies have since discovered "consensus" among scientists about climate change happening today. That few students of climate would disagree that there is climate change, and there has always been climate change, has come to mean that the use of carbon fuels by man is increasing the earth's temperature to the point that it poses a serious threat to human civilization. We should be careful because many of us want to believe in global warming: it appeals to our concerns about energy dependence and unwise human development and we love to assign blame, but however much hubris may lead us to suppose that man is capable of changing the weather, only God regulates the climate. Whether we are thankful or resentful, he is as fully in control of the weather and climate today as he was in the days of the Flood.

I could point to no better example than climate change to illustrate the social and political processes by which scientific knowledge becomes "established fact." The Central Intelligence Agency warns of the security threats posed to the United States due to global warming. During my childhood the same agency warned of the dangers of the United States falling behind the military capabilities of the Soviet Union.[138] In fact scientists, especially those with the greatest expertise in weather and climate, have never agreed about the dangers stemming from man-made global warming. Unfortunately, for funding, accredita-

---

[138] However falsely based, their warning was interpreted to mean that Americans were falling behind the Soviet Union in industrial and military achievement because Darwinian evolution was not taught in America's public schools (though the Soviets were actually teaching Lamarck's version of evolution). America's school boards complied and have been teaching Darwinian evolution ever since.

tion, and students, scientists must follow whatever dogma that society and government demand. In the case of global warming this is particularly sad because, as I know from designing infrastructure for developing nations, energy costs the poor a far greater portion of their income. Adding artificial costs to energy is an excessively regressive tax placed on the backs of the poor.

Concerns about future climate change have focused on the "drama" of rising sea levels caused by melting polar ice caps, and the trauma this will cause to those living near the sea. Those who make such predictions should know and base their prediction on how sea levels have changed in the past. Because Noah's Flood must have impacted the levels of the seas, I had to study the same. The most famous historical records of sea level change are watermarks on the Roman columns in the Bay of Naples. Charles Lyell included a line drawing of these in the introduction to his *Principles of Geology*, the book that convinced scientists to replace the biblical Flood with modern geology. His purpose was to point out that the sea had risen and fallen about twenty-five feet since the time of the Romans. Though this corresponds to the worst-case predictions of the current hysteria, observers and historians seem to have missed the great trauma this recent deluge caused the people of the earth.

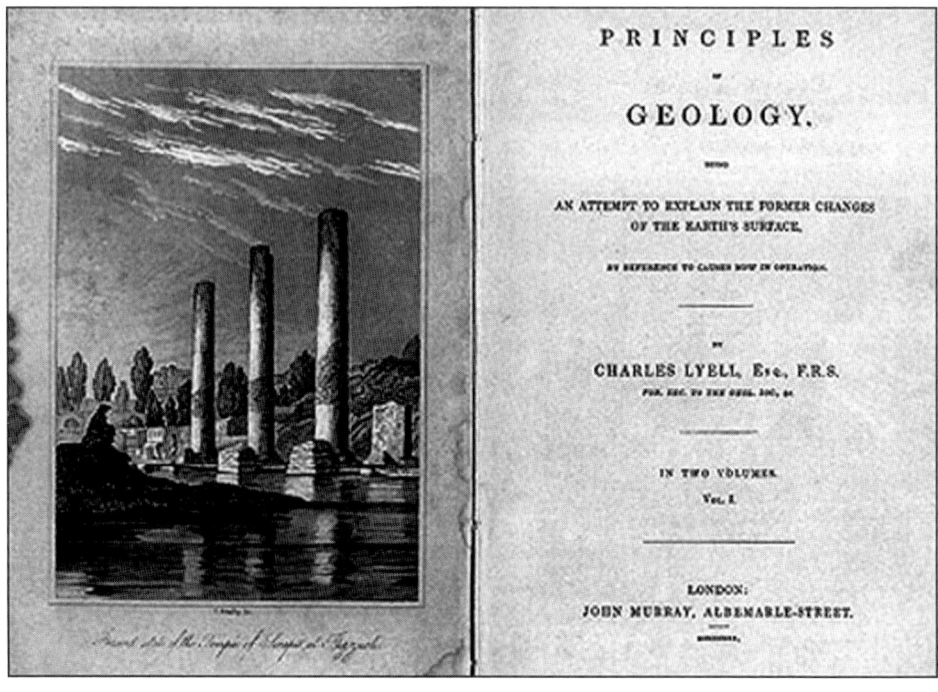

FIGURE 47   CHARLES LYELL'S *PRINCIPLES OF GEOLOGY*

Chapter 26   Climate change and dating the earth's history

Those claiming expertise in climate change ought to be familiar with the book upon which modern geology is based because aside from what can be gathered from history, the record of climate is contained in the geological record. Understanding climate change requires an accurate dating of the earth and an accurate way of gauging the temperature from the remains of the earth's past.

In Chapter 10, I noted that geologists studying the earth in the light of the Bible, though opposed by the Aristotelians, not only established that the earth had a history of development but also that the earth was much older than man.[139] The current scientific dates of the age of the earth pertain to the primary rocks, which the biblical geologists saw as appearing in the initial creation of the earth. A lot of assumptions other than what we might reasonably assume as a reliable rate of radioactive decay go into the present scientific dating of the earth, which now determines the oldest of these rocks to be about 4.5 million years. Whatever the accurate figure, it would in fact apply only to the creation of land, which appeared on the third day of creation. In fact the earth may be older than stars of the heavens, now supposed to be about three times the age of the earth. The earliest appearance of sea animals in the secondary levels of the earth's crust marks the beginning of the fifth day of Creation. Scientists date this Cambrian Explosion to about 500-600 million years.

Biblical geologists once attributed the Tertiary level, now dated to about 50-60 million years ago, to Noah's Flood. In fact that would be when the land animals appeared at the beginning of the sixth day of Creation. Biblical geologists determined that these animals had to be much earlier than the Flood because they failed to find evidence of man among the fossils of extinct animals. This meant that these deposits were not only unlikely to have been deposited by Noah's Flood, they likely predated the creation of man. They found Noah's Flood instead in the diluvial layer found in the valleys and plains belonging to a recent portion of earth's history. Though they were right, Lyell renamed them the Pleistocene, which he supposed to be a period of extremely long duration. Lyell needed a long dating because he attributed these remains to floods caused by the land falling below the level of the sea. Though subscribing to Lyell's extended dating, most geologists interpreted them as the deposits of an Ice Age. The soil and rocks in these deposits may in fact have come from millions of years of erosion and decay of vegetation, but almost all the artifacts and animals buried there date much closer if not to the very year of the Flood.

Also following Lyell, the Holocene, the period since Pleistocene, is now supposed to be the most recent period of the earth's history. Lyell determined the time elapsed from the end of the Pleistocene, now understood as the Ice Age,

---

[139] cf discussions in Chapter 10 and 20.

by revising American geologist Robert Bakewell's calculations of the time since the Flood. Everyone then agreed that the Great Lakes were caused either by the Flood, some tsunami (as Lyell believed), or as now commonly believed, by glaciers from the Ice Age. Bakewell's figures were based on the rate at which Niagara Falls was eroding. These famous falls had clearly begun eroding near Lake Ontario, about 7 miles down the St. Lawrence River. He measured the rate of present erosion, comparing that with accounts from local residents of the historical erosion, estimating that Niagara Falls was moving about 3 to 5 feet per year. That put the time since the Flood from 7,000 to 12,000 years.

Lyell acknowledged Bakewell's observation that the Falls must have been eroding more rapidly in the lower sections of the Niagara where the river is narrower than at the present Falls. He reckoned this uncertainty concerning the Falls' average rate of erosion to license him to guess the average rate of erosion as more like one foot per year! However disingenuous his reasoning, Lyell took every opportunity to stretch out periods of the earth's ancient history. His revised calculations put the end of the last Ice Age at about 35,000 years. Another American geologist made a similar measurement for St. Anthony's Falls on the Mississippi River near Minneapolis. He arrived at the span of time since the end of the Flood, or the Ice Age, of about 8,000 years. Compromising the difference, geologists settled for the end of the Ice Age at about 12,000 years.

I give a lot of attention in this book to Charles Lyell, who was so devoted, skilled, and influential in eliminating the biblical account of the Flood. The way this trained attorney imposed his uniformitarian dogma on the geological data with lawyerly advocacy was pointed out by geologists in his own day and has been a favorite subject of geological historians since. They have not been concerned with his impact on the biblical account of Creation, but on scientific geology. Advocacy is hardly objective study of the evidence. Lyell's attempt to steer geology away from the Bible came at the expense of empirical observations. Though he lauds Lyell for preparing the way for Darwin, Harvard's prominent paleontologist, the late Stephen Jay Gould, summarizes his complaint:

> I have tried to show how he set up his preferred form of geology as the right (and righteous) side of a strict dichotomy between vain speculation and empirical truth, defined, respectfully, as causes working differently on an ancient earth versus conviction that our planet has remained in a dynamic steady state throughout time.

> The reality of history is so much more complex and interesting; the irony of history is that Lyell won. His version became a semi-official hagiography of geology, preached in textbooks to the present day. Professional historians know better, of course, but their message has rarely reached working geologists, who seem to crave these simple and heroic stories.[140]

---

[140] Stephen Jay Gould, *Time's Arrow, Time's Cycle: Myth and Metaphor in the Discovery of Geological*

Chapter 26   Climate change and dating the earth's history

The Flood seems to have caused permanent climate changes. The remains of woolly mammoths found in Siberia and Alaska make it clear that the arctic regions were cold before the Flood, but were there much of an ice cap then covering the poles, these grazing animals would have starved. In recent years, archaeologists and paleontologists have found their own reasons for doubting the ice ages. They have discovered men and animals living in these northern regions in the very era when they were supposed to have been covered with the glaciers of the Ice Age.[141] Young Earth Creationists are correct in rejecting a pre-Flood Ice Age, but they follow Agassiz and Lyell in proposing a post-Flood Ice Age to explain away the actual evidence of Noah's Flood. That allows them to use their "Flood" to explain the deeper fossils, thereby defending their young earth theology.

Another great permanent change made to the climate of the earth by the Flood occurred between the temperate zones and the tropics, in the desert belts circling the earth above and below the equator. Before the Flood, the great deserts of Sahara, Saudi Arabia, Australia, South Africa, Western America, Mexico, and the Pacific coast of South America were home to flowing rivers and lakes and to numerous human settlements. The remains of some of these settlements,

FIGURE 48   SOME OF THE 100,000 BURIALS UNDER THE SANDS OF BAHRAIN

now buried under dunes, are pictured below. [Figures 48 and 49] When they

---

Time. (Harvard University Press, 1987), 111-112.
[141] Pavel Pavlov, John Inge Svendsen, and Svein Indrelid, "Human presence in the European Arctic nearly 40,000 years ago," *Nature* 413 (September 6, 2001), 64-67.

Part VI   *The Flood's Implications for Science and Scholarship*

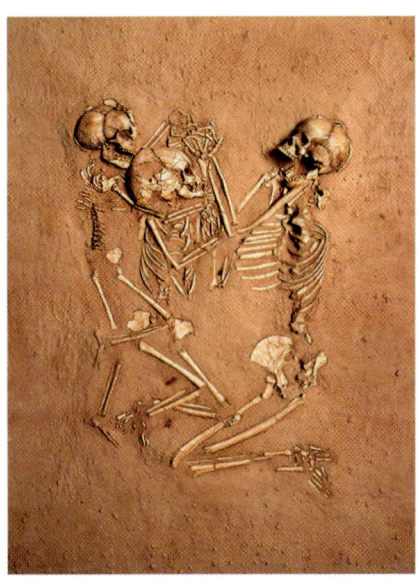

FIGURE 49

MOTHER AND CHILDREN

BURIED UNDER THE SAHARA

were in use, as recently as 4,500 years ago, the Arabia and the Sahara were tropical.

Though it is clear that a different kind of hydrological cycle existed before the Flood, the matter of the pre-Flood climate needs far more study. Even the earth's present hydrological cycles and vegetation ecologies are less understood than one might suppose. As has been the case from ancient times, scientists today can predict the weather only from expected seasonal changes and by observing weather patterns, which are constantly changing. Sun activity, sea temperatures, ocean and air currents give us the most fundamental and longest-lasting weather patterns, but what is driving those changes? Unpredictability is not the same as inherent randomness, as presumed by the chaos theory of a completely materialist meteorology. God has in fact designed the earth with self-correcting mechanisms to stabilize changes,[142] but naturally speaking there is no reason why some of these should not break down. Why doesn't the earth become so torrid that that its surface water evaporates or so cold that the world's food supply becomes insufficient? Why haven't the sea levels risen to drown all the people of the earth? Though scientists cannot, the Scriptures provide an answer to the providential sustenance of our inhabitable earth. Just after the Flood the great Regulator of the weather promised:

> "As long as the earth endures, seedtime and harvest, cold and heat, summer and winter, day and night will never cease." [Gen. 8:22]

While hubris causes man to suppose that *he* can both change and protect the earth's climate, we have the reliable promise of the earth's Creator that the earth will continue to be inhabitable. Though the climate and the different environments over the surface of the earth have often changed, God has been regulating the earth from the beginning of Creation. Before the earth's surface would be suitable for animals and man there had to have been a long period of cooling. Heat from the forming of the earth may have provided the warmth needed for

---

[142] These mechanisms rely on what systems engineers call negative feedback.

Chapter 26   Climate change and dating the earth's history

plants before God created the sun. Presumably the background infrared radiation from light created on the first day, still observed to this day though at a longer wavelength and lower intensity was then of sufficient intensity to allow photosynthesis to occur. This might explain the surprising dual spectrum light absorption capabilities of chlorophyll, allowing photosynthesis to take place in the infrared as well as the visible spectrum of light. God had in fact to tune the elements and the systems of the earth to be suitable for life on the third and fourth divine workdays of Creation, as he had also to do for the fifth, and sixth. The universe is not in fact a self-existing system, but has always depended on the rule of an all-powerful God. If our great Regulator does not continue to adjust the earth to accommodate changes to earth's history, including any supposed from man, life would soon perish from the earth.

Currently, knowledge of early climate is obscured by the deceptive re-interpretation of the Flood as being the Ice Age and by numerous artificially imposed epochs of the earth's history. The era of man before the Flood, now interpreted as the Ice Age, may not have lasted for millions but perhaps for less than two thousand years. The excellent preservation of the remains from this era definitely favors the chronology of the Bible. The large sizes of modern species of animals found in these deposits may indicate that the earth was in fact colder before the Flood, but the mere presence of these animals means the land was never in fact covered with ice. Knowledge of early climate as well as everything else in the supposed Ice Age, including the remains of man, is obscured because there is no reliable way of dating the era of history before and since man first roamed the earth! Of course, many chronometers have in fact been proposed: counting strata in lake varves; measuring the seasonal deposits and the depth of ice-cap and ocean-floor bores; and examining the layers of earth found along the beaches of rivers, lakes, and seas or elsewhere on wet or dry earth. Likewise, numerous thermometers have been proposed for ancient climate: measuring various chemicals, isotopes, pollen, shells, or microscopic animals embedded in the bores or strata.

Despite all the studies of ancient climates, the important key is still missing. I have explained the limitations of radiocarbon dating earlier than the historical period. The *theoretical* capabilities of radiocarbon are limited to items younger than about 50,000 years, while potassium argon, the next most suitable alternative radiometric with a half-life of more than a billion years, is useless for dating things that are less than a million years old. The problem with all these chronometers is that we have no way of calibrating or checking whether the methods used are reliable for anything older than historical times. With regard to reliance on the depths of various kinds of strata, we should understand that a single storm or catastrophe might be responsible for adding or removing many

[Handwritten annotation: Incorrect assumption with no evidence. The presence of these animals simply prove the earth was colder after the flood which brought on the ice age.]

millennia of normal, periodic, or aperiodic accumulation from ordinary deposits. At least this is the explanation for why the geological column never appears just as it is supposed. Great spans of time may be missing due to erosion, while much of the depth may have been deposited by a single event. Depth of strata bears only the roughest accord with time, and correlating strata from distant points of the earth is a great challenge. The missing key is some reliable way of gauging the rate of accumulation of ice, snow, seafloor, coral, or stratified soil over centuries and millennia.

Lake varves that reveal seasonal strata in the same manner as tree rings are frequently mentioned as a way of dating the past. There is a good reason why they are more mentioned than used. Consider what shore and what shallow body of water, either coastal or inland, is never exposed to storms, floods, earthquakes, or other activities that regularly disturb the earth. In addition, burrowing and scurrying animals disturb layers both on land and on the floors of oceans, seas, and lakes. Just one disturbance over a period of five thousand years will destroy the sequence. An interruption in what might appear a continuous sequence will be difficult to spot unless the strata are correlated with patterns from distant places. Coral reefs have been claimed as a chronometer because reefs build over time. The problem in using the buildup of reefs, as I will explain, is that the ocean floors have also been sinking and the ocean levels keep changing.

One might suppose that at least the patterns of either varves or bores from distant parts of the earth's surface might somehow be correlated. Some have thought they have detected correlations, but patterns in rocks and soil like those in clouds are highly subjective. Because local geology and ecologies vary so greatly, why indeed should the buildup follow the same patterns at different places across the surface of the earth? A better possibility is that certain chemical tracers might be found from volcanoes, catastrophic comets, or meteorites. These certainly exist in the regions surrounding various volcanoes, or at meteorite impact sites. If these disturbances can be archaeologically or historically dated in strata at distant parts of the surface of the earth, one does have a chronological marker such as the one I have attributed to the Flood. This might suffice at least to determine relative time. The problem in correlating such tracers before the historical period is having reliable chronological columns where one might search for such tracers. Ice core strata disappear some distance below the surface due to the fusion of the strata from the weight of the ice above. I know of no sea or ice-borne tracers for the Pleistocene, the "Ice Age." If any do exist we have good reason to doubt this whole business of prehistoric tracers.

Among soil samples, there is at least one tracer for this period: the Younger Dryas. The Dyras is an arctic flower whose pollen has been found in soil much further south than places where it currently grows. It is believed to mark a

Chapter 26   Climate change and dating the earth's history

colder epoch in the recent climate of the earth. It probably does because the temperatures of the temperate zones were also colder before the Flood, but due to the complications I have discussed, knowing just how long ago that might have been is a problem. Even if the date for such a climate change could be determined, we may not know whether the cause of the cooling or warming is some change over the entire earth or to the rising or dropping of local elevation. Changes in temperature might also stem from changes in the patterns of the ocean's major currents, perhaps also due to the effects of the Flood.

Badly needing some kind of chronometer for the prehistoric period, scientists tend to look favorably at whatever some eminent worker has proposed; after it has been grabbed by ambitious workers and defended by more speculation, at whatever is currently fashionable; and, after it has become established at whatever is now accepted. The less one knows how these sausages were made, the better they suit one's palate. You have heard that science is based on repeatable results. Indeed, these measurements and studies have much the same look and flavor. They should because they come from the same factory. Everything must conform to the standard view to be accepted.

If earth scientists really had confidence in their various chronometers they would have long ago conducted and published blind tests of soil, ocean, or ice core bores from around the globe. One will search in vain for such studies, as one will search in vain for similar blind tests for dating the deeper or greater geological column. It appears that absolute dating in the pre-historic era, whether from conventional science or from Young Earth Creation science, is largely a house of cards. This not to say that scientist should not continue trying to develop some better chronometers, and someday reliable measures may be developed. Today we have micro-imaging and the world-wide web. If these chronometers exist, serious scientists and organizations will make them available to their colleagues and to any who want to know.

For now, it is important that scientific instruments, formulas, graphs, and tables not be allowed to give what are in fact mere speculations and assumptions the wrongful appearance of scientific objectivity, turning mere speculation into a mass delusion. Absent divine standards, it seems that the Sophist philosopher Protagoras was correct when he declared man the measure of all things. Everything must be interpreted.

The problem in the earliest periods of the earth's history is lack of human records or some other reliable means by which we can calibrate or correlate chronometers. This is why I chose to make an archaeological rather than a geological search for the Flood. The chronological marker of the Flood that I have proposed works in the case of archaeology. I don't need to hear very much about a certain kind of newly found archaeological site before I know just when

Part VI   The Flood's Implications for Science and Scholarship

it is likely to be dated by radiocarbon tests. Alternatively, if I know that a site dates to about 4,000-5,000 years from the present, I know that it will likely be a complex site, probably containing graves of the type I described in Chapter 18.

— 27 —

The origins, antiquity, and migrations of man

THOSE WISHING TO know man's origins – when, where, and how he originated; when, from where, and how he scattered across the earth in different ages; how the populations of scattered nations have grown and shrunk, or how some may have been destroyed; how and when new populations arose from surviving remnants or new migrations; and how those populations have once again connected as we observe in the worldwide community of today – can seek answers in two fundamentally different ways. One way is to respect and critically use the best accounts passed down by our fathers, chiefly those from ancient texts. The second way is to construct an account entirely from philosophical principles and scientific data. While moderns have been taught to mistrust the history passed down by our fathers as enveloped in religious myth and political agenda, they have supposed scientific reconstructions to be objective. In truth, many ancient texts accurately record history, but nothing was ever more subjective and more the product of political agenda and fleeting fashions than have been the scientific reconstructions of the past.

If there is to be a definite account of man's past, some source or account must become the touchstone for testing conflicting accounts. But not all accounts are equally true or useful. The more an account accords with identifiable things in history, the more it can be tested and expanded by comparing it with other accounts. Because it so accords with identifiable things in history, the Bible is an excellent standard for judging other accounts, but for the same reason it has itself been subjected to the most critical attention and judgment. The reconstructions of the past by science are less easy to connect to what is known from history and thus have been subjected to far less criticism, but they especially need testing.

For the reasons I explained in Chapter 3, the most complete and useful source of history passed down by our fathers is the Bible. This is especially the case for the events of mankind's earliest history, made even more useful because this history connects to the origins of the nations. The Bible of course concerns much more than man's history and the veneration of this book is due to many things, not least being the distinctive Spirit of its words and how these have served those who trusted them. That it is venerable may not mean that it is based on uncritical acceptance, but to the fact that it *has* been so well tested. It may be that our fathers had good reasons to trust the Bible and for judging competing views of the past as mythical or unreliable. We may make these judgments today, but with far greater resources.

Though the best means of knowing and testing history are from the chronicles of the past, we can also test and perhaps expand our received account by comparing it with what we may surmise to have happened by examining similarities and changes in archaeological remains, in ancient and modern languages and cultures, and in the physical appearances of living and ancient men. Only available in recent times, we can now test accounts of mankind's past by studying similarities and differences in the cellular genes: the DNA of living people and of what we suppose to be the remains of ancient man. While an accurate history cannot be composed from scientific data alone, the scientific data does provide an excellent means of checking and expanding the history that has been passed down.

The need for critical judgment means that the best histories require erudition beyond the specialties of ordinary scholarship: an excellent knowledge of one's native history as well as that of other nations and cultures; knowing how to relate the accounts of other nations to the history passed down in one's own culture; and understanding what can be learned from certain applied sciences. The earliest of these histories that have been preserved by the Western world are those of the Hellenic historian, Herodotus (fifth century BC), and Josephus, the Jewish historian of the first century. Herodotus was limited not only because he lacked a basis for critical judgment, but also because he had no framework for relating the most ancient accounts he learned from the nations he surveyed to his own nation's history. Though basing his history on the Bible, Josephus supplemented it with a discriminating use of memories retained by specific nations. From late antiquity to medieval times, Christian historians followed his path, though they soon began dating events according to what we now know as the Christian calendar. Seventeenth century polyhistors, including Joseph Scaliger and James Ussher, composed the last influential histories of the world intending to be faithful to the Scriptures. They began supplementing and testing older accounts by new knowledge from astronomy and history, but influenced by the humanists, they incorporated a too uncritical account of the histories of the pagan nations.

Chapter 27   The origins, antiquity, and migrations of man

Isaac Newton placed *more* confidence in some of the pagan histories than in certain accounts of the Bible. But he had complete confidence in the mathematical principles of natural philosophy that he himself discovered. The fact that Newton's theory employs linear time does not mean that he looked at the world as an historian who anchors his account in the chronicles passed down from the fathers. Despite his extensive studies of biblical history and prophecy, Newton anchored history including the chronicles of the Bible to the calendar of the astronomers, what he called Absolute Time. He falsely assumed that the mathematical theories of the physical heavens that he discovered, supplemented by divine decisions (that according to him have not been perfectly preserved in the current text of the Bible), accurately govern all material and visible things. Newton's "high" regard for the Bible was his supposition that it was the best preserved wisdom of the ancients.

Beginning with Newton, scholarly and scientific studies of the ancient nations gradually loosened their anchors in the Scriptures, shifting them to various philosophies and producing the current views of the past that are based entirely on scientific constructions. More recent accounts of man's past have placed little trust in the ancients, especially the Bible, but the practice of imagining the world and its history from principles based on man's observations and studies of physical things did not start with Newton. This began with the ancient myths, was incorporated into Greek philosophy, and then into Jewish and Christian theology as these teachers turned from the Bible to philosophy. Augustine's theology of history based on philosophical principles was likewise essentially a mythical view of history. Protestant theology developed from Augustine and Aquinas, all of them essentially following the philosophies of Plato and Aristotle. I have explained how Newton's science is itself a development of Protestant theology. To the extent that a theological or scientific history of man is imagined, one may regard it as either theoretical, philosophical, or mythical. Of course moderns no more see scientific accounts as mythical than Jews and Christians saw their theological accounts as fictional. The scientific myths are constructed from current science rather than that of the past, but so is science fiction.

No one should suppose that scientific accounts are more empirical than historical accounts based on chronicles that have been passed down from our fathers. To the contrary, history is intrinsically empirical because true chronicles of the past are likely from someone's first-hand experience, whether human or divine. Those from the past probably had a better understanding of their times than us.[143] In any case, no less trust is required for accepting philosophical or

---

[143] The great logician and philosopher of science, C.S. Peirce, regarded ancient traditions as more reliable than modern speculations about the past.

223

scientific accounts of the past that cannot possibly be based on firsthand experience. These are likewise human accounts, which may just be what someone wishes to be true. As Thomas Kuhn explained, the great scientific worldviews become established for reasons other than the honest determination of the truth. As I will explain in this chapter, those who developed the scientific accounts of man's past did have agenda other than the truth; hence the minds of scientific workers may have unknowingly been encased in myth. I will point to evidence that this is in fact the case.

> One problem with the scientific reconstructions of the past is that, to the extent that they interpret the data, it limits how much they can in turn be used for testing accounts of the past.

However much modern scientific accounts may be based on data gathered from empirical sources such as archaeology, languages, and genetics, all are *theoretical* reconstructions because they are not based on chronicles of history. The scientific histories are constructed from circumstantial data without the benefit of witnesses, but data does not interpret itself. They need to be tested, but one problem with the scientific constructions of the past is that, to the extent that they interpret the data, it limits how much they can in turn be used for testing accounts of the past. As I explained in Chapter 13, accounts based on history are more testable by scientific methods than are theories deveoped from scientific data. Nonetheless, these imagined histories deserve testing no less than the accounts passed down from our fathers.

The most damning charges against the scientific accounts of man's past are that they are theoretical speculations rather than firsthand accounts, and are particularly susceptible to political and social fashions and prejudices. In Chapter 5, I explained how the first modern histories of man's past were based on an anthropology that employed a racist understanding of man created specifically to reject the close kinship of all men taught by the Bible. The racist anthropology was developed according to the Great Chain of Being, but the evolutionary account came from shifting the Great Chain of Being to a temporal basis. The evolutionary paradigm itself came from a willingness to accept almost any plausible evolutionary history of man however much based on supposition. Anthropology, the antiquity of man, and much else in modern science was in truth developed in conscious opposition to the Bible. Even in rejection, this makes the Bible essential to the scientific account! Moreover, this biased the scientific accounts no less than if they were developed to accord with the Bible.

Today, studies based on cellular DNA are replacing those of former years based on a scientific anthropology that judged age and relationships according to racist judgments of physical appearances, behavior, and native accomplish-

Chapter 27   The origins, antiquity, and migrations of man

ments. Yet, notwithstanding the supposed objectivity of genetic studies, there remains a problem: the genetic findings are embedded in the scientific history that retains the results though astutely avoiding the language and reasoning of the earlier racist anthropology. These influence the new studies from genes that must depend on judgments of the human remains being tested. Otherwise, these DNA studies are the most useful and objective of the scientific methods. Fortunately, some of the most valuable, including those of ancient human populations, became available just in time to be included in this book.

The history of man that I present in this book is anchored in the Bible and takes into account our present knowledge of the histories of the world's peoples. I have used numerous sources, including those from the science of genetics that were unavailable to earlier historians. Because it is difficult for modern readers to stay abreast of constant changing scientific accounts of man's past, I will summarize and explain the most influential of these accounts, beginning with their origins and explaining the reasons for important developments in these scientific histories.

Current science subscribes to the *antiquity of man* according to the geological scale of time put forth by Charles Lyell, to the *origins of man* according to the theory of evolution put forth by Charles Darwin, and to the *migrations of man* according to a variety of sources: archaeology and anthropological studies; the remains of ancient man as dated by radiocarbon; real and imagined histories as determined by the studies of languages; and more influential today, to studies of the genes of ancient and living men.

I address first the matter of the antiquity of man. As I have pointed out, aside from the Bible there is no historical consciousness. The notion that a long period of life on earth preceded the history of man came from studying the earth in the light of the Bible and then failing to find evidence of man in the Tertiary levels that contain the evidence of ancient mammals. Even so, there should have been evidence of man in the diluvial level lying near the surface of the earth – if, as William Buckland rightly proposed, those were the levels from the Flood. I refer to the geological remains now ascribed to the Ice Age. In fact there had long been reports of artifacts and human remains found in these deposits, together with those of animals such as the elephant, hippopotamus, and hyena, which no longer roam Europe – perhaps because they were eliminated by Noah's Flood! The problem was that the conjuction of humans with extinct animals conflicted with what leading scientists then believed. Napoleon's troops had discovered a modern looking cat depicted in the art of the ancient Egyptians. This seemed to confirm the great paleontologist Georges Cuvier's opinion that the earth's animals have existed in modern form since the appearance of man. That also suggested, contrary to the arguments of the evolutionists, that no evolution had occurred over the long period since man has existed. That being the case, evolution had perhaps not occurred at all. Eminent men of science subscribing to the view that men were not present when extinct animals roamed the earth included William Buckland and Darwin's mentor, Charless Lyell.

William Buckland had himself found human bones in the levels he attributed to the Flood. Because this skeleton, the so-called Red Lady of Paviland, was associated with animals that no longer roam Britain, Buckland attributed it to an intruding deposit from Roman times. Thus, far from the religious agenda commonly attributed to Buckland's diluvial hypothesis, he in fact introduced it for scientific rather than religious purposes. Charles Lyell likewise dismissed reports of human remains found in the diluvial levels. He was concerned that these might be seen as the result of Noah's Flood rather than the accumulated deposits of what he was claiming as a long geological era that he named the Pleistocene.

Among the reports Lyell dismissed were those of Jacques Boucher de Perthes who had found human remains with those of elephants and rhinoceroses in diluvial deposits at Abbeville, France. In 1847, the formerly obscure Perthes published a new report interpreting his finds as evidence of man among the prehistoric animals. It was a shift in Perthes's explanation from diluvian (man who died in the Flood) to antediluvian (man who lived before the Flood) more than his find that sent John Evans and John Prestwich to Abbeville to report their observations to the 1859 meetings of the Royal Society and the Society of Antiquaries. As President of the Geological Section of the British Association, Lyell declared himself at last "fully prepared to corroborate the conclusions." The same evidence that Lyell had refused due to his denial of the Flood he now admitted as evidence of the antiquity of man!

And this is how cavemen would come to be seen as roaming the earth during the Ice Age: by re-envisioning the same evidence formerly regarded to be from those who had died in the Flood. This story has been spun by triumphalist champions of scientific prehistory who suggest it was those who believed in the Bible and in the Flood who denied the presence of the remains of man with those of extinct animals. To the contrary, the denials were based on then-current scientific dogma and concerns that geology should *not* confirm the biblical Flood! Certainly the Young Earth Creationists, who believe in the Flood, have no problem believing that extinct animals roamed the earth in the era of man. It was a combination of scientific dogma and prejudice against rather than for the Bible that was responsible for holding back the progress of science. Ironically, modern science has been perverted by the Bible, but only because of its hostility to this book of truth.

Chapter 27 The origins, antiquity, and migrations of man

Ever since Lyell, scientists have reckoned the era of true *homo sapiens* to correlate with what he called the Pleistocene period of geological history, but what almost everyone besides Lyell and Darwin were coming to regard as the Ice Age. Understanding that these remains in fact belong to the antediluvian world, that is just what we should expect. There soon appeared Lyell and Lartet's zoological clock for dating the remains from the Ice Age. Because the Ice Age, dated by the wavering geological and zoological clock, is supposed to have lasted from one to two and half million years, this same period is now described as the era of *homo sapiens*. This explains why the Paleolithic era of man precisely corresponds to what Lyell called the Pleistocene and what others were beginning to call the Ice Age. But we should not take these million years dating for ancient man seriously. As I explained in the last chapter, due to the limits of radiocarbon dating, there is no way of accurately dating things belonging to this period of history. The Paleolithic, Mesolithic, Neolithic, Calcholithic, and Early Bronze remains may in fact be overlapping, and attributable to less than two thousand years of human occupation!

The next subject concerns the origins of man. In *The Descent of Man* (1871), Darwin frankly acknowledged the lack of any connections in the fossil record between man and the animals, even the higher primates. To Darwin's credit, he acknowledged the challenge this posed to his theory. Transitional links to humans, the newest species of "animal," ought also be the best preserved. Human remains are so recent they do not depend on the rare special conditions for creating fossils. In fact, aside from some exceptional situations, the remains of actual men have all been preserved in a non-fossilized state.

If constructing monster men from human or animal remains had previously been assigned to the imagination, due to Darwin's high status among geologists and his discovery of a supposed mechanism for evolution, these same exercises were suddenly reckoned as particularly scientific. The new evolutionary perspective required adjusting the zoological clock with one from anthropology, a new Paleolithic clock being added to the zoological markers of the Pleistocene clock. The markers on this Paleolithic clock were skeletons and artifacts. The hands of this clock would be manually placed to whatever marked various imagined stages of human development. According to the evolutionary clock, man's first use of fire and the large chipped stones he used to hunt the larger animals were the earliest markers of man's development.

The latest marker of time for the men of the Pleistocene was the presence of drawings in caves in France and Spain. Those who drew these beautiful and life-like images of Ice Age animals on the walls of the caves of Cro-Magnon had to be "modern" humans like us. Cro-Magnon skeletons are indeed like our own. An earlier marker on the skull-and-bones dial of the anthropological

Part VI   *The Flood's Implications for Science and Scholarship*

clock points to the Neanderthals. Neanderthal man was already recognized as a somewhat unusual example of humans, but Darwin's theory badly needed an intermediate species between man and what was reckoned as his closest relative among the animals. The German prehistorian Rudolph Virchow (1821-1902), founder of the science of pathology, judged this specimen to have been afflicted by child rickets and adult arthritis. Though he was found with human artifacts and was obviously human, naming him *homo neanderthalenis* re-envisioned him as a less than fully human ancestor of man.

The supposed appearance of Neanderthal men depends on the fashions in science and society. Recently, anthropologists have tried to correct these earlier images by explaining that, if walking along a public sidewalk, Neanderthals would seem well within the range of ordinary humans. New DNA studies have removed all doubt: Neanderthals were in fact intermarrying with Paleolithic humans. What this means of course is that the Neanderthals are not a separate species from modern humans. The same kind of imagination used for the Neanderthal was at work in the artistic renderings of what has been called *archaic homo sapiens*. It was the zoological clock of the Ice Age that dated a lower human jaw from the earliest species of homo sapiens, Heidelberg Man. Currently, *homo heidelbergensis* is reckoned *archaic homo sapiens* due to his supposed six-foot average height and muscular appearance. We might likewise reckon NFL and NBA players, *homo pigskinitus* and *homo roundballitus* according to their large skeletons and peculiar artifacts, different species of mankind.

All these finds are clearly *homo sapiens,* but there is a world of difference between these remains and those of their presumed ancestor: as great as the difference between men and apes. If ordinary human skeletons can be so divided into an evolutionary picture of man, imagine the possibility with the very real differences among the species of apes. We can date this problem to Carl Linnaeus (1707-1778) placing primates according to the Great Chain of Being under the category of humans and creating the *troglodyte* classification for an imagined race of cavemen. Aside from speech, this acclaimed scientific genius saw no difference between men and monkeys. Classification is the magic that turns ordinary things into scientific "truths," all the more so if the names are in Latin.

Promoting ancient primates to the status of man *(homo)* creates *homo erectus* as man's ancestor species, notwithstanding such consistent skull and bone markers of the former as much smaller brain case, sloping forehead, protruding jaws, massive and prominent teeth, ridge of bones above the eyes, and all this pertaining just to the skull. Wherever you find the skeletons of fossil apes – whether Java man in Indonesia, Peking man in China, or Lucy in Africa – some anthropologist has proposed it as the homeland of our earliest ancestors. A few famous missing links, the Piltdown Man in Great Britain and Nebraska Man in

Chapter 27 The origins, antiquity, and migrations of man

America, were actually manufactured to fill the great gap between man and the apes. If now universally acknowledged as either deliberate frauds or mistaken constructions, this discarded scaffolding served more than any other evidence to get a then skeptical public to accept the evolution of man. This also points to the problem of using unique finds rather than patterns as the basis of scientific history. Science refuses to recognize miracles because they do not conform to recognized patterns. But is evolution science?

Notice that anthropologists usually find skeletons from *young* adults and females, due to most apes having smaller stature than men. Darwin guessed that man evolved in Africa from an ancestor he shares with the great apes. His focus on apes as the closest cousin of man had not so much to do with their large size as the lack of tails among the great apes that could stand upright. What his family passed down about human tails from grandfather Erasmus, friend of Lord Monboddo, must have greatly impressed young Charles. But tales or no tales and tails or no tails, the jungles of Africa have been home to the greatest number of apes. Before the Flood, now understood as the end of the Ice Age, even the deserts and savannahs of Africa were homes to these animals. This explains why the reigning view of the source and place of man's origins is the same as Darwin's. It is where we find the tailless apes, which he regarded as man's closest cousin.

Paleontologists understand that most of these ancestors of man could be better argued as a species of some primate. Gibbons and other primates that roamed Europe and Asia during the "Ice Age," like other animals of this era, were especially large, thus their brain cases were also larger, but no one sells a lot of books or gets attention and funding by finding another ape skeleton or even a new species of ape. Man's antiquity will continue to increase because the industry of promoting man's earliest ancestor will amply supply the market.

Darwin did not believe that humans sprang from apes. Though neither those who believe the Bible nor those who believe Darwin's theory may be pleased, both declare the descent of all mankind from a common human ancestor. Like those trusting the Bible, Darwin opposed the polygenetic views of man's ancestry deriving from the Great Chain of Being, still popular among racists of the nineteenth century. Harvard's Louis Agassiz's famous opposition to Darwin's theory was not the fact that Darwin's theory of evolution conflicted with the Bible, but because *like* the Bible, Darwin taught the common descent of all mankind from a common ancestor. Like most pioneers of scientific anthropology, Agassiz was a passionate racist. Though tracing man to a common ancestor of the Africa's tailless apes, Darwinian theory allowed that the common ancestor of all the races of mankind might have first appeared outside of Africa. This was in fact the assumption for many years due to the presence of Archaic *homo sapiens* in Europe together with the then popular Aryan theory that Europeans arose in southern Asia – supposed homeland of all *Caucasians!*

Genetic studies of living African peoples, which show a significantly greater diversity than is found among the peoples from other continents, eventually pushed man's origins back into Africa. Genetic diversity is equated to genetic distance and because genetic distance is equated with time, this is supposed to support the fact that humans in Africa have greater antiquity. This created a problem because the dates for the oldest modern humans in Africa were understood to be younger than those of "archaic" *homo sapiens* found in Europe. Of course, as I have explained, there is no reliable way of dating any remains for this period of history; hence the genetic studies prevail. Thus Africa must be seen not only as the source of the pre-human ancestors of man, but also of modern humans. Currently modern humans are supposed to have appeared on the coast of South Africa. We should not be too surprised by that because, due to marine diets, the coasts of every continent yield the most ancient radiocarbon dates. Because the sub-human ancestor *homo erectus* had already left Africa, this discovery required a second out-of-Africa dispersion, bringing us to the topic of how humans dispersed throughout the earth.[144]

There are more sound ways of explaining Africa's greater genetic diversity, one of them being the diverse migrations to Africa from the various branches of Noah's family as might be noted from the map on the end-sheets of this book. But even more important in creating and perpetuating genetic diversity is Africa's still prevalent tribalism, which discourages marriages between members of different tribes. The rural character of much of Africa has also helped keep tribes physically separated. Thus, what the genetic studies of Africans chiefly show is that there is less intermarriage between the studied human groups in Africa than between the studied human groups on other continents.

Revisionist history or not, to keep up with the latest in genetic studies, still a third out-of-African dispersion will be required. This is because the newest studies just available for the present book show living humans more closely related to one another than to their Paleolithic and Neolithic ancestors. This requires a third worldwide dispersion of mankind's ancestors, and a second worldwide dispersion of modern humans. The latter, at least, is just what we should expect due to the history of man given in the Bible!

---

[144] None of the migrations discussed in this chapter should be confused with what has become a controversial out-of-Africa revisionist history, the spread of civilization from Africa. Popular today in Black Studies, it in fact goes back to the *Hermetica* and to Isaac Newton's belief, institutionalized in freemasonry, that Egypt is the oldest civilization. These theories prevailed early in the twentieth century with views that mummies and pyramids found throughout the world mark the spread of civilization from its origins in Egypt.

Chapter 27   The origins, antiquity, and migrations of man

These new findings from DNA studies would not have been so confusing or troubling until the latter half of the twentieth century. Until that time, archaeologists reasonably assumed that many of the peoples living in Europe from the earliest days of historical mention, as well as many of the world's populations native to their land by the time of the European explorations, came from new migrations rather than from Paleolithic or Neolithic ancestors. In the nineteen-sixties, reacting against those asserting that agriculture and civilization arrived from the Ancient Near East, prominent European archaeologists asserted that Europe's Bronze Age settlements originated from their own Neolithic ancestors. As the politics of natives asserted their influence over national antiquities and as archaeologists took advantage of the opportunity afforded by the deceptive objectivity though in fact vagaries of radiocarbon dating, prehistorians began assuming all the earth's native populations as essentially deriving from their land's earliest inhabitants.

Even more recently, geneticists had to challenge this picture due to extensive DNA tests of Neolithic and Paleolithic remains. These show that modern humans are far more closely related to one another than to any of these ancient peoples. Of course this is just what we should expect if those Paleolithic and Neolithic remains in fact belong to the people eliminated by the Flood and if all living humans descend from a single family from that era.[145] Though confidently denied by the skeptics of Noah's Flood, a second dispersion of mankind was one of the three criteria for which I was searching as evidence of that event.

For several years following my discovery of the disappearance of the Early Bronze Age population in the land of Israel, I was much concerned with what appeared a sizeable population in Syria and Mesopotamia at that same time. This challenged the notion that the entire population of the earth had only recently been reduced to eight people. It was several years before I understood the problems in dating Syrian remains of this period due to the conflict between the chronologies of Egypt and Mesopotamia.[146] More significantly, I had yet to discover the connection between the numerous religiously interpreted graves created by the Flood and how so many of them were improperly assigned to the period just after the Flood. Only then did I realize just how few were the actual remains from the Middle Bronze Age, and just how large had been the earth's population in the Early Bronze Age only a few years before.

---

[145] I predict that geneticists will discover the people of the Early Bronze Age to be more closely related to those of the Neolithic and Paleolithic eras than to those of the Middle and Late Bronze Ages who inhabited these same localities.

[146] cf Chapter 22.

Part VI   *The Flood's Implications for Science and Scholarship*

Sargon the Great lived within a few centuries of the Tower of Babel. Repeated mention of this famous king in Ancient Near Eastern texts has caused historians to suppose the Akkadian era to be the high point of civilization in the Ancient Near East, but notwithstanding his glorious exploits and his famous building programs, the archaeological remains of Sargon's time are tiny.[147] As we can determine from "those who ate at his table," Sargon appears to have had a standing army of about five thousand. The numbers of his troops are not out of line with the account of Abraham's battle with kings from the same region. Abraham and the troops of the kings allied with him, numbering perhaps one thousand, used a surprise attack to rout a policing force from those regions. Still, neither the biblical account nor the accounts in Ancient Near East texts fit the great population and the enormous violence that we see in the archaeology of the Early Bronze Age. Misunderstanding these considerable Early Bronze remains underlying the cities that Sargon built, which were actually from the pre-Flood era, may explain why the military exploits of the great Sargon have been so touted in both recent and ancient times. But in the Middle Bronze Age when Sargon and Abraham lived we are not looking at highly populated civilizations like those of the Early Bronze Age but at frontier settlements.

Eventually I came to understand just how plastic are the growth rates of the human populations, whether of specific populations or the world as a whole. Some of the highest population growths ever recorded for human beings were among the Jewish survivors of the Holocaust and among settlers in the early American wilderness. Population seems to grow most rapidly immediately following great losses of life as well as when people settle in isolated wildernesses. We have both conditions in the era that immediately follows the Flood. On the other hand, the recent growth in the world's population has followed the productivity of the Industrial Revolution. The slowing of the population growth since can be linked to the increasing general prosperity of that same Industrial Revolution! The numbers of children that can be counted in typical families of the American colonial era discourage any set predictions concerning population growth. Mankind can multiply like rabbits or become as infertile as pandas in American zoos. So much for those who have tried to prove the truth of the Flood based on the growth of world population.

That explains the rapid recovery of population in the Ancient Near East just following the Flood, but what about the population on the other continents? Reflecting the great skepticism deriving from the nineteenth-century scientific "refutation" of the Flood, University of Michigan geologist Alexander Winchell (1824-1891) asked "whether the table of nations in Genesis 10 implied that regions beyond the limits of the Middle East were vacant immediately following

---

[147] Harriet Crawford, *Sumer and the Sumerians* (Cambridge University Press, 1991), 16, 36.

Chapter 27   The origins, antiquity, and migrations of man

the Flood?"[148] Rather than accepting the glib suppositions of the skeptics, we have sufficient archaeological detail to examine the evidence. In fact, Winchell's insightful question points to specific predictions that allow testing the historicity of the Flood, a matter that I carefully checked using the numerous regional archaeological texts listed in the bibliography.

In the parts of the world outside the Ancient Near East there is indeed a considerable hiatus of population in the next millennium or so following the Flood. For most of this time, Northwestern Europe is mainly a great silent forest awaiting the arrival of the Indo-Europeans and the Celtic axes of the Iron Age to clear its trees. The former would spread the urnfield cultures into Europe from the Mediterranean and the Black Seas beginning near the end of the third millennium and the latter would arrive sometime around the middle of the first millennium before Christ. During the same period most of China, India, Western and inland Africa, and America are mainly unoccupied. The new dispersion from the Shang and Chou eras spread slowly from the original home of the Chinese along the Yellow River. Most of India seems not to have been resettled until the Iron Age. The same is true of western and inland Africa. The tropical interiors of the African continent were among the last places settled by man after the Flood. As in northwestern Europe, settlement of the great forests of Africa had to wait until the Iron Age when axes were available to clear these rain forests. America was resettled from a new population that first settled in Ecuador a thousand years or more after the Flood. Archaeologists who carefully study the regional patterns may acknowledge this hiatus in population, but ordinarily they fail to see it because they assume that the previous inhabitants are all this time still living and burying folks in those elaborate graves. But they do not tell us where we may find the settlements occupied by those buried.

The Flood skeptic Alexander Winchell also asked: "Had the black tribes of Africa and Australia and Melanesia and the brown nations of Asia and America and Polynesia been produced from the posterity of Noah during the interval which separates us from the Flood?"[149] However much an advocate of evolution, Winchell ignored Darwin's observation that selective breeding creates a wide diversity of appearances within a few generations. Darwin observed similar diversity among geographically isolated species. But the three wives of Noah's sons – who presumably did not descend from Noah and his wife – explain the three major racial divisions of mankind whose initial dispersion is shown on the map printed inside the cover of this book. Lacking an explanation, scientific anthropology has chosen to blind its eyes to what most everyone sees.

---

[148] from Davis A. Young, *The Biblical Flood* (Eerdmans, 1995), 175.
[149] ibid, 175.

233

The genetic "clock" that might appear to disprove the Flood is no better a guide for determining the time of our earliest ancestors than measurements based on the growth of population. It doesn't work for people and it doesn't work for animals. Genetic distance, presumed to measure genetic time, is determined by successive isolation of interbreeding populations. A genetic clock might have some meaning if breeding populations were becoming isolated from former populations at a constant rate. That doesn't happen except under special conditions, and when populations mix again, the so-called genetic clock goes into reverse.

Though the genetic clock does not provide an accurate measure of the passage of time from common ancestry, genetic distance is useful for determining ancestral relationships. Genetic studies have confirmed the recent ancestry of human beings now living on the earth as must be the case if all living humans descend from Adam, Eve, and Noah's family. Very interesting is the fact that mankind's mother Eve as determined by studies of mitochondria DNA is supposed to have lived about 160,000 years ago while our oldest common father as determined by the genetic studies of the Y-chromosome lived only 60,000 years ago. Bear in mind that the genetic clock is calibrated to the oldest human remains according to currently fashionable anthropological theory. Ignoring the fact that it is impossible to calibrate the genetic clock in order to know just how long ago our first ancestors lived, can we explain mankind's more recent common father? According to the Bible, that had to have been Noah. Noah's wife, on the other hand, could not have been the common source of mitochondria DNA. The actual source would have been a common female ancestor of the three wives of Noah's sons, the earliest being Eve, the wife of Adam.

Pre-Flood settlement in Africa appears to have also spread from the Ancient Near East, which means that Africa's first human settlers may not have had dark skins, while those then living in Europe, Asia, or America may have had some of the features now seen among the peoples of Africa. Darwin's theory of common descent, as opposed to the polygenetic theories that were popular in the nineteenth century, would not allow that black Africans could have a link to the great apes separate from other men, but the pictures of early men being used to illustrate anthropology well into the second half of the twentieth century illustrates how much the racism so rampant in this era assisted in the general acceptance not only of evolution, but also Darwin's theory of man's origin in Africa.

As I explained, the Enlightenment's rejection of Noah's Flood was due to their economic interest and to Eurocentric chauvinism, and resulted in their deeply racist scientific views of man. Contemporary myth stands history on its head by holding the Bible responsible for creating and perpetuating racism. Like any text, the plain words of the Bible can be twisted to conform to almost

Chapter 27 The origins, antiquity, and migrations of man

any perspective. Consider the way that Supreme Court Justices interpret the American Constitution. But the polygenetic anthropology of the Enlightenment, pro-Aryan German nationalism, and the Darwinian version of evolution, all claiming the mantle of science, put forth racist views of mankind as foundational facts. Whether based on differences in climate, language, culture, or biology, racism seems inseparable from some or another scientific understanding of man. But nothing challenges racism so much as a personal God who created in his own image the man from whom all humans descend, together with the even more recent ancestry of all men in Noah's family.

> **Whether based on differences in climate, language, culture, or biology, racism seems inseparable from some scientific understanding of man.**

I must however address the racist interpretations that many have read into the biblical text. The first concerns the chosen people of God. The notion that the chosen people are a *biological* race developed from the racism of modern times, including concerns from eugenics: ideas taken from animal breeding and applied to the biological purity of the races. The Abrahamic covenant is in fact based on circumcision, the Lord's way of pointing out to the Israelites that their membership in his covenant would *not* be based on natural birth, however much that would favor their biological descendents. Ishmael and Esau were just as much biological descendents of Abraham as Isaac and Jacob, and Esau was the biological seed of Isaac. This was true as much in the Old as well as the New Covenant. The New Testament shows Gentiles still joining the covenant through circumcision in the days of the Second Temple, though the practice began with Abraham. Like the New Covenant, the Old Covenant was based on adoption! This explains why the Jews in the days of the Apostle Paul made circumcision not ancestry the basis of Judaism.

The second racist interpretation was also read into the Bible in modern times. The Scriptures recognize the darker skins of some of the children of Ham, but in no place does the Bible (nor did early Christians) attribute skin color either to Ham's sin or to Noah's curse. Darker skinned Africans were prominent leaders in early Christianity, as is becoming the case again. In fact, Noah did not curse Ham, but his son Canaan, condemning him to be a slave of slaves. The same Canaanites who settled in the Promised Land of the Bible invented chattel slavery. In this kind of servitude slaves are regarded as mere property devoid of all human rights. This is very different from bonded servitude among the ancient Israelites, which was but the ancient form of employment. Many Europeans began their life in America in a similar capacity, as indentured servants. This type of servant could sell himself into slavery to survive in difficult times and circumstances, but the laws of Moses protected the rights of servants.

Anachronistic and ideologically motivated discussions of slavery and the Bible resist making these important distinctions.

The Greeks called the Canaanites *Phoenicians,* which is actually the name for the purple dye that the Canaanites sold. They noted that the Canaanites were unbearably cruel until conquered, in which case they were naturally docile. Just as Noah had cursed them, they were a nation of slaves, who were slaves to slaves. Archaeologists in the land of the Bible can distinguish the villas and slave plantations of the Canaanites from the first permanent dwellings of the Israelites who displaced them in ancient Israel. The dwellings of the latter are small and egalitarian, differing from the Canaanite villas much as early American log cabins differed from the slave plantations of the deep South. The Greeks and Romans themselves adopted their colonial and chattel slave cultures after conquering the Phoenician colonies in Sicily, North Africa, and Spain. The Greeks began regarding their slaves as "talking stock" (domesticated animals). This slave culture spread continuously from the ancient land of Canaan to the Mediterranean and North Africa, and ultimately to the New World.

The Bible also makes it clear that, rather than one of biology, the Lord's judgement of the Canaanites concerned their evil practices and false religion. From the time of the Patriarchs, those from biological families of Canaanites became part of the chosen people due to intermarriage, while those Israelites who followed the same evil practices were subject to judgment no less severe than that which he ordered concerning the Canaanites. As the Lord used the Israelites to punish the Canaanites, he used the nations to punish his own Israelites. Judgment upon future generations also stemmed from inheritance of righteousness or wickedness rather than DNA.

Seeing God's people as merely a biological race was never anything but scientific racism read into the biblical text. It was in fact the professors and ministers who wanted the Bible "to keep up with science" who introduced racist readings of the Bible. Not surprisingly, professors and ministers trained in Europe and supported in their professions by plantation owners, land speculators, bankers, and others who benefitted from slavery brought these readings into America, making them part of the culture of the older American South. Because they have been retained in later times by less educated Southerners, they no longer seem progressive. But the same desire to make the Bible keep up with science causes the "progressive" Christians of today to read evolution into the early chapters of Genesis because the business and professional classes have long favored the theory of evolution over special Creation. As always, scientific theories that avoid a literal reading of the Bible serve economic and cultural interests. A literal reading of the Bible, on the other hand, truly portrays all mankind as created in the image of God. Reading the Bible literally, we see in the account

Chapter 27   The origins, antiquity, and migrations of man

of Noah's family how recently and how closely related are all the varieties of mankind. Scientific theories notwithstanding, we are all descended from one family that lived on the earth not so long ago. The truth concerning the Flood has humanitarian as well as theological consequences.

— 28 —

Anthropology

ANTHROPOLOGY IS THE study of man: either some philosophical, theological, or scientific explanation. It is a vast subject, encompassing archaeology, physiology, ethnology, sociology, economics, medicine, law, education, history, prehistory, art, music, religion, languages, literature, psychology, and psychiatry – the last two fields having been created to explain away the spiritual dimensions of men. To master their subject, anthropologists must understand everything essential about humans including all they are capable of creating, requiring comprehension of the finest literature and the potential of the greatest minds – a task requiring nothing less than the mind of God! Anthropology that supposes people to be objects for scientific study rather than subjects who might be known through encounters is either a confused idea or a fantastic dream.

Historical accounts of man such as those found in the Bible do not explain man in this way. These concern specific individuals and their specific relationships. But regardless its vast ambition, if anthropology does not altogether ignore man's specific actions, personalities, and relationships, it does not see them as essential. To the extent that scientific anthropology does recognize relationships, they are treated in the associated science of sociology. But scientific sociology studies men in political, economic, and cultural terms. Specific relationships are no more important in sociology than in anthropology. That includes the relationships we inherit from our families or discover over our lifetime, including any that we may have with a personal God. Notwithstanding the ambitions of anthropology, because created in the image of God, man cannot be rightly reduced to an object of *scientific* investigation. At best a soft version of the methodology of Hitler's scientists, it is dehumanizing to view people in this impersonal manner.

As I noted in Chapter 3, the Bible is less a book of science and more a book of history. Whatever the Creator has to say to us or about us, the Lord addresses us with dignity, the subjects of his special concern. Individuals are in fact just what they are and they do not need to be psychologically or scientifically *explained*. By contrast, individuals have no great meaning for science, which aims to explain *what* things are, using universal concepts and laws. Mankind's written records better serve for understanding people because they introduce us as individuals and teach *why* men did those things that have created history. Those who chronicle history use concrete language to address the facts of man's existence, adding purpose and meaning that are lacking in scientific explanations.

I have explained how, beginning with the Enlightenment, moderns replaced the biblical and historical account of man with one based on the new science of anthropology. Since then, scientific anthropology has aimed to explain away man's special relationship to his Creator by ascribing all our purposeful and spiritual activities to determinative materialist causes. In this chapter, I will explain a few characteristics of man from his history as given in the Bible, and then, beginning with John Locke, show how modern science avoided and deviated from that history by creating what is now known as anthropology.

The Genesis account of early man and his history is brief but rich with significance. God seems to have prepared the earth especially for man, the last thing he created, the only creature he made in his image, and the one to whom he gave dominion over the earth. This explains two things that naturalism cannot: why the world is hospitable and why humans differ so profoundly from the animals. The once supposed continuity between the higher animal species and the "lower" human races never existed but in the racist imaginations of early scientists. Some animals do acquire human-like emotions and attachments from living with humans, just as human beings with a close and special relationship with the living God acquire some of his divine character, but the offspring of animals never become persons. Scientists have yet to explain the biological divide between humans and animals, thus some point to similar biology as evidence of common origins. If true, it only demonstrates that something more than biology distinguishes man from the animals. What amounts to proof of the limitations of science should not be regarded as "evidence" that humans do not essentially differ from the animals.

Classifying man as one of the animals did not begin with the theories of evolution, but with scientific anthropology based on the Great Chain of Being. Carl Linnaeus's classifying man with the primates brought with it the problem of how man acquired speech. The Enlightenment philosopher Etienne Condillac (1715-1780) supposed that speech arose from the grunts and pointing of primitive men, as happens with children. My early studies in communications theory caused me to understand that the creation of speech *cannot* be explained by scientific principles, but speech or some form of communication is essential to our existence as persons. It need not be audible speech, for touching will do, but the minds of children unspoken to cannot develop beyond that of an animal, while adults no longer spoken to degenerate into a vegetative state. The souls of children are spirit and not flesh. They are not a product of biology but of those who truly parent them, whether their biological parents, those who adopt them, or perhaps some parent unseen.

By giving man life from his own sacred breath and meeting with him each evening, the Lord God himself gave man speech. By allowing man to name the animals, God enabled him to create the language pertaining to the things of the earth.[150] As does the rest of his creativity, man's speech reflects his Maker. While animals are indeed conscious beings and some of them act or respond as if human, their creativity is limited, especially in the absence of humans. In truth, the creation of art, artifacts, and language are things that distinguish humans from the animals. This allows scientists to recognize the artifacts of man from the constructions of animals: beaver dams, bird nests, geometric spider webs and sea shells, and the far less interesting and less skillfully made tools of primates, so often claimed as showing the closeness of apes and humans. If studies discover that apes learn new things, so do most animals. However much scientistic drivel may suppose these trite observations to be profound truths, because animals are not created in the image of the unlimited God, their consciousness cannot develop beyond the limits given by their Creator.

The Genesis account reveals that all of us spring from the same first family who began their history under the favorable conditions of the Garden of Eden. Thus, our ancestors knew nothing of many thousands, much less millions of years of foraging before learning to herd and plant as anthropologists now suppose. They were never so mentally slow, being no less bright than we are. Challenges also birth creativity. Agriculture – working the land rather than simply gathering the fruit of God's Creation – came immediately after our first family was expelled from the nourishing garden. It was not long before men were making tents, those portable dwellings suitable for migrating through the earth. Metallurgy and musical instruments soon followed.

Even if curses sprang from their increasing disobedience, having recent communion with our Creator, our earliest ancestors knew nothing of the fear and superstition or terrible practices such as cannibalism or disposal of the weak that have been observed among the scattered tribes of mankind, even to the modern age. Notwithstanding the dogma of progressive evolution and the myth that all our ancestors were noble, all nations have experienced both degeneration and progress in their spiritual, intellectual, and material development. Still, all the

---

[150] That explains why, though God's words are unchanging, men's words are mere conventions with meanings that vary according to the men who use them.

earth's people can claim the same ancestry and history until our most recent common origins in Noah's family. Such is early man and the nature of man as seen in the light of the early chapters of Genesis.

Anthropology and sociology derive first from the philosophy of the ancient Greeks, and secondly from Christian theology that also depends on Greek philosophy. Theology gave Christians a language apart from the sacred Scriptures for explaining God, Creation, and man, but we must never confuse what the Bible teaches about God, Creation, and man with the teachings of theologians. Moreover, we should not mix what the Bible teaches about the nations of the world with what it teaches about the separated people and Kingdom of God. Christians who tilt socially to the political left tend to apply the teachings intended for the separated people of God to worldly governed society, while those tilting to the social right tend to impose the rules for the people of this world upon the free but separated people of God. Anthropology, whether from systematic theology, philosophy, or science has obscured the vital distinctions between the people of the world and the called-out people of God.

The thinkers of the Enlightenment began the creation of scientific anthropology by removing the theological wrappings of what were once supposed to be divine institutions and basing their new theories of government on what they claimed to be divinely created laws of Nature. They insisted on using only General Revelation, what we would now call science, to oppose the political and religious traditions of the ancient order. The men of the early Enlightenment believed that the Bible was in fact in harmony with their natural laws, just as their conservative opponents supposed that the Scriptures supported their religious traditions. In truth, rather than using the Scriptures as the true basis of their political theories, both parties merely used isolated passages as proof texts. Both were opposed to a strict use of the literal teachings of the Bible.

The development of anthropology began in earnest with John Locke's attempt to justify Parliament's right to depose one king and establish another of Parliament's choice, as happened during England's bloodless Glorious Revolution in 1688.[151] Locke wrote against what Sir Robert Filmer (1588-1653) had declared as the divine right of kings and what the royalist Thomas Hobbes had explained as the right of kings based on the laws of Nature. Opposing the actions of the Puritan Commonwealth, Filmer traced the divine right of kings to what he saw as the Bible's implicit patriarchal order. John Calvin's theology had presented man's nature as intractably wicked, but the atheist Thomas Hobbes

---

[151] Even more than did the Puritan Revolution, the Commonwealth, or the regicide of the previous generation, the uncertain basis for Parliament's decision confused the rules that had long governed succession and shifted the debate about the basis of government from religious to philosophical grounds.

saw this view of man as a fact of nature. Filmer's theology and Hobbes' science agreed that men should not be allowed to choose their own government. While not denying the sinfulness of men, Locke explained that government arises naturally from man's self-interest.

Locke modeled his theory of the natural state of man on what he believed to be the order of society among the American natives. He declared that all men began in the state then prevailing among the native Americans. By envisioning the original state of man as a plurality of anonymous "Adams" in the larger garden of Nature, his natural theology bypassed the historical ancestry of man in the family of Noah as found in the Bible and removed from anthropology the importance of specific relationships for understanding man's present condition. Following the lead of Hobbes, but seeing ultimate power as belonging to the people rather than to kings, he saw society as a social contract between the people and their leaders. Though Locke supported his theories with arguments both from the Bible and history, he aimed to derive his principles of sociology and anthropology entirely from natural rather than from revealed theology. "Natural law," which many evangelicals champion today, was deliberately created as a source of government and morality independent of the Bible!

Despite his claims to empiricism, Locke ignored what most observers had reported about the natural state of the native Americans, in fact more in line with man's nature as explained by Hobbes: solitary, poor, nasty, brutish, and short. As has been the case of most societies, native American society was tribal rather than based on contract, but having himself written one of these constitutions, Locke used the order of the commercial European colonies as the basis of his political theory. Locke did have one example of a social contract among American natives, likely the inspiration for some of his ideas. These were the social contracts in the towns of New England's praying Indians, established by the missionary John Eliot (1604-1690). These American natives used the same kind of self-government then existing in the English colonies, all of them modeled on the first at Plymouth Rock.[152] Eliot published an account of these in London in 1670.

It is likely that Locke was also familiar with and inspired by Eliot's *The Christian Commonwealth: or, the Rising Kingship of Jesus Christ* published in London in 1659. His book was censored and Eliot was forced to write a retraction of his challenge to the divine right of kings, but he believed that men are subject only to the invisible King of Heaven. Locke assumed as possible for all mankind the kind of government that can only work when a substantial populace is committed to a common faith in Jesus Christ and accept a governing order of

---

[152] Democratic self-government as it exists in the world today stems from the first at Plymouth Rock.

a priesthood of believers among those of the same faith. But following Locke's example, liberals would continue to assume an order possible only in the Kingdom of Jesus Christ as natural law applying to all mankind.[153] In fact, justice and liberty for all requires the light of the gospel.

Challenging the view of Hobbes and Filmer that mankind's selfish nature denied them the right to self-government, Locke saw the same traits as leading them to form a government of laws. His insistence that the king not confiscate property without due process made Locke's theories popular with both of England's new political parties: the Tories who favored the interest of the landed lords, and the Whigs who favored the Crown's expansion of foreign and commercial affairs. In seeing the chief role of government as protecting private property and the pursuit of happiness as man's natural right, Locke's socially based theory of government focused on the material side of man, leading to the modern theories of economics. Less like the teachings of Moses and Jesus than the law code of Hammurabi, Locke's social contract focused on property rights rather than on humanitarian welfare and justice.

Disagreeing that government ought to be based on self-interest, Locke's student Anthony Ashley-Cooper, Lord Shaftsbury (1671-1713), developed a vision of society on what he believed were natural laws of morality. In line with Locke's empiricism, in which the laws of nature could be observed by the physical senses, Shaftsbury posited that man also possesses a moral sense for determining laws of justice. Combining that with Neo-Platonism, he proposed a teleological view of a world advancing as morality becomes ever more elevated. His teachings would influence Gottfried Leibniz and the Enlightenment views of the progressive evolution of civilization. Though Shaftsbury did not deny the helpful contribution made by religion, by insisting that moral actions be taken for their own sake without regard to rewards or punishments or any religious concern, he separated morality from religion. Thereafter, liberals would embrace this assumption. Unfortunately, separating morality from its source turns it into an impotent abstraction, obscuring the source of all righteousness in God, himself true righteousness. The Bible reveals God and righteousness as inseparable.[154]

Bernard Mandeville (1670-1733) challenged Shaftsbury's moral theory, declaring that the good of society actually comes from private vices. His *Private*

---

[153] Indeed, freedom from earthly rule is possible only if men willingly submit to a Heavenly King who has authority above all earthly and heavenly powers. If this kind of faith ceases, so will freedom, equality, and justice in the earth.

[154] The sacramental justification of the Catholics and the forensic justification taught by Martin Luther each separate justification from righteousness, and thus may have led to the notion that righteousness may be separated from the God of the Bible.

Part VI   The Flood's Implications for Science and Scholarship

Vices, Publick Benefits included a poem, the "Fable of the Bees," with subtitles "'The Grumbling Hive' or 'Knaves turn'd Honest'" that envisions England as a prosperous hive spreading its multiplying inhabitants to new hives in various colonies. Though the hive hums with prosperity, the hardworking bees complain of an excessive amount of corruption. Irritated by their constant complaining, Jove turned the hive into a society of honest workers. To everyone's surprise, the prosperity of the newly virtuous hive also ended as entire professions – policemen, lawyers, judges, auditors, brokers – are without work and entire industries – wineries, arms workers, brothels, taverns – are without purpose. To save the economy, Jove reverses his decision. The hive reverts more than ever to vice and corruption, but its economy is once again humming.

Against Mandeville, Frances Hutcheson (1694-1746) defended Shaftsbury's view of morality as the basis of society's laws. Teaching that morality could be understood as disinterested benevolence rather than in terms of self-interest, he began what would be called mental (or moral) science. Notwithstanding Hutcheson's influential moral focus, his student Adam Smith (1723-1790) returned to Locke's way of looking at society in terms of self-interest. Like Mandeville, Smith explained self-interest as a public good and a necessary part of the economic system. This was an integral part of the Scottish Enlightenment's shift from the Puritan expectation of the Kingdom of God to seeing progress as a law of Nature. The optimism of the former carried over to the latter, and America would inherit both.

The turn to seeing human nature as formed by Nature instead of attributing it to God or social relationships was pioneered by the French philosopher, Baron de Montesquieu (1689-1755). Better known for the theory of the separation of powers employed in the United States Constitution, Montesquieu was also inspired by England's Glorious Revolution to discover natural laws for governing men's actions. Borrowing ideas from the ancient Greeks, he taught that men's varying natures are determined by climate. People living in warm countries are hot tempered, while those in northern countries are icy or stiff. His own nation France was just right for producing temperate men. This is how climates like that of France came to known as temperate. In seeing men's natures as determined by different homelands instead of a common ancestry, Montesquieu established the foundation for the Enlightenment's racist anthropology.

The Scottish Primitivists Lord Kames (1696-1782) and Lord Monboddo (1714-1799) pioneered a history of early man based strictly on the laws of Nature apart from any considerations of the Bible. Kames saw man as developing in four stages: from hunter-gatherer, to pastoralist, to agriculturalist, and finally to a market society. Monboddo looked at man's development along the Great Chain of Being, believing that orangutans are as capable of learning speech and culture as any species of wild man. Influencing Charles Darwin's grandfather Erasmus Darwin and Jean-Baptiste Lamarck's mentor Comte Buffon, Lord Moboddo fathered the modern theories of human evolution.

By the early nineteenth century some thinkers began to notice that human "progress" was not uniformly positive. The increasing prosperity enjoyed by a fortunate few brought increasing misery to others. While slavery in far-off America might be loudly deplored and European's exploitation of the natives of Asia and Africa silently ignored, the misery of factory workers at home too obviously challenged these optimistic evolutionary views of the progress of civilization. Thomas Malthus (1766-1834) deemed the plight of the industrial workers to be the inevitable result of human fertility: the more workers were fed, the faster they bred. The only way to control the population was to limit their bread. Malthus supported the Corn Laws that limited the import of wheat, driving the price beyond what factory workers could afford. In the manly custom of Enlightenment, he opposed labor reforms and humanitarian assistance to improve the plight of the workers. In his view nothing could be done in the way of humanitarian assistance to change what he saw as a law of Nature. Herbert Spencer (1820-1903) saw this struggle for existence as bringing forth the survival of the fittest. According to Spencer, this principle had been at work since the beginning of time, making the cosmos ever more diverse and interesting. Moving away from the Enlightenment's natural theology, the agnostic Spencer supposed the origin of the cosmos to be unknowable. It was Spencer, not Darwin who popularized the theory of evolution, especially in America.

Following Spencer, Charles Darwin (1809-1882), projected Thomas Malthus's dismal observations of England's industrial and social conditions into a law of Nature. Bringing his reasoning full circle, he then saw Nature as determining man's own inherited nature. By abandoning the optimistic unilinear view of the evolution of human societies and replacing it with the competitive elimination of unfit species, Darwin introduced into evolutionary thinking the biological racism that was implicit in the earlier polygenetic view of the races. The subtitle of Darwin's *Origin of Species* is *the preservation of the favored races in the struggle for existence.* Alfred Russell Wallace (1823-1913), Darwin's co-discoverer of natural selection had noticed that the natives of the East Indies were not so different from Europeans. Darwin protested, explaining to his colleague that this observation threatened their mutual "discovery."

Darwin invented neither evolution nor racism, but he did introduce racism into evolutionary theory. Polygenesis, deriving from the Great Chain of Being, was a conservative form of racism, but Social Darwinism was aggressive, rationalizing neocolonialism and imperialism well into the twentieth century. Darwin resisted some of the more inhumane consequences that some drew

Part VI   The Flood's Implications for Science and Scholarship

> **By abandoning the optimistic unilinear view of the evolution of human societies and replacing it with the competitive elimination of unfit species, Darwin introduced into evolutionary thinking the biological racism that was implicit in the earlier polygenetic view of the races.**

from his theory, but his brand of evolution was popular with those who wanted neither laws nor organized labor protecting consumers or regulating the treatment of workers. As these believed, however many the losers and whatever their fate, a competitive struggle was important to the development of man and to the elimination of the unfit and could not or should not be changed by laws or social policies. If it created fitter creatures it should be welcomed rather than resisted. Those holding to this view were concerned not only with labor reforms proposed by the Evangelicals but also with the cooperative vision of Robert Owen (1771-1858), the utopian socialism of Saint Simon (1760-1825), and the communes based on the ideas of the eccentric Charles Fourier (1772-1837).

That economists and evolutionists should suppose social problems created by industrialization to be a matter of concern was brought to light by Karl Marx (1818-1883) and Friedrich Engels (1820-1895) who fled from Germany to England to continue promoting their radical views. One of the left-wing Hegelians who shifted from idealistic philosophy to a scientific view of the development of history, Marx developed the evolutionary view of man's social and intellectual progress being espoused by the Protestant liberal theologians Friedrich Schleiermacher and Ludwig Feuerbach (1804-1872). As did the latter, Marx developed an avowedly atheistic and materialist version of the progress of man. For the earliest stages of mankind's development, Marx and Engels were attracted to the theories of the American sociologist Lewis Morgan (1818-1881). Subscribing to the Aryan theory that mankind's roots sprang from Central Asia, Morgan saw mankind advancing in successive stages from savagery, to barbarism, to civilization. His anthropology provided a prehistory to Marx's dialectical materialism which saw society moving to a capitalist stage before reaching its communist utopia.

Whether in liberal or racist form, progressive evolution dominated the thought of the nineteenth century. One of Saint Simon's students, the French philosopher Auguste Comte (1798–1857), regarded knowledge as advancing in three stages: mankind's first stage in which religious explanations developed from fetishism to monotheism; a second stage where understanding was based on the abstractions of philosophy; and ultimately the third and highest, the era of positive science. Comte proposed a version of socialism modeled on the Catholic Church rather than the state, but one in which a secular scientific elite would rule and teach all of society. He boldly designated scientists as a new priesthood to replace the Christian clergy. Comte went so far as to propose liturgies and creeds to formally recognize the role that scientists must now play in society. To the present day, societies devoted to Scientific Humanism or to keeping religion out of the public sphere continue to function much as do religious sects.

The heart of the nineteenth century's great shift in allegiance from the Bible to science was the elimination of the historicity of Noah's Flood. In the early part of the century, the plentiful human remains that I have explained as resulting from the Flood were understood to be diluvian. As this biblical interpretation was eliminated, the Scandinavian founders of archaeology attributed them to a stone age of man, to be followed by bronze and iron ages. Charles Darwin's neighbor and childhood friend, John Lubbock (1834-1913) divided the Stone Age into the Old Stone Age and New Stone Age, what we now call the Paleolithic and Neolithic periods. Incorporating Darwin's evolutionary racism into his anthropology, Lubbock described the unsavory practices of the world's various indigenous species of men: how they mistreated children, murdered aged parents, ate human flesh, and practiced human sacrifice. They lived in filth, were controlled by their passions, and were incapable of abstract thinking. This was not due to their having drifted into darkness but to their primitive level of evolutionary advancement.

Another advocate of cultural evolution was Edward Burnett Tylor (1832-1917) who introduced the notion that early man's religion was animistic: seeing the things of Nature as alive with conscious aims. Tylor was not a racist in the mold of Darwin and Lubbock. Holding to the earlier evolutionary model, he held a patronizing view of the isolated native peoples, seeing them as still in the childhood state of "primitive" man. As did Lubbock, Tylor strenuously denied that this primitive state stemmed from the degeneration of an earlier society, a view held by those who maintained the recent ancestry of all human beings in Noah's family. But for those who denied the Flood, there remained the problem of explaining the plentiful human artifacts and graves of entire families and cities found all over the world. One of Comte's disciples, the sociologist Emile Durkheim (1858–1917), provided the solution: these remains were evidence of the religion upon which the entire society of early man was organized. In contrast to Edward Tylor's proposed animism, Durkheim saw man's earliest religion as based on totemism. Primitive man taught and preserved his religion through symbolism and art.

A religious interpretation of ancient burial sites seemed natural to those who deemed belief in the supernatural to be the product of unenlightened primitive men. These philosophers were of course only projecting their European

Part VI   *The Flood's Implications for Science and Scholarship*

Auguste Comte   Emile Durkheim
FIGURE 50   FATHERS OF SCIENTIFIC SOCIOLOGY

experience of abandoning traditional faith for philosophy and science onto the history of early man. In man's earliest times, as today, those living in difficult circumstances or situations beyond their control are more likely to seek assistance from some unseen power; but the highly liturgical and art-dominated religion that these anthropologists projected onto the remains of ancient man only appears in the kind of society that is least likely to fear the gods. This particular form of religion can only be sponsored by the affluence and leisure of the few who can take their good fortune for granted. It was of course the kind of religion familiar to these nineteenth-century Europeans.

An actual study of peoples living in primitive conditions would have made it clear that the primary concerns of ancient man had to have been the ordinary concerns of all people: the need for survival, and taking advantage of opportunities for a better life. But imagining a religious interpretation of artifacts and sites is far easier than studying the ancient remains for their true functions and circumstances because few rules exist to constrain religious interpretations. Any artifact could be imagined as an idol, a ritual object, or votive offering, and at vast numbers of archaeological sites most objects have in fact been explained through just such a religious lens. Ironically, secular science has become obsessed with explaining man in terms of the subject it least understands.

An obvious question that evolutionary prehistorians must answer is how mankind, whom they have seen as astonishingly slow in developing and improving the first artifacts during their first million years or so of existence, suddenly became creative. Man's sudden burst of creativity has been linked to the melting of the glaciers at the end of the Ice Age. Why the melting of the glaciers should have had such a profound effect has yet to be explained. Even more difficult to explain is how this burst of creativity appeared simultaneously among all the various nations and tribes who, according to the dominant view, dwelt in isolation since the time of their original migration. The scientific anthropologists have given two answers. One offered by the German polymath, Adolph Bastian (1826–1905), posits the psychic unity of mankind. Bastian developed his theory from Herder's naturalistic spiritualist views of the development of mankind. He opposed Darwin's views that the minds of men are determined by their physical nature.

Those determined to find a physical cause for similar developments among isolated peoples attributed them either to migrations or to the diffusion of inventions and styles arising from contact and trade. Influenced by Darwin and Ernest Haeckel (1834-1919) to seek racial and material causes for evolution, Friedrich Ratzel (1844-1904) declared tradition so strong and innovation so rare that it is unlikely that even the simplest inventions were ever made twice. He explained the spread of inventions like the blowpipe and the bow and arrow as deriving entirely from diffusion. Ratzel modified Herder's theory of nations to incorporate expansion beyond national homelands. Imperial Germany used Ratzel's concept of the growing need for living space to justify its neocolonial expansion into Africa and Asia, but the German emigrant Franz Boas (1858-1942) brought Herder and Ratzel's historical approach to archaeology to the United States. Boas was more interested in the diffusion of cultures than inventions. He established a framework in American archaeology for uncovering historical patterns and connections of the peoples belonging to pre-Columbian America.

Old World archaeologist Oscar Montelius (1843-1921) used typologies and seriation to discover a spread of civilization from the Ancient Near East. European archeologists saw this "light from the ancient East" more as confirming beliefs that civilization had spread from Egypt or, in accordance with German nationalism, from someplace in southern Asia than as confirming the Bible. Grafton Eliot Smith (1871-1937) explained the technologies of embalming of the dead and the building of pyramids and megaliths found on many continents as emanating from Egypt. But Gustaf Kossinna (1858-1931) proposed Germanic origins in northern Europe as the roots of civilization, views that would be embraced and elaborated by the Nazis. More from anthropological evidence and reasoning than from the biblical record, Lord Ragland (1865-1964) chose Mesopotamia as the source of civilization.

Whether progressive evolution was seen as unilinear due to the psychic unity of man or as variable due to racial and ethnic differences, its popularity caused anthropologists to reject the notion that mankind's civilization and culture ever degenerates whether from spiritual causes or difficult natural circumstances. But this has not been the case over the historical period of man's existence. Mark Twain compared the sad state of Palestine during the nineteenth century to the glories of the place as described in the Bible. Material and spiritual decline also occurred in ancient Egypt, Iraq, Iran, and Greece; in Rome during the Dark Ages; and in Spain during the nineteenth century. The same occurred in the American South following the Civil War, and inner cities in America during the middle of the twentieth century. "Primitive" conditions could just as well be a more advanced state of degeneration.

The English historian Arnold Toynbee pointed to my Appalachian ancestors as "the melancholy spectacle of a people who have acquired civilization and then lost it." I have recently heard Toynbee's nation described the same way, but historians do not usually distinguish between material, intellectual, and spiritual degeneration. Those who leave the comforts of civilization to settle in distant wildernesses necessarily experience material degeneration, what I prefer to call *rustification*. Rustification occurs as artifacts have again to become homemade due to a sparse population and the loss of access to industry and trade. This happened to the ancestors of us all immediately following the Flood, and to those who first settled in the distant wildernesses of Europe, Africa, the Pacific, and the New World after the Flood. It happened again among the first European settlers in what is now the United States.

Spiritual degeneration does not necessarily follow the loss of material and cultural refinement. As happened with the Flood, with the Israelites delivered from slavery in Egypt, and with some of the first European settlers in the New World, a loss of material refinement may be accompanied by episodes of spiritual renewal. Spiritual revival is badly needed because troubled souls often head to the anonymity of the wilderness, as happened in the Appalachians and among some who settled the Wild West. Degeneration of culture and a coarsening of society also occurred among those who first settled sub-Saharan Africa, Australia, and the Pacific, due to the harsh brutalities of wilderness or war. Greeks and Romans believed that the world once knew a golden age. They regarded degeneration as the rule of mankind. But whereas degeneration is natural and to be expected, progress towards life, prosperity, and peace are indeed exceptional and should be attributed to some extraordinary cause.

There is something exceptional about each individual, family, and nation and about all the religions, languages, nationalities or causes in which people claim their identities. Philosophers and scientists want to know the ways in which people are alike, but historians are interested in how and why they differ. The specific ways in which people understand their identity fascinate those who claim the same identity: nationalists, genealogists, and sectarians. While a common history explains identities, imagined histories create identities with terrible consequences. I have already explained the creation of a mythical German history. The world has experienced the consequences of that, but numerous nationalisms seeking a return to or a preservation of some partially real, partially imagined past still foment atrocities and wars. Tracing mankind's origins to

Noah's family dilutes these dangerous passions by showing that all nations own a common and close identity.

There is of course an exceptional identity apart from the nations that is also rooted in the Bible: the chosen people of God. This identity may also be mythical and misconceived, but when biblically and rightfully considered, rather than wars and injustices it brings peace and blessings, and not just to the chosen but to all nations. This is because the chosen people of God are a servant rather than a ruling nation. Rather than dominating other nations and seeking to impose their culture, as have Greeks, Romans, and modern Westerners, it is a nation created by a voluntary covenant and when faithful to the covenant, they are sought by all peoples due as they spread light and blessings. In truth, all nations should seek or compete to become part of God's chosen and servant nation. That Christians were destined to share in this heritage of the chosen nation was foretold in the prophecies of the Old Testament. This identity is no longer much sought after because it requires sacrifice and suffering and strict discipline by God on the part of the people of the chosen nation.

As unlikely as it may seem today, much of the world once agreed that the first nation to establish its independence from colonial Europe was an exceptionally good nation and a beacon of hope for the rest of the world – even in the eyes of a French sociologist! Alexis de Tocqueville (1805-1865) traveled to America to study the secrets of the new nation's success. Whereas France's own revolution had turned Europe into a reactive and conservative direction, Americans became even more optimistic and progressive after their "revolution," because whereas Europe viewed the French Revolution as a disaster, Americans viewed their War for Independence as a success. Not only had America escaped the terrors unleashed by the French Revolution and the brunt of the Napoleonic wars that followed, they seem to have avoided the evils associated with England's Industrial Revolution: what the poet William Blake (1757-1827) described as England's dark Satanic mills. This gave rise to American Exceptionalism, the belief that America could escape the vagaries of history, including the decadence and decline that the "science" of history declares must be the fate of all nations.

Secular and religious thinkers gave different reasons for America's Exceptionalism. For the former, avoiding the corruption of the Old World meant that Americans had to maintain the virtues of an agrarian nation modeled on the ancient republic of Rome. For most Americans, the nation was blessed because America was then the world's most Christian nation. That the millennial Kingdom of God might begin in America was a hope developing from the First Great Awakening. The Second Great Awakening beginning in 1800 centered on the Kingdom of God. Unlike the First Great Awakening, this revival was not so much focused on individual salvation, but on social reform beginning in the church and sweeping into the community and nation.

In his classic *Democracy in America* (1835), Tocqueville noted how the nation's social life and public spiritedness extended far beyond the centralized powers of government. He attributed this to the nation's religious life, which was separated from the government powers. Though few Americans have ever wanted the government to be involved in religion, no one expected that religious ideas would not inform government. From the nation's beginnings, education from the finest colleges to the local schools was created and sponsored by the nation's churches. Thomas Jefferson wanted the churches to establish their seminaries to work closely with his secular University of Virginia and until the twentieth century, America's public universities required mandatory attendance at Chapel. American's religious concerns deeply influenced the social and public life of the nation, and without the patronage of government. America was great, Tocqueville concluded, because America was good. But he was cynical of the nation's prospects for sustaining its greatness: "When America ceases to be good, it will cease to be great."

That would happen as America prospered and as Americans educated in Europe found it embarrassing to explain the nation's success and future to sophisticated Europeans either in terms of republican innocence, or by Christianity and biblical prophecy. To compete with the embarrassing religious explanation of American Exceptionalism, a new breed of progressive American sociologists sought to follow the example of Germany in promoting patriotism over Christianity and science over the teachings of the Bible. As happened in Germany, public schools and universities began countering "reactive" teachings from church and home. Two new scientific views of American Exceptionalism competed with the older rationalizations.

With his trademark phrase "root hog or die," Yale's William Graham Sumner (1840-1910) attributed American success to a new gospel: unrestricted private enterprise.[155] Holding forth the premise that an unbiased pursuit of truth required the teaching of naturalistic science, Sumner pressured Yale's President to allow him to teach Spencer's sociology. However much Spencer's agnosticism challenged the basis upon which the school was founded, Sumner claimed the mantle of academic freedom, demanding to teach Spencer's agnostic form of so-

---

[155] Though a small business libertarian, Sumner condemned the expansion of America's interest for the purposes of expanding trade. Nor was capitalism yet added to the equation for explaining America's success. Strongly condemned in America from the time of America's founders, especially leading up to America's War for Independence, it would become baptized as American and Christian through the sociology of Max Weber (1864-1920), the rise of large corporations, and the ideologists of the Cold War.

cialism. Though Sumner won his case, evolutionists would deny the same right to Creationists when the evolutionist view became established in America's formerly Christian universities. Just as no one should be surprised that democracy in Islamic nations fails to support the rights of religious minorities, no one should have been surprised that a view based on the elimination of competitors failed to support academic freedom.

This economic explanation of America would have to struggle with a more socialistic version of America's future. Mainline church leaders educated in Germany, especially those responsible for churches catering to immigrants and industrial workers, wanted America to adopt a more socialist system like they were seeing in Germany. They attributed progress to government-sponsored education and social programs. Those who worked in education and social programs tended to prefer government programs while the business communities preferred the system of free enterprise for everything, it seems, but national defense and education. Both schools of thought turned Americans from the Bible by attributing America's success to a superior economic and political system – either based on private enterprise, as Republicans would come to prefer, or scientifically-guided government involvement, to which Democrats were more sympathetic.

Tying American nationalism to science trivialized the humanities and gave American archaeology and social sciences their scientist flavor.[156] Excessive scientism entered everything from biology to the humanities and was to be seen in archaeological schools bearing names such as Functionalism, General Systems Theory, or the New Archaeology. Appearing in the sixties, the New Archaeology extolled new technologies, methods, and abstract processes as if they equated with understanding what was being studied. In this vein, archaeological assemblages, seriations, and periods defined by process and procedures succeeded in obscuring American prehistory more than anything except the post-processional methods that would follow.[157] The new scientific methods helped in understanding ancient agriculture and economic systems, but American anthropology deliberately turned its attention from the archaeological and cultural connections and continuities that would have provided a clearer and more historic understanding of pre-Columbian archaeology.

Increasing in popularity as the nation moved into the twentieth century were views challenging American Exceptionalism and cynical of the light provided by the nation. Following the rise of postmodernism in academia, the study of

---

[156] For much of the previous discussion of American Exceptionalism, I am indebted to Dorothy Ross, *The Origins of American Social Science* (Cambridge Press, 1991).

[157] That the technical terms (which can be found in the Glossary) in this paragraph will be unfamiliar to most readers points to the problem of the New Archaeology.

Part VI   The Flood's Implications for Science and Scholarship

American prehistory moved in the direction of ethnology and ideology, while American history moved towards pluralistic views of the nation's beginnings. Native tribes officially recognized by the government and obtaining increasing right from US Courts asserted their control over American prehistory. This new view of America has consequences far beyond the view of American history. With the Bible and Christianity pushed to the margins, America's "melting pot" no longer sustains community even among the children of earlier generations of Americans, much less blending the numerous new kinds of arrivals. Badly needed is a pot that can meld peoples from all languages, ethnicities, and countries into a righteous, peaceful, and productive nation. This would be possible if people from all nations rediscovered their identity in the same God who saved our ancestors from the fragmentation and conflict that once before engulfed all the peoples of the earth.

> Author claims to use the Bible as basis of history, yet denies that the Bible declares Everything was made in 6 days and died 1 day after he claims they were created. Of course, to believe this you must deny Biblical truth of 1 day being 1 day in which God would be the worst historian ever. 6 days or 6 thousand years for creation. Rained for 40 days or 40,000 years. Jesus in tomb 3 days or 3,000 years. The Bible clearly states 1 day is 1 day. It never says 1 day is 1,000. It says to the Lord 1 day is *as* 1,000 because God is not limited by time, that is God the Lamb of God was slain from foundation of the world. Additionally author denies evolution then claims to believe in, in that scientist claim dinosaur evolved from birds. There is NO scientific evidence to this just as no evidence man came from an ape.

— 29 —

How animals and plants were affected by the Flood

Those animals filing up the ramp to be saved with Noah and his family, could they all have fit within the Ark? According to the Lord's instructions, this super barge with a cargo capacity of over one and a half million cubic feet needed to hold only a single pair of each of the kinds of animals that live on land – not all the earth's animals. Still, there are supposed several million species of animals and the Ark had also to contain food and water to feed these representative pairs for as long as a year.

Notwithstanding the claims of Young Earth Creationists, it is not likely that dinosaurs and most prehistoric species were aboard the Ark – at least not in the form by which paleontologists identify them. Those who study dinosaurs have discovered that these creatures were genetically related to birds.[158] Dinosaurs would have been among the great swimming and flying creatures that God created on the fifth day of Creation, but dinosaurs in the form found in so many fossils did not survive into the sixth day when God made mammals and men. Long before God created man, the dinosaurs had perished from the earth.

Some may wonder why he allows or causes varieties of animals that he created to perish, but not withstanding our romantic imagination of the innocence of animals, the accounts of the Garden of Eden and Noah's Flood show God holding animals accountable for deceiving or killing human beings.[159] As he brings individuals and nations to judgment, he does the same with animals and species. Animals are not robots: that view comes from Descartes rather than the Bible. If animals know how to obey God, as was the case of those who came to the Ark, they may also disobey him. In truth, whatever has life has some degree

---

[158] cf Horner, Jack and James Gorman, *How to Build a Dinosaur: Extinction Doesn't Have to be Forever* (Dutton, 2009).
[159] Genesis 3:14, 9:5

Part VI   *The Flood's Implications for Science and Scholarship*

FIGURE 51   *PEACEABL KINGDOM* BY EDWARD HICKS

of freedom. The account of the Flood does not mean that God had never before judged individual creatures or entire species.

Most existing species are creatures that live in streams, rivers, lakes, or the oceans, none of which needed space in the Ark. Of the remaining species, most are insects and other invertebrates that could fly or crawl in through the air vent at the topmost section of the Ark. The Bible tells us that God caused the animals to come into the Ark of their own accord. To determine the necessary space on the Ark, we have mainly to consider the vertebrates that live on or fly above the earth. Again, most of these are tiny, even as mature adults, and most are birds that could roost in the rafters of the Ark. We have only to consider a few thousand species that are larger than a rabbit but smaller than a sheep, and another several hundred species that are larger than a sheep but no bigger than an elephant.

It is easy to know what constitutes a biblical *kind*. The Bible defines the various types of animals as those that breed after their own kind. Currently,

Chapter 29   How animals and plants were affected by the Flood

some kind of wolf is regarded as being the father of all the various kinds of dogs known to man. It takes only a few generations to create new breeds through selective breeding, and many of the current breeds of dogs were created in the nineteenth century as Darwin was composing his theories. Through selective breeding, one can create almost any kind of dog from a Chihuahua to a St. Bernard; but he will never produce a cat from any of these dogs. Humans create various hybrids by mating closely related animals or closely related plants, but in the wild, hybrids are sterile. In the Nature that God created, animals breed with others of their own kind. That seems an eminently sensible way of classifying animals.

The problem is in knowing what constitutes a modern *species*. The Latin classification system of Carl Linnaeus serves more to obscure than to solve the problem by making classifications seem more objective than they really are. While avoiding the biblical way of classifying, this system has no clear alternative criteria for defining and distinguishing species and sub-species, if not also for genus and family. Charles Darwin showed that most of what we now call species were created by natural selection,[160] but Darwinists have an interest in obscuring the meaning of species. What the Darwinists do not want is a clear distinction between the types of animals that can be created by natural or artificial selection and the fundamental kinds of animals that cannot. For answers, I studied the writing of the late Ernst Mayr (1904-2005), the most eminent of the Darwinists regarding the issue of species. Mayr treated geographically isolated populations as species, though these still interbreed with other species whenever the isolated populations become mixed.

Despite later denials by the Darwinists, the leading nineteenth-century zoologists such as Georges Cuvier and Richard Owen (1804-1892) had discovered the fixity of basic species as fact. If this were not the case, neither living nor fossil species could be identified. Darwin's missing links between fossil species are still missing, and despite all the intelligence and knowledge of modern biology and medicine, no new kinds of animals have ever been created. Until we have precise answers for the number of true species or kinds, we have no exact way of calculating the space needed for food and animals on the Ark, but there is no reason to believe that the Ark was particularly crowded.

John Fleming (1785–1857), a Scottish Presbyterian minister, declared Noah's Flood an event so tranquil that its slowly rising and receding waters would have left no record in the earth. Apparently that included no sign of the abrupt extinction of animals that might have be understood as evidence of the

---

[160] "Natural selection" may in fact be partially or completely divine selection, both in the providential preservation of ecological habitats and in the selective preservation of particular populations of interbreeding species.

Flood. Fleming searched for reasons to suppose that the faunal extinctions that Buckland had attributed to the Flood were in fact gradual. Following Fleming's declaration of gradual extinctions, Lyell stretched the zoological remains from the Flood into Pleistocene extinctions lasting hundreds of thousands of years. Contrary to Fleming and Lyell's decisions, these sudden Pleistocene extinctions "at the end of the Ice last Ice Age" are now universally acknowledged.

It is clear from the mega-fauna extinctions at the end of the "Ice Age" that various subspecies did not make it into the Ark. This includes the woolly mammoth, the saber-toothed tiger, the giant cave bear, and the giant sloth. Interestingly, it seems to have been *large* animal subspecies that did not get their boarding pass. This does not mean that Noah's Flood eliminated these "species." The Indian elephant is more closely related to the mammoth than either is to the African elephant. Likely these ancient species could still be bred or would have reappeared had their species returned to the same places and climates that existed before the Flood. As the Bible suggests and archaeology demonstrates there was a great change in geography and climate following the Flood. Animal species have adapted somewhat differently in the differing habitats from before and after the Flood.

There is plenty of evidence for great changes in fauna at various places of the earth from before and after the Flood. Once, elephants, camels, and horses ranged the Americas, but Europeans did not find them on their earliest visits. In all, twenty-eight genera in the animal kingdom suddenly vanished from the New World at the end of the last Ice Age.[161] More interesting still, many species of animals then found in America are now found in the Old World, while some species then ranging Europe and Asia now range in America. The mega-fauna extinctions also occurred in Australia. We now have the answer to the mega-fauna extinctions associated with the end of the last "Ice Age." It was Noah's Flood rather than some the end of the "Ice Age" that was responsible for these extinctions.

The pre-Flood art of the ancient Near East shows a close relationship between animals and men. Plaques and seals from the Early Bronze Age depict large animals such as lions and deer sitting and dining at tables. They seem to be enjoying themselves as if they were teenagers. Interestingly, the skeletons of lions and other wild animals are found in some of the houses that the Flood turned into tombs. We may remember from the account in the Bible that Eve was deceived by one of the animals. All this might explain why the animals were included in the judgment of the Flood. After the Flood, as the Bible informs us, the Lord caused the fear of man to fall upon the animals.

---

[161] Richard B. Lyttle, *People of the Dawn* (Atheneum, 1980), 75.

Chapter 29 How animals and plants were affected by the Flood

Understanding of the obstacles presented to the animals in getting to the Ark is obscured by numerous changes to the earth's topography that may have resulted from the Flood, including the possible loss of land bridges. If the latter is the case, there were even greater obstacles in the paths of animals in getting from the Ark to their present habitats. Of all these potential migration paths, the most difficult to envision seems to be the route that animals would have taken to South America. I gained insight some years ago when I learned that in 1995 fifteen iguanas clinging to a mass of uprooted trees were carried by a hurricane across hundreds of miles of open water in the Caribbean.[162] Pondering this report, it occurred to me that the massive foliage from tropical rainforests must have created floating islands soon after the Flood. Whenever these islands

Figure 52   Floating Islands

were in the rivers or near the shores of continents, animals would have fled to such places, their predators following.

Not long after I read that report, a colleague related to me that floating islands have been documented in historical times.[163] There are nineteenth-century reports of great floating islands off the coast of West Africa.[164] Hurricanes and currents would have gradually carried these islands to the upper coast of

---

[162] Carol Kaesuk Yoon, "Hapless Iguanas Float Away and Voyage Grips Biologists," *New York Times,* October 8, 1998.
[163] My appreciation to Vlatko Dir.
[164] Chet Van Duzer, *Floating Islands: A Global Bibliography* (Cantor Press, 2004).

South America. That would explain why so many South American animals are tree dwellers or climbers. Due to the demonstrated obedience to their Creator of the animals that were saved by the Ark, and to similar providence, Australian passengers may have enjoyed the same kind of voyage. Only by the same providence would their island ship have departed before predators arrived at their port of embarkation.

The fact that these islands have largely disappeared indicates that they were created by a recent historical event rather than being an ordinary phenomena. Such passages were also available to the people and animals upon which the Flood came. This probably explains why God allowed the waters to cover the earth over such an extended period. The Flood remained until every insect and creature that flew above or crawled upon the earth that was not in the Ark drowned, starved, or otherwise perished from the earth.

Likely, floating islands and smaller clumps of vegetation and flotsam were the means of preserving the seed stock of trees, brush, and other wild land plants. The domesticated plants animals that survived the Flood would have been aboard the Ark. Other plants and animals were domesticated immediately following the Flood. In both the Old and New Worlds, the wild varieties from which domesticated crops and animals derive often mark the original points of dispersion. In the Old World, such an area stretches from Armenia along the arms of the Fertile Crescent. Here are found the original stocks of sheep, goats, wheat, grapes, and various kinds of fruit trees that spread to Europe, China, and, eventually to the rest of the world.

Other kinds of plants and animals were domesticated in Southeast Asia and in the country of Nigeria in West Africa. The chicken, for instance, is thought to have developed from some species of bird in Southeast Asia. We cannot be certain because fowls are difficult to study using archaeology. Their soft bones do not survive the ravages of time. This explains why we find so few fossils of small birds, though they have been around since the disappearance of their close relatives, the dinosaurs. Regardless of the place of their domestication, important Old World animals such as sheep, goats, cattle, horses, pigs, chickens, dogs, and cats and crops such as wheat, barley, olives, types of beans and grapes followed the new spread of mankind from the Ark.

The Ecuador region of northwestern South America is not only the home of the original New World dispersion of people. The surrounding area on the Pacific coast of the Americas from Peru to southern Mexico is also the homeland of the domesticated crops that Europeans found in the New World. These include maize, squash, tomatoes, potatoes, and pumpkins. Few domesticates seem to have made it across the waters from the Old World to the New World in the first dispersions of mankind after the Flood. Not surprisingly, cotton and

Another anti-biblical and anti-Christ evolutionary theory claim

Chapter 29   How animals and plants were affected by the Flood

gourd seeds, plants that are useful for ships but not for eating, were exceptions. Somehow Old World coconuts and bananas also survived some of the earliest crossings. Among domesticated animals, as we can learn from the observations of the earliest Spanish explorers to visit America, only the tiny Chihuahua dog and perhaps chickens made it across the ocean with man's first crossings to the New World after the Flood.

The Flood would surely have presented numerous ecological challenges for all land animals, for all the earth's plants, and even for numerous species that live in the sea. Most species are not nearly so adaptable as are human beings and the parasite species that depend on man and his domesticated animals. Nonetheless, they are far more adaptable in diet and habitat than is suggested by ecologists with various ideological, political, or environmental agendas. If this were not the case, every species of animal would long ago have perished from the earth, with or without a Flood. We must keep in mind that the "zookeeper" arranging and conducting all these affairs was the same one who created these animals, who feeds them regularly, and who knows when a single sparrow falls to the ground. He has the assistance of countless angels that are constantly watchful of his Creation. If one thinks it most improbable for Noah's Ark and all its creatures to have made it through the Flood, consider the larger ark that is our present earth. Without the same guiding hand, how improbable it would be that we have survived until the present day.

— 30 —

A geological understanding of the waters of the Flood

THE SOURCES AND present location of waters sufficient to cover the highest mountains of the earth has long been a mystery eluding defenders of the biblical Flood. The Bible does not claim ordinary sources: rather "the fountains of the great deep burst forth" and "the floodgates of heaven were opened." From the beginning of my quest for the Flood, I understood how difficult it might be to translate these reports into concepts and terms that we now understand.

There does exist empirical evidence that only a short time ago, geologically speaking, the highest mountains of the earth were far lower than today and that the earth's largest ocean was much shallower and warmer during the era of early man. It is remarkable that the earth's topology should have radically changed in so recent a time. Could this be have been caused by the Flood? For example, scientists recognize the highest mountains to be the earth's newest. Though they can determine relative age, geologists have no reliable way of determining the mountains' absolute age. Typically, geologists use twenty-five million years as the age of the Himalayas. Mount Everest is still growing at a rate of about 2.4 inches per year. At that rate, it should have grown from sea level to its present height in only 150,000 years, much closer to the date of the Flood than to the age presumed by the geologists.[165] Had the Flood initiated the growth of these mountains, we might assume that the world's highest mountains grew much faster in the centuries just following the Flood.

Studying the remains of vegetation, animals, and humans now found at high elevations, but which could have lived only at much lower and warmer levels is a more precise way of estimating the age of the mountains. One example is the

---

[165] Rather than eroding the mountains, as supposed by the modern geology founded by Hutton and Lyell, rivers and streams are themselves elevated with the plains and mountains.

Chapter 30 A geological understanding of the waters of the Flood

vegetation found in the stomach of Ötzi the Ice Man, discovered in the Alps. [Figure 35] Either Ötzi had just completed a remarkably long and arduous climb, or more likely the mountain on which he was found was much lower at the time that he died than it is today. The mountainous plains of Ararat and Armenian show evidence of plants and domesticated species that can survive only at elevations thousands of feet lower than the present plain.[166] The discoveries of Pleistocene and Neolithic remains in these mountains together with those that William Buckland found in the Himalayas[167] make it reasonable to suppose that the highest mountains of the earth have grown considerably since the time of the Flood.

Geologists have long been aware of the remains of modern fauna found beneath the lava-covered plains of Italy and France. Charles Lyell used what he presumed to be a lava flow dating to ancient times to prove the great antiquity of animal species. In fact these animals had roamed the earth in the days just before the Flood. What the evidence actually proves was how recently these volcanoes appeared. Contrary to Lyell's assertions, volcanoes can appear and grow to great heights in the space of a few years. The notion that volcanoes have always grown at the rate observed in recent history for Mount Etna was more of Lyell's dogma imposed on the data.

Looking at geology in the light of the Bible rather than Lyell's Deep Time theory of geology, we might guess that the growth of mountains points to the source of "the fountains of the great deep." As geologists recognize, rather than from runoff coming from rain, the steam we see gushing forth and exploding from volcanoes comes from primeval water. One sees such water coming forth as geysers in places like Yellowstone National Park. Extremely hot water is also spraying forth from vents in the ocean floor, some of it hot enough to cut holes through the steel plate in the hulls of deepwater vessels. This super-heated water must be coming from deep within the earth.

Geologists have given little attention to the sources of this primeval water. But water, being lighter than rock, should not be found so far below the earth's surface. A geological principle known as isostasy requires the heavier parts of the earth's crust to settle more deeply into the liquid mantle below, just as heavily laden ships settle more deeply into water. According to this principle, we might expect the surface of the earth to be covered with water, and in fact two-thirds of the surface is covered with water. But why do the continents float higher than the oceans upon this liquid mantle? Surely heavier continents and mountains must settle more deeply into the liquid mantle than the ocean basins, which are

---

[166] David M. Lang, "Uratu and Armenia." In Arthur Cotterell, editor, *The Penguin Encyclopedia of Ancient Civilizations* (1980), 118.
[167] See Chapter 10, p. 91.

filled with lighter water. Since the continents are in fact higher with mountains sticking up like great icebergs, we must reckon that the continents upon their basins must be lighter or less dense than the oceans upon their basins. Only great amounts of water or gas inside the continental basins can explain why the continents float. Regardless of all the water emptied from the continents during the Flood and since, we should expect still more water beneath the continents than is contained in all the earth's ocean basins.

Because we are not accustomed to thinking of the solid earth as floating, it may seem that the crust should be heaviest and densest where the highest mountains stand. Earlier geologists thought so, but when they actually measured the gravity in the Himalayas they were shocked to learn that the gravity from this part of the earth's crust is actually lower than any place on the earth's surface.[168] They later discovered that gravity is greatest upon the ocean basins. The ocean basins must accordingly be denser and heavier than the continental basins. Based on that, one might reckon that the ocean basins consist mainly of heavy rock. It must also mean that deep within the continental basins there are caves, great caverns, or more likely, porous rock filled with hot air, steam, or water. There may be all of these; but likely it is mainly some form of water and steam, and some state of the hydrogen and oxygen that these produce.

I suspect there is even more water below the upper mantle of porous and liquid rock. What I mean is that the interior of the earth below the outer mantle of porous or liquid rock must be filled with water. The Scriptures tell us that the earth was formed of water.[169] On the other hand rocks are heavier than water and therefore porous or liquid rock should be heavier than water. That is certainly true at temperatures and pressures similar to those near the surface of the earth. It may not be true fifty miles deep in the earth where exist temperatures and pressures capable of creating diamonds. Imagine the pressure and temperature five hundred or four thousand miles below the surface.

Much depends on the relative compressibility of water versus hot porous or liquid rock. At temperatures and pressures with which we are familiar, we can mainly ignore the compressibility of either. Under the weight of the deepest waters, the oceans compress only about 100 feet. Hundreds and even thousands of miles deeper into the crust the pressure is far greater than anything we have been able to study. Though presently we have no way of knowing how compressible is either water or rock at those temperatures and pressures, we do know that water is unique in that it becomes more compressible with increasing temperature. It is possible that deep within the earth, we can put five gallons

---

[168] Naomi Oreskes, *The Rejection of Continental Drift: Theory and Method in American Earth Science* (Oxford University Press, 1999). 23-24.
[169] Genesis 1:2, 6; 2 Peter 3:5

Chapter 30   A geological understanding of the waters of the Flood

of water (as measured at surface temperatures and pressures) into a two-gallon bucket. At those temperatures, liquid rock may expand, even under such great pressure. In either case, deep within the earth water may have greater density and be heavier than liquid rock. [170]

The main data for determining the composition of the interior of the earth are taken from acoustic refractions and reflections generated by earthquakes and by detonations used in the exploration for oil. These only give information concerning the depth where whatever is below changes from solid to liquid or from liquid to solid. It does not tell us the composition of material deep inside the earth. Fortunately, there is a more direct source for knowing what lies inside the earth. Drilled by the Russians, the Kola super-deep borehole extends almost eight miles below the earth's surface.[171] Russian scientists expected to find a transition from granite to basalt because, as now believed, basalt would have been formed from the cooling of the liquid rock or magma in the mantle. Instead, they found metamorphic rock saturated with water. They also found hydrogen gas, probably indicating the breakup of water molecules at enormously high temperatures and pressure. Judging according to the best available evidence, the interior of the earth is water!

**Figure 53
Russian stamp commemorating the Kola Super-deep Borehole**

In the light of this, we might now have some better explanation for volcanoes. The very fact that rock is coming forth from these vents in liquid form indicates a molecular composition that has a lower melting point than ordinary rock. That might also explain why it is mixed or saturated with water, and is becoming less dense as it is pushed towards the surface of the earth. Owing to the great heat, and to lower pressure as it rises, the volcanic magma may dry before or as it reaches the surface.

Likely, the water breaking forth in the Flood was not nearly as hot as we now see gushing forth in some places. Having had ages to cool since the formation of the earth's crust, it would be more the temperature of the water now found in the great underground aquifers still watering some parts of the earth. As I have already explained, it is not only the account in Genesis but empirical evidence from Neolithic times that point to the earth having had a different kind of hydrological cycle in those days.

---

[170] Evan H. Abramson, J. Michael Brown, and Leon J. Slutsky, "The thermal diffusivity of water at high pressures and temperatures," *The Journal of Chemical Physics* 115 (December, 2001).

[171] My appreciation to Mark Williams for pointing this out.

Part VI   *The Flood's Implications for Science and Scholarship*

There is also the issue of explaining what happened to all the water covering the mountains in the year of the Flood. The answer is obvious. Aside from creating various great lakes and deepening inland seas, the waters ran into the oceans. Africa's large Lake Victoria seems to date from the Flood. So do America's Great Lakes. The Caspian Sea and the Great Salt Lake were far larger a few thousand years ago than they are today. The continents are still draining water and rising.

We have evidence that just before the Flood, the oceans were much shallower and warmer than today. This comes from studies made of the remains of deep sea catches found in middens of the pre-Ceramic civilization of Peru, dating from about five thousand years ago.[172] The fish being consumed then were types that are found only in much warmer waters, suggesting that the Pacific Ocean has become much cooler since that time. This would have happened if the oceans sank under the extra weight of the waters from the Flood. In the process of sinking, the ocean basins would have pulled down continental shelves to the offshore locations where many of them are found today. This is why we find the remains of Neolithic settlements off the shores of Florida and the eastern Mediterranean. Similar remains are found in the Caribbean and in the Yellow Sea off the coast of China. Whatever bronze or metal might have been among these "Neolithic" remains would have long ago corroded. Black Sea remains recently given as evidence of the Black Sea flood (if they indeed date to the Neolithic period) are instead evidence of the Flood that covered the entire earth.[173]

In the aftermath of the Flood, the oceans would have had to expand and stretch to accommodate the new waters. Indeed, studies of the variation of the magnetic field along the ocean basins reveal stretch marks paralleling the places where the ocean floors are spreading. As the ocean basins are sinking and spreading in accordance with the principle of isostasy, the continents and their mountains are rising. To be sure, the sinking oceans are pulling down some of the continental shelves, but this action is balanced by the rising of mountains and plains in the continental basins. Volcanoes would naturally break forth in the cracks being created by the rising continents and sinking oceans. This explains what is known as the "ring of fire," the volcanoes surrounding the great Pacific basin.

Currently, the magnetic stripes on the ocean floor are interpreted as resulting from periodic reversals in the earth's magnetic field dating from hundreds of millions of years ago, making these stripes far too ancient to have been created by the Flood. But that is but an interpretation. The earth's induced magnetic

---

[172] Andrus, C. Fred T., Crowe, Douglas E., Sandweiss, Daniel H., Reitz, Elizabeth J., and Romanek, Christopher S. 2002. Otolith d18O record of mid-Holocene sea surface temperature in Peru. *Science* 295: 1508-1511.

[173] William Ryan and Walter Pitman, *Noah's Flood* (1998)

Chapter 30   A geological understanding of the waters of the Flood

field dominating, the degree and orientation of paleomagnetism is inferred from differences in intensity of the measured field. In truth, any shifting in the ocean floor or on the sides of volcanoes will likely create a variation of magnetic field. These stripes in the ocean look astonishingly like the stretch marks of a pregnant woman. The majority and greatest of them were perhaps created over the space of a year as the waters from the Flood settled into the oceans, stretching and cracking the basins. The orientation of paleomagnetism then in the ocean floor and most especially along the walls of the cracks would have shifted, giving rise to the presently observed phenomena.

In truth, apart from some special miracle of God, it is unlikely that the magnetic field of the earth can ever reverse. The current theory of the earth's magnetic field supposes it to have been created by a hypothetical current flowing deep within the earth. Earth currents do exist, and I have measured them, but they are driven by potentials above the surface of the earth, none of them greater than that which comes from lightning strikes or electrical power lines and having no general orientation to create a stable magnetic field for the whole earth. In truth, the interior of the earth does not contain a dialectic (non-conducting medium), which is necessary for potential differences to exist deep inside the earth, thus the earth will short-circuit any attempt to create an internal electrical current, whatever may be flowing deep within the earth. The truth is that the earth everywhere is at ground potential.[174]

The dialectic necessary for obtaining the earth's magnetic field is in fact to be found between the surface of the earth and the ionosphere. If you place the fingers of your right hand towards the rising sun, which is the direction of the turning of the earth and the direction of the movement of these positive charges called ions, your thumb will point to magnetic north. To confirm that magnetic fields derive from ionospheres, we observe that the magnetic fields of the other planets follow the intensity of their ionospheres and their rate of rotation. The exception is the magnetic field of the sun. It is likely that solar winds sweeping ions across its surface create the sun's magnetic field. We can confirm this by considering the chief gravitational force creating these solar winds, which must be the planet Jupiter. The magnetic field of the sun reverses every eleven years and, as we should expect, corresponds with the duration of Jupiter's orbit. Either these moving ions – those far above the sun's surface and those far above the earth's surface – produce magnetic fields, or else Maxwell's famous equations describing the behavior of electromagnetic forces and fields do not apply to the ionospheres of planets and the sun.

Geologists have had a lot of fun in recent years with plate tectonics and the supposed "conveyer belts" circulating deep within the earth, which are believed

---

[174] Which makes it dangerous to stand on the earth and touch a high voltage wire.

Part VI   The Flood's Implications for Science and Scholarship

to move the "great tectonic plates." This video-game geology moves continents back and forth across the oceans, each time shoving up new ranges of mountains. Bear in mind that those "ocean plates" subducted beneath continental shelves are but drawings and video productions. The rising mountains, the spreading ocean floors, the earthquakes, and the ring of volcanoes are indeed related. They are just what we should expect as a result of the Flood. What is in fact mythical are those conveyor belts moving tectonic plates – the same theoretical constructs as the chthonic currents supposed to produce the earth's magnetic field.

As I explained above, the continents do spread and move, but not so radically as explained by the currently popular theory. Permanent magnetism in the shifting crust of the earth varies the magnetic field slightly and accordingly from place to place as the continental surface has shifted. This is due to centrifugal forces on the elevated continents stemming from the earth's turning, along with changes resulting from the Flood. It is reasonable to suppose that early in the history of the earth, the earth's mantle and crust were less solid and the continents swung or shifted to the general positions where they lie today. Together with other changes such as the rising mountains, sinking oceans, and sinking continental shelves arising from the Flood, this created the magnetic declination that keeps compasses from pointing true north.

As I have already mentioned, according to historians of geological science the theory of plate tectonics was a return from empirically determined geology to the speculative theories prevalent in the early eighteenth century. If we are going to speculate on that level, we need to be constrained by the empirical data and we also need guidance from the cosmic dimension. Indeed we need the light of the Bible to understand the earth.

— 31 —

Understanding cosmology in the light of Genesis

THE ORIGIN OF the world in water as taught in the Bible and discovered in other Ancient Near Eastern texts may not have been due to the imagination of the ancients, but to an ancient communication from the world's Creator. This is not to say that the ancients did not envision this communication from their limited experience of deep waters. But the Ancient Near Eastern poets were not the last to fashion an understanding of the world and its origins based on their limited experience of the cosmos.

Modern cosmology began with Copernicus's observation that the earth turns on its axis and orbits the sun. The telescope invented shortly afterwards revealed much of what we now know as the solar system. The sun was immediately suspected of being but one of a far greater universe of fixed stars. The Swedish engineer and mystic Emmanuel Swedenborg (1688-1772), who may have learned about space from his claimed visits to Heaven to debate the Apostle Paul, proposed the nebular hypothesis: how the solar system might have formed by gravity operating on particles orbiting the sun. Immanuel Kant, an examiner of this ghost seer's visions, proposed his own version, but Pierre Simon Laplace (1749-1827) was the first to express the nebular hypothesis in mathematical form. Rationalist scientists reckoned the greater universe to be an eternal system, of which earth's was but a passing moment.

As time went on, more powerful telescopes revealed that some objects that had earlier appeared as fixed stars were in fact great systems of stars called galaxies. Our own sun was but one star in a galaxy that was none other than the Milky Way. Still more powerful telescopes revealed that some of what appeared to be stars or galaxies were actually clusters of galaxies. The shift of light from some of these galaxies towards the red part of the spectrum indicated that most of these galaxies were receding from us at great speeds. This suggests not only that the universe is expanding, but that it had some moment of Creation. Even more recently, the Hubble Telescope revealed that not only is the universe expanding, but its expansion is accelerating! No physical force can explain this acceleration. Due to the finite speed of light, the far reaches of space show the universe in its earliest stages. Low intensity infrared light spread uniformly across the sky reaches us from a far ancient stage of the universe's creation. It is clear that the universe is no fixed system, but a creation that has changed over history.

The nebular hypothesis assumes that the solar system was formed from gravity operating on gases and solid materials such as meteorites found in interplanetary space. Based on the molecular composition of most meteorites, it has been suggested that the interior of the earth must consist of melted iron and nickel. Perhaps we think this the chief compositional material for the solar system only because (1) meteorites are dislodged when comets strike the surface of terrestrial planets, and (2) that kind of material best survives the fiery entry through the earth's atmosphere. The nebular hypothesis of the solar system and the current scientific cosmology of our larger universe can only assume that the deeper things of the solar system and cosmos are the same as what we see at the surface. In truth, both are superficial theories.

I suspect that it is not only the interior of the earth that consists mostly of water. The same is probably true of the planets, moons, and stars. It is certainly true of specific comets. As the Bible indicates, God formed our universe from water, separating the waters on the second day of creation to form space (the firmament).[175] Astronomers have only assumed that the universe is largely terrestrial or gaseous based on what they observe on the surface of planets, moons, and stars. If my thesis is correct, this is true only of the outer layers of our planet. Probably most of the matter of our universe still consists of some form of water.

If the universe began as water, that conflicts with the current scientific version that creation began as an ultra-hot "Big Bang." The Big Bang theory has numerous problems, including in its earliest stage the breakdown of the known laws of physics. This is not solved, as some suppose, by the *ad hoc* theory of Inflation. The theory of Inflation is only a myth created to fill a gap that the current theory of cosmology cannot explain. It is now supposed that the initial Big Bang was far too hot for atoms to have formed. According to the current theory, hydrogen atoms appeared as the universe expanded and cooled, while larger atoms were created by a series of nuclear reactions in the interior of stars or during great cosmic explosions. But if the universe is accelerating as it is expanding, it would have less energy in its earliest stages. Instead of being ulta-hot, it may have been cold.

---

[175] Genesis 1:2, 6, 7; Psalm 24:2; 104:3; 136:6; 2 Peter 3:5

Chapter 31   Understanding cosmology in the light of Genesis

Due to the uniform expansion that the current theory assumes for all the matter in the expanding universe, the present theory cannot account for the creation of stars and galaxies. But if the matter in the universe was not truly uniform how did it become so? The Genesis account does not have such a problem because it explains the creation of the universe not as one act of creation, but as several separate acts, all of which may be empirically verified. That is to say, these separate acts of Creation cannot be reduced to the work of a single initial explosion.

On the First Day, God created the waters, then he created light: what we now see as the universe's background radiation. On the Second Day, God expanded the waters, creating space. The initial Creation need not have been so hot that water could not exist. With nothing but water in the universe, gravity would be uniform in every direction.[176] Similar to naturally-occurring water today, it would have contained trace minerals suitable for forming rocks needed for the crust of the earth on the Third Day of Creation. Of course, this supposes a different order and source of creation for the various elements than supposed either by current interpretations of the Creation account in Genesis or by the conventional cosmological theory. It will be more testable and therefore more useful than the current theory.

God formed the moon, the planets, the sun, and the stars on the Fourth Day. The giant planets were probably too large for their waters and gasses to have become capped by a mantle of liquid rock that would form a crust of solid rock like that of the terrestrial planets and moons. Note that the terrestrial bodies are the smaller bodies in the heavens. Most of the light bodies near the sun have lost their surface water due to evaporation and low gravity. The largest bodies in the heavens, the sun and the stars, were far too large to be capped by layers of liquid rock, but as scientists believe, they were in fact large enough to generate pressures and temperatures conducive to nuclear fusion. Some of the energy created by nuclear fusion reaches our earth in the form of light.

If scientists don't know what is inside the earth, how would they know what is inside the heavenly bodies? Under heavy pressure, hydrogen atoms are stripped from water molecules, while helium is created by the fusion of hydrogen atoms. The deep interior of the sun and stars may consist mainly of some form of water, and the gases oxygen and hydrogen, as water becomes under sufficient temperature and pressure. We should not be surprised that on the surface of stars we see mainly the lightest elements, hydrogen and helium.

Much dark matter of the universe may simply be water that has not been formed into planets and stars. Some of this inter-galactic water has been

---

[176] Such as one might conceive "direction" in the unformed world of this earliest era of Creation.

detected,[177] and every year, more water is found in space. Each discovery of water is trumpeted as new evidence that life must exist somewhere in outer space. If water makes life probable, then the universe must be full of living organisms. So much for the claim that evolutionary science is based upon empirical findings! To the contrary, evolutionary science is forever determined to find facts to fit or justify its theories.

Finally, what about "the floodgates of heaven"? The heavens contain plenty of storehouses of water that God might have sent to the earth for the purposes of the Flood. As I explained in Chapter 10, William Whiston thought a divinely guided comet initiated the Flood. Had God done so, he would have sent it as a special act of his power. He may have sent many comets to accomplish his purposes. Perhaps God used some such source of heavenly water to break the crust of the earth, releasing the "fountains of the deep." These warm waters from below would have created super-hurricanes, and plenty of new floodgates from above. This could have happened even if the comets had only impacted the oceans, the effect rippling and spreading across the entire surface of the earth. As I have already noted, the greater miracle of God is not so much his cosmic power in causing the Flood as his preservation of mankind in the earth before, during, and since the time of the Flood.

---

[177] Martin Harwit, et al, "Thermal Water Vapor Emission from Shocked Regions in Orion," *The Astrophysical Journal Letters* 497 (April 20, 1998).

— 32 —

Ancient writing, scripts, and texts

Writing in the early years of the twentieth century, Hermann Gunkel taught scholars to understand the biblical text using his new art: the highly subjective methods of form criticism. He expected modern Christians to view the plain teachings of the book of Genesis as legend. Believing literacy to be a recent invention, Gunkel scorned the notion that records as detailed as a modern ship's log might have been preserved from so long ago as the days of Noah, but he was oblivious to the discoveries of ancient texts and scripts dating more than a thousand years before Moses. The evidence negates his stated necessity for the oral transmission of history even as late as the records of early Israel, more than a thousand years after the Flood.

I could not ignore the evidence of ancient writings, since the Bible suggests that only one language survived the Flood. The survival of several pre-Flood scripts and languages contradicts my criterion concerning the discontinuity of culture that must necessarily have resulted from the Flood. Likely, many languages and scripts disappeared as a result of the Flood. Indeed, a script of an undeciphered language that dates to the Flood has been found at Harappa along the Indus River and another has been found in the ruins of ancient Iran. Deciphering any language requires either that they be closely related to languages known from historical times or that some "Rosetta stone" be discovered relating them to a historically-known language, a most unlikely possibility. The fact that these two languages are among the few ancient texts that cannot be deciphered buttresses the case that they date from before the Flood. Still, the matter much concerned me because (as I then understood) *two* historical languages – Sumerian and ancient Egyptian – do in fact appear in pre-Flood remains!

The Egyptian language was most troubling. It appears not only on the walls of the Pyramids, which certainly date to a later remodeling of these great structures as tombs for the kings, but also in the interior of the Pyramids which I knew dated from *before* the Flood! It was in fact used to mark stones quarried for building the Pyramids. Egyptologists remind us of Egypt's long and continuous language and civilization, a chief means of denying the history of man found in the Bible. The roots of this language, including the famous and beautiful hieroglyphic script in which it is written, are supposed to date from Egypt's First Dynasty. Egyptologist believe the First and Second Dynasties, as evidenced by the archaeological ruins of the great necropoleis of Abydos and Saqqara, existed even before the building of the Pyramids.

Searching for solutions, I pondered the possibility that new arrivals in Egypt somehow learned to read the ancient language from text they found in the ruins of the Flood, perhaps by a "Rosetta stone" among older texts they already possessed. As this became their language of literacy, they may have adapted it as their spoken tongue. But that was just *ad hoc* theory proposed only to save my version of the Flood. Rather than making things simpler, it added a highly speculative hypothesis. In truth, my theory was failing the important test that I had proposed as evidence of an historical worldwide Flood.

FIGURE 54
THE NARMER PALETTE

It would be years before I learned that the popular writers on Egypt from whom I had learned either do not understand or else fail to remind their readers that Archaic Egyptian, the language belonging to earliest Egypt, has in fact never been deciphered. In truth, the necropoleis of Abydos and Saqqarra, where the Archaic Egyptian texts are found on such artifacts as the famous Narmer Palette [Figure 54] were once cities of living people, turned into cities of the dead by Noah's Flood. Note that the fear and violence appearing on the Narmer palette perfectly fit the era just prior to the Flood. Though historical Egyptian kings may have placed monuments in these elaborate remains and written upon the monuments and walls, their language using the hieroglyphic script is not the Archaic Egyptian language of the Narmer Palette.

Archaic Egyptian has never been deciphered because it does not appear to be related to the historical Egyptian language. Though never the primary script for any period of the historical Egyptian language, some of these beautiful hieroglyphic scripts were eventually borrowed as an alternative script for the Egyptian language and used on the walls of the Pyramids. Such a pictorial script can be as easily borrowed to write any language, including English. The Museum of the Alphabet in Waxhaw, North Carolina contains an exhibit with labeled stamps, allowing visitors to write their name in this ancient Egyptian script.

Chapter 32   Ancient writing, scripts, and texts

Figure 55   "Philip" written in hieroglyphics

I had to sort through mountains of popular writings about Egypt before I learned that those most expert in the ancient Egyptian script do not hold the view that the Archaic and historical Egyptian languages are necessarily continuous.[178] Linguists can only guess the meaning of the Archaic Egyptian letters, but I doubt that the name of founder of the Egypt's great civilization was "Smelly Crayfish"as some Egyptologists read the name on the Narmer Palette. The so-called Horus names, currently proposed as alternative names of the Pharaohs, are likewise guesses. Whatever the Horus names meant, they belonged to the original owners of the Pyramids – not the Egyptian kings who remodeled these structures as tombs.

Like numerous problems that now confront Egyptologists, the facts make perfect sense when we understand that the Pyramids and the cities of those who built them date from before the Flood. This new perspective should help Egyptologists develop a simpler and more reasonable understanding of Egypt's ancient history, important not only for Egyptian history but for the entire history of the Ancient Near East since it is now based on that of Egypt. The current Egyptian chronology is already known to be in serious error due to the artificial and wrongly conceived chronology developed by Flinders Petrie, but we now have a means of resolving the problems.

Understanding the changes made by the Flood should also be useful for understanding the scripts and languages of ancient Sumer. Named for the descendents of Shem, this language seems also to have been that of all mankind before the division of tongues and the scattering from Babel on the plains of Shinar. But it may not have been spoken in Mesopotamia before the Flood. This is because the names of the Tigris and Euphrates Rivers and certain ancient cities of Mesopotamia are not themselves of the Sumerian language. Perhaps Noah's

---

[178] W. V. Davies, *Egyptian Hieroglyphs* (The University of California Press/British Museum, 1987).

Part VI   *The Flood's Implications for Science and Scholarship*

family retained the pre-Flood names of these rivers and cities first explored by Noah's great grandson, Nimrod.

Archaeologists and historians tend to see things the way that Nature and circumstance preserved them, but I doubt that the medium used for the world's most ancient writing was either stone or clay as generally supposed. The conditions of preservation bias archaeology and ancient history towards graves and caves; towards the powerful ancient civilizations that did write upon stone monuments and clay tablets; towards desert civilizations; towards oxygen-deprived peat bogs; and towards remains created by various kinds of sudden destruction. Unfortunately, organic remains such as books are rarely preserved through the ravages of time, giving those who suppose earliest man unsophisticated an excuse to deny that he was capable of writing.

To overcome the bias of accidental preservation in the study of archaeology and history one must look at what the broader picture suggests about the technologies, capabilities, and history of the ancients. Some form of pictorial or hieroglyphic script was used for the earliest phonetic writing, and the bark paper medium favors that script. Wood is far more widespread, more robust and lighter for transporting letters and messages than clay tablets. It is likely that the oldest medium used for writing was bark or wood tablets. In fact, our word *book* is rooted in more ancient words for *birch* or *bark*. Where available, papyrus is a better and less costly way to make paper than bark. Clay tablets are even less expensive, but they are cumbersome, fragile, and less portable and too bulky for libraries except those owned by wealthy kings. They do have the advantage of long preservation if they are deliberately or accidentally baked to the hardness of pottery.

The earliest writing on animal skins or parchment is currently dated to the era of the Persians. Some date it later, as an innovation due to the embargo on exporting papyrus by one of the Hellenistic kings of Egypt. But it is unwise to make judgments concerning the earliest appearance of organic artifacts based on surviving remains. I doubt that it took people so long to learn how to write on leather and to discover what a robust and convenient medium this can be for keeping important records such as family and national genealogies. In a pastoral society, the most convenient and economical media for preserving important writings is leather. I would guess that parchment dates from the time of Patriarchs, if not from before the Flood.

After the Flood, pictorial forms of writing spread over the ancient Near East, through the Mediterranean into Egypt and Europe, and even to China, the East Indies, and Central America. The discovery of hieroglyphic and cuneiform scripts dating respectively from antediluvian Egypt and Early Bronze Age Iraq suggests that both kinds of writing were in use before the Flood. Widespread

Chapter 32   Ancient writing, scripts, and texts

use of hieroglyphics soon after the Flood points to the almost certain use of a hieroglyphic script as the primary script used by Noah's family, which in turn points to the literacy of those embarking from the Ark. Because there exists evidence of narrative writing around the time of the Flood and continuing afterward – however shocking this might be to Hermann Gunkel – it seems likely that Noah carried books written on bark paper in a hieroglyphic script with him in the Ark.

Linearization of scripts occurs naturally as a shortened form of writing, but the existence of cuneiform before the Flood and evidence of cuneiform soon after the Flood causes me to conclude that cuneiform writing was either retained as tablets carried by Noah on the Ark, or else waited restoration at ancient Babel. Some of the earliest forms of this type of writing have been found in the remains of the city archaeologists know as Late Uruk and which I have identified as ancient Babel. A noted change in the direction of writing of the cuneiform script may have resulted from restoration of cuneiform following the Flood.

Whatever the medium or script, confirming what I explained in Chapter 3, evidence for basic literacy and writing can always be found wherever and whenever one finds the servants of the God of the Bible. This extends from places in the Ancient Near East associated with the Patriarchs to the mountain and jungle tribes where missionaries go today. Serious belief in the Scriptures and popular literacy are always to be found together because the Bible gives ordinary people both the need and the desire to read and write. That widespread literacy always follows the Bible is a principle that has powerfully assisted my study and understanding of ancient history.

What I have to say here and in the rest of this chapter and the next is not what you will learn from biblical scholars, linguists, or scholars of ancient history and the Ancient Near East, but in the light that I have used, the facts of ancient history are simpler and clearer. It appears that the descendents of Shem, the Sumerians, were the most literate of the sons of Noah. The descendents of Shem who settled in China, the East Indies and America preserved writing. The evidence both from the Bible and Ancient Near Eastern texts point to the Hebrew branch of the Chaldeans as perhaps the most literate if not also the most learned line of Shem's descendents.

The Hebrews were the sons of Eber, from whom they derive their name. Most of the ancient nations were agriculturalists, but the Hebrews were pastoralists who made their living with flocks and herds of animals: sheep, goats, donkeys, and camels. While most of the Shemites lived north and east of the Euphrates River, the Hebrews crossed over the River to take advantage of the uncultivated but more easily traveled area in Syria and lands south.[179] The contact of these

---

[179] That may have led to their name coming to mean "across the River" or "across the Flood" in

wandering Aramaens[180] with many nations gave them opportunity and need for knowing numerous languages, and serving kings as scribes and messengers.

Failing to see mention of camels in certain texts from Egypt, an earlier generation of biblical scholars claimed that camels were not domesticated in the era of the Patriarchs, a rash conclusion against the historicity of the biblical text. But absence of evidence is not in fact evidence of absence. More recent studies have discovered the camel domesticated as early as the third millennium.[181] Moreover, those like Abraham who traversed lands where water is rare would have been most likely to have needed and to have used camels. To follow their flocks and herds to wherever they might find pasture, the Hebrews had mainly to live in tents. But however profitable it may have been, nomadic life is also strenuous. This might explain how much Abraham may have desired a suitable land where he could settle and rest in his old age – a land promised to him by the Lord God. Of course, this does not mean that he was not also looking beyond to a more enduring city than what his dimming eyes could then see.

It would be reasonable to suppose that Abraham sold wool and many of his sheep to the merchants of such ancient cities as Ebla, Sodom, and Gomorrah. Due to the chronological mistake associated with Late Uruk, the recently discovered ancient city of Ebla is currently dated a few centuries too early. I think it likely that the famous Ebla archives, where is found some of the earliest evidence of the Canaanite language, date to the era of Abraham,

Abraham's servants may also have served as couriers for letters between ancient cities. In ancient times, like today, there was a need for long-distance communication. Women who married foreign kings or joined the households of migrant pastoralists wanted to remain in touch with their families. New colonies wanted to hear news from their mother cities. Kings needed to make alliances and solve disputes with other kings concerning matters of regional interest. Compare this era to the colonists of early America who tried to stay in communication with their kinfolk, governments, and business partners in Europe using whatever reliable courier might be available.

Abraham would have obtained servants from many of these nations and cities, giving members of his household knowledge of many languages. The household of the widely trusted Abraham would have wonderfully served as translators and couriers. We do know that those speaking a language related to ancient Hurrian served as ancient scribes for various nations and kings. The couriers may have been Hebrews or the Habiru, the name by which some of these wandering Arameans are called in Ancient Near Eastern texts. Likely, the

---

the language of Canaan.
[180] Deuteronomy 26:5
[181] cf Richard W. Bulliet, *The Camel and the Wheel* (Columbia University Press, 1990).

earliest Arameans (or Syrians) are those living in the same land but currently identified as Mittanians, a language of the same family as Hurrian. Eventually, the descendents of all these groups adopted some form of Akkadian or, like the Hebrews, the language of Canaan.[182] The Caananites were merchants, hence their language became the languages of commerce, much as English serves our world today.

It is likely that what we now know as the Aramaic and Hebrew languages were just different branches of the language spoken by the Israelites at the time of David and Solomon. Due first to the great kingdoms of David and Solomon, and second to Aramean and Israelite captives serving as scribes for Assyrian, Babylonian, and Persian kings, the Aramaic (Syrian) language eventually became the *lingua franca* of the Ancient Near East. Supposing that Aramaic, as well as Hebrew, developed from the language of Israel at the time of David, by the era of King Hezekiah those speaking the Hebrew and Aramaic dialects were no longer able to understand one another's language.[183]

---

[182] Isaiah 19:18
[183] 2 Kings 18:26

— 33 —

Higher Criticism of the Bible

However much a vain world and our human nature dislike criticism, we should view it as our friend. True criticism comes from the Spirit of truth and uses as the basis of its judgment the Word of God. Certainly, criticism in the form of careful, expert, and honest judgment is necessary for preserving, translating, and obtaining a deeper understanding of the Bible. In ancient Israel, criticism – the job of distinguishing the sacred from the profane, the true from the false, and the clean from the unclean – was the job of the Levitical priests. The priests were charged with preserving and teaching the words of God, the written form being the sacred Scriptures. In Chapter 39, I will return to the biblical way of determining truth and there explain some of the ways that the Lord used to safeguard the sacred Scriptures.

Figure 56
Ark of the Covenant

The ancient Levites carried the testimony of God in the Ark of the Covenant. The Ark was simply a wooden box, but this chest contained the witness of specific things that God had said and done that he charged the Israelites with remembering. The Israelites had to recognize this in order to meet with God. Thus the Ark of the Covenant rather than the numerous high places found throughout ancient Canaan marked the one place of Israelite worship.[184] After the Babylonian exile, the Ark of the Covenant was no longer to be found in the Temple. The wooden box was no longer necessary since the Lord's testimony was then contained in written Scriptures recognized by the worldwide community of Jewish believers. The Temple alone sufficed to maintain the unity of the Jewish community until the outpouring of the Holy Spirit, which now functions to maintain the unity

---

[184] Deuteronomy 11:12

Chapter 33   Higher criticism of the Bible

of God's holy people. The Holy Spirit fills only those who believe and trust God's Holy Word.

In the New Covenant, criticism is still required, but the Lord has assigned these former Levitical functions to his priesthood of believers. Indeed, the Bible provides the same functions once provided by the Ark of the Covenant. As once did the Ark of the Covenant, the Bible now contains the Word of God and is still to be carried by human beings who are devoted servants of God. God's presence attends *only* those who recognize the authority of his Word. Only these have drawn close to his unseen presence.

As was the case of the Levites, some who carry the sacred testimony in their hearts and minds must necessarily be scholars and expert in the languages in which the Scriptures are preserved. Scholars who are not believers provide valuable information for the preservation of the Scriptures, but it is only believers – those filled with the Holy Spirit – who can determine just what is sacred or inspired and what is not. Unfortunately, recent discussions about inspiration and canon have violated the divine separation of the sacred and the profane. The sacred can never be reduced, as some have insisted, to that which is accessible by the profane, whether a legal decision pertaining to the canon or intellectual propositions pertaining to the sacred text. The Holy Spirit, which unbelievers fail to possess, will always be necessary for knowing God and, as now appears, even for preserving truth.

Scholars divide study of the Scriptures into lower and higher criticism. Lower criticism is concerned with determining the best text and translation of the Scriptures. Higher criticism concerns itself with such things as the authorship and circumstances in which the Scriptures were written. Using as the basis of their judgments the unexamined opinions of mere men, unbelieving higher critics have challenged and obscured the truth of the Scriptures. Notwithstanding these great sins, higher criticism by those who believe only develops a deeper understanding of the text and is useful for spreading the eternal Word of God into the larger realm of history. Unlike unbelieving scholars, believers can understand these ancient texts. Though written in ages different from our own, the Holy Spirit creates a common understanding among believers of all ages. J. G. Herder notwithstanding, God can indeed speak the same truths in many tongues and he also provides interpretation.

After comprehending the historicity of Noah's Flood and the accompanying events so precisely recorded in the Bible, it will be clear to most that it is past time to retire the kind of literary and narrative criticism of the Bible that dominates higher criticism today. I refer to the kind biased against the Bible's account of history, which assumes that the Bible cannot be understood as speaking to believers of the present age, and which refuses to acknowledge the Scriptures as inspired by the only God. Most importantly, studying the Bible should be understood as the sacred task that it is. The realm of profane studies must no longer be allowed to confuse and contaminate the truth. I trust that it is clear to the reader of this book that those who have followed this route from the time of the Enlightenment have thoroughly disgraced themselves as searchers for truth. The search for and preservation of truth – biblical studies especially – should return to the province of the believing community regardless of the institutions or circumstances in which believing scholars may presently work. In part, this is already happening as believers are once again beginning to command the field of biblical scholarship.

Such a negative judgment does not apply to much wonderful work that has been done in textual criticism, canonical studies, or historical criticism. These are essential for preserving, translating, and understanding the Bible. Nor is there anything wrong with a study of the history of the composition of the Bible so long as it recognizes the history and truth plainly taught by the words of the Bible. We need not be captive to rabbinic myths about the authors and composition of the Bible, to Catholic myths about who is responsible for the Bible, or to Protestant doctrines of textual inerrancy that are based on humanist concerns. All these defend the Bible in ways that the inspired Scriptures specifically reject. Fortunately, these distracting issues bear in only a minor way upon the important question: whether the message plainly taught by these Scriptures is true and whether the living God inspired them.

As I explained in Chapter 7, the aim of higher criticism in modern biblical scholarship has been to trace the origin of the biblical documents to some later time than suggested by the Scriptures themselves. I have explained how such scholarship was not only deeply biased against the Bible but operated under rules that preclude the very possibility that the biblical documents might give a true account of what they witness. This does not mean that higher criticism and composition history concerning authorship, canon, or text are themselves illegitimate undertakings. Properly executed, they will give us a better understanding concerning cultural and historical matters of the Bible. Nor is it illegitimate to suggest that those who wrote the books of the Bible under the inspiration of the Holy Spirit worked from or knew various sources. The inspired writers of our Bible mention these sources: numerous books of genealogy kept by various tribes, which also contained historical notes [Genesis 5:1], the Book of Jasher [Joshua 10:13; 2 Samuel 1:18], the Book of the Wars of the Lord [Numbers 21:14], the annals or chronicles of the Kings of Israel and Judah, and other records.

It is also likely that, as in the New Testament, various documents had characteristic ways of referring to the LORD of Israel and to the Father, God Most

High, but this method of determining the authors of the documents, used by those guessing the composition of the historical portions of the Bible according to the widely used JEPD hypothesis, is unreliable. Christians today also have characteristic but varying ways of referring to God. Scholars guessing supposed documents used in the composition of the Bible seem to assume that the inspired writers of the Bible possessed one-dimensional personalities and moods. In fact, one-dimensional thinking has been chiefly that of the modern biblical scholars.

Those who have attacked the truth and inspiration of the Bible have supposed that the discovery of various Rabbinic, Catholic, and Protestant myths about authorship, canon, and text licensed them to do so. The fact that pious myths have been invented as misguided though perhaps well-intentioned means of defending the Bible does not in any way mean that the Bible is myth.

Having discovered that the earliest chapters of Genesis shed the light we need on ancient history, the question before us in this chapter is this: what does it tell us about how these accounts came to appear in our Bible? Of course God is capable of dictating such documents to one of his prophets such as Moses. He could even have told Moses the accounts of Moses's own death and the events following. The question is not whether God could have done that, but whether he in fact did so.

Referring to the Torah as "the Books of Moses" is legitimate, regardless of the composition or time of composition, because four of the five address the era of Moses. Moses had also to preserve the books that Israelites then had in their possession, which would have included the accounts found in Genesis. God appointed Moses Israel's Teacher until the time of Christ, the Prophet to whom the Torah of Moses instructs Israel to listen.[185] To be obedient to the Torah of Moses we must be obedient to Jesus and his commandments. But if we do not listen to Moses, we will not listen to Jesus.

From Hellenistic times, the Torah has also been known as "the Law." Calling these books "the Law" rather than "Teachings," which better translates *Torah*, dates to the Greek translations. In fact *spirit* far more than *law* describes the character of the God and people of the Bible. For us today, the word *law* carries a legalistic meaning stemming from the Greco-Roman tradition we have inherited. Greek kings needed a translation of books containing the customs or laws of their subjects, thus they may have sponsored the first translation of the Torah into Greek. Alternately, wealthy Greek-speaking Jews may have sponsored the Greek Bible. Because the Greeks were proud of their laws or customs, and their lawgiver, Solon, it would have made sense for Hellenized Jews in the Second Temple era to refer to Moses as "the Lawgiver of the Jews."

---
[185] Deuteronomy 8:15; Acts 3:22

The greater question is the one raised by Gunkel: whether books of ancient history existed at the time of Moses. This is to say: did Moses and the Israelites in Egypt have accurate knowledge of their own history and of the history contained in the first eleven chapters of Genesis? Moreover, did Noah and did Abraham, Isaac, and Jacob possess the accounts or the knowledge found in the first eleven chapters? If Abraham did not possess reliable books containing this history, he was indeed like the illiterate Arab sheiks, as Julius Wellhausen supposed him to be. This assumption is not only patronizing, but also lacks acquaintance with the world and writings of the Ancient Near East. Supposing ancient man to be void of such skills, Wellhausen and Gunkel were in fact unaware or ignored evidence that writing existed from the era of Noah.

Writing dates no later than the Early Bronze Age, the time of Noah while writing suitable for historical narrative dates to around the time of the Flood. In fact, the Flood narrative contains too many details of time and place to be accommodated by oral transmission. Despite myths concerning the reliability of oral transmission by various religions, we can evaluate the reliability of oral transmission by comparing the biblical record of the Flood to the sketchy and distorted accounts of this event preserved by numerous nations. Though containing certain germs of truth they are in fact unreliable with regard to details. Gunkel's tradition and form criticism that assume oral transmission are but ways of hiding unconstrained and uncritical speculation behind a learned veneer.

While oral transmission is hardly reliable, we must not suppose that the nations had no knowledge of the things taught in the early chapters of Genesis. Unfortunately, both Rabbinic Jewish and early Christian teachers seem to have supposed that both revelation and history began with the Torah of Moses. In the same manner, they have supposed biblical Hebrew to be the oldest language. This type of thinking is indeed the way of myth, but not the way of a faith based on truth. In truth, the events of history must precede or accompany the recording of history. For sure, everything recorded in the book of Genesis happened long before Moses' birth. The Exodus narrative, for example, does not even make sense if those being delivered from slavery did not already possess some knowledge of what is recorded in the book of Genesis.

As I have mentioned, the most ancient accounts of this history would have been written in the earliest Hebrew language, resembling or perhaps identical to what we now call Hurrian, which is not a Semitic language. The descendents of Shem would not have spoken a Semitic (in fact *Hamitic*) language until they entered the land of Canaan. Yet, due to their presence in the land as a small group of strangers, long before the Exodus, the Israelites had long before adopted the language of Canaan, what we now know as biblical "Hebrew."

Chapter 33   Higher criticism of the Bible

We have no lists of the books in Israel's most ancient possession and no physical evidence of books written on perishable organic media survives from this era. We are fortunate to have in the Dead Sea Scrolls Old Testament texts copied in the time of Jesus. Only a few fragments of our Scriptures are known from a few centuries earlier than the composition of the earliest of these scrolls. Notwithstanding, preservation of accurate history from the days of the Flood requires that these records were in fact preserved in written form from earliest time. It is reasonable that Moses himself translated and preserved the portion of world and Israelite early history written in ancient languages. He may have translated and compiled these into a form very similar to the present book of Genesis. This history would have been essential to the giving of the Law, which refers to the six day Creation as given in the book of Genesis.

Another reason for supposing Moses to have composed the book of Genesis is the fact that it was written in an alphabetic script. Currently, Phoenicians (as the Greeks knew the Canaanites) are credited with the invention of the alphabet. These Canaanites were certainly early adapters of the alphabet, but it is unlikely that they were the alphabet's inventors because Canaanites continued to use cuneiform as their language well into the first millennium before Christ, while recent archaeological evidence show Israel using the alphabet from the very beginning of the same first millennium BC. The evidence therefore points to the Israelites rather than Canaanites, more commonly called Phoenicians, as having likely invented of the alphabet.

Another reason for thinking this so is that the alphabet depends both on the language of Canaan and the script of Egypt. As sojourners in Egypt, the Israelites had to have known both. But whether it was Joseph, Moses, or some other speaker of the language of ancient Canaan who invented the alphabet, we do know that it was at just this time and place in the history of the world that the earliest evidence of the alphabet appears. The most important reason for believing the Israelites to be the inventors is that, unlike the Phoenicians, Moses and the Israelites had an important need for the alphabet and need drives invention. The Law of Moses required all Israelites to write commandments on their doors and clothes to remind both themselves and their children. The giving of the Law of Moses was the first time in history when families of all statuses and income levels needed to read and write. The alphabet would be required for this kind of popular literacy. Confirming this, archaeological evidence of the earliest common literacy appears first in the land of ancient Israel.[186] Throughout history, the Bible and popular literacy have always spread together.

---

[186] For the current explanation of the development of the alphabet, and summary of earliest evidence of Israelite literacy, cf. Hershel Shanks and Frank Moore Cross, *Conversations with a Bible Scholar* (Biblical Archaeology Society, 1994), 65-66, 93-94.

Next, consider the books that existed prior to Moses and which were available to him for his inspired composition. Was Noah pondering history passed down from the time of Adam when he found grace in the eyes of the Lord? Was Abraham pondering ancient accounts of the acts of God from books in his possession when the Lord asked him to leave his family and homeland and go to a land that he would show him? Was Moses studying such things when he became interested in helping his brothers during the era of their enslavement to the Egyptians? I think all are likely scenarios. God's servants have always loved and preserved his testimony.

The last question in these considerations of how we got the Bible is how the history of Israel and the teachings of Moses came to appear in their present form. Consider that the kings of Israel were required to make a copy of the Law of Moses so as to understand these commandments and teach them to the people and to the nations. Royal scribes and recorders worked closely with Temple scribes and priests. A biblically sound conclusion for the first five books of the Bible is that they were publications of the earliest kings of Israel. The reason for thinking thus is that so much history in the Bible pertains to the era from Samuel to David. Moreover, Genesis *looks back* to the time when there were Canaanites living in the land, and before any King of Israel reigned,[187] while prophets writing in the eighth century are referring to the things recorded in these books. On the other hand, nothing truly requires a date later than the time of Solomon. Though their entire content was long known in ancient Israel, it is likely that the five books of the Torah were published in essentially their present form during Solomon's tenth century reign. The Bible that we have is in fact the Law of God that went out from Zion to the nations.

---

[187] Genesis 13:7, 36:31

— 34 —

Summary

I COULD CONTINUE writing interesting things about ancient history and correcting scientific and scholarly matters in the light of these earliest chapters of Genesis. I could also address in more detail issues in the specific fields and subjects that I have already covered. There is of course opportunity here for those specializing in various fields to advance the work in their chosen field using the powerful light of the ancient Scriptures. I will mention a few areas where further study along the lines suggested should yield reliable and fruitful results:

1. MAKING A STUDY of the settlements and migration paths of early mankind – that is, mankind before the Flood – employing as a baseline the chronological marker of the Flood. Such a study would collapse the time frame of the "Ice Age" to that of settlements and civilizations buried by the Flood. As the great confusion and errors owing to the Flood burials are erased, an archaeological trace of the pattern of earliest migrations should appear

2. DEVELOPING A RELATIVE archaeological chronology of ancient man based solely on archaeological considerations, then dating archaeologically clear samples from these levels by radiocarbon. This will not only provide a more reliable and clearer picture of the settlement history of ancient man, but will better reveal sources of systematic errors in the current radiocarbon dating.

3. DEVELOPING A LINGUISTIC historiography in the light of the table of nations in Genesis 10 using the corrections that I have suggested. These include the *Shemitic* family of peoples and languages that I have newly identified; seeing the original Hebrew language as part of this family, either related to or identical to what is now understood as ancient Hurrian; seeing Aramaic and related languages as deriving from the spread of literacy from ancient Israel during the reigns of David and Solomon and from subsequent Hebrew servants who served as scribes for the rul-

ers of the Aramaen, Assyrian, Babylonian, and Persian empires; and understanding that the Japhetic or Indo-European languages of India and vicinity likely derive from the Persian conquest.

4. DEVELOPING A MORE accurate historiography of the world from this corrected linguistic history, which recognizes that nations adapt new languages and which takes seriously the light of these earliest chapters of Genesis. Studying the records of ancient historians, tracing the spread of archaeological and historically known migrations, and making studies of the cultural and genetic relationships between human groups should inform this study.

5. STUDYING THE TECHNOLOGIES, economies, climate, ecologies, and the likely scientific understanding owned by the world destroyed by the Flood. This might help us understand how the Pyramids were built and how they once functioned. It would also give us a better understanding of the relationship between humans and animals during this era, as I discussed in Chapter 29.

6. REVISING THE HISTORY of the Ancient Near East from the time of the Flood. This includes a major revision of the Egyptian history and chronology, and seeing the Late Uruk period of ancient Mesopotamia as beginning in the middle years of the third millennium.

7. STUDYING ANIMAL SPECIES and their present and former habitats in the light of the changes resulting from the Flood. Much needed is a clearer understanding of the basic kinds of animals, and revision of the current species classifications based on these basic kinds.

8. TAKING A FRESH look at the geological column unconstrained by dogma. Separate geological columns, one for land and one for the oceans, should be developed and correlated.

9. FURTHER DEVELOPING GEOLOGY and astronomical cosmology based on understanding of water as the fundamental matter from which the earth and the cosmos are composed. The new cosmology would recognize the singularities created by the various acts of Creation during the first four days of Genesis. The simple way that geological and cosmological data will likely appear will demonstrate the superiority of the Genesis-based paradigm and unify the currently fragmented knowledge of our physical universe.

According to the greatest philosophers of science, such as Charles Peirce, Thomas Kuhn, and Karl Popper, and the greatest of modern scientists such as Albert Einstein and Niels Bohr, the simplicity and fruitfulness – which one might summarize as 'successful predictability' – is the ultimate measure of any scientific theory. In Chapter 13, I proposed extending this judgment to test the validity of historical accounts and claims. There, I noted that the test of a light is how much and how clearly or simply it allows us to see. Consider how much I have been able to simply explain with this light of Genesis, how well it integrates our knowledge in numerous scientific and scholarly fields, and how simple and clear things look in the light of the Scriptures inspired by the God of Heaven who created our world.

This book has focused on the early chapters of Genesis because that is where the deepest challenge to the truth of the Scriptures has been leveled, licensing the general skepticism about the historical truth of the Scriptures. Understanding that the Bible reliably preserves the truth of the most ancient times should give us confidence that the entire Scriptures are the revelation of God preserved for mankind's salvation.

The aim of this book is only to present the big picture of Noah's Flood and ancient history, and demonstrate how this impacts the natural sciences and related scholarly fields in fruitful ways. Even so, a lot of information and new ways of thinking about familiar science and history are packed into what I have written. I must therefore give everyone a chance to ponder these things and adjust to the light of the Scriptures for understanding both history and science. The last section of this book will concern issues of our present day.

Part VII

The Flood's Meaning for Today

— 35 —

The days of Noah and the Day of the Lord

In Parts III and IV, I explained how early modern thinkers ceased believing in the Flood and the rest of the Bible for reasons other than an unbiased search for truth and how many of us have unknowingly replaced the Bible with their speculative and misleading ways of understanding our origins and ancient history. In Parts V and VI, I showed how recognizing that history and creation were accurately recorded in the Bible simplifies the now-muddled explanations of ancient history and the now-fragmented understanding of the natural sciences. I put forth powerful and detailed evidence that the Flood recorded in the Bible, one that covered the entire earth, occurred at the end of the Early Bronze Age, in the middle of the third millennium before Christ.

The Early Bronze Age preceding the Flood was a period of extensive worldwide population, technical accomplishments, and prosperity – an era much like our own. It was a materialistic age when everyone seems to have been pursuing fleshly pleasures and gain. As suggested in Genesis,[188] exploitation of people and the desire for revenge probably gave rise to violence, for which plentiful evidence from those days is found on every continent. It was a busy world until the very day that Noah and his family entered the Ark. Though the onset of rain may not have seemed ominous, archaeological evidence indicates that drowning from the Flood was sudden. Likely that happened as tsunami-like waters swept over the earth. This would preclude temporary escape by climbing mountains as taught by the Young Earth Creationist science and depicted in traditional paintings of the Great Deluge.

The closest thing in recent history to which we might compare the suddenness of the Flood is the awful tragedy of 9/11. On that day business came to a standstill as the world's attention was riveted on this unexpected event. Drowning by the Flood was a more humane ending of an earlier world filled with the kind of vengeance and violence that ruled on 9/11. Sudden drowning by

---

[188] Genesis 4:23-24

Part VII   The Flood's Meaning for Today

FIGURE 57   "AS IN THE DAYS OF NOAH..."

Noah's Flood was even more humane than the recent tragedy when Hurricane Katrina gradually flooded New Orleans. Otherwise, the New Orleans flood is a fit comparison. The plentiful human remains found inside dwellings suggest that the onset of rain caused most in the ancient world to retire to their houses. The royalty of Ur took advantage of the occasion by preparing to party.

As Jesus replied to those who noted similar tragedies, those who suffered may have been no more deserving than those who escaped. Still, he pointed to the events as reasons for the people of his age to repent lest even greater destruction come.[189] However great his mercy, God would be unwise to save those who repeatedly reject his righteous rule and all his warnings, which only leads to greater wickedness and sorrow. Indeed, Noah's Flood is something that we should remember. If we acknowledge and become obedient to the truth, as in the case of Noah and his family, our Creator has the power to wondrously save those who repent even as he brings his great judgment on a world that does not.

When truth is embraced, it comes with power to set us free from the darkness that leads to such destruction. Though they will be skeptical at first, even the most learned who have a commitment to truth will revive their interest in the Flood. I base this on experience with family and friends, those usually the most difficult to convince. As they absorb this new understanding, traditional skeptical arguments melt away. What they have been taught as edifying legend and unsophisticated belief is history, carrying with it all manner of implications for science and learning.

Of course, the meaning of Noah's Flood for today is not only the light it sheds on history and science, but also the truth of biblical faith. Those interested in the truth about the Flood extend well beyond Christians. Traditional Muslims and Jews believe in the Flood. Almost every nation once believed in the Flood, whatever gods they worshipped or whatever religion or philosophy they followed. But for Christians, the truth concerning the Flood touches the very heart of our faith. I focused on this particular matter because I knew it was

---

[189] Luke 13:1-5

Chapter 35 The days of Noah and the Day of the Lord

the linchpin of the modern challenge to the truthfulness and hence the authority of the Scriptures and Jesus. The fact that the same Jesus who revealed to me his great authority and love also referred to the days of Noah meant that I could not ignore the Old Testament's history of the earliest days of mankind.

For biblical faith to have meaning it has be telling us the truth, just as the Bible proclaims it does. Were Jesus' words not reliably transmitted by his chosen Apostles and preserved by the church, the solid foundation of our faith would have been lost. A Jesus mistaken as to the truth that he spoke is obviously not divine. We could not trust him concerning the future, nor could he be an acceptable sacrifice for our sins. Were Jesus fallible or in darkness about the past, we would be denied the wonderful hope I discovered the first time I read that little book of John.

For the same reason, a God who failed to understand how the earth was made cannot possibly be its Creator. Nor is a God who assumes that the entire world is confined to the Ancient Near East and Europe truly God. Of course, it was "enlightened" Europeans and not the Bible or Jesus who thought in such parochial terms. They simply projected their limited vision onto the Bible and onto Jesus. When they discovered the true extent of the world they presumed it was the Bible and Jesus rather than themselves who had been mistaken.

But Jesus accurately recalled the Flood. The reference that he made to the days of Noah was not aimed at teaching people the Flood's historicity, something almost everyone then believed. He was explaining that his glorious Second Coming would surprise the world just as the Flood surprised Noah's world. Some point out that this promised coming has been proclaimed for two thousand long years. Thus few today take Jesus' Second Coming seriously, let alone his admonishment that we be ever vigilant for that day, as were his chosen and faithful Apostles.

Few took Noah seriously. It is instructive to compare the faith and patience for Jesus' Second Coming to the faith of Noah. The Scriptures also refer to the Flood as a type of the great Day of Judgment when everyone will be destroyed except those preserved by God's special provision.[190] Early Christians understood Christ to be a new Noah's Ark who would save people from a world slated for destruction.[191] Though they were looking for salvation on the great and terrible Day of the Lord, the cohesiveness of their community also preserved Christians from the destruction of Jerusalem in AD 70 and after the collapse of the Roman Empire in the following centuries. The truth of Jesus' Coming has all along been relevant, but never so much as today.

---

[190] Luke 13:1-5

[191] cf Jeroslav Pelikan, *The Christian Tradition: A History of the Development of Doctrine,* Vol. 1, *The Emergence of the Catholic Tradition (100-600)* (University of Chicago Press, 1971), 157.

Part VII   *The Flood's Meaning for Today*

In times of trouble, many types of religion and false teachings flourish, but only those built on truth can foster the lasting togetherness that is needed for a community to survive. This explains the survival of biblical faith despite its worldly disadvantages and weakness. Because the Bible is about truth, faithfulness to its teachings is the key to creating and preserving the greater family and community essential for survival in the most difficult of times.

Truth is never popular because like a sword it cuts through and exposes our popular and private illusions. It is our nature to like those who tell us what we want to hear and dislike anyone who tells us the truth about our present condition, however much we may need it. The prophets of the Bible were never popular. We do not elect politicians who speak truth that has become politically incorrect, and nothing is ever so politically incorrect as the truth. For example, few want to acknowledge the conflict between pursuing profits, pleasure, and our own interests and doing what is right. Only naïve idealists expect academic, religious, business, or scientific organizations that depend on patrons, government, or profits to make truth their priority. Manifestly, neither the ways of the world nor of the establishments of the present world are ways of truth. As Jesus explained, the way to truth and life is narrow and few find it.[192]

Because the Bible is the book of truth, those who refer to the plain meaning of its words are unpopular. Jesus' Second Coming is an especially unpopular part of the Bible because it is about judgment or accountability. However important and profitable it may be for ourselves and for the world, none of us enjoy accountability. We love Jesus when he tells us *not* to judge, but not when he is the Judge. The Scriptures tell us to leave judgment to God, but God has appointed a day – the great and terrible Day of the Lord – when he will judge the world by Jesus. That is when he comes to purify the world to prepare it for his long reign of peace.

At his first coming, Jesus declared that the words he spoke then, and which his Apostles recorded for us as our Scriptures, will judge us on that Day.[193] The Scriptures judge us because they *are* in truth God's inspired words. The way to save the things upon which we have spent our labor and time, if not our very lives, is to allow the Word of God to judge us *before* that Day. That requires total surrender to the Word of God. It effectively ends one's present life and associations, however fit one may suppose them for God's Kingdom. One exchanges his old life for a new and better life in the Spirit, which God freely gives to all who believe and ask. Only those who make such a complete commitment fit properly into the body of believers led by the Spirit of the living Jesus, and will

---

[192] Matthew 7:13-14; Luke 13:23-24
[193] John 12:48

rule and reign with Christ, but everyone who humbles himself in his inmost heart to the Lordship of the risen Jesus will be saved.

For whatever part of our lives that has not been devoted to the Lord, judgment comes on the great Day – the baptism of fire or the "great tribulation" that comes on the whole earth. The Word of God is indeed the Ark of salvation for that great and terrible Day of the Lord. Those purified on that Day will become a light visible to the whole earth. That which will preserve our lives on the Day of the Lord is the same Word that has preserved the community of faith until the present day.

At the time of Jesus, Second Temple Judaism provided a community for the survival of Jews throughout the world. In a world dangerous to travelers and strangers unaccompanied by armies, Jews could expect to find a synagogue or Jewish community in every city. Jews who were in great danger or need could find refuge and help from their community in whatever country they happened to find it. The earliest Christians were Jews, but their devotion to one another exceeded that of their brothers. Christianity became victorious in the Roman Empire and in Europe because Christian community survived as Jewish and Roman institutions fragmented and collapsed. The early Christians had no armies. They were victorious not only by surviving but by thriving during the collapse of the ancient world.

Christianity continued to be the glue that held together Western Europe turning it from one of the most backwards to the most prosperous region of the world. The same biblical faith was also the pot that melded together early Americans from various nations of Europe. Though divided by ethnicities and denominations, the core communities in those days held allegiance to the Bible. Like ancient Israel, upon which early Americans modeled their society, America prospered.

Also like the Israelites who imagined their prosperity to be the work of their own hands,[194] Europeans and Americans turned from the faith by crediting their wealth and security to their institutions, military strength, and science. As our biblical foundations crumble it becomes increasingly clear that not only is the West's relative prosperity being challenged, but so are the world's general prosperity and security. Ideologies, political parties, and all our institutions – whether secular, commercial or religious – that have purported to replace the biblical foundations are no substitute for them.

As I noted in the first chapter, by abandoning the literal belief in the Bible upon which Christian identity and community depend, Christians too have become increasingly divided, usually in the same ways as the world is divided.

---

[194] Deuteronomy 8:17

Part VII   *The Flood's Meaning for Today*

This indicates that Christians hold other things to be more important than their common faith. Whatever they are, the greater attachment reveals them as idols.

Some abandon the Bible for a supposed "Jesus" who is manifestly not the Jesus of the Scriptures. No such Jesus can save us. Non-Christian religions – Islam, Judaism, and Hinduism – also acknowledge another Jesus. From the time of the Gnostics until today many have wanted to deny the fleshly or earthly Jesus who is known only from the witnesses in the New Testament. Their fruit is the same as those who have denied the Old Testament and the historicity of our faith. We can neither separate the Bible from Jesus, nor separate Jesus from the Word of God contained in the Bible.

> **We can neither separate the Bible from Jesus, nor separate Jesus from the Word of God contained in the Bible.**

Though the incarnation or fleshly appearance of Jesus is found only in the New Testament, the Spirit of Christ who inspired the Apostles also inspired the Prophets who wrote the Old Testament. Thus from beginning to end, the Scriptures are Messianic. The entire special revelation we call the Bible is the proclamation of the Word of God given for salvation. We must therefore return to the strict truth of the Bible, the very oracles of God.

These same Scriptures also foretold the great turning from the faith that would occur among those who formerly believed. The generation of the Last Days began at Jesus' first coming. They will not pass away until everything concerning them has been fulfilled. Fortunately, that includes not just the great turning from the faith, but also the proclamation of the gospel of the kingdom to all the peoples of the world.[195]

The latter will require an end-time revival and a church more glorious than any since the days of the Apostles. Thus, just as Scriptures foretell the great darkness that appears at the end of the present age, they also declare that there will then be a great light.[196] In a dark world, this light from Jesus will

Figure 58   **The Jesus who came in the flesh**

---

[195] Matthew 24:14
[196] Matthew 13:40-43

shine through a church built on the solid Rock: the Word of God. However small it may be, a truly united body of Christ will enjoy the Spiritual power and effectiveness that believers haven't experienced since the days of the Apostles.

— 36 —

What the Scriptures literally say

Though themselves coherent and true, the Scriptures do not provide the single faith that can build Christians into a united body unless we understand them the same way, or at least in coherent or non-contradictory ways. Some tell us that the Bible cannot function as the common basis for Christian faith because it must be interpreted.[197] We should qualify such pronouncements by pointing out that indeed the Bible cannot provide a common basis for our faith if it is spun by interpretation rather than these inspired words being taken at face value. To do the latter we must read and believe the divinely inspired Scriptures literally, that is as meaning just what they say.

No one's communication fails to say what it means on its face unless it is poorly communicated or deliberately encrypted. Though some seem to believe it so, God's revelation to all mankind would not be poorly communicated. Nor would it be given to us in code. We need someone to translate the Scriptures into the various languages that we understand today, but it is presumptuous for anyone to put any meaning on them other than that intended by the very words and Spirit of the Scriptures. Surely the God who made man is sufficiently articulate to communicate without patronizing human interpreters.

This does not deny that a literal understanding of the Scriptures is sometimes challenging, especially for those who do not believe. To take the Scriptures at face value, we must first understand the Scriptures, and that also entails believing them. The things the Scriptures say range from natural or ordinary things that anyone can comprehend to deep things that are impossible to understand without spiritual maturity. To understand the latter, we need an increasing amount of light from Jesus, which comes only from the fellowship of his suffering.

---

[197] cf Ronald H. Bainton on 'sola Scriptura,' *The Cambridge History of the Bible*, Vol. 3, *The West from the Reformation to the Present Day* (Cambridge University Press, 1963), 1.

Nor is this to deny that we read the Bible with presuppositions, as must be the case with any communication, but these presuppositions ought themselves to be those of the Bible. Scholars call this proper *exegesis* or contextual reading, which they contrast with *eisegesis* (or *isogesis*), that is to interpret the Bible through some light that is external to the inspired Scriptures. The context must not only be that of the passage surrounding the text, but the context of the entire canon. We must also understand the Scriptures as communication to us from the only true and living God. Regardless of the pretensions of unbelieving scholars, it is impossible to understand the Scriptures aside from the true church or believing community![198] Faith is key to obtaining the Holy Spirit present in the community of believers, but not among scholars who read the Scriptures in the light of the world they understand. In Chapter 39, I will explain how believers may come to a common understanding that transcends the various traditions through which we have come to understand the Bible.

My original purpose in reading the Scriptures just as I would any communication was to understand the Bible so I could fairly refute the book still cherished by the "uneducated." The unexpected but joyful discovery of what the Scriptures plainly declare led me to hold a literal understanding of the Bible in high esteem. Afterwards, I could not in good conscience turn from a plain understanding in the case of those Scriptures that troubled me. Jesus took the historical passages in the early chapters of Genesis as referring to events in human history. Even though science and the modern world have challenged the literal truth of the early chapters of Genesis, I had to embrace them as intending to be history. Happily, this straightforward and simple way of reading the Bible also led to a better understanding of history and science. The Scriptures are indeed a great light if we trust them enough to use them.

A literal understanding of the Bible has often been derided as lacking sophistication. This is hardly the case, even if a literal understanding is in fact the simplest way of understanding the Scriptures. Strictly speaking, a contextual literal reading is not an interpretation and it is the only kind of reading that is not, explaining why the best scholars try to understand their text in this simplest and most straightforward way. As I explained in Chapter 4, the scholars of the Renaissance revived a literal understanding of the Scriptures. They taught Christians to read the Scriptures as if they were speaking directly to people today. That led to the Reformation, scholars and professors in the lead.

One reason for a negative view of literal understanding is that the term *literal* is ambiguous. It carries numerous meanings, many of them contradicting one another, and several of them even contradicting what the Scriptures literally

---

[198] I appreciate Les Scofield for pointing this out and insisting that it remain central to our understanding.

teach! In the sense I recommend, a literal understanding refers to the meaning of the words read in the context of the passages as they appear in the Bible, and in the light of the Jesus who is revealed in the Bible. In this sense, a literal understanding is not an interpretation, but opposed to interpreting (or deflecting) the Scriptures' plain meaning.

A method of *literal* interpretation that I do not embrace gives meaning to individual letters and words apart from the context in which they appear in the Scriptures. Developed by medieval rabbis, this method also influenced medieval Christian interpreters. Cabbalists developed an extreme form of this focus on the letter rather than the meaning of the text and some even claimed that secret messages were coded in the very letters and form of Scriptures. Messages actually contrary to the Scriptures were taught by interpreting individual words and sentences through ancient commentaries. Endless commentaries and commentaries on commentaries from rabbinic and church traditions gave teachings actually contrary to the Scriptures the veneer of ancient authority. An "amplified" Bible is in fact a diminished Bible because it adds to the inspired words of Scripture the light of men. We still see these commentary Bibles today, but a Bible published with interpretations (not meaning translation or historical notes) of what the Scriptures mean is corruption or additions to the biblical text.

Another problem comes from supposing that some traditional interpretation is also the literal interpretation, especially when, as is usually the case, the traditional interpretation has been specifically championed as the literal interpretation. Traditional interpretations that are not in fact literally taught by the Scriptures will seem literal readings for those who were trained to read the Scriptures in such a light. This is because the traditional light by which Scriptures are interpreted function as unconscious paradigms, as I explained in Chapter 12.[199] We will not be aware that our unconscious assumptions are external to the biblical text until we encounter other ways of reading the Scriptures.

As I noted, proponents [~~opponents~~] of the Bible hold up the Young Earth Creationists' twenty-four-hour-day reading of the days of Genesis as the foremost example of "biblical literalism." Most today assume that is indeed the natural and literal reading of these passages because our modern age has taught us to read it like that and because this reading is pronounced as clearly a "natural" reading by presumed authorities who cannot possibly know what they confidently pronounce. The duration of the days of Creation looms large in current readings, though until Isaac Newton brought the subject up, in reading those passages believers focussed on the fact of Creation, the Creator himself, and what was specifically created in various days. Regardless of their duration, and however

---

[199] See Figure 14C. Author continues to speak of Biblical literalism, while constantly denying it. He only believes the word of the Bible when it supports his belief.

interesting the question of their duration, they are necessarily "literal" days if in fact God did create the world and in just the order given.

The passages in Genesis do not in fact literally declare them to be 24 hours in duration (or solar days), but of course one can defend those days as being 24 hours in duration from other passages of Scripture. Some point out that the Lord instructed the Israelites to observe the Sabbath to remember that the Lord created the earth in six days and rested on the seventh. But we can challenge that interpretation by noting that the means by which we remember need only be a token of that which we remember. For example, by the Lord's Supper, the broken bread and cup, we remember his death and suffering until he comes. We can also use other Scriptures to support extended days of Creation, for example, pointing to those that say that God continues to rest from the seventh day of that first week.[200] One of those first seven days has lasted for about six thousand years. I don't think the duration of the days was the point he had in mind. If so, the seventh would have been something of an exception. But it does appear that the legalistic controversies pertaining to the Sabbath that afflicted Jesus days on earth persist to the present day.

FIGURE 59 LIGHT *ON* THE SCRIPTURES OR LIGHT *FROM* THE SCRIPTURES?

A more common misunderstanding of literal interpretation is to conflate *literal* understanding with *natural* or this-worldly understanding – even when the Scriptures literally declare the opposite. This is not an issue when it comes to historical events such as Noah's Flood where the natural and literal meaning are the same, in which case anyone from unbelievers to small children can understand. Though not everyone believes in the historicity of Noah's Flood, even children can understand the account. Everyone (aside from modern theologians) understands that the account is intended to convey an episode in the his-

---

[200] Hebrews 4:10

tory of man. Nor for most people is there a problem understanding Scriptures that refer to ordinary and visible things, and to matters pertaining to the visible world. On the other hand, the Scriptures also speak of invisible or spiritual things that cannot be comprehended by anything that has appeared in history, even if these passages of Scripture must necessarily use words referring to things that are or have been visible.

Spiritual maturity follows our development from a natural to a spiritual understanding. As the Scriptures suggest, the natural comes first.[201] From birth, we learn to understand things in a natural way, the way the world – at least, that part of the world that we come to know – understands things. This allows us to function in the present world, but a spiritual understanding, one that sees things according to God's purposes and values, will be contrary to how the world values and sees things. None of us are spiritual when we first hear the message of the gospel, though if our hearts are sincere we can understand the historical message in the Bible and the great examples there of faith, hope, and love. As Jesus explained to Nicodemus, we must first believe the earthly things pertaining to the Kingdom of God before we can understand spiritual things. What is true of our individual spiritual growth is also true of the order of God's revelation. Israel's experience under the Old Covenant created the language necessary to communicate the New Covenant. Then God became flesh so that earthly men might know him. As we die with Christ to the things of the earth – having submitted our desires to Christ and becoming indifferent to what interests the world – we resurrect with him as spiritual beings.

When applied to prophecy, assuming some natural meaning to be the literal meaning often result in obsolete or bizarre messages with little meaning other than mechanical fulfillment.[202] Contrary to the literal words of Scripture, some suppose that these prophecies refer to matters of ancient history while others suppose a future fulfilment in a way that Jesus or the Apostles did not teach. This was an important issue around the time of the Reformation when, attempting to translate the Scriptures and return to a literal understanding of the Scriptures, the Reformers had to learn Hebrew from Jewish rabbis. During the Middle Ages, the Karaites and rabbis had developed what was then called the *Judaica exposito,* and since then there has been a tendency of Hebraists to suppose this the literal interpretation of the Scriptures. The rabbis supposed certain Old Testament prophecies to apply to the prophets' own times, denying any oracular meaning, or when they did allow a future fulfilment beyond their own day they supposed it to require a worldly messiah instead of a suffering servant

---

[201] 1 Corinthians 15:46

[202] For numerous examples of such a mechanical fulfillment of prophecy, cf Paul Lee Tan, *A Pictorial Guide to Biblical Prophecy* (Bible Communications, 1991).

like Jesus. The *Judaica exposito* is in fact more often a natural or this-worldly interpretation which for that reason might indeed be favored by a scientific mind, but it is not how Jesus, the Apostles, the Early Church, and the Second Temple Jews who wrote some of the Dead Sea Scrolls read and explained prophecy. All these interpreted the Scriptures in a Christological sense.

Following the great French scholar, Jacque Lefevre d'Etaples (1455-1536), Martin Luther distinguished two types of literal interpretation: the literal-historical sense and the literal-prophetic sense.[203] The latter is essentially the Christological sense. Here the historical matters serve as types for the spiritual realities. Even among these two senses there were levels of meaning. To depict these different understandings, Luther used the example of Mount Zion. Mount Zion was an ancient barren mountaintop in ancient Israel. It also referred to the central place of worship in ancient Israel. It could be a name for those who assembled in Jerusalem for worship of God. Finally, it refers to the Church, or to the Heavenly assembly. I would add that more precisely, it referred to the Church of Jesus' Apostles, wherein the gospel went out to the nations.[204] All these are literal meanings of Mount Zion, though some are natural and historical and some are spiritual and Heavenly. But today, some proponents of popular prophecy limit the meaning of Zion (or Jerusalem) to a certain geographical spot in the Middle East.

If we take the Scriptures literally, and if they are to have meaning for believers, it is necessary to understand the prophecies Christologically. The Apostle Paul claims that the Apostles were speaking spiritual truths to spiritual men using spiritual words. Notwithstanding what the Apostle plainly says, some stand the message of the Kingdom of God on its head by making a virtue of reducing the spiritual things in the Scriptures to a carnal understanding on the grounds of not "spiritualizing" away the Scriptures. What they may mean is that they do not want to *allegorize* away the Scriptures. They may have seen the error of conflating the Kingdom of God with some transcendent ideal that removes it from visible actualization in history: the promised historical advent and Kingdom of God when the saints will visibly reign with Jesus in the earth. But those like Origen and Augustine who denied a future Millennium also denied the historicity or literal truth of the Scripture when referring to the theophanies in the book of Genesis and to other descriptions of God and Heaven in the Scriptures that they found to be too anthropomorphic and embarrassing. In fact, this does not address a matter of spiritualizing but one of changing the message of

---

[203] For a recent discussion of this, cf Alister McGrath, "The Patristic Testimony. In *The Intellectual Origins of the European Reformation* (Blackwell, 1987).

[204] Interestingly and appropriately, the principle physical assembly of the Apostolic Church seems to have literally been on the Mount Zion section of ancient Jerusalem.

Scripture to philosophy by viewing it as an allegory. Origen and Augustine and others who followed them falsely claimed to be giving the spiritual sense of the Scripture and wrongly claimed a future Millennium of an earthly rule of the saints to be a "carnal" understanding. A literal Millennium does not have to be a carnal Millennium, that is, a future Millennium focussed on carnal affairs, even if popular prophecy today seems to conceive it just that way.

Origen and Augustine's kind of allegorization was invented by the pagan Greeks in Alexandria, Egypt to rationalize the embarassing behavior of their pagan gods as found in Homer, the sacred writings of the Greeks.[205] Philo the Jew, Origen the Christian, and all the Jews and Christians who have followed them have denied the historicity and literal truth of Scriptures by declaring them to be allegories for a transcendent and abstractly understood God. Whereas the pagan Greeks used the method of allegory to explain away the embarrassing behavior of their gods, Jews and Christians used allegories to explain away what they have seen as the embarrassing anthropomorphic depictions of God in the Scriptures. Their error and the reason for their embarrassment was to suppose the literal depiction of God in the Scriptures to be referring to fleshly rather than spiritual realities. Unable to understand or accept them as spiritual but appropriately described real entities, they simply supposed them to be allegories for some aspects of their transcendent and abstract philosophical "God."

Whereas in Scripture fleshly and historical things may be types of spiritual things, the spiritual things they depict are no less concrete, in fact, even more real than the physical things used for the depictions. This typological language must be distinguished from the willful allegorizing of those such as Origen who reject the Scriptures as referring to literal spiritual realities. Allegories may be useful for illustrating the plan of God in the Scriptures, but they can also be used to avoid the convicting words of the Scripture by changing its message to philosophy in order to accommodate Christianity to worldly thinking and ways. The Gnostics aimed to entirely replace the historical faith of the Bible with philosophy but, as I explained in Chapter 4, Christian theologians also allegorized away the plain meaning of Scriptures when they turned to philosophy for understanding the faith. Though they claimed that they were staying faithful to the literal sense of the Scriptures, even preferring it as the primary sense, that meant only that they saw the necessity of allegorizing away the literal meaning rather than dismissing it as did the Gnostics. But their philosophical and allegorical teachings which they claimed as the spiritual meaning ran contrary to the inspired words of Scripture, to the Spirit, and to the truth.

---

[205] Likely this concern arose when the pagan Greeks encountered the high moral character and concerns of the Lord God in the biblical Scriptures in this same city and during this same era.

These false claims for a spiritual understanding in no way refute the fact that Jesus and the Apostles taught a spiritual and presently otherworldly Kingdom of God and the fact that they used the historical language of Scripture as types or references to these spiritual realities. As the book of Hebrews explains, the earthly or natural patterns of the Kingdom of God as revealed to Moses are only a shadow or type of the spiritual realities in Heaven. Likewise, the earthly Kingdom of Israel ruled by King David was but a shadow of the Kingdom of Heaven promised in the Scriptures: the Israel of God as it will one day be manifested in the earth. Regardless of the fact that the unbeliever, the natural or worldly mind, finds the Scriptures foolish, incomprehensible, or false, the inspired Scriptures *literally* teach that they have spiritual rather than natural or worldly meaning.[206]

The eighteenth-century British scholar Robert Lowth (1710-1787) discovered that frequent use of parallelisms suggested that much of the Old Testament Scriptures were originally composed as poetry. Whether originally composed in this fashion, parallelism certainly makes for easier memorization, which is why meter and rhyme were commonly used in ancient times for oral compositions. It is reasonable to suppose that oral composition styles influenced the written style of the Bible, but to German scholars of the nineteenth century, *poetry* suggested that the Old Testament was *romantic* (imaginative) poetry. Discovery of Ancient Near Eastern poetry with similar language and motifs as that of Genesis seemed to settle the question that many of the Old Testament passages were in fact myth.

Some of these myths drew on sagas pertaining to sea monsters, themselves the imaginative product of battles with creatures living in the sea. According to scholars who supposed that the ancient Sumerians lived in a watery plain, that they imagined a world composed of water was a natural conclusion, and it explained why the Scriptures declare that the world itself was formed out of water.

These are some of the same passages that I have taken literally to develop the geology and cosmology in Chapters 30 and 31. Of course, I projected this light of Genesis on the way we currently understand our modern cosmos. Doubtless those of the Ancient Near East envisioned the cosmos in the terms that they knew, but the accounts of a world being formed by a divine Creator from water are essentially the same. The "monster of the sea" is of course the Great Dragon or ancient serpent called Satan. In the Scriptures, the sea also refers to peoples, languages, and nations, that is to say to the Gentiles or to the world under the sway of Satan.[207] It seems that the struggles to birth the Creation mirror those to birth the New Creation.

---

[206] John 3:10-12; 1Corinthians 2:13-14
[207] Revelation 17:15

Part VII   *The Flood's Meaning for Today*

We should not be surprised to learn that a water-based cosmology was present not only in the Bible, but prevalent throughout the Ancient Near East. The early chapters of Genesis were not, as some traditionalists seem to assert, to create but rather to restore knowledge of God and the earliest history of man. Can we imagine that Noah knew nothing of the truth that had been owned by his recent ancestors, some of whom walked with the Lord? It seems evident that Noah passed this knowledge on because native peoples throughout the world still preserve remnants of a teaching that sees the world formed of chaos and of water. It is now clear that these teachings are reliably preserved only in the early chapters of the Bible. Regardless of the fact that the ancients had no way of viewing the extent of the universe, their water-based cosmology was in truth a superior understanding of the essence of the greater cosmos than are the latest scientific myths.

Since the nineteenth century, the supposed disproof of the early chapters of Genesis has been the chief excuse for attacking a literal understanding – really, for attacking the Scriptures. Hence this book has focused on the historical truth of the Scriptures. Moderns have also challenged the moral message of the Scriptures. Today, it is popular to attack a literal reading of the Scriptures by quoting the Law of Moses: the severe punishments necessary for the survival of a tribal society; and the ceremonial prescriptions necessary to safeguard the separateness of God's servants. Firstly, these charges assume that modern man is a competent judge of a people, an era, and a God he does not know. But these charges are made as if the Scriptures did not teach the New Covenant that followed the death of Jesus, the mercy of God and the great softening of society benefiting from the influence of biblical Christianity.

As in the case of a young earth, outdated cosmologies of a flat earth, a column-supported sky, or an earth-centered universe have been claimed as literal readings of the Scriptures. European professors taught that the ancient world of the Bible was enveloped in crude myths, marking "the childhood of early man." According to them, things outside the European experience or that are not believed by learned professors simply could never have existed. Hearing this spoken with the authority of an imperial officer, as was the manner of the university professors in Germany, must have intimidated and impressed the minds of their young students who brought their manner of pronouncing dogma to the universities of America. Saying it so makes it so? Having rejected that the God of the Bible had this power, these professors assumed it for themselves.

Projecting what are now seen as primitive scientific views onto the words of the God of the Bible is patronizing and arrogant. Falsely rationalized by the dogma of historical distance, those charges are disingenuous, unreflective, and pedantic. Hardly as critical as they claim to be, modernists tend to believe in the finality of the latest scientific cosmology as much as earlier scientists, the Aristotelians, believed in their earth-centered universe. Everyone is limited in his understanding, but the Scriptures serve as a light to develop an increasingly deeper understanding of the world that God created.[208] Fortunately, rather than using changing cosmologies or specialized scientific terms, the inspired words of the Bible speak from the universal human perspective that we still use today.

The Scriptures are in fact not imaginative poetry. They refer to the determinative spiritual reality that underlies and sustains the physical world. Because we live in bodies with physical limitations, physical things seem far more important than they are. Science implies that ultimate reality can be measured by our dull physical instruments and our senses and understood by reductionist, scientistic thinking. Materialistic thinking is in fact the way that children think. In truth, the world that we experience with our physical bodies and understand with our present minds is but a faint reflection version of the spiritual reality of invisible Heaven.

Yet, contrary to what philosophers such as Plato, Augustine, and Aquinas have taught, the spiritual world that our physical eyes fail to see is no less concrete than the world that we know from our fleshly senses. Far from the vague abstractions and ideal forms preferred by these philosophers, it is more specific and detailed, far richer, more concrete and meaningful than the world we know from our physical senses and understanding. It is no less real and no less rich with significance than the greatest events of human history – the latter having been great for the very reason that they also involved the participation of Heaven. Beyond the understanding of scientists and the imagination of the philosophers, that more fundamental reality can only be experienced, and the joyful part of that experience comes only through the presence of God's Spirit given to those who trust his eternal Word. Thus, we should not be surprised by the reactions of those who experience God in his glory. Theophanies recorded throughout the Scriptures reveal that God's presence overwhelms all but the pure in heart.[209]

The Bible teaches that God sustains the world by his powerful Word. Though spiritual, such words are literally true. Our physical cosmos is literally subject to the Lord's commands. The underlying spiritual reality can transform our physical world, as in the case of miracles, and at the time of the Flood. Someday the presently visible world will be removed, but the Word of God will remain forever.[210] The Lord has indicated that the visible world *will* change at his Sec-

---

[208] 2 Peter 1:19
[209] Judges 6:22; Isaiah 6:5; Luke 5:8; Matthew 5:8
[210] Isaiah 50:9

ond Coming.[211] Everything but the Kingdom of God will then be shaken. To be sure, it seems that the physical structure of our world has already changed several times since his first coming. I refer to the world as experienced by those in the Bible, then as learned Christians shifted successively to the views of Plato, to Aristotle, to Isaac Newton, all the way to our postmodern world of today. Our world will change yet again. Quantum physicists understand that the physical world does in fact depend on the way that we perceive and experience it. If the way that we perceive the world also changes the world, this does not, as suggested by the Eastern religions, deny the reality of the physical world, nor does it deny God's concern for the same. It only means that it is not the physical world that is the ground of our being but instead the unchanging Word of God.

Yet the greatest problem in understanding the Scriptures does not stem from the mistaken literal meanings supposed by scholars but from theologians and sectarians who advocate *non-literal* interpretations. They insist on ignoring the plain words of the Scriptures and interpreting them through some kind of theology or religious tradition. But those who challenge the plain sense of the Scriptures require the words to be read in some light other than the words of the God of the Bible. Because interpretation determines meaning, any interpreter who is not God effectively replaces the light of God. Whether it be a religious authority, a government court, an expert or professional, our own opinion, or our most trusted friend, our ultimate interpreter – the authority whom we refuse to question or to whom we cannot appeal – becomes effectively our light or our "God."

If the literal or straightforward meaning of a text makes perfect sense, why would anyone propose a non-literal meaning? The reason can only be that one does not understand, does not believe, or does not like what the text plainly says; or else wants it to say something that it plainly does not. None of these are valid reasons for rejecting the plain meaning of the inspired Scriptures. The motive for avoiding a literal interpretation of the Scriptures is always present for those who are not completely devoted to God because the Scriptures plainly require our complete submission.

We would show disrespect to any great and honorable official or person by not taking his words at face value. How much more the inspired words of God! If we are still in rebellion to God, we want to avoid his words by explaining them away, whether by reducing them to allegories or by deflecting their application from speaking to us and our condition, assigning them instead to some other time or people. Theologians who explain away the troubling Scriptures have been highly esteemed. As I explained in Chapter 4, this occurred early in church history as the formerly otherworldly Christians became an accepted part

---

[211] Matthew 24:29; Isaiah 13:10

of the present world. In Chapter 38, I will explain some newer ways in which theologians deflect the inspired Scriptures from speaking directly to the hearts of Christians today.

So many conflicting interpretations may seem discouraging, but Jesus has promised to guide us if we seek him and remain faithful to what he has given us. Historians must also contend with conflicting accounts of the past. The renowned historian Herbert Butterfield (1900-1979) is reported to have remarked, "Hold fast to Jesus and question everything else." If this is the case for history, how much more so the Scriptures. Certainly those who insist that their light is the authoritative understanding of the Scriptures are playing or replacing God and are among the many false messiahs that Jesus prophesied would deceive the world. This is why the Messiah must be the only interpreter and why the body of Christ must necessarily be a priesthood of believers. Jesus is our only Master or Teacher. Thus, we read the entire Bible in the light of his words and his Spirit.

It seems that the proponents for non-literal interpretations of the Bible are chiefly sectarian zealots dividing the flock by drawing disciples to themselves instead of to the Scriptures and to the Spirit of the living Jesus.[212] They want to make the Bible agree with what they teach. Sectarian churches are those who preach and teach their church, their ministry, or their theology rather than Christ and the Scriptures. These of course see other churches as sects or cults. But God's Church is the Jerusalem above to which we all belong when we worship him in Spirit and in truth. Whenever we do this, *God's* church becomes visible to the people of the earth.

---

[212] Acts 20:29, 30. My appreciation to Jay Ferris's monograph, "Grievous Wolves" for pointing this out.

— 37 —

Restoring biblical community as a light to a world in trouble

BIBLICAL FAITH IS unique among religions in God's special concern for human beings, not only for their afterlife but also the welfare and future of those living in the earth. It is natural that this should be the case since the Lord God is the Creator and only God. Of all his creatures, he made only man in his own image. Unlike the impersonal and distant Creator "God" of the philosophers, the God of history, having plans for his Creation, remains active in the affairs of the earth. This makes the behavior of human beings, including our government, education, and welfare uniquely his concern. This does not mean that God either programs or compels his creatures to obey him. Like the father of the prodigal son, he allows us to pursue our own destiny, and if ever we see the error of our ways, he joyfully welcomes our return.[213] God does not wish us to serve him merely out of fear or compulsion, but because we truly appreciate his love. This means that true biblical faith is and has always been voluntary, but this voluntary character of faith means that God's servants must separate from those of the world who are pursuing their own ways.

Even if faith in God is voluntary, at some point and at some time there must be an accounting of all mankind if for no other reason than the pain, suffierring, and injustice caused by disobedience and wickedness. This accounting begins first in the earth and first among the family of God to prepare them for the return of Jesus.[214] God's judgment of the earth begins at that time, to be followed by a long era of rightousness and peace. Though many have ignored the promise of Jesus' Second Coming, it is God's plan that invisible Heaven join visible earth. He plans to restore the paradise lost due to man's first rebellion. Preparation for God's restoration also began long ago with the calling of Abra-

---

[213] Luke 15.
[214] 1Peter 4:17; 1 Corinthians 6:3

ham when first he separated the servants of God from the people of the earth. The restoration of all the nations began at the first coming of Jesus. Since that time, the faith has been gradually spreading throughout the earth.

Though we may not like what we presently see, though as at the time of the Flood God himself may not like what he sees, it is a fact that the Lord himself, only Son of the Most High God, is now ultimate ruler even of our fallen world, and has been since his resurrection from the dead.[215] Were the Lord not the highest ruler, it may be pointless for us to pray, for he would not necessarily have the power to grant our requests. He does in fact appoint and ultimately command the governments of the present world. Although our allegiance is to the Word of God, Christians must honor and respect the governments of the present world for their function of providing security and defense in a world that does not fear God. Because they serve people of all religions or none, these governments also provide public services such as roads and economic infrastructure. To pay for these things, they collect taxes. Regardless of the earthly means by which these governments establish and preserve their power, the Lord raises them up and puts them down. Wise governments understand the fragility of their power, and how much their rule depends on circumstances that only God controls.

Though it can preserve order in a fallen world, there are limits to worldly power, the most important being that it cannot change the hearts of men. As Jesus explains, worldly governments (kings) give favors so as to be known as benefactors.[216] We should not be surprised that genuine concern for those outside one's own family, servants, or tribe – even for those who are not concerned about us and who we may even regard as enemies – is uniquely rooted in the faith of the Bible. Until modern times when governments influenced by Christianity replaced them, only Christians provided what are now known as the human services: education of the masses and care for the poor, the sick, widows, orphans, and strangers – provisions for the physical as well as spiritual needs of the weaker members of societies, those whom the pagans exploited or discarded. In recent times, Christians in America have largely forfeited to the secular government their traditional responsibility for peaceful and humanitarian services, even for services to the Christian community! Americans did so with widespread belief that we were giving up these functions to Christian governments – local, state, and federal.

Due to their nation's birth in the wake of the Reformation, Americans have somewhat of a special history with regard to the Bible. If the Protestant state churches of Europe soon abandoned the principle of *sola Scriptura*, not so for

---

[215] Mathew 28:18; Ephesians 4:8-10; Colossians 2:10
[216] Luke 22:25

many who fled to America. The thirteen colonies differed even from other English-speaking colonies in the Caribbean, Canada, and later in other parts of the world due to the fact that these colonies specifically harbored religious refugees. This was perhaps the first time since the formation of ancient Israel that a nation was created from religious refugees, in both cases the refugees focusing on the God of the Bible. Another thing making America different is that many of the refugees, such as the Pilgrims of Plymouth Rock, sought separation even from a nominally Christian state church and society as those of England and Holland. Separation of church and state was thus built into the consciousness of many Americans long before the composition of the US Constitution. Americans therefore preferred from the beginning that they be served by a government that restricted its concerns to matters of the present world: military defense, international affairs, interstate commerce, and physical infrastructure such as roads and canals. They were also things in which scientific knowledge was important. In the formative days of the new nation, education was still in the hands of the churches and that education was at least nominally based on the Bible. Few Americans saw the possibility that scientific knowledge and biblical knowledge, both concerned with truth, would ever conflict.

This conflict was already developing in Europe, as I have explained in this book, but Americans were long insulated from these developments. Late in the nineteenth century, influential Americans sought to replace the Bible with scientific teaching and state-sponsored schools modeled on those of Germany. Also following Germany, they sought to replace Christian community based on the Bible with nationalism or patriotism. They explained all this as "progress." Because of this the universities and public schools of America developed into competitors to America's traditional faith. Supposing they were separating church and state, they only created a new established "church," and one that has became ever more hostile to its main competitor: faith and understanding based on the Bible. However one may view this, whoever or whatever takes on the role of teaching society has become its new priesthood. In effect, America has developed an established church teaching a statist version of truth in what amounts to a rival religion.

Whether the American government was ever truly Christian and for whatever cause they ceased to be so, it is no longer the case. Moreover, the matter is no longer an *American* issue because both the American system of government and Christianity have spread thoughout the world. Most importantly, Christians today have given up their traditional teaching functions – including the discovery and determination of knowledge – to the scientific and secular priesthood as now recognized by Western nations. Considering that Christians were so long the world's teachers, this is as astonishing as it is appalling. Pushed

Chapter 37 Restoring biblical community as a light to a world in trouble

into the religious ghetto, churches seem to have become content with telling those who believe them how to go to heaven. Because the world has no good answers for what follows death, it doesn't much mind if Christians limit their concerns to death. But addressing the issues of death more than those of life is certainly not *biblical* faith. It seems that Christianity in America is no longer much concerned to be a light to the world, no longer rejoices in being persecuted for the sake of the gospel, and no longer much tries to reach out to the other fragmented parts of Christianity so as to be a more effective witness. Some Christian leaders, calling for cultural relevance, wish Christians to become one more party in an increasingly divided world, but the world only the more despises Christians who imitate them.

For those who worship the great and living God of the Bible, conformity to the world is a contemptible end. Ironically, today the world teaches and influences the church. The church no longer teaches or influences the world. The world has become the head. The church has become the tail. In fact, this is just the fate God promised his disobedient children.[217] Though the modern world increasingly teaches the church not to see itself in terms of Old Testament prophecies, what believers face from the world today was put forth long ago in the Scriptures:

> Your tormentors… said to you, "Fall prostrate that we may walk over you." And you made your back like the ground, like a street to be walked over. [Is. 51:23]

This passage goes on to call God's church to awake, shake off the dust, loosen the chains from her neck, be clothed with strength, put on her garments of splendor, and sit enthroned with the King. But we cannot do so until we understand and confess that we are dirty from sin, ineffective for the purposes that God intended for us, and that it is unacceptable for us to be so. Refusing to acknowledge our need to repent is due to pride, a most un-Christian vice and one that greatly displeases God. Religious pride only keeps Christians in the dirt, but humility and repentance in the form of genuine change are prerequisites for restoration. We must confess that the calamity besetting us is not at its root because of the world, which God uses to correct his own erring children; or due to a lack in God's power for helping us; or due to his lack of interest in changing the world, but it is due to an unbelieving and sinful church! All today's Christians can truthfully say is that Jesus Christ has faithfully loved us, even if we have not been faithful to him.

Repentance entails that Christians, once again, separate from the world. This no longer means heading into a wilderness to build a new nation, but separating from worldly institutions, even worldly religious institutions, especially where

---

[217] Deuteronomy 28:44

participation requires compromise. Separation from the world certainly does not mean that Christians should separate from other Christians who are fully devoted to the Lord. Such separation was a leading cause of forfeiting education and social responsibility to the secular governments. In ancient Israel, local idols threatened the unity of the ancient biblical faith. Today any tradition, organization, or authority that keeps Christians from being united in the Word and Spirit of the living Jesus – which puts sect or tradition, institutional, or local church or ministry ahead of the unity of the body of Christ – is an idol.[218] There may be different tribes in God's Israel, but the good things in various traditions are good only if they are subservient to the Word and Spirit that unifies Christians into one body. The Temple of God is a house of prayer for *all* people.[219]

The Scriptures tell us that sectarian separation is evidence of worldliness.[220] Selfishness, jealousy, and religious pride cause Christians and leaders to avoid accountability and fellowship with other Christians. Folks seem more important in their small worlds away from the greater light that is present in the unity of Christ and his people, but in the sunlight of Christ individual stars are hard to see. The recent challenges to Christianity from the world makes it clear that the fortune of the greater Christian community is more important than whether our separate denominations, churches, or ministries succeed or fail. We must have first in our hearts the greater work of the kingdom of God in the earth. Christ's royal blood – if we truly have it – gives us concern for his greater kingdom. In God's house, wherein the Lord himself is in charge, all God's children sense that they are home.

Our unity must not be in any earthly church or ministry but in Jesus and in strict submission to his words. Long misuse of the word *church* explains why I prefer *community* to refer to the unity of the body of Christ. Community points to the wider body of Christ, the communion of the saints in the kingdom of God. Those who are willing to be led by the Word of God in the Scriptures and by the Spirit of Jesus *will* be united. No one need organize or plan it because the living Jesus builds and adds to his church by the outpouring of his Spirit. Thus, we must not confuse the spirit of unity with the unity of the Spirit. The former is to replace the Spirit with human organization, which will always trump the loving and gentle Spirit of God in every institution. We must understand the spiritual nature of the Lord's church, and how to seek, wait on, and be led by the Spirit of Christ. No matter how busy and important we suppose ourselves to be, no one should be in a hurry when meeting with the

---

[218] cf Herbert Schlossberg, *Idols for Destruction: Christian Faith and its Confrontation with American Society* (Regnery Gateway, 1990).
[219] Isaiah 56:7; Mark 11:17
[220] 1 Corinthians 3:1-4

Chapter 37   Restoring biblical community as a light to a world in trouble

great ruler of heaven and earth. There is of course a need and a place for human organization, even more for leadership and correction, but where the Spirit of the living Jesus is present, organization and leaders bow to the Word and Spirit of Christ. This means that regardless of any institution's order and rules, leaders in God's House must be able to recognize and submit to the Word and Spirit of God, and expect others to do the same. However few, those led by the Spirit will become a light that the whole world will see. In the last days, the world will recognize them as Jesus' servants.

All restoration begins with widespread, heartfelt repentance. This includes all those who presently suppose they are "saved." No revival, either during or since the time of the Bible, has ever occurred without repentance from those who were accustomed to thinking themselves already saved or already in a satisfactory relationship with God. Not only does religious pride keep people from repenting, it turns them into enemies of God. But being "saved" will not excuse anyone from the promised baptism of fire that will test the authenticity of everyone's faith. The Scriptures make it clear that salvation requires us to remain faithful to the end.

As must now be clear, restoring truth to the foundation of the Bible requires wholesale revision to the way in which knowledge is discovered and imparted. This does not refer to technology and systems, though as in all other great eras of biblical and church history, providential technologies assist wholesale changes in teaching and communicating God's truth. In previous changes, it was the alphabet, the codex book, and printing press, but now it is the Internet. More importantly, the education of believers must return to a *separated* Christian community, one that is uncompromisingly built upon the Word of God. This requires a big shift in Christian self-understanding, and a return to how the church ought to function rather than how it has come to function. Despite the modern abandonment of key parts of its teaching function to science and the secular world, teaching the important truths regarding God, man, history, and the nature of the world is still the function of the Christian ministry. Believers must take back their historical functions for teaching – not just about God, but also about the origin and the nature of man and the world. These must be taught together. The truth concerning all these can only be known from the light of their Creator.

I am not addressing what the governments and institutions of the present world ought to do. They function by their own rules. Of course they can benefit from light and truth, and in fact, to survive and prosper it will be necessary that they find them. As the ancient world fell into darkness, governments found the church to be an essential ally. The Scriptures suggest that the surviving govern-

Part VII   The Flood's Meaning for Today

ments will once again look to the light of the church.[221] They will need the help of the church and the blessing of God, though hardly in the way presently thought: that is, to execute government plans and programs. The Scriptures clearly command believers to separate from the world. We are ambassadors from another Kingdom preparing this world for the arrival of our Sovereign, the Creator of all. When he does arrive, every eye will see and every tongue will confess the Lord of all the earth.

Authentic revival, the restoration of the family of God, always begins with the preaching of truth.[222] Thus the first thing in restoring Christian community is restoring truth to the church and people of our day. There are precedents for such wholesale shifts in understanding and teaching, shifts that have changed both the church and the world. Each began with a small group of reformers and each became the greatest of revivals. The Reformation was one such shift. Catholics teach that obedience to the Church is sufficient for salvation. To be saved, Catholics needed only to be obedient to the Church, but Protestants, teaching salvation by faith alone, had to understand and confess their beliefs.

FIGURE 60   ALCUIN OF YORK (735-804), FATHER OF EUROPE'S SCHOOLS

This explains why public preaching more than liturgy became the focus of Protestant churches. It also explains why the Reformation and eventually the Catholic Reformation as well initiated the modern systems of public education. The system of higher education that created the Enlightenment and the international scientific revolution developed from a small group of Puritan professors in seventeenth-century Cambridge, England, working together with Pietists from the Continent. Unfortunately, owing to pride in the success of that project, the authority of science and of the knowledge of man would come to replace the authority of the Bible.

A previous revolution occurred in the eighth century. When Rome was in its Dark Ages, Charlemagne obtained a few clerics from Britain to begin the educational system for Europe, from which the Latin system of Western education derives. Of course the greatest previous change to education and understanding

---

[221] Isaiah 60:3
[222] Romans 10:14-15

Chapter 37 Restoring biblical community as a light to a world in trouble

of the world was that set up by Jesus and the Apostles, teaching the Bible to the Gentiles and introducing the gospel of the Kingdom of God to Jews and Gentiles alike. Whatever we do today must be strictly in accordance with what they taught and did.

In Chapter 1, I mentioned the possibility that the light of Genesis might prove to be more productive for scientific advance than the current theory of evolution, putting those using this light in a similar position to those who pioneered the scientific revolution. I explained how that would put Darwinists in a similar position to the one occupied by Aristotelian science when the scientific revolution took hold. This wonderful reversal of fortunes between believers in the Bible and Darwinists seemed but a dream. But it is not in fact a dream. It is just the wonderful fortune that lies before us. There is not so much need for those who believe the Bible to battle the darkness. It is only necessary that we turn on the light.

— 38 —

A bright future for a dark day

THE LIGHT OF the church planted by Jesus burned brightly during the era of the Apostles. Despite poverty, persecution, and opposition from both Jewish and Gentile rulers, the Apostles accomplished their mission, laying once and for all time the foundation of the church: our New Testament, the Apostles' written testimony of Jesus. Because the church has possessed that witness from the time of the Apostles, one might suppose that Christians have ever since been preaching the same message, but this has not been the case: unlike the message of later Christianity, Jesus and the Apostles focused their teaching on a wonderful future for the suffering church in the earth upon the return of Jesus. This expectation of the Kingdom of God and the reversal of the suffering church's present circumstances gave meaning and reason for their great sacrifices and hard service in the face of great opposition and persecution.

The Apostle's message of the corporate salvation of the church was largely ignored, if not forgotten, as a comfortable and seemingly victorious institutional church came to see itself as no longer in need of salvation. An institution replaced the Spirit of Christ as the government of the Church. As this occurred, the gospel became transformed into a message focusing on *individual* salvation, while the Church's leaders neglected and even opposed the exciting promises of the coming Kingdom. Individual salvation had previously been taught by the mystery religions, but no other religion has ever conceived of the world being wonderfully changed by a coming Kingdom of God. If the first step in a transformation to a completely individual salvation occurred when the Catholic Church came to regard itself as already the promised Kingdom of God, replacing the returning Jesus as the savior of individuals, the last step followed the Reformation, as the Church itself no longer seems essential to an individual's confessional salvation. Alternately, one could say that Protestant baptism of secular callings turned the Kingdom of God into a Christian society that was hardly separate from the world. As these changes occurred, Jesus no longer

Chapter 38   A bright future for a dark day

seemed so close to his church, leading and guiding a close-knit body of believers as appears in the book of Acts and the letters of the Apostles.

In truth, people cannot be saved from the kingdom of darkness unless there is a kingdom of light to receive them. In view of the present darkness we surely need the safety of God's Kingdom however much its presence must be spiritually discerned. But Jesus and the Apostles also warned that many false prophets and teachers would exploit their work. Jesus referred to these false teachings as weeds that would grow in the world together with the wheat that he planted, until the harvest of the last day. Though the truth planted by Jesus has been multiplying like yeast hidden within bread, divisions among believers and teachings that confuse those who might believe have dimmed the bright light of the Apostolic church. Today, scandals and divisions exist even within the great institutional churches, all of which have been losing prestige and influence. However great the number of Christians, as I noted in Chapter 1, our faith has never seemed so fragmented and irrelevant to the world.

By contrast, the early church functioned as one great family, allowing it to prosper even as the ancient world headed into the Dark Ages. A divided church can hardly serve as an ark of survival for a world that is also getting dangerously in trouble because of the same kind of divisions and confusion. The world badly needs the light of a pure church, but before truth and faith can be restored to the world, as the Reformers once declared, they must be restored to the church. These hopes were delayed because Jesus' parable of the wheat and tares promises a complete separation of the righteous from the wicked only at the end of the age. At that time, Jesus declares, the righteous *will* shine as the sun in the Kingdom of the Father.[223]

If Christians have changed the message of corporate salvation associated with preaching of the coming Kingdom of God, it is useful to know more completely than this brief summary just what teachings have replaced it and how these changes have hindered progress to the goals set before believers by Jesus and the Apostles. This is vital because our vision of the church will powerfully determine the church's future. Where there is no vision, the people perish.[224] But with a clear vision, believers will know how to prepare for what is coming on the world. As I examined the history of science to discover how erroneous views arose and kept the world from recognizing Noah's Flood, I had also to examine the teachings of the church in light of those of the Bible. We need to know whether it is possible or proper to return to the message of the Apostles and whether, due to the differences between their situation and ours, that message might be understood differently today. I will briefly address four views that

---

[223] Matthew 13:40-43
[224] Proverbs 29:18

have dominated the church's self-understanding since the time of the Apostles. We should not be surprised that each embodies some portion of truth taught by the original Apostles. Indeed, each arose as a reaction to so much of the church and outward Christians having departed from the message of the Apostles. At the same time, each new view brought with it new traditions and theologies that were contrary to the foundational message, but whose bitter fruits would not be immediately seen. Each of these ways of looking at the church also developed characteristic ways of opposing any correction.

Some of these views were important in the creation of particular movements and the reformation of particular churches, though today these views are diffused among the members of most churches and among the numerous small groups of Christians. These views are commonly characterized by different ways of relating to the Millennium, the thousand years mentioned in the twentieth chapter of Revelation: the time when the saints will rule and reign with Jesus. I will note the varying millennial perspectives while using characterizations that better express the practical differences between the four views. Many of us will want to identify with at least one of these views of the role of the church and its characteristic vision of the church's past and future. It may be that your understanding of that view will not altogether be the way I describe it. To show how some have misused the particular views we hold, I will not refrain from the severest criticism of each. As I will explain in the next chapter, truth can withstand the most severe criticism. Hence, we need to keep all these views at an objective distance so we can together move towards that truth that will help the church function as a bright and effective light in the present dark days.

The first view is that of an *established church*. It is believed to be the order of the church instituted by Jesus and the Apostles, which would in fact function as an institution. This catholic understanding replaces a priesthood of believers under the direct authority of Christ with a clerical hierarchy understood to have inherited the authority of the Apostles. Early church leaders developed this perspective to protect believers from purported secret teachings of Jesus and from those who rejected some or all of the writings of the Apostles. As this view developed, servant leadership of a persecuted church as taught and experienced by the Apostles was replaced by one in which leaders reign as monarchs over a church that believed itself to become more or less victorious in the present world, perhaps something the Apostles did not expect to occur until the return of Jesus! This perspective is particularly associated with state churches, Catholic and Protestant, and with those church traditions that derive from them. The best features associated with this view are its sense of continuity with the Apostles, and its desire to be the great and influential Christian community that the church should be. Though in decline due to secularization, this view has long dominated the teaching of church history because of the established church's association with the worldly powers.

Closely associated with the view of the established church is the concept of orthodoxy: correct worship and belief. We may forget that in distinction to the inspired Scriptures, orthodoxy is a human creation. Deriving from a religious version of what we now call political correctness, orthodoxy has been mainly the creation of various worldly states, in earlier days enforced if necessary by banishment or by the death penalty. The opposite of the volunteer way of the cross, it is a religion under the head and sponsorship of worldly governments.

Because the proponents of orthodoxy see the church as already established, they suppress eschatology by seeing the great changes for the church foretold in the Scriptures as already fulfilled or to be fulfilled at the end of the world and thus of no immediate consequence. Subscribing to a view known as *amillennialism,* they reject the future Millennium depicted in the book of Revelation when Christ will reign in the world with the saints. But in truth, biblical faith *is* eschatology. Until Jesus returns it will be always a gospel for the Last Days. Removing the Millennium from the future of Christians also removes our hope for a coming Kingdom of God, turning the joyful Christianity of the Apostles into orthodoxy's long-faced piety.

The established church understands itself, to use Karl Barth's apt phrase, as "the blessed possessors of the truth." The blessed possessors have difficulty conceiving of any important deficiency in their knowledge and faith or any crucial need to obtain more. Fortunately the church *is* the blessed possessor of the faith put forth once and for all time in the Bible. But anything else is adding to or removing from the foundation of the church. These additions include the traditions and affirmations of orthodoxy, the rules of faith through which the orthodox would interpret the Scriptures.

Unfortunately, the blessed possessors do not expect that the established church may ever become apostate, believing that apostasy can only come from individuals and from those who have left or been expelled by the church. Because of its monopolistic claim on divine authority, it refuses correction except by its own leaders. That is not the way taught in the Bible, where the Lord raised up prophets as he chose to correct the leaders and people of God. The Scriptures know nothing about a people in the present world who cannot become apostate. Jesus warned the church of apostasy and the Apostles pointed to the history of ancient Israel, in which apostasy was the norm more than the exception, as instruction to the church.[225]

The second influential vision, which does recognize that the church can become apostate, is the opposite of the view held by the established church. It is

---

[225] 1 Corinthians 10:1-11; book of Hebrews; 2 Peter 2:1; Jude 5

the *restorationist vision* that developed from the early Reformation. Though the Protestant state churches returned to the established view as quickly as they became established churches themselves, the restorationist view continued to be championed by the Puritans, early American Christians, and many others who have wanted to move closer to the ideal of the Apostolic Church by looking directly to the authority of the Bible. Because they saw the established Christian church as corrupt, some restorationists returned to the early Christian view that the Millennium would not appear until Jesus returns. Holding the antichrist responsible for the established church's long history of apostasy and persecution of the faithful is one way their *historical premillennialism* differs from the futurist version of premillennialism now popular, which I will explain below as part of the fourth view of the church.

Restorationists have either a low view of the present state of the church or else a high view of where the church once was and to which it can somehow return. The restorationist is the most radical and challenging of the various views of the church, though the extent of its radicalism depends on how low one sees the state of the present church or how glorious one expects the restored church to be. There are restorationists who seek to restore the church to other eras since the days of the Apostles. Some want the church to function as it did during the time of the early church fathers. Others look to the Middle Ages, the Reformation, or some earlier time in America to find their ideal church. These lack the grand vision that sees the church of the Apostles with its purity and power as the model for the church today.

Because they aim at reformation of the church and share the corrective spirit of the prophets of the Bible, restorationists have been unpopular. But we should keep in mind that Jesus warned his disciples that they would suffer the same fate as the prophets. Indeed, both traditional and contemporary churches have developed numerous ways, refined or brutal, of silencing their prophets. This means that those promoting a restorationist view are going to experience deprivation and suffering.

These challenges help explain why today's restorationists usually assume they have already achieved restoration, or have become content with their status as perpetual outsiders. Instead of prophets with Christ's love for the church they become merely church bashers. Many have exploited hopes for a restored church in order to create new cults. They may even persecute their own prophets who have not lost sight of the original vision of something better. Once they are no longer radical or effective, most restorationists turn into just more examples of established churches that are comfortable in the present world. If, on the other hand, some hidden church does have a light, this is the time to let it shine.

Chapter 38 A bright future for a dark day

Some believe they have indeed become a light, giving rise to the third influential vision, the traditional *evangelical view*. Though most common among American Protestants, it is not just a Protestant or American view. Martin Luther has been regarded as the father of evangelicalism, but the Catholic Reformation was also driven to convert the world, if with a different version of the gospel. Evangelicals see the church advancing ever forward in its efforts to win the world for Christ. This accords with Scripture, which teaches that the Kingdom of God grows and spreads throughout the earth. The best examples of this view hope to see the church advancing in truth and righteousness as well. The Great Awakening, for example, opened a new mission field for evangelicals: nominal Christians who needed to be born again, giving rise to the modern revivalist tradition.

Still, because it sees the present church as the Kingdom of God, the evangelical view has much in common with that of the established church. Success in obtaining converts may blind the eyes of evangelicals to the possibility that they are bringing converts to a worldly and apostate church. This is indeed a danger because due to their focus on growth, it is easy for evangelicals to compromise with the world. As the established view of the church owes much to control of the church by worldly governments, the evangelical view tends to be too much influenced by popular culture and worldly success.

Having perhaps a too-high view of the church, evangelicals tend to look to human resolve and efforts rather than divine initiative and the supernatural power of God to accomplish his purposes in the earth. Though stemming from the historic premillennialism of the restorationists, this focus on the work of the church encouraged a new view of the Millennium in which the church is able to convert the entire world before the return of Christ. In the nineteenth century, American evangelicals began turning to a view first taught by Daniel Whitby (1638-1726) and Jonathan Edwards (1703-1758) that Christ would not return until the end of the Millennium, during which the church would clean the world and restore all things for his return, a view known as *post-millennialism*.[226] The progressivism in this view develops naturally into liberalism or even nationalism akin to that of imperial Germany or patriotic America. With the help of a compliant church, a "Christian nation" may take the place in our hearts of identification with believers throughout the world. Among those who seek to avoid that error, it may develop into the internationalism characterizing the ecumenical movement, believing that peace on earth can be achieved through

---

[226] Postmillennialism is frequently conflated with evangelical amillennialism, but in fact postmillennialism sees the Millennium as future, just as does premillennialism. In the postmillennial view, the Millennium does not begin until the church becomes the government of the whole earth.

human institutions. Because their focus is on human action, evangelicals may fail to notice when the church simply turns into society or the world. Evangelicalism has become the traditional cultural Christianity of America and the West, whether the nationalist version of the right or internationalist version of the left.

While the evangelical view is the most optimistic regarding man's abilities to accomplish ever more of God's will on earth, a fourth view of the church which I will call the *escapist view* is the most pessimistic. It is fatalistic regarding the prospects that the church can ever return to becoming a light to the world, no matter how much the church may repent and devote itself to God. Nonetheless, it has come to be the most popular view of the future of the church. If my criticism of this fourth view seems particularly severe, the reader should also know that perhaps those that I love most in the Lord and particularly those of my own culture hold some form of this view of the church. It is because this is the most recent of the views, because few of the great number of Christians who hold this view have considered its implications and consequences, and because inclined to this view due to our disappointments with organized Christianity, it is also the most damaging to the restoration of Christian community that is essential to the church again becoming a light to a dark world. Indeed we need an escape, but not from truth.

This dark vision of the future was originally accepted by numerous serious believers due to the tendency of leading evangelicals to identify Christianity in America and the West with the Kingdom of God just it was becoming too obvious that Christianity in America was becoming ever more worldly and unbelief was entering the highest ranks of the mainline churches. Some resented the church's involvement in movements such as anti-slavery and labor reforms, but others believed that social programs and political involvement were ineffective as well as useless because the church would never be able to bring about the Kingdom of God. That would have to await the return of Jesus. Before that advent, they expect the church to become apostate – aside from a remnant that will someday be "raptured" to heaven. The *rapture* refers to the Apostle Paul's mention of Christians being *caught up* to be with Christ as he returns to the earth.[227] In their case, it means being secretly *caught away* from the earth and into heaven *before* Christ returns! They posit *two* Second Comings of Jesus: the first secret coming when he comes *for* the church, the second public coming when he comes *with* the church.

This secret rapture was first taught in nineteenth-century Great Britain through a system of theology known as Dispensationalism. According to this system, the rapture brings the end of the Dispensation of Grace, or what some

---

[227] 1 Thessalonians 4:17

Chapter 38 A bright future for a dark day

of them call the age of the "gentile church." In truth, a gentile church is an oxymoron. In the Scriptures, gentiles (the heathen) refer to the world; but God's church are those called out from the world. But this view does not identify what they call the "mysterious church" with the chosen nation of God. The Dispensationalists teach that most of the Bible was not written to the church! They claim that neither the commandments nor the wonderful promises of Scripture were intended for Christians during the present "Dispensation of Grace."

The Dispensationalist view sees the mysterious church being replaced sometime after the rapture with the modern geopolitical State of Israel and an ethnic group defined as Jews who will have rejected Jesus as their Messiah until that time. Humanist scholars trained to read Hebrew by medieval rabbis introduced into Christianity this political interpretation of Zionist prophecy. The scholars mistook an anti-Crusader version of Jewish Zionism, the *Judaica exposito*, for ancient Hebrew exegesis. Martin Luther found the rabbi's exclusive claims to the promises of the Old Testament useful for his theology and for his anti-Catholic program, but his acceptance of the Rabbinic view of Judaism may also have been responsible for Luther's anti-Jewish polemics later in his life. An ethnic rather than a religious view of Judaism developed from the same roots, a product of German nationalism as I discussed in Chapter 6. Rooted in anti-Semitism and perpetuated by scientific myths about history, biology, and genes, and replacing the proper religious understanding of Judaism with a racist identification, it is neither historical, nor biblical, nor what Rabbinic Judaism teaches. Nor are most Israeli Jews happy about being the subjects of this dangerous real-life experiment in popular Christian prophecy. Astoundingly, whether ethnically Jewish or Gentile, faithfully believing in Jesus in the present age seems to disqualify one from God's future kingdom in the earth. We should not be surprised that rabbis developed this type of Zionism in response to the Crusades, but why have Christians come to believe such things?

What, in the Dispensationalist perspective, is the future for those who have faithfully believed in Jesus? They teach a variety of post-rapture roles for Christ's bride, both in the earth and the sky. Some have Christians ruling gentile cities, perhaps occasionally coming to Jerusalem to visit their bridegroom who will then be busy giving his attention to another favorite. These differ as to whether the spiritual Temple has reverted to one made by human hands. Others have believers ruling distant planets, an idea they may have learned from the Mormons. The more heavenly minded have them playing harps on clouds, as parodied in Mark Twain's *Letters From the Earth*. Though Jesus' bride will be with him forever, this "co-ruler" is also safely tucked in some Docetic heaven. According to the Dispensationalists, God never had the members of the church in mind as part of his great plan of history as recorded in the Bible. Our opportunity for a heavenly dwelling came from a temporary interruption in God's plan because the Jewish leaders rejected Jesus when he came as a suffering servant. Dispensationalists are vague about the future. Since we do not talk about what does not excite us, perhaps this is the Dispensationalists' way of acknowledging that their "Heaven" is not so interesting as the earthly things they do so love to discuss.

Many who believe in the rapture do not identify themselves with Dispensationalists: thus I have termed it the escapist view. The rapture is definitely escapist. The most escapist version of this view expects the rapture of the church before the onset of the great tribulation and the appearance of the antichrist. This antichrist is not one of those principalities or powers in heavenly places, but a flesh-and-blood man, perhaps an apostate Jew, who will rule the world for a short time as depicted in recent novels and Hollywood movies. According to this perspective, the Scriptures have not been pointing to the long history of persecution that the faithful have suffered, and in many countries are still suffering today, but to a short end-time scenario from which Christians may escape. This seems in every way an escapist view.

Because this group sees the Millennium as a future event, it is premillennial, but this *dispensational premillennialism* is very different from the older historical premillennialism. Some proponents of the older view believed there would be a total conversion of Jews before the coming of Christ, but expected these Jews to become part of an Israel consisting of Jews and Gentiles together in Christ. Dispensationalists point out that the Old Testament prophecies have to be fulfilled. Having rejected the Israel of prophecy as the body of Christ but with a theology that particularly emphasizes the fulfillment of the Old Testament prophecies, they recognize the need for a this-world fulfillment of the prophecies concerning all the ancient nations: those deriving from Noah's family and from the scattering at Babel whose fate is recorded in the prophecies along with the restoration of Israel. Along the lines of some varieties of historical premillennialism, the Dispensationalists envision the recreation of those ancient nations according to geopolitical boundaries. I have traced the ancient dispersion and have found none of the ancient peoples to be the same as the geopolitical nations of today. Even if the geopolitical boundaries were redrawn, they would not be the same as the nations of the Scriptures, who were *peoples* and not geopolitical boundaries. In truth, these prophecies pertain to the spirits that have governed the peoples of the world since ancient Babel. These spirits still rule various kinds of people in the earth, even Christians, though in ways that transcend political and ethnic divisions. That would include everyone not ruled by the Spirit of Christ, while those devoted to him alone are indeed the Israel of God.[228]

---

[228] Galatians 6:16

Chapter 38 A bright future for a dark day

An important and valid aspect of the Dispensationalist view is that it points to an important distinction between Israel, the servant body of the Lord, and the gentiles who recognize the authority of the Lord, though not as his devoted followers. Much of our problem is that, notwithstanding the Catholic doctrine of *corpus Christi*, Christendom was never the body of Christ, a family of devoted believers filled with and following the Spirit of Christ, as was the church of the Apostles. Though from earliest times the distinction might have been equated to the one between clergy and laity, it became obscured when the church allied itself with the powers of the present world and many of the "laity" proved more devoted followers of the Lord than the clergy.

While many Americans did once view their nation as the New Israel, Christ's suffering body of believers will never be a people defined by some *worldly* state, whether Christian or Jewish. Here we must not confuse a *state*, a nation defined by a government of the present world, which obtains its power from the coercive and unspiritual ways of worldly governments with the nation headed by Jesus, one that possesses the power of God that comes through the weakness of the cross. It is in truth the former type of rule that the Lord purposes to replace.[229] Whether one understands God's people as Israel, as his church, or both as the same people, his people have always been and must ultimately be completely devoted to him, holy and separate from the gentiles (the heathen), what Jesus and the Apostles refer to as the *world*.

While the evangelical view tends to altogether ignore the supernatural, at least the escapist view is apocalyptic. In expecting great changes in the end times to require the supernatural acts of God, it is in line with the Bible, however pessimistic it may be. But if evangelicals put too much responsibility on believers, this view assumes no responsibility for a sinful church, even for preaching repentance. It "leaves everything to God" though because it does leave everything to God it may not be obedient to that which God has instructed *us*. Indeed, those looking for a coming antichrist to rule the world are not expecting their present efforts to win the world for Christ to succeed. Some nonetheless do preach repentance, but why expect a restoration of a glorious church if it has no future in the earth?

A sad aspect of the rapture is that it offers only a dark earthly future for Christians. It is particularly damaging to children and to the young not to be part of a church or community with a vision for an earthly future, and so different from the hopeful view of the future put forth by the Apostles. Formerly, Christian parents have striven to leave at least the Christian part of the world better than they found it, for the sake of their children. Unfortunately, the escapist view has excused Christians to turn their hearts from their children,

---
[229] 1 Corinthians 15:24

leading the children to turn their hearts from their fathers. This explains why so many young people leave such churches at their first opportunity. At least for the current age, the world seems to offer more meaningful callings.

> It is particularly damaging to children and to the young not to be part of a church or community with a vision for an earthly future.

The chief task, and it seems the only task, this view assigns to believers of the present age is in "getting people saved." Dispensationalists are either highly cynical of the church or else completely indifferent and accepting of the church in its current state. Either is highly destructive of Christian community. Many see the rapture as license for Christians to ignore or forget their obligations to their brothers and sisters in the earth – except, perhaps, to convert them – and to focus on their natural families, their own church or ministry, or some huddled and fearful group of Christians. With no burning vision for the Kingdom of God on earth, it is natural that Christians will turn their attention and affections towards their personal affairs or to some non-Christian calling rather than to the Kingdom of God. "Family values" that is the valuing our natural families above the believing family of Jesus may in fact contradict Jesus' teachings that *his* family be first in our hearts. Not only does this view explain the "great reversal" of social concern among American Christians from the nineteenth to the twentieth century,[230] it helps explain why Christians have also abandoned social responsibility even for the members of their own church to the systems of this world. It surely does not see the church as ultimately victorious or as a Noah's ark that can survive God's judgment of the earth. Not surprisingly, this view has come to dominate a very worldly popular Christianity.

From the Lord's perspective, the most serious defect of Dispensationalism must be that it takes away the inspired words of God as speaking directly to the hearts of believers. As to which if any of the Scriptures might speak to believers, the Dispensationalists differ among themselves. There are hyper-Dispensationalists who remove all the Scriptures as speaking to believers, replacing even the commandments of Jesus with a theology of grace sufficient for saving those who have "confessed Jesus." This Jesus they would have us confess has a different teaching for believers than the one in the Scriptures, which they claim speaks only to Jews of the past and future. Denying that the Scriptures speak directly *to* believers, they teach Christians *about* the Scriptures. Offering nothing to our hearts, Dispensationalists speak to our head. Just as medieval theologians allegorized away the plain meaning of the Scriptures, those who hold the escapist view have Dispensationalized them away. Since the Scriptures are not reckoned as speaking directly to us, no wonder so many today leave their Bibles unread.

---
[230] Carl F. H. Henry, *The Uneasy Conscience of Modern Fundamentalism* (Eerdmans, 1947).

Of course, many believe that the "rapture" is just what the Scriptures do teach. They have been taught, and everyone in their Christian experience seem to believe, that the Scriptures about the catching up to be with Jesus forever is the rapture, failing to see that this passage does not refer to a secret snatching away, but to the gathering of the saints to Jesus upon his return to the earth.

These four views of the church can also be combined, however contradictory the combinations. There are those who hold both the established and the escapist views. Others hold both the established and the evangelical views. There are even restorationists who believe in the rapture. Many Christian teachers have no coherent or well-thought-out vision of the church or its future. Depending on different days, moods, and speakers, they may be trying to win the world for Christ, but on other days looking to the rapture to escape the coming antichrist! If worldviews affect the world, church views certainly affect the church. The church today exists in a state of muddled confusion, which helps explain its lack of effectiveness. But clear vision is required for building Christian community.

Is it possible today to return to the simple view of the church as the suffering but devoted servants of Jesus eagerly expecting to be part of the soon coming Kingdom of God in the earth? May we believe the message of the Apostles just as they taught it to those who first heard? A better question is whether it is possible to be faithful believers without being faithful to the gospel of the Kingdom as preached and taught by those whom Christ appointed. Hopefully, the only difference between what the Apostles preached and what should be preached today is that the apostasy, the great "falling away," lies behind us. Certainly we need a gospel message with a future. Our future cannot be part of a dark world that is soon to pass away, but it must be as a separated community throughout the world who will reign with Jesus at his coming. To truly encounter God's Spirit, we must have more than a sense of being saved as individuals. We must have a sense of being part of the body of Christ.

Though we can accomplish nothing without Christ, God does answer the prayers of those who humble themselves and turn from their own ways. If Jesus has set us free, we are free to pray for restoration. The God of the Bible responds to what his people choose and do. Having his Spirit makes available the Lord's righteousness and power. The Scriptures show Christ working together with his servants and family in the earth, Christ's Spirit leading and guiding them.

A place to start might be to look at the experience of some earlier Christians who had similar aims: those who fled to the New World in order to return to Christianity as they believed it was taught in the Bible. Our world's present knowledge of early America is in a state of darkness, almost as dark as that pertaining to earlier historical times. Misunderstandings exist on the part of believers as well as those who do not want to recognize Christianity as having

Part VII   *The Flood's Meaning for Today*

FIGURE 61   THE FIRST NEW WORLD FEAST OF THANKSGIVING

either a significant or positive impact on American history. I hope to address these matters in another book. The point here is that these Christians, our forefathers, owned a vision with a great spiritual future: expecting the Kingdom of God in the earth.

There are differences between our situation and that of early Americans. They came to the difficult wilderness of America seeking religious freedom and to escape what they saw as the darkness of the antichrist. Contrary to what is widely believed, almost all the early Americans were looking for the imminent return of Christ, seeing their struggles as preparation for a future Millennium. Because they were willing to suffer, many have enjoyed freedom, prosperity, and the blessings God promises the children of those who suffer to serve him.

The very wildness of the New World and its preference for commercial goals above religious conformity allowed for the religious freedom they sought. Early Americans accordingly patterned their society on that of the early Israelites who traveled through the wilderness to a new land of promise. Like the early Christians, they understood themselves as God's New Israel. As I pointed out in Chapter 28, also present in their New Canaan were those wanting to make the land a haven for building wealth, either through owning slaves, selling merchandise, or lending money. Within American souls and institutions, spiritual battles were being waged, as they are still being waged today. Unfortunately, as Americans prospered, their vision of God's New Israel changed from a spiritual body of the faithful into a political nation operating as part of and according to the rules of the present world. Instead of the New Israel, America has begun to look more like a new Babylon.

Today, the church in America and throughout the world does not face a wilderness so much as it faces a great worldly City. As were the Jews in Babylonian captivity, the church today is in captivity to the world. Ancient Babylon was a city of commerce that dominated the whole world, a city where *everything* was for sale. Today, even Christianity has become dominated by business concerns. Sadly, the gospel has been prostituted as a means of gain in the business-dominated culture that rules our world. The mystery of Babylon in the book of Revelation could have only foretold of the international economy of today. No such economy incorporating the entire world has existed since ancient Babel. This economy is underpinned by a worldwide system of government and laws that the Scriptures depict as beasts. At least from the time of the ancient empires, governments formed by systems of laws do in fact function as impersonal beasts. Trusting our future to governments that depend on military power and economic strength is effectively worship of the beast. As believers, we must not trust or place our hopes in the kingdoms or enterprises belonging to the present world. Instead, we must come out of Babylon, which would be any entanglement with the present world. Otherwise we too will receive her judgments. We must seek first the Kingdom of Heaven, and we must seek it *apart* from the world.

The return of the Jewish exiles from Babylon to Zion is a wonderful model for the church today. The Zion to which they returned was outwardly in ruins, overgrown with vegetation and wildness. Compared to the great City of Babylon, Zion may have outwardly seemed insignificant. The ancient Jews had to have courage and love for the Lord to be willing to endure the temporary hardship of returning to Zion and rebuilding the Temple. Most of their nation preferred to remain in Babylon. Likewise, most Christians or nominal Christians prefer to remain attached to the world with its temporary privileges and pleasures. Today, no less courage and sacrifice is required of believers to return to Zion: the place of those uncompromisingly seeking righteousness and truth rather than success in a world that is soon to perish. Christians who are penalized for speaking the truth in the establishments of the present world must sacrifice their comfortable livings. Else, we are cowardly. If we expect to reign with Christ, we must suffer with him. If we are ashamed of him, he will be ashamed of us. While the Scriptures point to Babylon as the place of worldly success, the Bible calls Zion "the City of Truth."[231] It is a place where neither worldly power, nor wealth, nor opinion trumps truth. Rebuilding it is a calling worthy

---

[231] Zechariah 8:3

of sacrifice and devotion. Zion is also the place from which God's truth goes out to the world. Though small and insignificant in terms of what is recognized as important by today's world, God promised in the last days to lift up Zion to become the most notable place on earth. All the world's people will stream to Zion to receive blessings and light.[232] The prophet Haggai declared that the glory of the latter house shall be greater than the glory of the former.[233]

This temple of God is the body of Christ, a church headed by his Spirit.[234] With his leadership, we can look forward to a latter day church more glorious than the church of the Apostles – the one to whom the Lord is shortly to return as he becomes glorified in his holy people and marveled at by those who believe.

---

[232] Micah 4; Isaiah 2
[233] Haggai 2:9
[234] Hebrews 3:6; 1Peter 2:5

— 39 —

The biblical method for determining truth

A NY SERIOUS ENDEAVOR – whether in science and technology, a business or military operation, or a secular or spiritual community – depends on working from some measure of truth. Successful advance towards goals depends on distinguishing and discarding untrue claims that have been holding back progress because they have not been challenged. No less is required for recovering for today the understanding of the Kingdom of God as taught by Jesus and the Apostles, thereby developing the kind of community that will allow the church to become a light to an increasingly dark world.

The scientific method contains many essential principles for arriving at truth: peer review, testable predictions, testing claims against an accepted body of knowledge, and basing that knowledge on well-supported facts rather than traditions, fantasies, or fashions, called idols of the tribe, cave, marketplace, and theater by Sir Francis Bacon in his *Novum Organum* (1620), the book setting for the principles of inductive reasoning. Using these principles, numerous specialties have accumulated the basic skills for developing technologies and testing new scientific claims. Within narrow but practical fields, these methods have been and will continue to be successfully used. The source of confusion about the greater issues, including history and cosmology, was not the scientific method but how it was so ignored by those claiming the mantle of science.

Scientific progress also requires community: building on the knowledge of the past and testing proposals and claims by the widest community of peers. Science expects to advance by correcting its errors and moving to an ever better understanding. How much more the ministry of the church, those charged with teaching the things of God! Unfortunately, owing to the doctrine of "the blessed possessors of the truth," theologians and biblical teachers have shown little interest in the biblical way of determining truth. The Bible has a lot to say about it. Its commandments pertaining to the pursuit of truth include every useful aspect of the scientific method and every wise practice of successful scientists.

Examining, testing, and preserving are essential both for scientists and for the biblical priesthood. These disciplines are explicitly put forth in the Law of Moses and exemplified throughout the Bible. In the New Testament we are admonished to test things for their accordance with the Scriptures and with the truth – to test even apostles and prophets, and be aware of false teachers, even among leaders of the flock. No divine dispensation excluded kings, priests, or prophets from accountability either to God or to the people of God. Unlike the arrogant, the immature, or those with something to hide, Christian leaders should not mind being questioned. As did King David, God's anointed today should be humble enough to receive correction, even from their enemies. Christians should have a reputation for humility as well as integrity and righteousness, even before a hostile world.[235]

The prophets and priests of the Old Testament had different functions. Prophets delivered the Word of God, but it was the priests' responsibility to determine that each message really was his Word by comparing it to the truth they were already charged with preserving unchanged. Further protection came from the fact that although prophets could come from any family in ancient Israel, priests could only come from priestly families. The endogamic provisions of the Law of Moses prohibited high priests from marrying foreigners, which included the wealthy and powerful families of allied nations that would divide their interests from the Lord and his people. Given no great tracts of land as an inheritance, the priests and Levites depended on whatever offerings the Israelites might freely offer to God. Instead of their interests being tied to their plantations and patrons, their dependence on the Lord maintained their interest with their Heavenly provider. The three-fold separation of prophets, priests, and kings in ancient Israel preserved the truth of the Bible by guarding against the development of a self-serving oligarchy or ruling establishment as found among the gentiles.

Likewise, in the churches of the New Testament anyone could prophesy, while the entire body of Christ was a holy priesthood charged with determining the true prophecies.[236] They were not to change what had been passed down to them from Jesus by way of the Apostles. Of course, though it is necessary to retain what has been passed down to us, simply possessing the witness of the Apostles and Prophets is not sufficient. The touchstone of truth is the Word of God from the Scriptures written on the minds and hearts of the body of Christ.

---

[235] Matthew 5:16
[236] 1Corinthians 14:31

And how can it be written there, unless believers are truly obedient to the commandments and are fully devoted to Jesus?

As priests of the new Kingdom of God, they were to remain separated from the world so as not to be corrupted. We must have independent watchman who are willing to speak the truth concerning the established powers and popular trends. A free and open society benefits from the same accountability and discipline. "Christian" or not, running communities, churches, universities, and institutions for money, power, or worldly success corrupts justice, righteousness, and truth. Instead of depending on institutions or patrons, God's servants today must be fully devoted to him and to those who have made the same sacrifice. They must become a living body of people who are fully devoted to Christ and to one another. Those who have his Spirit love their fellow believers and their love overflows to the world, but they abhor pretension or hypocrisy. Thus the biblical method of preserving truth requires vigorous challenge to unrighteousness and untruth by those who would be leaders in the body of Christ.

The Bible advocates open rebuke of leaders who sin and a more severe judgment of teachers than those who are taught.[237] We see the prophets, Jesus, and the Apostles rebuking kings and religious authorities of Israel and Judah, God's chosen nation.[238] Their correction was not aimed at worldly sinners, but at the sins of the leaders and the people of God. They did not see those whom they rebuked as enemies to be destroyed, but leaders needing correction in order to save them and the people they led. As do all wise and loving parents, the God of the Bible chastises or rebukes those whom he loves – and so long as they submit to him, he does it through his prophets, instead of through the rod of an unloving world.[239]

The Apostles taught that leaders should be rebuked *publicly* so that the people could learn righteousness and truth.[240] The Apostles did in fact rebuke one another publicly.[241] Peter, James, and John had previously experienced public rebukes from Jesus. In the Old Testament, the Lord rebuked David, the king after his own heart, in the most public and humiliating way.[242] The Lord chooses the most severe discipline for his favorite sons because they are to represent his great holiness and because of his great love for them.

Jesus and the Apostles limited the objects of such public or harsh rebuke to leaders and insiders, that is to say, to mature elders. Thus serious issues such as

---

[237] Luke 9:55, 17:3; James 3:1; Titus 1:13; 2 Timothy 2:15
[238] Matthew 23; Luke 3:19
[239] Hebrews 12:5; Revelation 3:19
[240] 1 Timothy 5:19-20
[241] Galatians 2:11-14
[242] 2 Samuel 12:11-12

Part VII   *The Flood's Meaning for Today*

the sins of public leaders should be addressed among elders, absent the participation, though not necessarily the presence of either the tender or the spiritually immature. The latter may observe and learn, but cannot endure such public discipline themselves. They will not recognize the comforting rod of correction spoken of in the 23rd Psalm as powerful love and acceptance. Jesus explains that brothers should be first admonished privately. Even so, those who do not repent are to be publicly rejected. The immature, like sinners in the world, find it difficult to accept any type of rebuke. They must be handled as newborn babes in the Lord. The church however badly needs as leaders mature men who can humbly receive public discipline. As demonstrated by the Apostle Peter, that is the highest mark of maturity, what it takes to be a living stone in God's building.

Institutions and organizations are forms of worldly power. Because such power always corrupts, God accomplishes his work from the Spirit, and from the weakness of the cross. It is due to the corrupting nature of power that institutions, whether religious or secular, cannot be reformed. Even in the fast-moving world of technology, the successful development of new projects requires quasi-independent enterprises that can function independently of corporate bureaucracies.

In worldly diplomacy and in political gatherings, truth cannot even be spoken. The same hypocrisy may be seen among Christian leaders who prefer not to hold their peers or associates accountable lest they themselves be subject to accountability and lose their status and privileges. This makes them popular with a sinful world and with sinful Christians who fail to see their hypocrisy in criticizing those whom they see as "critical" men. Profitable criticism can come from anyone, but it should be judged by whether it has the interest of the Lord and the Lord's church at its heart. When worldly leaders do hold one another accountable it is only to protect or expand their joint interests and privileges. That kind of community among Christians will provide no light to the world.

I was very fortunate to be prepared for this task not only by the demanding rigor of scientific and industrial experience where my colleagues were accustomed to challenging one another fiercely and productively, but also from my memory of 'the threshing floor' in meetings of the early twentieth-century School of the Prophets.[243] This threshing floor was a forum for separating true teachings from the untrue, and for gleaning the kernels of truth from the chaff that enveloped them. The School of the Prophets believed in close and permanent as well as growing fellowship, but remaining faithful to the original Pentecostal convictions, they refused to join or form new Pentecos-

---

[243] cf Elmer T. Clark, *The Small Sects of America* (Abingdon Press, 1949), 105.

Chapter 39   The biblical method for determining truth

FIGURE 62   ANCIENT THRESHING FLOOR

tal organizations.[244] As the organized Pentecostals were refusing to fellowship with their theological opponents, the School of the Prophets practiced an open platform, allowing any believer to share his revelation, teaching, or correction, regardless of his denomination or theological persuasion. But whatever was shared was subject to the 'threshing floor.' Like the noble Bereans,[245] they examined any revelation or teaching against the Scriptures. When people know they are going to be questioned about what they have said, they speak less, they speak more carefully, and they speak more from the heart. Sharing in the general assembly of God's people ought to be recognized as the solemn and sacred task that it is.

As spiritual Christians, the School of the Prophets expected that the anointing Spirit should be present in their meetings to teach truth and to confirm truth whenever it was spoken. Like early American ministers, they were expected to speak from the Spirit and from the heart rather than from planned sermons or lectures that limit the flow of the Spirit. They believed in seeking and following the direction of the Spirit. That required constant and reverent

---

[244] cf Walter J. Hollenweger, *The Pentecostals* (SCM, 1972), 29 and Frank Bartleman, *Azusa Street* (Logos Books, 1925).
[245] Acts 17:11

> **When people know they are going to be questioned about what they have said, they speak less, they speak more carefully, and they speak more from the heart.**

focus on the Lord. This did not mean that they did not insist that participants prepare themselves with much study and prayer. Participants had to learn self-control, to speak the truth kindly, to gracefully overlook and be quick to forgive those who offended. They could be severe or uncompromising in their testing, but when the discussions ended, fellowship and love among those participating would be stronger than ever. Such a forum certainly requires mature leaders who have love for all participants and a heart for the truth, two things that come only from the Spirit of Christ.

The objective of the threshing floor is not winning an argument, as is the case with debate. Debaters may find it disadvantageous to discover something valuable in what their opponent might say. Those who debate may not love the truth, and therefore do not belong on the threshing floor. By whatever name we call it, dialogue must never degenerate into unprofitable debate that displeases the Spirit and fails to feed the soul. The greatest delight in *threshing* is recognizing another's point of truth and confessing one's own error – because the objective of threshing is discovering and rejoicing with the truth, the truth that makes us free.

To conduct a profitable threshing floor we must share a common hunger for testing teachings in order to discover truth. The people of God's Zion are those who have a hunger for truth. However unpleasant the truth sometimes seems, it is the only means of salvation. Yet most churches and ministries follow the dogmatic method characterizing the schools of Greek philosophy. Originally, the Greek word *dogma* described the manner in which Greek philosophers excluded any opinions that challenged or conflicted with their own.[246] We see the same methods in the politically-correct world of today. Some churches and ministries speak with confidence only because they allow no forum for anyone to question their teachings or present other views. They cannot stand on the threshing floor unless they speak the truth and speak it from their heart.[247]

Certainly, parents and church leaders alike need to protect children and new believers from untruth by supervising what they are taught. Nonetheless, it is vital that there be a general forum in the body of Christ for determining and testing what should be taught. Appropriately, the ancient city of Zion was built

---

[246] Academic freedom in fact develops from biblical rather than classical roots, while, as Karl Popper explains in *The Open Society and its Enemies* (Routledge and Kegan Paul 1945), Plato advocated the view of education found in modern totalitarian societies.
[247] Psalm 15, 24

on a barren rock, suitable for threshing wheat. Solomon's Temple itself was built on a threshing floor. So too is the Church of Jesus.[248] It is very clear that Jesus allowed his listeners to ask questions, even difficult questions. Unlike proud religious leaders, the Creator of this world humbled himself to submit to being questioned, only refusing to reply when his enemies had an agenda other than the truth. Then he silenced his opposition with questions of his own.

Truth is a powerful sword, but righteousness is a strong shield. Those with nothing to hide do not mind being exposed. Authentic experts love those who ask the hardest questions. Nor do they mind admitting what they do not know. Of course, questioners should respect and not abuse those whom they are interrogating. Those who are trying to honestly respond, rather than evading honest questions, should not be exploited but given opportunity to answer as best they can. The threshing floor should be a safe place for participants to speak their hearts, free of any political correctness. In our day the Internet provides a wonderful opportunity for responding in a public forum in an unhurried but timely fashion. But whatever the forum, a threshing floor will never be better than the purity, kindness, and boldness of those who listen, question, and speak from the heart.

---

[248] Matthew 3:12

— 40 —

Acknowledging the truth

JUST AS THE first step towards righteousness is humbling oneself and confessing one's sin, the first step in discovering truth is being humble about what we know, honest and forthright about what we do not. Mistaking humility for weakness, the immature limit those from whom they will learn to whomever they suppose is admired by their peers or the world. I have discovered that the most accomplished scientists, scholars, and leaders are willing to learn even from those of no reputation. Yet while admitting our lack of knowledge is essential, so is acknowledging the truth, if we ever find it. The truth changes us as it also changes the world. Once we discover truth, we cannot continue in our old traditions and ways. In popular spirituality, one learns that seeking truth is more important than discovering it. However important it is to travel the lonely road of truth, should we celebrate being eternally lost?

We should not mistake skepticism for humility, as did those who discovered the limitations of modern science but did not return to pre-modern faith in the Bible. Amusingly, no one is so trusting of science as the postmodernists. They believe that if science cannot provide truth, none is to be had. They have turned to postmodernism because that is the most up-to-date, the *modern* thing to do. Postmodernism is in fact not *post* but *hyper*modernism.

We must not be immature Christians, tossed back and forth by waves of fashion or swayed by every wind of teaching.[249] When we do not acknowledge, hold to, and act on the truth that we have found, we do not actually love it. In both mainline and evangelical Christianity, exhortations and polite criticism have become liturgical flagellation rather than a cause for serious action or change. Coming from the serious business and scientific world, I was disappointed to discover a lack of seriousness among so many Christian endeavors. Such a lack demonstrates the presence of hidden agendas, reminding me of the

---

[249] Ephesians 4:14; James 1:6

Chapter 40   Acknowledging the truth

rationalizations for ill-conceived research projects and business enterprises that proved to be bottomless pits. The road to truth may be difficult and long, but if one is never making progress or if one's spiritual progress seems to be permanently slipping, I would seek those who are serious about the Kingdom of God. Ministries and entire churches or groups that are not advancing in truth or as an example of light should do the same. One's future and one's soul are too important to entrust to the incompetent or those with hidden agendas, even out of loyalty to tradition. This kind of loyalty too easily becomes idolatry, yielding only bitter fruit.[250]

Whatever is declared to be true must be tested. Both new and traditional Christian teachings need to be tested for their accordance with the Scriptures. Those who would challenge old teachings and those who would present new ones should offer them to the threshing floor of the body of Christ. It would be a good learning experience for all to see this publicly done and for all to feast on the truth they discover. But as in the case of scientific specialties, testing requires some standard, some body of knowledge or truth by which we test. If we do not already have truth, or if we do not recognize or acknowledge the truth we do have, we will have no such means for testing. As Jesus explained, those who have will be given more, but those who do not have, even what they do have will be taken away. As long as we do not acknowledge, hold to, and act on the truth that we have found, we will not find more. If we have truth, we must put it to work rather than burying our gift in the ground.

The Bible recognizes that the people of the world have wisdom pertaining to the present world, and the truly wise everywhere recognize the wisdom found in the Bible. When it comes to wielding specific technologies, arts, or wisdom, it may matter little whether the scientist, artist, or guru is atheist, Christian, Muslim, Buddhist, or tribalist. There was a time when Christians viewed science as an independent or complementary way for discovering truth not only concerning specialized knowledge but for the great issues of our world, and even the truth given in the Bible. As we now see, that only proved to be a deception, producing a generation who do not fear God and who will no longer allow truth to be spoken when it is politically incorrect. It seems that serious Christian faith is necessary for the preservation of academic freedom.[251]

For Christians, the Scriptures and the Spirit of Christ are the two exclusive witnesses by which we test truth. If anyone's wisdom does not conform to these two witnesses, it must originate from the forces of darkness. There is

---

[250] Deuteronomy 29:18
[251] cf George Marsden, *The Soul of the American University: From Protestant Establishment to Established Unbelief* (Oxford University Press, 1994).

343

no fellowship between light and darkness.[252] Hence, assertions that attack the foundations of our faith in the inspired Scriptures should be challenged and rejected. If such a challenge is impossible – as thought those who believed science disproved the Flood – and truth is to be found elsewhere, we should not be so disingenuous or sentimental as to call it Christianity. If we pursue Christianity without truth, we are on the road to apostasy, darkness, and eventual destruction, worse than if we had never been enlightened. If we honestly pursue truth, we will not be satisfied until we humble ourselves and return to where our hearts and minds should be dwelling, the Promised Land that we know as our Bible. That, together with those who have the Bible's message written on their hearts is the only place where the God of all the earth can be sought and found

The Bible, like the Holy Spirit, is a gift from God. Preserving the Bible requires the true servants of God to thresh matters concerning the manuscripts to determine the precise boundaries of the canon and the precise understanding of the text. If we are to preserve, translate, and understand the Bible, we must allow historical issues to be discussed and our present understanding to be challenged, but we must not test God by doubting his inspired Word. Christianity follows the way of faith. Those who reject faith cannot profitably contribute to the threshing floor of the body of Christ.

I have explained how some have used unfair and distorted means to attack the Bible. I trust I have shown that such falsehoods cannot bear the light of truth if that light is seriously used. Jesus advocated letting our light shine, because truth is meant for the whole world. He warned against claims that the truth giver was "in an inner room" or "out in the desert." Today, many rave about this guru, that preacher, some church, or some tradition. Very well. Who is testing their claims? Where is their response to those who have questioned their claims? We need friends or colleagues who hold us to strict accountability more than we need those who flatter or applaud us. The right questions need to be asked, and those who are sufficiently familiar with the matters being discussed need to ask them.

> **Immature Christians, sectarians, sycophants, and institutional representatives will champion someone, some party, or something other than the truth.**

We must exclude from this assembly of truth seekers those who are under the authority or sway of anyone but the invisible Christ of the Bible. Neither do those with institutional or cultural commitments have the independence to be peers in the assembly of truth seekers. Immature Christians, sectarians, sycophants, and institutional representatives will champion someone, some party, or something other than the truth.

---

[252] 2 Corinthians 15:23

Chapter 40   Acknowledging the truth

If we really have truth we will go, as did Jesus and the Apostles, to the courts of God's spiritual temple. His house of prayer for all people is accessible to everyone who believes in the one God, the Father of all spirits, and in the unique authority of the builder of his temple: the one Lord, Jesus Christ.[253] Those who seek God are hungry to discover and discuss things pertaining to the Kingdom of God. We will want the best and most qualified among those with the appropriate knowledge to challenge whatever we offer that is not perfectly true. We should hear the objections of anyone whose agenda is righteousness and truth.[254] If we have discovered falsehood that has kept people in darkness, we will shout it from the housetop. If we have good news, we will proclaim it from a high mountain that all may know.[255] The temple of God, the body of Christ, consists of those who are fully devoted to God and who submit to the Word and Spirit of Christ. The Holy Spirit is also the spirit of truth. These members of Christ's body have different gifts but they are peers sharing one head, who is Christ.[256] They will be prepared to humbly submit to correction. They will also fully address every argument and pretension that sets itself up against the knowledge of God, to take captive every thought and make it obedient to Christ.[257]

This book is based on extensive experience in science and industry, on careful research of the best scholarship and on strict attention to the Scriptures. Though I consulted primary sources, documents from hundreds of languages were unavailable to me, as they are to anyone who investigates such a vast realm as the entire scope of ancient history and contemporary science. In documenting specific areas, I was never sure how much to presume that most readers would know. Though I had much more to say and reference for every subject, I did not want to destroy the flow of this book by excessive detail or pedantry.

I am an experienced systems engineer accustomed to developing successful practical systems that boldly challenge conventional knowledge, and I am deeply familiar with the Bible. I also have confidence in what I have written. Nonetheless, I am human. That means I am fallible. I had to depend on the scholarship of those whom I judged honest and competent but who, like me, are fallible. I have discussed these things with colleagues in many of these fields, but no one or no school is expert in all. The community of peers working on a subject of such vast scope can only be reached with the publication of such a

---

[253] Matthew 21; 26:55; Luke 21:7; Acts 5:42
[254] Acts 17:11
[255] Matthew 10:27; Isaiah 40:9
[256] 1 Corinthians 11:3
[257] 2 Corinthians 10:15

Part VII   *The Flood's Meaning for Today*

book as this. Those who know the Bible can also judge how what I have written accords with the Scriptures.

In fact, everything that I have written *should* be thoroughly checked by those with the appropriate experience, knowledge, and skills. I would appreciate hearing from those who do this, whether privately or publicly. Public questions allow others to learn. I appreciate those who criticize my work as much as those who understand the difficulties and the labor behind it. Until they were discovered, crucial errors in my earlier work kept me from understanding vast areas of important knowledge. I know that the removal of every speck of error from this work will make for a clearer and brighter light.

I have pioneered too many new projects and new ways of thinking not to understand that any great change, especially a return to the truth of the Bible, will not be without great opposition and struggle. But I have also discovered how powerful is truth. Though the darkness is great, the light of the God of the Scriptures will overcome the darkness. His light will shine on those who love truth. In its wings comes healing to the people of God and to the world.

Truth is that which does not change in better light. When at last we discover truth it will be impossible to fairly challenge it. More light only reveals how profoundly true it is. That is what gives me confidence in the Bible. The hope of this coming age lies with those who have this book firmly written in their minds and hearts.

Figure 63   **The End**

Epilogue

Discovery on Mount Ararat

Discovery on Mount Ararat

I HAVE WRITTEN this 400-page book on Noah's Flood with the barest mention of the many searches and claims for the discovery of Noah's Ark that get so much attention in the media. It is not that I am uninterested in the subject. As I explained in Chapter 21, I traced a new dispersion of mankind almost to the foot of a mountain in the region of the ancient kingdom of Uratu, a name that scholars translate as Ararat, the place where the Bible says Noah's Ark came to rest. Bible scholars and proponents of other mountains as the resting place for Noah's Ark love to point out that the Bible does not say that the Ark landed on Mt. Ararat, but upon the *mountains* of Ararat. In fact only one mountain in the world can match the biblical description of the Ark's resting place: somewhere high in the mountains of Ararat where lower peaks would only become visible after ten additional weeks of receding waters.[258] That greatly narrows the places where one should be searching for Noah's Ark. The Ark should not only be on Mt. Ararat, but near the very peak of this mountain.

Landing near the peak of one of the world's highest mountains greatly benefitted those in the Ark where food stores would soon be exhausted. Unlike the lower elevations, which would still be submerged for months, here fresh food was waiting for the animals as soon as the door to the Ark was opened. Of course, no less than in the case of a NASA mission, that could happen only by expert planning and guidance. The biblical account points to divine providence.

I also knew of ancient accounts that the Ark was still to be found upon a mountain in Armenia, part of which is in now in eastern Turkey. That description points to Mt. Ararat. Josephus tells us that Berossus, a Babylonian historian active at the beginning of the third century before Christ, mentions that bitumen relics from the Ark on this mountain were being marketed as amulets. According to Josephus, the Ark was still on the mountain in his own day. Throughout the Christian centuries, there continued reports that the Ark rests on Mt. Ararat and has been visited by pilgrims. Marco Polo (1254-1324),

---

[258] Genesis 8:5

Epilogue

the first European to visit Asia since the Islamic conquest, wrote that Noah's Ark rested on a cup-shaped mountain in Armenia. Again, this describes Mt. Ararat.

I have also met or corresponded with some of the modern searchers for the Ark, but I discovered that they knew little about archaeology and were surprisingly uninterested in the subject. I was unimpressed with the patterns of rocks that the most celebrated Ark searchers have hyped as the vessel's fossilized remains; not just because they did not find these on Mt Ararat, but because fossilization in just five thousand years seems most unlikely. Far more interesting are accounts by some who claim to have visited the Ark remains on Mt. Ararat over the last two centuries. Some of these reports have the ring of truth and describe the remains in similar ways, but why have these witnesses been unable to guide others to the site? The same is true of interesting phenomena observed in satellite photographs of Mt. Ararat.

Since fires, insects, rot, and re-use of timbers mean that few wooden structures have lasted for so long as four thousand years, I doubted whether the remains of Noah's Ark would ever be found. The truth is I did not want this carefully researched book burdened with controversies over claimed sightings of Noah's Ark.

My thoughts on this changed suddenly in 2008 after I received reports of an archaeological discovery in eastern Turkey. Two items from the report attracted my attention. The first was the involvement of the archaeological authorities. Aside from needing search permits, the competitive Indiana Jones-style Ark searchers have tended to avoid the archaeological authorities and anyone else who might ask pertinent questions concerning their "evidence." Though some Turkish authorities believe that the remains of the Ark exist, they cannot afford to be embarrassed by archaeological fraud. It was thus significant that whoever made these new discoveries were in fact working with the Turkish authorities and with archaeologists.

The second reason for my interest was the mention of caves. Due to my study of archaeological evidence from ancient times, I knew that wooden structures, once buried, often appear to be ditches or caves. A buried Ark would also explain two mysteries: why the many modern explorations of Mt. Ararat have failed to discover it, and how its remains might have been preserved. Even if the snow and ice cover melts on hot summer days, the remains in caves below may never thaw, keeping the Ark in a frozen state. But a search for more information ended in an enigmatic Chinese website.

Early in 2010, I was ready to publish this book and had heard little else about this discovery. Then, in late April 2010, my mother called down the stairs: "Philip! Turn on ABC News." I was already watching Diane Sawyer's stunned face as she reported an announced discovery of the remains of Noah's Ark on

Discovery on Mount Ararat

FIGURE 64

THE NAMI ANNOUNCEMENT

Mt. Ararat, including wood that radiocarbon tests dated at 4,800 years old. Given a few hundred years for the trees to mature, that suited the biblical date for Noah's Flood. The report had come from Hong Kong-based Noah's Ark Ministries International (NAMI), the same group responsible for the earlier report that had so interested me. Joining them for the announcement were scientists and officials from Turkey, the country in which the discovery had been made.

What a wonderful report in the very year I was to publish this book! My friends wanted to celebrate. But even before we got to the restaurant, news reports began focusing on claims that the announcement was likely based on archeological fraud. My bubble of elation burst like a punctured balloon. The reports of fraud seemed themselves incredible, but if confirmed they would seriously damage interest in Noah's Ark and Flood. I could not allow my work of over twenty years to become associated with a hoax. We spent our evening of "celebration" in anguished reflection on how anyone could fabricate the evidence being reported.

I spent the next day tracing the reports of fraud to their sources. One came from Robert Cornuke, an Ark searcher whom I knew. A few years back, I had been unable to dissuade him from making a highly promoted announcement of the possible discovery of Ark remains on a mountain in Iran. Convinced he had seen Noah's Ark in those rocks, he could only see fraud in any competing evidence. The more widely reported and far more damaging source was from Randall Price. Dr. Price is an end-time theologian and popularizer of biblical archaeology in the interest of biblical prophecy, better known for his interest in another Ark, the same Ark of the Covenant sought by Indiana Jones, which Price supposes to be hidden beneath the Temple Mount in Jerusalem. Some years before, I had reviewed his book on biblical archaeology, and was disappointed to find that it was only a survey of what others had written.

The astonishing thing was that he claimed to be *the* archaeologist on the Hong Kong team that made this discovery. He ended his associations with NAMI based on rumors from a rival mountain guide, whom he refused to name. Price asserted that NAMI's guide had fabricated the site on Mt. Ararat with timbers carried from the Black Sea coast. Though not accusing the mem-

351

Epilogue

bers of NAMI of dishonesty, he was condescending of their judgments. He sent his claims of fraud in an email to the supporters of his rival search for Noah's Ark, but someone posted it on a website and it got leaked to the press. Though he had not meant them to be publicized, Price stood by his claims.

Documents that Price himself published on his website made it clear that rather than resigning from his brief association with the team, he had in fact been expelled by NAMI's guide, Mr. Ahmet Ertugrul, also known as Parachute (Parasut, in the local language). I found Parachute's concerns most understandable: Price's insistence on climbing the dangerous mountain in bad weather,[259] and associating himself with a rival guide and climbing party at such a sensitive time in the new discovery. Price misrepresented his original association, having himself requested to become part of NAMI's team following their original announcement. His mistrust of Parachute contrasts with the respect accorded him by Bruce Feiler in his best-selling *Walking the Bible*. Feiler called Parachute the most impressive person encountered in all his travels. The sincerity and credibility of Parachute's claim to have seen a timber on Mt. Ararat, even if he refused to reveal the location to Feiler, is vouched for by the notable Avner Goren, an Israeli archaeologist with long experience working in the Arab world. No biblical literalist, Goren would not be an easily impressed by such a report.

Unfortunately, the media and detractors on the Internet ignored the discoverers' account, preferring to report Price's charges, probably without examining the details of those charges. Otherwise they could not have missed the fact that they were based on an anonymous source. In truth, both the media and public were tiring of unfounded claims about the discovery of Noah's Ark and were looking for any excuse to ignore this report. Perhaps they were becoming so tired as to miss the fact that while the new report was backed by the appropriate archaeological authorities, the detractors were rival Ark searchers, responsible for hyped reports of their own.

When it came to professionalism, NAMI and their Turkish partners contrasted favorably even with the archaeologists at ASOR,[260] one of the most prestigious organizations concerned with biblical archaeology. Sadly, a few archaeologists associated with this venerable organization responded to the report in swashbuckling fashion, as if promoting a new calling to police biblical archaeology. Most surprising was their charge that NAMI had not yet revealed the precise location of the discovery. Could they be unfamiliar with practices for

---

[259] Price's protest about climbing notwithstanding, the guide was not exaggerating the dangers from the precarious location of this discovery. As I write, I am reading reports that a climber may have lost his life attempting to visit precisely this site. Price's insistence on overruling the judgment of an experienced guide gives us some insight into his judgment.

[260] American Schools of Oriental Research (ASOR)

protecting new archaeological discoveries? One ASOR archaeologist acknowledged that NAMI's announcement differed from previous claims by actually producing evidence. Why then his criticism?

Perhaps the most surprising opposition came from prominent leaders in the Young Earth Creationist movement, those who have long believed in and taught a worldwide Flood. Though initially seeming to treat the announcement with an open mind, astute thinkers in the movement could see the discovery as troubling. For instance, radiocarbon tests supporting the biblical date of the Flood could seem to demolish their theories concerning the unreliability of radiocarbon dating for the pre-Flood era. In addition, the identification of this particular peak as Mt. Ararat challenged their geological theory that it was formed in post-Flood times. Not all Young Earth Creationists hold the opinion that the Ark does not rest on Mt. Ararat. Some have become early enthusiasts of the NAMI discovery.

Even more interesting is the fact that "believers" seemed untroubled that Randall Price challenged NAMI's discovery by quoting the great skeptic David Hume: "The greater the claim, the greater the evidence needs to be to support it." Hume's circular reasoning dismisses any evidence against reigning dogma for the simple reason that it challenges what is widely believed. His dictum is famously used to question the miracles of Jesus and cast doubt on the reports of his resurrection. The discovery of a ship this high on Mount Ararat might have satisfied even David Hume, but why are believers allying themselves with the great skeptic? Not only did Young Earth Creationists seemed pleased to ally themselves with David Hume, but conversely, many who disdain literal belief in the Bible enthusiastically quoted Randall Price's attacks on the discovery. Atheist sites championed the most eminent popularizer of end-time prophecy as an authority! The new discovery was producing strange bedfellows.

Following my investigation of the announcement made by NAMI, I published a blog reporting my favorable judgment of the discovery, and addressing the accusations against it. I pointed out that while NAMI was providing evidence, the detractors were rival Ark searchers giving unexpert opinions and making charges from unidentified sources. I also addressed criticism concerning the supposed impossibility of finding spider webs and straw on a mountain so high or inside a relic so old. This act connected me with

FIGURE 65   THE DISCOVERY

Epilogue

the members of the NAMI team, who were delighted that someone was addressing the matter from an archaeological and scientific perspective.

I soon learned the story behind the discovery. These explorers did not go to Turkey in search of Noah's Ark. A prominent Hong Kong Christian developer had built the first full-scale replica of Noah's Ark on an island between Hong Kong's airport and the city. He intended this huge vessel to be operated as a hotel, restaurant, and biblical theme park. The developer invited a Christian media organization to operate the museum inside the Ark replica, who sent researcher Clara Wei to go to Turkey and Armenia to collect information and stories about the Ark that had been preserved by the local people as part of their traditions. The media company formed NAMI to provide content for the museum.

After a few years of research and filming, trust and respect developed between the local villagers and the Hong Kong researchers, who were keenly interested in the villagers' traditions about Noah's Ark and their experience of living near the mountain of Noah. NAMI also developed a close working relationship with Parachute and other members of the Mt. Ararat rescue team. The villagers showed the Hong Kong film team how their ancestors used to climb the mountain. Visits had ceased following the earthquake of 1840 that broke the Ark into three sections, burying them under volcanic rock and ice as pieces of the Ark slid down the side of the mountain. Due to their relationship with the Turkish locals and because they were filming rather than searching for Noah's Ark, NAMI was able to obtain climbing permits that were being denied to American Ark searchers. The villagers shared with NAMI and Parachute, information that would eventually lead them to the wooden remains on Mount Ararat.

The group's first discovery was something that their scientific partners determined to be petrified wood. Reading about this on the NAMI website dampened my enthusiasm because wood from that era is unlikely to be petrified. Though seemingly unconnected with their later discovery of the actual remains, it served to generate interest in the team's research. NAMI alerted the Turkish authorities, including Mr. E. Muhsin Bulut, Director of Cultural Ministry for Turkey's Agri Province. Information about the discoveries was also sent to Dr. Ahmet Özbek a geologist at Kahramanmaras Stugcu Iman University in Turkey; Dr. Özlem Çevik, an archaeologist at Trakya University; Professor Otkay Belli, Director of the Institute of Eurasian Archaeology at the University of Istanbul; and Dr. Selim Pullu of Afyonkarahisar Kocatepe University. The Turkish and Hong Kong teams jointly developed a plan for exploration and investigation.

By the summer of 2008, Parachute's climbing team began uncovering and photographing the astonishing remains. Showing these photos to the NAMI team, Parachute explained the precarious location of the caves and the danger this posed to potential visitors. Because of the danger, the researchers invited Panda Lee, trained as a professional climber by the British Army, to verify Parachute's report. When he climbed the mountain soon after receiving this call, Panda became perhaps the first verifiable foreign visitor in modern times to see the remains of Noah's Ark. After exiting the caves where he observed the remains, Panda sent

FIGURE 66   PANDA LEE CONFIRMS THE DISCOVERY

a brief text to the NAMI organization in Hong Kong: "Mission accomplished!" This led to a joint visit to the site by NAMI and the Turkish members of the

expedition. The team made videos of the discovery on their second visit, a portion of which was published in conjunction with the announcement in late April, 2010.

Soon after this announcement, aiming to remain true to their mission as makers and publishers of documentary films about Noah's Ark, the NAMI team visited the United States to record initial reactions to their discovery. I invited the NAMI representatives to my hometown in Charlotte, North Carolina to present their information before a small delegation of biblical archaeologists, university professors, scientists, seminary officials, and interested individuals. This took place on June 7, 2010. Whatever doubts that NAMI had been guided to a recently fabricated site ended as those in

FIGURE 67   BENEATH TONS OF GLACIER ICE AND VOLCANIC ROCK

Epilogue

attendance saw the video documenting the vast amount of wood, the various rooms, the obvious antiquity of the remains, and their similarity to the biblical description. On that day, it became clear to us that an important discovery had been made. We were no less impressed with the account of the discovery shared by Clara Wei: how she had conducted her research with the local villagers, and how that became the key to the discovery. We noted her refusal to rush to judgment concerning NAMI's discovery.

From this meeting and the resulting interviews came NAMI's invitation to address the National Conference on Christian Apologetics meeting in Charlotte on October 15-16, 2010. It would be their first opportunity to speak to a large audience of leaders in biblical and Christian apologetics. This conference was particularly appropriate because it has refused to serve as a forum for any of the parties within the Creationist community, trying to get young earth and old earth partisans to discuss their differences in polite and open discussion.

Not everyone involved with the National Apologetics Conference was delighted that NAMI should appear in this venue. Those who protested claimed to be speaking for the interests of biblical archaeology, the Bible, or science. Although a great deal of pseudo-archaeology has been passed off as biblical archaeology, especially pertaining to Noah's Ark, this was perhaps the first time that pseudo-archaeologists have themselves taken the lead in expressing these concerns. In truth, the heat is on this new discovery precisely because it threatens the support if not the very existence of numerous schools of teaching about Genesis and the Bible, of skeptics and believers alike.

Some objected to NAMI's appearance at the conference by claiming that their conclusions were premature, ignoring the fact that NAMI believes a definite decision should await further scientific analysis. I suspect these objectors do not trust ordinary folks to look at the evidence and draw their conclusions before having the opportunity to spin the evidence in their party's light. Most disingenuous were suggestions that NAMI's discovery had no credibility unless supervised by Western scientists and archaeologists, the very organizations who have declared ancient Flood accounts myth, and who disdained to become involved in investigating the discovery themselves.

In fact what is on trial is neither NAMI, who do not claim to be a scientific organization but a ministry led to their discovery by prayer, nor the Turkish archaeologists who are in fact hard-nosed scientists, nor the discovery of this joint team. At stake is the credibility of the Western scientific institutions that have long claimed the mantle of authority for matters of science and history. Those who charge that the radiocarbon dating is suspect because performed in Iranian laboratories echo a new episode in the sad tradition of the ugly American. Turkey has yet to bring on line their planned radiocarbon laboratories,

Discovery on Mount Ararat

thus their archaeologists employ the services of the closest and most convenient laboratories: those in Iran. Likewise at stake is the credibility of evangelical organizations and leaders who have either distanced themselves from or opposed this discovery, some even suggesting that such a profound challenge to modern disbelief of the Bible is of little consequence for biblical faith! Such obliviousness to the impact of the scientific challenge to the Bible can only be attributed to judgment blinded by complacency and pride.

Despite a stellar panel of speakers, registrations to the National Conference on Christian Apologetics had been falling far below previous years. This was in part due to a planned boycott by the Young Earth Creationists in response to the appearance of a prominent old earth Creationist, defender of a local Flood. Following the last-minute announcement of NAMI's appearance, Young Earth Creationist leaders called off their boycott and registrations soared.

No one seemed more interested than the critics of the new discovery, especially Randall Price, the theologian who accused the NAMI guide of fraud. Price, who now holds a chair at a prominent evangelical university, had sympathizers among the highest level of evangelical leaders and apologists. Presumably owing to his concern for science, he peppered the conference host with calls, attempting to stop NAMI from presenting their discovery, but their appearance had already been announced. NAMI's Panda Lee and Parachute, the guide he accused of fraud, have invited Price to bring his concerns to an open discussion in the United States, reflecting the kind of forum that I advocate in Chapter 39. This would have been an excellent opportunity, but Price preferred that NAMI not be heard. An important backer of Bob Cornuke did bring his concerns to the conference, agreeing that this should be the proper procedure, and that whatever the outcome, we would remain friends.

On October 13, NAMI representatives Wing Cheung Yeung, Panda Lee, and Clara Wei came to North Carolina to explain their discovery. Prior to their appearance at the National Apologetics Conference, I requested them to present their findings at a venue I had rented on the campus of our local university. Again, NAMI did not hype their discovery. They simply told the story, showed

Figure 68 **NAMI's Wing Cheung Yeung (center) with the author (right)**

Epilogue

FIGURE 69   CLARA WEI ADDRESSES NATIONAL CONFERENCE ON CHRISTIAN APOLOGETICS

video footage taken inside the discovered structures, and answered questions. Each session allowed a one-hour question and answer period with the audience. Though a less academic audience than the select group I had called in June, these sessions ended with most attendees convinced that Noah's Ark had been found.

On the evening of October 16, the NAMI representatives gave the final address of the 2010 National Apologetics Conference. Many had decided to attend this year's conference precisely for this time, while others who learned of the presentation after arriving at the conference delayed their departure to witness the highly anticipated presentation. The atmosphere was electric as the packed audience waited patiently through a 45-minute technical delay. NAMI explained the circumstance of the discovery, showed a ten-minute video filmed in different compartments of the caves, and addressed possible explanations for what they had found. The conference ended with a standing ovation in honor of the guests from Hong Kong.

Following NAMI's appearance at the National Conference on Christian Apologetics, Randall Price increased his attack on the Mt. Ararat discovery, this time including NAMI and Clara Wei in his charges of fraud. The attack first appeared in the form of a special report, which he posted on his *World of the Bible* website. This report was supplemented by a video featuring a short plank of charred wood supposed to demonstrate how Ahmet Ertrugrul "built" NAMI's archaeological discovery. The report and video contained a picture of the anonymous informer, a mask covering his face due to what Price claimed were dangers to the informer's safety from Ertrugrul, or Parachute [pictured in yellow jacket on front row, Figure 72]. At the end of his special report, seemingly incidentally(!), Price mentions that he himself had likely located the Ark on Mt. Ararat at "17,800 [sic] elevation."

Price's co-author and "scientist" Don Patton, previously known for championing claims of finding human footprints among the dinosaur tracks along the Paluxy River near Glen Rose, Texas, is not new to archaeological controversy and charges of fraud. It is perhaps not surprising that of the media, only Pat Robertson's CBN and the online newspaper *World Net Daily*, both located in the home state of Price's Liberty University, and one radio program on biblical prophecy elected to carry his sensational report. In these interviews, Price claimed that his own life was endangered by the influential and powerful leader of the Mt. Ararat rescue team.

While many had been paying too much attention to Price, some were not paying sufficient attention. I contacted both news organizations as well as the university and seminary where Price served as an adjunct professor. CBN removed the report from their website as the leaders of Price's university began investigating his activities and claims. The immediate results of this investigation and my expressed concern about Price's use of anonymous sources may have been the reason that a purported affidavit from two Turkish brothers, Davut and Ergan, soon appeared on Price's website. According to Price's posted translation of this letter, the brothers worked for Parachute, helping him build movie sets. The letter explained that they were shocked when they learned that this movie set had been claimed as the remains of Noah's Ark. Unusual for an affidavit, the letter gave neither the last names nor addresses for those who wrote the letter.

Probably no one was more shocked than Randall Price when an angry Davut and Ergan Gimrin, claiming to be the only brothers in Turkey with their first names who were mountaineers and licensed guides, suddenly appeared on NAMI's website. Both brothers displayed their Turkish identification cards. They had never seen the letter posted on Price's website until notified by NAMI. They did in fact work with Parachute, but they trusted him as if he were a member of their own family. The brothers showed their signatures and compared them with the obviously forged names appearing in Price's letter. Price immediately pulled the letter from his website, leaving a note declaring that the source of the

Epilogue

letter was under further investigation. One might suppose that Dr. Price would have thoroughly investigated such serious charges *before* posting them. After a few weeks, the note disappeared, but the other anonymous charges remained. So long as charges remain anonymous it is impossible for innocent parties to address them, explaining why they violate journalistic, scientific, and especially biblical ethics.

In truth, there had long been reason to know that Price was also unsure of his original charges of fraud. As indicated by his quote of David Hume, he was open to being convinced by further evidence. If Price was uncertain of the charges, he was repeating gossip and in the process injuring the Turkish nationals, Clara Wei, and his brothers and sisters at the Hong Kong-based Christian ministry. I mentioned Price's logical and ethical inconsistencies in a letter to Dr. Norman Geisler of the newly established Veritas Evangelical Seminary, where Dr. Price serves as an adjunct professor. Disappointingly, Dr. Geisler treated my letter about his professor's use of anonymous sources as the basis of defaming charges with disdain: to the point of retaining the link to the now-removed CBN interview on his seminary's website. This is the Dr. Geisler who has been a leading voice in Christian apologetics, who writes and lectures on the subject of ethics.

The reporter for *World Net Daily* informs me that he is eager to report the results of the investigation into these matters. What he reports may be more interesting than anyone has expected. Ironically, Price's ongoing activities did give rise to an important and exciting element in the discovery of Noah's Ark. It is not the structure that Price's "scientific" testing has revealed at the depth of twenty meters at "17,800 elevation" on Mt. Ararat. Likely, what Price's team has discovered under the glacier with their ground penetrating radar is the mountain itself. Rather, I refer to the transcripts of emails from Clara Wei and the photographs of pottery that NAMI furnished to Randall Price during their brief association. Price published these emails to explain why he dismissed the NAMI discovery and why he expects us to do likewise. Some of the photographs, including one with a tree at the entrance of a cave and others with running water, pertain to caves that NAMI and other expeditions had been exploring prior to the important discovery. The most interesting email is the one that Price dates to July 25, 2008 in which Clara Wei informs Price of Parachute's discovery of the Ark.

> I would like to share some confidential information here and everyone please keep it to yourself. Parasut has climbed Mt. Ararat since last weekend. He said the ice melt was up to 5,000m. He is convinced that he finally found the Ark. We had brief communications by SMS and telephone over the past few days. He is still on the mountain now. He told me he found a large wood structure on 4,900m and also ventured

Discovery on Mount Ararat

inside for several times. According to him, he found a lot of stuff inside, including pots, 2 meter long stick, food and etc. He said the structure was not horizontal but sliding downwards. To his puzzle, lot of the pots were half full of food. He asked me why but I was unable to answer. I warned him not to take anything away and he agreed. From the earlier communications, I found him rather shocked and excited. He has not decided what to do next. I asked him whether I could share the information with you and he said alright. But he refused to show any photos.

I am not sure the direction of the location but he said is in the region the Americans applied for permit (he meant ArcImaging). I think this location is higher than your one.

Uncharacteristically for an archaeologist, Price covers the pottery in a single paragraph of his 31-page report. In fact, he understands it as evidence *against* the authenticity of the discovery. In point six of his report, labeled "Missing Artifacts from the Paraşüt/NAMI 'Ark,'" he writes:

> None of the Press Conferences have mentioned (to our knowledge) the claim by Paraşüt that a large assemblage of pottery filled some parts of the "Ark". In July 2008, when the U.S. team was asking questions of Paraşüt through Clara Wei before agreeing to send their part of the required fee of €60,000, the sum of $17,000 was paid to Paraşüt for photographs (see below) of these pottery artifacts because it was hoped these photos would provide proof of the antiquity of the structure. As an archaeologist, Dr. Price felt he might be able to determine the age of the pottery once he studied the photographs. When the photographs were received Dr. Price looked them over and also sent them to an expert in regional pottery in eastern Turkey. His conclusion was that the pottery came from Iran, and Dr. Price, as well as two Israeli archaeologists who looked at the photos, agreed that many of the pieces were wheel-made, and therefore of a much later period than that of the biblical Ark. Paraşüt also provided a photo of an **animal figurine** (see below) he said was with the pottery. Despite the later date of the pottery, it was supposed that the animal figurine, as well as the pottery, may have been votive objects brought to the site by those in past centuries that revered the site. The figurine may have been to commemorate the people or animals preserved on the Ark, and the pottery may have contained food offerings. This, of course, was speculation, but we were trying to explain to ourselves what its purpose might have been given it was on the structure Paraşüt identified as the "Ark". However, it was the appearance of old, gray, wood planks in the background of the pottery photos that seemed more persuasive. Although Paraşüt told us that he had taken much of the pottery to his home, Clara said he admitted that the photos were taken inside the "Ark." Paraşüt also gave us in October 2008 photos of himself inside a wooden structure (some of the same photos being circulated by NAMI today). Two of these show an old stone vessel filled with "food" (according to Paraşüt) and Paraşüt kneeling beside this vessel (see photos below). Where are these objects and why have they never been shown by NAMI? Why was the stone vessel with "food" not shown in the NAMI film? The answer must be that if they were displayed, they would reveal to archaeologists that the objects were planted (if

Epilogue

they were ever there).

Wheel-made pot 1 (side view)

Hand-made bowl 1 (side view)

Wheel-made pot 1 (top view)

Hand-made bowl 1 (top view)

Left: **Figurine (heads missing)**

Above: Stone vessels inside wooden structure

Rights [sic]: Paraşüt and vessel with "food"

Wheel-made pot 1 (bottom view)

Hand-made bowl 1 (bottom view)

I have not included the photographs of the pottery from the Ark because they are proprietary. This may be one of the strangest cases of archaeological analysis ever undertaken, but one that delightfully attests to authenticity. Note that Parasut "admitted" that the photos were taken inside the Ark. Note also Clara Wei's professionalism: her concern that the archaeological provenance not be disturbed so that these discoveries remain under the control of Turkey's archaeological authorities. NAMI has not made an announcement about them until the Turkish archaeological authorities complete their analysis and report.

Price's archaeological experts conclude that *wheel-made* pottery precludes these artifacts as belonging to the era of the biblical Ark. Of course mainstream archaeologists no longer study archaeology in the light of Noah's Flood, but Price is referring to his fellow Young Earth Creationists who push the Flood back to the primitive period of mankind's existence in order to explain their inability to point to archaeological evidence of humans from before the Flood. Typically, they declare that the Flood occurred during the Paleolithic era when there exists no pottery at all. Thus, according to Price, wheel-made pottery has to have been from a later period.

According to the Bible, the Flood occurs around 2345 BC (to use Bishop Ussher's calculations). That is almost identical to the date of the Flood that I determined from the statistical analysis of calibrated radiocarbon dates in Japan, India, and Stonehenge in England. In the Ancient Near East, this corresponds to the high point of the Early Bronze Age, as revealed by the construction of the Pyramids of Egypt and the amazing artifacts from Sir Leonard Woolley's excavations of the royal tombs of Ur. Contrary to the claims of the Young Earth Creationists, not only is the pottery of this era being made by the wheel, much of it is being made on the fast wheel. There was, as I pointed out, a temporary loss of the fast wheel due to the Flood. The first pottery appearing after the Flood I

Still a matter of opinion. According to many the Bible supports 1650 BC Flood date

identified as the Khirbet Kerak, also called Transcaucasian, which archaeologists have traced to the upper regions of the Kura and Araxes Rivers. As the archaeologists have noted, "Kura-Araxes traditions apparently emerge during a rapid burst of cultural evolution, the early stages of which remain undocumented or unrecognized." [Peter Glumac, *Chronologies in Old World Archaeology* (University of Chicago Press, 1992), 203.]

What I did not mention when I discussed this in Chapter 21 was my secret hope that this pottery might somehow be found on Noah's Ark. At the time, I thought it unlikely that the Ark would be found, or even if the Ark were somehow found, that pottery would be found inside. Hence, I was surprised by what I learned from Price's unauthorized revelation and publication of this proprietary knowledge.

Stone vessels were common just prior to the Flood, then suddenly disappeared. The discovered stone vessels point to the era in the Ancient Near East just prior to the Flood and were likely brought aboard the Ark by Noah's family. The wheel and hand-made pottery lack distinct markings, pointing to the rustic character of the Khirbet Kerak pottery assemblages. It appears more like the burnished gray ware common in this area just prior to and just after the time of the Flood. The pottery that Price reveals show no handles or lugs, which were soon to be common, but the wheel-made, flat-bottomed pottery foreshadows the shape of some of the Khirbet Kerak pots. More significant are the black marks that may point to the curing of the pottery in open fire, which does match the Khirbet Kerak. It definitely seems a prototype, as I suggested earlier, of this distinctive tradition that identifies the very campsites of Noah's family.

If there is any doubt about this, note Price's mention of animal figurines. I have added the bold letter emphasis in his report to draw attention to the fact that animal figurines were also found in ancient camps on the Kura-Araxes plateau. [See last paragraph of Chapter 21]. Clara Wei informed me that Price declared the figurines to be of Hellenistic era, when in fact they date to the transition era between the Early and Middle Bronze Ages. These animal figurines are not "votive offerings" nor is it likely that the food in the pots has any religious significance. As I noted in Chapters 17 and 25, when archaeologists do not know what something is, they resort to religious interpretations. Since almost anything can be supposed a votive offering, these have become the favorite explanations of lazy minds. During years of studying the archaeological trace from Mt. Ararat, I had often considered the meaning of these animal figurines. Their ubiquitous presence makes it likely they originated before the descendents of the survivors had greatly scattered. The tradition of making toy Noah's Arks filled with model animals may go back to the original, beginning with the stories that Noah's family shared with their grandchildren. Perhaps

Epilogue

one of Noah's sons took his children back to visit the Ark, then abandoned this broken figurine.

As attorneys understand, there can be no more credible evidence in favor of a claim than that introduced by an opponent or hostile witness. Unwittingly, Price has confirmed the very moment of discovery and what was immediately reported concerning the find. He likewise documents the professional care practiced by NAMI and Parachute to protect the archaeological integrity of their discovery. He has given us powerful archaeological evidence that what NAMI and Parachute, using information provided by the Turkish natives, have discovered and announced to the world is indeed Noah's Ark.

Though I have demonstrated increasing interest in this new discovery, until this point I have not declared whether I believe these remains to be the very Ark that the Lord God instructed Noah to build some five thousand years ago. My scientific training and experience require me to thoroughly investigate and test things before stating conclusions. That was surely the case before I could accept that there was in fact no archaeological evidence of Noah's Flood. Before I became convinced that current science had in fact made great mistakes, I had to understand the precise grounds and the objections that have caused scientists and modern scholars to reject the Flood. Before I rejected the Young Earth Creationist account of the Flood, I had to understand their account. I continue to follow the new trends and spins from both schools of modern thought.

As have members of NAMI, I have discussed this new discovery with both secular and biblical archaeologists and scholars, those whom I admire and respect and who are deservingly prominent in their particular fields. Due to the relatively modest coverage in the media and scholarly circles, and because so many who did cover the discovery carried only the hoax charges along with standard rebuttals of the Flood and Noah's Ark, I had first to bring their attention to the seriousness of the new discovery. Unaware of the scientific investigation being conducted by the group of scientists and the involvement of the Turkish cultural authority, a few scholars wisely suggested setting up the proper procedures for investigating the discovery. NAMI and their current scientific team will surely benefit from the addition of archaeologists and scholars, whom they have already sought to recruit: those with relevant expertise in the many and valuable new techniques now available to assist archaeology. All this requires planning, funding, and patience.

At the same time, we must recognize that this discovery is not like that of the Dead Sea Scrolls, whose great significance was only gradually appreciated. The team making this discovery has already completed the careful and gradual steps that revealed this massive, ancient artificial structure. NAMI has also conducted a careful analysis of whether this might be some more ordinary structure such as a human settlement, a monastery, a church, some type of animal pen, or military post. Their analysis clearly rules out each of these alternative possibilities.

Consider that the discovery location is more than a mile higher than Peru's Machu Picchu, long noted as a remarkable site for ancient peoples due to its great elevation. Ancient peoples could

FIGURE 70   THE ARK'S DECAYING REMAINS

climb mountainous heights, but lacked the technology and resources to create buildings or settlements at such sites. Most importantly, this discovery is not only located on a high mountain, far above the tree line, but portions lie under ice and volcanic rock on a steeply inclined slope, dangerous even to climbers with modern equipment and training. Were people even able to access these heights, they would not have chosen to construct a building there. Not only is it geologically unstable, but the evidence points to it having long been so. In Chapter 21, I noted archaeological evidence indicating that these mountains and plains have been steadily rising over historical times. Notwithstanding what had to have been easier access in ancient times, no settlements have been found at the higher elevations of this mountain, the highest being signs of slight occupation in a few caves thousands of feet below the discovery. There are no signs of permanent buildings in these caves.

The curved walls of some parts of the structure and the tight construction produce an appearance remarkably like the hull of a ship, but there is no nearby body of unfrozen water. Neat rows of seven wooden pegs are found near the top of some compartments, as if for tying animals. Most compartments have the look of a barn or animal stable, and contain rope and straw. An offensive smell, strong in certain compartments, pervades the structure. Something besides straw and wood has also been long preserved upon these frozen heights. As I mentioned, the pottery found inside appears to be a clear prototype for the kind that archaeologists trace to

FIGURE 71   THE REMARKABLE WOODEN PEGS

Glosssay

FIGURE 72   DISCOVERERS OF HISTORY'S GREATEST ARCHAEOLOGICAL FIND

these mountainous slopes, with no known antecedents. So steadying ourselves to maintain our scientifically correct attitude, we ask with pompous pretension: "What on earth can this possibly be?"

Was this discovery not made on the very mountain, probably the only mountain in the world that can match the description in the book of Genesis as the resting place for Noah's Ark? Is there any mountain more identified by tradition as the resting place of Noah's Ark? Was it not found at the same great heights suggested in the biblical account? Do not local traditions report ancient visits to the Ark resting on this very mountain? Have not peoples throughout the world traced their ancestors to the survivors of a world-destroying Flood, and has not this been the only type of worldwide disaster reported by the numerous peoples of the world? Have not many of them noted the preservation of their ancestors on some type of ship? Do not these accounts alone indicate a far more recent dispersion of mankind throughout the earth than currently believed?

The frozen remains of so large a ship so high on this famous mountain will long outlast the skeptics. But how do we explain our hesitation to draw the one simple conclusion that might make sense of this discovery? I have been astonished at the pious response of so many Christians: all this evidence is unimportant because they simply believe the Bible. If the Bible is myth, as so many claim today, it would not be important. In reality, the Bible is about history, about things that really happened. This response is not unlike those who would believe in Jesus' resurrection, even if his tomb had not been empty. That is not a "faith" worth having. The Bible is significant because it truthfully reports what has happened, what is the case today, and what will someday happen.

Doesn't our reluctance reveal that we secretly hold a too-high opinion of the wisdom of the present world and a too-low opinion of the plain words of the Bible? Upon what basis have we determined the simple words of the Bible to be false, and the current scientific knowledge reliable? Do we even know? Or, is it because we fear man and love the present world more than we fear God and love the refuge he has provided? Do we hide our face from the one who is coming, or do we rush to receive him? If we are embarrassed by his promises and words, will he not be embarrassed by us? Shall we remain part of a world that is soon to be destroyed, or shall we look forward to new beginnings? The decision must soon be made and it shall certainly come from our hearts.

Glossary

Absolute Despots Rulers of Prussia who claimed absolute authority over their subjects. Being Europe's first rulers to embrace the Enlightenment, some were also described as Enlightened Despots.

Acheulean An archaeological culture defined by artifacts from Abbeville, France. Originally understood as remains from the Flood, contemporary science supposes them to define an epoch in the Pleistocene ("Ice Age").

Adena An Eastern American archaeological culture belonging to the *Woodlands* stage and lasting c. 1000 BC to 100 AD. The remains are found beneath the great "Indian" mounds, extending from the Ohio River to New York State. These elaborate "tombs" include a rich assemblage of weapons and furnishings. More modest graves and remains are occasionally found in the upper levels of these mounds. [See Hopewell, below]

ad hoc [Latin] A reactive modification to a theory.

agglutinative Forming words by sticking elements together rather than by changing their form (inflection).

Age of Reason Also called the Enlightenment. The era of European history beginning in the late seventeenth century and ending with the French Revolution when many turned from the Bible to the authority of reason.

ancien regime [French] The old order of Europe in which social and political privileges were inherited and could not be acquired by merit. The order was often defended as established by divine appointment.

Akkadian A widespread language in ancient Mesopotamia dating from the later centuries of the third millennium BC. The language is named for the city of Akkad (Gen 10:10), capital of the empire of Sargon the Great.

alluvial Refers to the topmost layers of river sediment clearly deposited by rivers in their present courses. These layers are often found above a deep layer of non-stratified mixture of gravels and muds, formerly called *diluvial*.

amillennial Rejecting a future thousand year reign of the saints with Christ (Rev. 20).

amorphous Without definite form.

anachronistic Improperly viewing a matter from the perspectives of a different age.

Ancient Near East (ANE) The lands of the Bible during the times of the Bible. These include lands extending to northern Iran, eastern Arabia, western Turkey, southern Ethiopia and all areas between.

Anglican Pertaining to the established Church of England.

animism, animist Seeing spirits or supernatural powers in various things of Nature. One who views the world in this manner.

antediluvian Referring to the time before the Flood.

anthropology, anthropologist The study of man, and one who studies mankind, usually referring to studying the remains and culture of the earliest humans.

Glosssay

anthropomorphic Having human form or characteristics.

antichrist Literally "one opposed to Christ." One who denies the fleshly (historical) appearance of the Christ (1 and 2 John). Traditionally conflated with the beasts of Revelation 13, "the little horn" of Daniel 7, or the man of lawlessness (or sin) in 2 Thessalonians 2.

antidiffusion Opposition to the notion that native or ancient cultures were owing to influences or people from other continents and lands.

antinomian Denying that Christians are subjected to laws, sometimes supposed to be a consequence of God's incomprehensible Sovereignty.

antiquity Ancient times.

anti-Semitism Hostility or prejudice against Jews stemming from the notion that they derive from a race determined by an inferior or repugnant language. Anti-Judaism.

apocalyptic Pertaining to the revelation of things hidden, specifically the surprising acts of God at the end of the age.

Apollo, Apollonian Greek god of wisdom and light associated with the sun. Concern with proper external appearance.

apologetics Defending the Bible from attacks against its truth, morality, or inspiration.

apostasy Defection or falling away from the faith. Rebellion against Christ.

Apostolic Church The church of the New Testament.

a priori Belonging to the mind prior to any experience.

archaeology, archaeologist Also spelled archeology. The study of the ancient remains of man, and one who engages in such a study. For the study of the remains of ancient animals, see paleontology.

Aram, Aramaen A son of Shem, or the name for ancient Syria. Referring to one from the ancient nation of Aram or Syria.

Aramaic The language of ancient Aram or Syria that became the lingua franca (see below) of the Ancient Near East in the latter half of the second millennium before Christ.

Ararat A mountainous region surrounding present day Armenia where the Bible says the ark came to rest. The famous mountain of the same name.

Aratta The homeland of the ancient Sumerians.

Archaic Meaning "ancient." The term is used for the cultures in America that predate those of the current natives.

Archaic Era A pre-Flood era in ancient American prehistory. Currently, this period follows the Clovis and Folsom periods of the earliest inhabitants and ends with the Formative cultures of America.

Aristotelian Characterized by the philosophy of Aristotle.

Aristotelian science The science of Aristotle, which taught currently rejected views such as an uncreated, earth-centered universe.

Ark of the Covenant The sacred chest where was kept the testimony of God.

Ark of Noah The large floating vessel that God commanded Noah to build (Gen. 6:14).

Armenia A modern country and ancient nation located in the highlands just south of and between the Black and Caspian Seas.

arrow of history The direction of history.

arrow of time The direction of time as provided by indicators from the natural world such as the expansion of the universe.

artifacts Things made by man as opposed to things made by God (occurring in Nature).

Aryans The inhabitants of ancient Iran, believed by some to be the ancestors of those speaking the Japhetic (Indo-European) languages.

asceticism, ascetic Avoiding fleshly indulgencies and pleasures, possibly including severe bodily discipline and celibacy.

Ashkenazi Jews who lived in Christendom during Medieval times. cf Sephardi.

assemblages, archaeological A set of archaeological artifacts with unique styles, subsets of which are found together indicating cultural unity or connection

Atlantis A city mentioned in Plato's *Republic* that disappeared beneath the ocean.

Augustinian Referring to the teachings of the Catholic theologian, Augustine of Hippo.

Aurignacian An era in the Paleolithic associated with Cro-Magnon man.

Babel The ancient city and tower built some centuries after the Flood from where mankind was scattered across the earth (Gen 11:1-9). As reflected in the words *baby, babble, barbarian,* **it also refers to unintelligible words.**

Bar Kokhba Meaning "son of a star." One claiming to be the Messiah who led a Jewish revolt against Rome in 130 AD.

barrow The term used in Great Britain to refer to a large hill covering the remains of the dead. These are similar to those "Indian" mounds of America that contain remains of the dead.

basalt A grayish or black fine-grained rock formed from the rapid cooling of volcanic lava.

Beth Yerah Israeli name of a town near southern mouth of the Sea of Galilee. Also known by its Palestinian name Khirbet Kerak.

bevel-rimmed bowls An unusual mass-produced molded vessel that serves as a marker for the Late Uruk culture of the Ancient Near East.

biblical minimalism Limiting the historical content of the Scriptures to the minimum required by widely-accepted extra-biblical evidence.

biblicist One who views the words of the Bible as true and authoritative. An expert in the Bible.

Big Bang Nickname for the notion that the universe exploded into existence.

bitumen Naturally occurring tar or petroleum that can be used to seal cracks.

Bronze Age An era following the Stone Age when early humans used bronze or copper, but before iron came into wide-spread use. The designation is primarily used in Old World archaeology.

burnished Reference to polishing the external surface of pottery by rubbing with a hard stone.

calibrated dates Earlier than 1500 BC, radiocarbon dates are known to give readings that are increasingly too young. Radiocarbon dating of tree rings can be used to provide corrective adjustments. Dates that have been corrected by these tables are regarded as calibrated.

Cambrian Explosion The sudden and simultaneous appearance of many forms of sea life in the geological record.

Cambridge A town north of London which is home to one of England's two established universities, to be distinguished from the town in Massachusetts that is home to America's Harvard University.

Canaan Grandson of Noah, whose descendents settled in Canaan (the Promise Land).

Canaanites Descendents of Canaan, and founders of ancient colonialism and chattel slavery. The Greeks referred to the Canaanites as Phoenicians.

canon Meaning "measuring stick." Writings recognized as Scripture. The term also refers to any tradition or law that the Church recognizes as binding.

catastrophism Belief that eras of the earth's geological history were ended by sudden catastrophes.

celibacy Abstaining from marriage and sexual relations.

Glosssay

ceramic Clay artifacts baked to the hardness of pottery.

chattel slavery Owning and treating slaves as if they were property like cattle.

Chavin The Formative native American culture of Peru and surrounding vicinity that begins around 1000 BC.

Chellean A Stone Age archaeological era named for finds in a suburb of Paris.

chevron A V-shaped pattern, similar to a sergeant's stripe, found on ancient pottery.

chiliasts Early Church and Medieval Christians who believed that Jesus would return to begin the Millennium, often persecuted as heretics in Medieval and Reformation times. In modern times, some of these ideas are described as *premillennial*.

Chou (Zhou) A dynasty of emperors that ruled an area of China centered along the Yellow River from 1122 – 256 BC.

Christendom The world as once dominated by Christians and Christian governments.

chronology The science of determining the dates of ancient events, people, or archaeological remains.

chronometer A standard marker for the measure of time.

church fathers Early Christian leaders who wrote after the Apostles but before the Council of Nicea in AD 327.

Confessions Formal or official beliefs subscribed by various Protestant sects.

Copernican, Copernican Revolution Understanding the earth as one body in the heavens, rather than center of the universe as taught by Aristotle. The consequence of the notion that the earth spins and orbits the sun as proposed by the Church astronomer Nicolaus Copernicus (1473-1543). Often regarded as the beginning of modern science.

corpus christi [Latin] The body of Christ.

cosmogony The history of the universe, often included as part of cosmology.

cosmos The world, usually referring to the physical cosmos.

cosmology Teachings or study of the character, shape, and extent of the universe, often including *cosmogony*, how the world came to be.

credentialism Excessive regard of formal academic credentials, especially at the expense of intellectual substance.

critical Discriminating judgment.

critical history A view of history supported by historical criticism.

Cro-Magnon Men of the Old Stone Age identified by a cave in southwestern France with paintings on the walls of the cave. Current science regards these as the earliest of the modern species of man.

cult A specific religion. A religion regarded as departing from the tenets of Christianity.

culture Styles or patterns in the language, artifacts, and modes of living that identify the time, place, or ancestry of various human groups.

cuneiform A form of writing on clay using letters formed by a wedge-shaped stylus.

cylinder seal An ancient marker of ownership in which a seal is imprinted on a small barrel-shaped roller.

Cynic Meaning "dog-like." A school of ancient Greek philosophy that despised material things and conventional opinions and values.

cynicism An excessively skeptical and dismissive view of the world.

Damascus Road experience Referring to the theophany of the Apostle Paul while traveling to Damascus (Acts 9:3). An experience that results in a sudden about-face of one's deepest beliefs.

Dark Ages Currently the period from about 600-1000 BC when literacy and learning largely disappeared from Rome. In Puritan theology, the era of an apostate church extending from the rise of the Papacy to the Reformation.

Day of the Lord The Second Coming of Jesus. In Old Testament prophecy, a time of darkness and judgment expected to precede the Lord's future visitation.

Dead Sea Scrolls Ancient writings on parchment and papyrus found in caves by the Dead Sea. These writings include portions of Old Testament books dating several centuries before Christ.

decadence A way of living associated with materially-advanced and prosperous cultures, often associated with injustice, moral decay, and indulgence.

Deep Time A dramatic and perhaps imagined extension of prehistoric time to allow for the supposition that all features of the earth or its organisms were created by presently-observable natural processes.

Deism, Deist Belief in a Creator God that rejects the Bible. Deists usually believe in human immortality and see revelation only from the "Book of Nature."

demiurge In Plato's philosophy, a divine being who fashioned the word from pre-existing matter, regarded as malevolent by the Gnostics.

demography, demographic The scientific study of human populations and settlements. Characterized by such concerns.

dendrochronology Dating things by counting and correlating patterns of tree rings.

Deluge Noah's Flood.

determinative Sufficient to fully define.

Deuteronomist According to the JEPD theory of biblical criticism, a supposed writer of Old Testament history including the book of Deuteronomy and most of the historical prophets.

dialectic In physics, an electrical insulator, a non-conducting medium. In philosophy, logic.

diluvial Belonging to the Flood. A layer of unstratified sediments and organic remains lying near the surface of the earth.

disarticulated Having no particular order or pattern.

disenchanted, disenchantment A worldview that does not recognize spirits or purpose.

Dispensation of Grace According to Dispensationalist theology, the period from the beginning of the Church until its rapture. The "Church Age."

Dispensationalism, Dispensationalists A system of theology that divides history into divine Dispensations, including a mysterious Church Age between the first and second comings of Jesus. Those who hold to such teachings believe that a remnant of Christians will be secretly "raptured" from the earth when Jesus returns to become king of an earthly Jewish nation usually understood as ethnic Jews living in the modern State of Israel.

DNA A nucleic acid found in the cells of organic beings or their remains. These contain chemical patterns called genes that can identify persons, or establish biological relationships.

Docetism, Docetic Belief that Jesus' crucifixion was an illusion. Associated with Gnostic denials of history.

Druid A priest or wise man of the ancient Celtic peoples. Pertaining to the religious beliefs of pre-Christian Celts.

Dryas An arctic flower. The presence of Dryas pollen may indicate a period of colder temperatures.

dualism In philosophy, the view that reality exists in the dual worlds of body and mind. In theology, belief in two competing Gods, one good and one evil.

Early Bronze Age The era of Old World archaeology prior to around 2300 BC when bronze was in widespread use and when urban development and populations of the Ancient Near East had reached a peak.

Early Church The church from the time of the Apostles (the New Testament era) until the Council of Nicea (327 AD).

ecology The environment necessary for sustaining certain forms of life.

egalitarian Favoring equality and opposed to social class systems.

eisegesis Interpreting a text by something external to the text or context. Also called **isogesis**.

empiricism, empirical Basing knowledge on observation and experience rather than theory.

encrypt Hiding the true meaning of a communication in some code.

endogamic Marrying only within a local community, clan, or tribe.

Enlightenment A term deriving from biblical prophecy, pointing to a later era of light. It now refers to the era of eighteenth century Europe when many came to believe that the Bible was an obsolete book.

Enthusiasm A term used during the Enlightenment to express opposition to those claiming immediate revelation from God. Also used against revivalists claiming a "born again" experience.

escapist view A vision of the Church's future held by many Christians, which envisions believers escaping the earth through the rapture.

eschatology, eschatological Study of "the end times." Pertaining to the Last Days.

established church The official church of a nation. A church assumed to have been established by Christ and the Apostles.

eternal ideas, forms A view taught by Plato that ideal forms (ideas) exist in an eternal transcendental realm.

eternalism, eternalist Belief that the world is uncreated, thereby minimizing the importance of history.

Evangelical Christianity Defined by spreading the faith through seeking conversions. Christianity that emphasizes personal faith.

exegesis A reading of a text from context rather from matters external to the context.

American Exceptionalism Belief that America's experience or its divine calling makes it an exception to the history of the nations.

fallible Able to make mistakes or to err.

Far East Eastern Asia, including China, Japan, and Korea.

fauna Animals.

Fertile Crescent A crescent-shaped region of the Near East believed to have been the place of the earliest farming and the first domestication of animals.

fideism Blind faith in the Church, usually the Catholic Church.

Final Cause In Aristotle's philosophy, the ultimate purpose to which the world strives, sometimes equated with God. The study of final causes is called teleology.

First Cause In Aristotle's philosophy, the ultimate cause giving movement to the world. Some Christians have equated this with God. For Aristotle, this would not be a Creator God, since he regarded the world as uncreated.

flagellation A ritual whipping or scourging of one's own body.

folk [German *volk*] The people of a particular language and culture.

form criticism Analyzing writings to discover patterns and forms, and using these to determine a document's meaning and composition.

Formative The earliest identifiable stage of various native American cultures in most cases, occurring from 1000 BC to 500 AD.

forensics Investigative science deriving from legal proceedings, including determining cause and circumstances of death.

Freemasonry A secretive and traditionally anti-Catholic fraternity that teaches enlightenment by initiation into the secrets of ancient religion.

Functionalism A school of modern archaeology seeking to understand artifacts according to how they functioned in human societies.

Fundamentalism, Fundamentalists Beliefs of early twentieth-century Christians who resisted modern claims to knowledge by insisting that certain fundamentals are essential for Christian faith. Those who hold to "the Fundamentals."

genera A biological classification higher than the species level, but lower than the family level.

General Revelation Also called natural theology. What God reveals by his Creation ("Book of Nature") rather than by Special Revelation (the inspired Scriptures).

General Systems Theory The science pertaining to all-encompassing systems, whether naturally occurring systems or those made by an intelligence.

genetics The science of the biological mechanisms that determine inheritance. Pertaining to biological genes.

genetic clock Determining the supposed time of separation of biological populations by studying the degree of similarity of genes.

genetic distance A measure of the genetic dissimilarity of genes.

genetic time A concept of time determined by causal relationships rather than quantitative measure.

geological column Order of the earth's strata believed to demark periods of the earth's history.

geology Study of the earth.

geopolitical Referring to a nation defined by its geographical boundaries and government rather than the origins of its people.

ghetto [Italian] A neighborhood and community isolated from the larger society.

Gilgamesh An Ancient Near Eastern king who claimed to have built ancient Uruk. An ancient Near Eastern Flood epic.

Glacial Kame An Archaic-era [pre-Flood] archaeological culture consisting of burials and found under hills in Michigan, northern Ohio, Indiana, and Ontario. Glaciers from the "Ice Age" are thought to have formed these hills.

Gnostics, Gnosticism Early Christian heretics who denied the humanity of Jesus and an historical or biblically-based faith. Beliefs of those who deny historical meaning and the goodness of the physical world.

God of the philosophers God as defined by and understood through philosophy.

Great Awakening A revival of experiential Christianity in the eighteenth century that involved all the American colonies and most churches, and which created the distinctive revivalist form of American Christianity. The revival also had roots and branches in the Anglican, Puritan, and Pietist Christianity of Europe.

Great Chain of Being A classification of forms of life from lowest to highest order. Popular during the Enlightenment, this philosophical system for classifying Nature was eventually temporalized to create the modern theories of evolution.

hagiography Writing the lives of saints. Excessively adulatory or idealized biography.

Hamitic Of the children of Ham, son of Noah. A family of languages named for Ham.

Harappa An ancient and materially advanced civilization on the Indus River. As presently believed, the civilization was destroyed by floods.

Hardaway An Archaic American culture defined by a North Carolina archaeological site of this name.

hedonistic Referring to the pursuit of physical pleasures.

Hegel, Hegelian Influential German philosopher (1770-1831) who developed the dialectical way of imagining history. Hegel's method of dialectic proposes a thesis, then an antithesis, and finally a synthesis of thesis and antithesis. The synthesis then becomes a new thesis that continues the dialectic of development.

Hellenes, Hellenic Terms used by the classical Greeks to refer to themselves and their culture. The Romans referred to Hellenes as Greeks, after a tribe in Italy speaking the same language.

In the east, they were called Ionians, after Javan, son of Japheth.

Hermes, Hermetica In Greek mythology, messenger of the gods. Egyptian writings from the early Christian centuries falsely believed to have dated from the most ancient Egyptian civilization. The magical teachings of Hermes.

hieroglyphics A pictorial script.

higher criticism The study of the time and circumstances of the composition of writings such as the Bible.

historical criticism A historical understanding of literature or of the history found in literature.

historical distance The degree of language and cultural difference resulting from the passage of time.

historicism, historicist A philosophical view of history or understanding history as determined by historical laws.

historicize To reduce the meaning of historical writings to the matters of the world that produced them, often in an anachronistic and patronizing manner.

historiography The study or understanding of written history. The view of history from particular historians.

Holocaust A horrific genocide of the Jews in Nazi death camps. Generally, the mass destruction of a specific group of people.

Holocene According to current geology, reference to the latest or post Ice-Age period of geological history.

Hopewell A wealthier form of the Adena or Woodland culture, presently dated from 200 BC - 400 AD. The sand-tempered pottery and simpler burials of the Mississippian, the Formative culture of the Eastern native Americans, are also found on some of these mounds.

Hsia [Xia] The earliest Chinese dynasty or culture located on the upper Yellow River and ruling from 2100 – 1600 BC.

Huguenots French Protestants, largely Calvinists, who suffered persecution, many of whom were driven from France.

humanists Ancient pagan writers and artists. Renaissance scholars who studied ancient writers and artists.

Humanist Reformers Renaissance scholars whose reforms of the learning and morals of the Roman Catholic Church resulted in the Reformation. Also called **Christian Humanists.**

Secular Humanist A modern use of the term *humanist* for someone who seeks truth and meaning apart from religion.

humanities Originally, the literature of the ancient pagans regarded as of enduring value. Currently, learning based on the study of language and literature.

Hurrians An ancient Near Eastern people living in ancient Assyria (northwestern Iraq and Syria) whose written language is neither Semitic nor Indo-European.

ice-core bores Sections of ice removed from glaciers and permanent ice caps, believed capable of revealing the weather from ancient times.

idiosyncratic Having a highly specific or identifiable pattern.

imam One who leads prayers at a mosque.

Indo-European Formerly **Aryan** or **Indo-German.** The scientific designation of a family of languages originally identified as belonging to the family of Japheth, son of Noah.

Industrial Revolution A vast increase in productivity beginning in late eighteenth-century Great Britain, owing to mechanization and other technological and infrastructure advances.

infrastructure Physical structures such as roads and utilities and the organizational structure necessary for economic productivity.

inspired Literally "God breathed." Deriving from God or motivated by the Spirit of God.

institutional church A church defined by its government rather than its people.

Glossary

Intelligent Design A movement, beginning in the nineties, to recognize things of Nature whose creation must have required some intelligence.

ionosphere The portion of the earth's upper atmosphere were exist atoms stripped of electrons, thereby giving the atoms a positive charge.

isogesis Improperly reading a text from a point of view external to the context. Also called **eisegesis**.

isostasy A geological principle which states that the height of the earth's surface reflects its relative underlying density and thickness.

isotopes Radioactive or stable forms of matter as determined by the numbers of neutrons in its atoms.

Japhetic Belonging or descending from the family of Japheth, son of Noah. Indo-European.

JEPD Theory of biblical composition based on four presumed sources: Yahwist (J), Elohist (E), Priestly Editor (P), and Deuteronomist historian (D).

Jesuits [The Society of Jesus] A Catholic religious order begun during the Catholic Reformation.

Jomon The earliest period(s) of Japanese prehistory.

Judaica exposito An interpretation of the Old Testament conforming to Rabbinic Judaism rather than the Christological understanding of the New Testament.

Karaite A Jewish movement dating from the Islamic conquest who reject the religious authority of the rabbis and the Talmud for the Tanakh (Old Testament) alone. Regarded as heretical and at times persecuted by Rabbinic Judaism.

Katrina Hurricane in 2005 that killed almost two thousand people following the failure of levees in New Orleans.

Khirbet Kerak The Palestinian name of a town near the southern mouth of the Sea of Galilee. An archaeological culture named for this town where it was first identified.

king lists Records of dynasties and kings and years of their reigns that are preserved in the records of the Ancient Near East.

King Midas An ancient king, whose legend claimed that whatever he touched turned to gold. His legend, preserved by the Greeks, is likely based on a historical king who reigned over a kingdom in ancient Turkey.

Kish A city near Babylon in ancient Iraq, perhaps named for Cush, the son of Ham. According to ancient Sumerian king lists, Kish was the first city after the Flood to have kings.

Kura, Araxes Two rivers south of the mountain range extending between the southern portion of the Black Sea and the Caspian Sea and just north of Mt. Ararat.

kurgans The Eastern European term for burial mounds, similar to those found elsewhere in the world.

Last Days Biblical reference to the time between the outpouring of the Spirit, and before the great and terrible Day of the Lord. Also, a time of increasing wickedness.

Late Uruk A widespread culture in the Ancient Near East named after the city of Uruk in southern Mesopotamia. Currently dated from 3200-3000 BC, it actually dates from about 2300-2200 BC.

Latitudinarian A party in the Anglican Church open to scientific progress and transcending the religious quarrels within the Anglican Church.

liberalism Originally referring to the beliefs of those seeking freedom from the constraints imposed by the ancient class order of Europe.

Liberal Christianity A movement in Christianity deriving from nineteenth century Germany that sought to accommodate the beliefs of the Christian faith to science and modern values and sought to be led by the modern state rather than "held back" by traditional beliefs.

libertarian A point of view that rejects or

Glosssay

wishes to limit government involvement in economic and social behavior.

linguistics, linguist The science or scholarship of language, and language relationships. One who studies languages.

lingua franca A widely-spoken language used for literature, government, and commerce, even by those who have other native languages. Though originally referring to the language of France, English serves this role in most of the world today.

literal An understanding that accords with the contextual sense of the words of a letter or literature, without eisegesis (interpretation).

biblical literalism Adhering to the literal teachings of the Scriptures.

literary criticism An understanding or pretended understanding of literature, aside from its content, often by assuming forms, beliefs, and prejudices for its composition.

literati Men (and women) of letters, sometimes referring to those sharing elite or highbrow cultural prejudices.

liturgy, liturgical Public forms of worship.

lost-wax A form of bronze working in which a wax likeness is used to form a clay mold for the bronze product.

lower criticism Textual criticism seeking the best text and interpretation rather than seeking the origins or questioning the truth of a text such as the Bible.

mainline Christianity Referring to the traditional, culturally-prominent Christian denominations that largely adapted to modernism.

Manichaeism A form of Gnosticism dating from the third century that viewed matter as sinful and ultimate reality as a contest between light and darkness.

mastaba Bench-shaped structures found by the Pyramids in Egypt, where are found the remains of the dead surrounded by elaborate provisions.

Mayan Referring to the Mayas or ancient natives of Guatemala and the southern regions of Mexico.

mechanistic science The science that studies the behavior of mechanical systems. Informing a view of the world as if all things are governed by deterministic mechanical laws.

Medes An ancient Indo-European people that ruled Persia and its Empire from the sixth to the late fourth century before Christ.

medieval Pertaining to the Middle Ages, the time between the ancient and modern worlds.

mega-fauna Large animals such as mammoths, elk, cave bears, and horses.

megalithic Great stone structures found in northern Europe and elsewhere dating to very ancient times. Burials are found among many of these structures.

megaron Elaborate multi-room dwellings with internal plazas. They are found in the Aegean and Near East and date from the Middle Bronze Age.

Mesopotamia The name for the land between the Tigris and Euphrates in ancient Iraq, where is found the oldest and most developed ancient civilizations.

Messiah, Messianic [Hebrew] Literally "the anointed one." "Khristós" in Greek; "Christ" in English. The Savior, or any would-be "Savior." Referring to or having characteristics of the Messiah.

metamorphic A type of rock believed to have been formed from existing rocks through great pressure and heat.

midden A heap of shells or refuse.

Middle Bronze Age An era before the widespread use of iron, but following a distinct change in culture from the preceding Early Bronze Age.

Millennium, millennia A thousand-year period referenced in Revelation 20. Thousands of years.

Minyan A type of pottery spreading through Eastern Anatolia (Turkey), the Aegean, and into Italy in the Middle Bronze Age (2200 – 1600 BC).

Glossary

Mitanni, Mittannian An ancient kingdom in Syria and western Iraq dating from the second half of the second millennium. The kingdom spoke a language unrelated to either the Indo-European or Semitic families of languages. Reference to this ancient kingdom.

modernism Belief in the superiority of science over faith. A belief in progress and superiority of the present over the past. An artistic movement opposed to classical and traditional forms.

monogenesis Offspring having a common ancestor. cf **polygenesis.**

Mousterian A Paleolithic archaeological culture named for a site in southern France and associated with Neanderthal remains.

mullah A teacher and leader learned in Islamic theology and law.

Murphy's Law The adage stating that "anything that can go wrong will go wrong," sometimes modified with "and at the worse possible time."

Mycenea, Mycenean An archaeological site in Greece believed to be the root of Hellenic civilization, possibly including pre-Greek remains. Characterized by this culture.

Mystery Babylon In the book of Revelation, the great wicked city that rules the world.

Narmer palette A decorative artifact, widely though inaccurately regarded as depicting Egypt's first Pharaoh.

nationalism, nationalistic Excessive devotion to one's nation, government, or country.

Nature The visible world aside from the influence of man. God's **Creation.**

nawamis Bee-hive shaped sandstone structures found in the Sinai desert.

Near East The lands of the Bible. They extend from Cush (Ethiopia) and Egypt in the South, to Persia (Iran) in the East, to Anatolia (Turkey) in the West, and Ararat (Armenia) in the North.

nebular hypothesis The theory of the formation of the solar system by the gradual consolidation of gases or particles of dust or rocks.

Neolithic The New Stone Age. An archaeological era identified by highly-polished and finely-constructed stone tools.

Neo-Orthodoxy A twentieth century development from liberal theology that emphasized the human condition and crisis, expressed in the form of classical Protestant dogma.

Neoplatonism A philosophy that combines the teachings of Plato and Aristotle and explains the visible world as eternally emerging from some primary source called "the One."

New Age Modern forms of spirituality that are not bound by the teachings of the Bible.

New Archaeology A movement in archaeology dating to the sixties which supposed that new technologies would revolutionize and dispense with the methods of traditional archaeology.

New Canaan Reference to a place as the new Promised Land.

New Christian A convert from Judaism during and following the Spanish Inquisition.

New Covenant A promised new covenant to replace the covenant of Moses (Jeremiah 31:31). The New Testament or the covenant of the Spirit instituted by Jesus.

New Science The early modern astronomical and mechanical sciences that replaced Aristotelian science.

New World Lands of the Western Hemisphere unknown to Europeans before Columbus's "discovery" of America.

Nimrod Son of Cush, grandson of Noah, a "mighty hunter before the Lord" and founder of cities in ancient Shinar and Assyria (Gen. 10:9-12).

ochre The color of yellow, brown, red or iron-pigmented clay.

Ockham's [Occam's] Razor A principle dating from William of Ockham (fourteenth century) to make no more assumptions than necessary because the simplest explanation is more likely.

Glosssay

Old World Refers to Europe, Asia, Africa, and the Near East, or the lands Europeans knew before they discovered America.

Olmec The earliest or Formative culture in southern Mexico, dating from 1400-1300 BC.

oppida The remains of ancient hill forts in Europe.

oracular Having meaning beyond the immediate circumstances and understanding of those who heard or wrote a prophecy.

organic chemistry Chemistry relating to extended hydro-carbon molecules, and to the structures of amino acids and living things.

orthodoxy, orthodox Right or correct opinion or forms of worship, usually in reference to established church teachings.

pacifist A form of faith or politics that does not believe in compulsion and holds that faith or political aims should be neither spread nor defended by force of arms.

paleography The science of ancient scripts and writing.

Paleolithic Belonging to the Old Stone Age and characterized by tools or weapons chipped from stone.

paleomagnetism Ancient patterns of magnetized earth, often thought to evidence ancient reversals of the earth's magnetic fields.

paleontography The use of imaging technology for scanning fossils and relics.

paleontology, paleontologist The study of fossils, the remains of ancient plants or animals. One who studies these.

parochial Of limited or narrow outlook and scope.

Passover A biblical feast commemorating the Exodus.

Pentecost A biblical feast commemorating the Israelite's meeting with God at Sinai. The day of the outpouring of the Holy Spirit in the book of Acts.

Pentecostal Reference to the coming of the Holy Spirit at the first Christian Pentecost. A form of Christianity beginning early in twentieth century which viewed the church in the book of Acts as normative for today, and which separated the experience of conversion from the reception of the Holy Spirit. Most Pentecostals came to view speaking in tongues as the initial evidence of the baptism of the Holy Spirit.

philology The study of ancient literature or letters.

philosophes French philosophers of the Enlightenment who believed in the superiority of philosophy or reason above religion and the Christian faith.

physicalist Reducing all phenomena to physical causes. Materialist.

philosophical history A view of history that accords with certain philosophical principles vis a vis seeing history freely determined by God and free creatures, therefore requiring empirical discovery. **Historicism.**

Phoenicia, Phoenician The Greek name for the people whose ancient home was the land know as Canaan in the Bible. Greek term referring to the Canaanites.

Pietists A movement among the Protestants of continental Europe following the Reformation that emphasized private Bible study, personal piety, and social action.

plano-convex A type of brick, flat on the bottom and curved on the top, used in the construction of Ancient Near Eastern buildings.

plate tectonics Presently reigning geological theory that assumes that the earth is composed of giant plates that move or slide under one another owing to conveyor belts of magma operating deep inside the earth.

Plato, Platonism A Greek philosopher of the fourth century before Christ. Embodying characteristics of Plato's philosophy.

Pleistocene Reference to the era of the "Ice Age(s)."

Plymouth Brethren A sect developing from influential nineteenth century British teachers who exited the Anglican Church, emphasized biblical prophecy, and created the Dispensational Premillennial school of biblical theology.

Pompeii An ancient city near Naples, Italy, whose inhabitants were buried by the eruption of nearby Mount Vesuvius in 79 AD.

polygenesis The belief that different races of human beings do not have common ancestors. cf **monogenesis**.

polymath One who is learned in many scholarly and scientific fields.

positivism A philosophy dating from the nineteenth century which holds that science based on verified physical sense experience is the highest or only valid knowledge.

postmodernism Skepticism owing to the discovery that science and other forms of knowledge inescapably depend on non-objective assumptions.

post-processual archaeology A post-modern form of archaeology emphasizing interpretation above objectivity.

practical reason As defined by Immanuel Kant, reason pertaining to morals that is separate from the pure reason supposed to undergird scientific knowledge.

pragmatism A form of philosophy created by American philosopher C.S. Pierce that recognizes the limits of speculative philosophy and gives validity to human needs and experience.

predestination The biblical teaching that those who will be saved have from the beginning been chosen by God for salvation.

prehistoric Referring to the time before history, applicable to the history of humans before they left written records.

premillennialism Belief that Jesus' Second Coming begins a thousand years of peaceful rule in the earth. In historic premillennialism Jesus rules with the Church. In Dispensational Premillennialism, he raptures the Church and rules in the earthly Millennium with ethnic Jews.

preservation bias Bias in archaeology determined by characteristics favoring preservation of archaeological remains.

preternatural Having a supernatural but dark character.

Primary [rocks] Geological features believed formed in the earth's initial creation.

primitivist Those seeking to return to the Christianity of the primitive (Apostolic) Church or seeking a return to the pristine state of Nature prior to its corruption, views popular in early America.

Progressive Creationism Belief that God created progressive forms of life at various intervals of history, as reflected in the days of creation in the first chapter of Genesis.

Promised Land The ancient land of Canaan that God promised to the children of Abraham. An earthly paradise.

proto- A precursor or primitive form.

Providence The belief that Creation and the events of history are beneficially and completely predetermined by God.

punctuated equilibrium Belief that evolution occurs in rapid bursts, making a fossil record unlikely.

pure reason According to Immanuel Kant, reasoning according to ideas fixed in the mind and not arising from experience.

Puritan A Protestant reform movement beginning after the Reformation and centered in England that sought to purify the English Church from traditions and to base faith strictly on the Bible.

Q [sayings] A hypothetical collection of sayings of Jesus that, along with a shortened form of the gospel of Mark, liberal scholars assume as the sources of Matthew and Luke.

QED [Latin *quod erat demonstrandum*]. Used to mark the conclusion of a formal proof.

Quaker Informal name for the Society of Friends. A movement in seventeenth century British Christianity emphasizing the egalitarian, pacifist, and spiritual character of early Christianity.

Glosssay

qualitative time Genetic time. A sense of time determined by dependent relations rather than quantitative division.

Quaternary The last major epoch in geology encompassing the Pleistocene ("Ice Age") and Holocene eras.

quantum physics A school of experimental modern physics teaching that matter consists of indivisible particles such as photons whose definitive physical properties cannot be both precisely and simultaneously measured.

rabbi [Hebrew] "Teacher" or "master." A religious leader in Second Temple and post-biblical Judaism.

Rabbinic Referring to the religious leaders of modern Judaism who reject Jesus as the Jewish Messiah promised in the Scriptures.

racism Viewing essential characteristics of mankind to be determined by race. Belief in the superiority of certain races.

radioactive dating Dating materials based on the breakdown of radioactive molecules and calculated from the relative abundance of the isotopes.

radiocarbon Carbon whose atoms contain extra neutrons created by cosmic rays impacting carbon-dioxide in the atmosphere, then decaying to a stable form of carbon. Radioactive carbon becomes part of living plants and of animals that eat these plants.

rapture The catching up of believers at Christ's return (1Thes. 4:17) when interpreted as believers being secretly taken out of the world a few years before the Second Coming.

rationalism, rationalistic Rejecting whatever does not conform to philosophically understandable principles.

rebuke The correction of an erring leader or brother.

reductionist The belief that any matter or report can be reduced to some materialist, physicalist, or rationalist basis.

Reformed A form of Reformation Protestantism associated with John Calvin and separate from the Lutheran and Separatist movements.

refraction Deflection of sound or light owing to a change in medium through which waves pass.

Renaissance A transition period between the Medieval and Reformation era characterized by a revival of interest in ancient times.

restorationist The theological belief that the church should be restored to the standards and vitality of some earlier point of its existence.

rigor, rigorous Demanding or difficult standards. Systematic subjection to these standards.

Romantic Escaping from reality into emotionally satisfying flights of imagination. The term comes from the Roman poets who pretended to believe in gods or in unusual things in which the Roman elite no longer believed. A similar period characterized the culture of Europe during the early nineteenth century.

Royal Society An organization begun in the seventeenth century and sponsored by the government of Great Britain for the promotion of natural philosophy (science).

rustic Rural living characterized by homemade artifacts.

sand-tempered Pottery composed of clay mixed with sand to strengthen its construction.

Sanskrit The earliest written language of India, deriving from Old Persian and following the extension of the Persian Empire into India. These linguistic roots gave rise to the myth of "Indo"-Europeans.

Sargon The name of two Ancient Near Eastern kings, the earliest being Sargon the Great (c. 2200 – 1800 BC); the second, an Assyrian king of the first millennium before Christ and mentioned in the Bible.

scepticism [UK] or **skepticism** [US] An attitude of doubt often based on principles rather than evidence.

scholastics, schoolmen Originally, members of certain Medieval or Renaissance schools known for their exacting but tedious theological or philosophical reasoning.

School of the Prophets Early American schools of biblical and spiritual training responsible for creating America's earliest colleges. An early twentieth-century Pentecostal fellowship.

scientism, scientistic Belief that science is the only reliable way of determining truth.

scientific method Variously-explained ways that distinguish how scientific knowledge should be obtained.

sciolism, sciolist Holding opinions on subjects in which one has only a superficial knowledge. One who does this.

Scriptural Geologists Geologists in the nineteenth century who insisted that the earth be studied in the light of the Bible.

seal A ownership marker for imprinting possessions and documents.

Second Coming The promised return of Jesus from Heaven.

Second Great Awakening A great revival that began in America (ca. 1800), especially active on the American frontier.

Second Temple Judaism The period of ancient Judaism belonging to the New Testament and the Dead Sea Scrolls. The First Temple was built by Solomon but destroyed by the Babylonians (ca. 587 BC). The Second Temple, built by exiles returning from Babylon (ca. 538 BC), was destroyed in AD 70.

Secondary [rocks] Features of the earth formed after the earth's initial creation but lacking evidence of those mammals and other familiar land animals once believed to have perished in the Flood.

sectarian Divisions or pertaining to divisions in the body of Christians.

secular Not religious. Pertaining to matters of the present world.

seminary A school for training ministers and for imparting a theological education.

Semitic From the German name for Shem, son of Noah. Improperly applied to those speaking languages such as biblical Hebrew, a form of Western Canaanite. A subdivision of the Hamitic family of languages.

Separatist One who believes the church should be separate from society and government.

Sephradi Jews from lands subject to Islamic rule. cf **Askenazi**

seriation Dividing artifacts according to some pattern supposed to reflect historical change and development.

Sermon on the Mount Jesus' teachings in Matthew 5-7.

Seventh Day Adventism A sect of Christianity formed in the wake of the Adventist movement in the middle of the nineteenth century and much influenced by the prophetess, Ellen G. White.

Shang A dynasty centered on the upper Yellow River that ruled China from 1600 – 1100 BC. Shang styles also appear in the Formative cultures of America.

Shemitic The author's proposed designation for the most ancient language of the descendents of Noah's son Shem. This family of agglutinative languages would include most native tongues found in Asia and the New World.

Shroud of Turin A relic some believe to have been the burial cloth used to wrap Jesus' body.

singularity A condition that can be expressed or given but which cannot be rationally explained.

in situ [Latin] Archaeological remains that have not been removed from their original location.

Solon Author of the laws of ancient Athens, which were less severe than those of the previous law-giver, Draco.

Son of Man The self-designation of Jesus. A human being rather than an angel or other heavenly being.

Sophist An ancient school of Greek philosophers emphasizing the wining of arguments above depth and truth, thus favoring materialist beliefs.

Sothic cycle A period supposed to have characterized ancient Egyptian calendars determined by the first appearance of the year of the star Sirius in the southern skies. Each period lasted for 1,460 years.

Special Revelation The inspired Scriptures. The Bible.

species A particular kind of plant or animal. A subspecies of plant or animal given a unique Latin designation.

strata, archaeological Layers of archaeological remains.

strata, geological Layers of earth with distinctive, usually horizontal, markings or composition.

stratum A single layer.

systems science The study of the organization, function, and development of man-made or naturally-occurring systems.

Sumer, Sumerian The earliest civilization of the Ancient Near East whose writings can be understood.

Supreme Creator A designation for a philosophical Creator God, sometimes understood to be distinct from the God of the Bible.

Susa A city lying in the lowlands of ancient Iran and near the Persian Gulf.

suttee In Hinduism, the accompaniment of a widow in her husband's death usually by immolation. Used generally to describe the sacrifice of family members and servants upon the death of an important person.

Table of Nations The descendents of Noah's family, the ancestors of ancient nations recorded in Genesis Chapter 10.

Talmud The sacred written traditions and commentaries of Rabbinic Judaism.

Tarim Desert Basin of Western China, whose cold, dry climate preserve ancient archaeological remains.

tel [Hebrew] or *tell* [Arabic] Hills in the Near East containing the buried remains of ancient cities.

temporal Referring to history rather than to that which transcends the world of space and time.

tenure Protecting the academic freedom of teachers by guaranteeing the continued employment of those granted such status.

Tertiary A geological phase of earth's history that reveals early mammals, once supposed evidence of Noah's Flood.

theistic evolution Belief that God guided evolution in creating the separate forms of life.

theology The study of God. Understanding the character of God and how he functions, whether from philosophy or from the Bible.

theophany An encounter with God.

tholos A round structure having an extended rectangular hall or platform, giving a keyhole shape to its foundation.

threshing floor A flat, hard surface for separating wheat from the chaff. It also refers to an open forum to allow teachings to be discussed and tested for conformity to accepted standards of truth.

Torah A Hebrew term meaning "Teachings" referring to the first five books of the Bible. Also called the Pentateuch or the Books of Moses.

totemism Religious belief that incorporates ancestors in a hierarchical order and reflects man's kinship with Nature.

TranCaucasion An archeological culture of the third millennium before Christ that is widespread throughout the Ancient Near East and which extends across the Caucasus mountains. Variously called the Khirbet-Kerak or the Kura-Araxes culture.

transcendent Beyond the physically-perceived material world.

tree-ring calibration Correcting radiocarbon dates to accord with absolute years counted from radiocarbon dated tree rings.

Glossary

the Tribulation or **the Great Tribulation** A period of great persecution or troubles that immediately precedes the return of Christ.

Trinitarian gloss The Comma Johanneum supporting a Trinitarian formula inserted into 1 John 5:7,8 in some versions (e.g. KJV) of the Bible.

typology As practiced by the New Testament writers, the use of historical types from the Old Testament to refer to realities in Heaven and in the coming spiritual Kingdom of God.

tumulus Referring to earth-covered burials. In some places called barrows, kurgans, or burial mounds.

unilinear evolution Supposed constant evolutionary progress.

Ur of the Chaldeans The ancient home of Abraham, believed to be the city in lower Iraq whose remains were excavated by British archaeologist, Sir Leonard Woolley.

urn A large vase.

Uruk A city in lower Iraq at the site of present day Warka that has been identified by this name in Ancient Near Eastern tablets. Called Erech in the Bible, it was the largest and most significant city of the third millennium before Christ and likely the site of the Tower of Babel.

varves Layers built up from annual deposits of sediment.

Vatican The governing body of the Roman Catholic Church headed by the Pope.

Villanovan A European Bronze Age culture centered in the upper Italian peninsula.

volk [German] Folk.

votive offering A gift that is buried as an offering to the gods. A common archaeological interpretation of buried artifacts found in prime condition.

vulgar Common. Lacking good taste or learning.

wattle-and-daub A type of building construction where clay is used to fill a wooden framework.

the West, Western Referring to western or formerly Roman Catholic Europe. The culture springing from Western Europe.

wiggle-pattern matching Matching tree rings by patterns of radiocarbon dates from successively dated tree rings rather than determining absolute dates by counted sequences of tree rings.

Windmiller An Archaic culture of North America defined by an archaeological site in California.

Woodland The era of Eastern American archaeological culture (1000 BC – 1000 AD) between the earlier Archaic and the later Mississippian periods.

Yiddish A dialect of High German spoken in the Jewish communities of Central Europe.

Young Earth Creationism A school of theological and geological thought that teaches the days of creation were 24 hours in duration, and the earth was created from 6,000-12,000 years ago.

Younger Dryas According to current science, a cold period in the early Holocene (9500-10800 BC) marked by a more southern appearance of the Dryas flower often linked to the birth of agriculture.

Zion The ancient hill in Jerusalem serving the general assembly of God's people.

zoology, zoological The science of animals.

Topical Bibliography

Journals and Periodicals 387

Ancient Texts and Histories 387
Ancient Legends, Myths, and Religion 387

Flood (General and Lore) 387
Vanished Civilizations and New Age Floods 388
Searches for and Studies of the Ark 388
Young Earth Creationism and Critics 388
Local Flood 389

Bible Dictionaries, Encyclopedias, and Reference Books 389
Biblical Text and Interpretation 390
Archaeology and the Bible 392
The Bible and the Reformation 393
The Bible and Science in Modern History 393
History of Christian Thought 393
The Bible in America 394

Philosophy 395
Philosophy and History of Science 395
Historiography and the Philosophy of History . 397
Anthropology, Population, Race, and Genes 397
Ancient Agriculture and Technologies 398
Languages, Scripts, and Writing Technology 399
Death, Burial, and Archaeological Excavation .. 399
Dating and Chronologies 399

World History 400
History of the Ancient Near East 400
History of Ancient America 401
History of Ancient Europe 401
History of the Ancient Orient 402

Archaeological History, Thought, and Science .. 402
Prehistory and World Archaeology 402
Old World Archaeology 403
Archaeology (Ancient Near East) 403
Archaeology (The Land of the Bible) 404
Archaeology (Mesopotamia, Arabia, Syria, and Iran) 404
Archaeology (Egypt) 405
Archaeology (Anatolia and the Aegean) 405
Archaeology (Europe) 406
Archaeology (Asia) 406
Archaeology (Australia and the Pacific) 406
Archaeology (Americas) 407
Archaeology (South America) 407
Archaeology (North America) 407
Archaeology (Africa) 408

Climatology and Environment 409
Cosmology 409
Geology 409
Geography 410
Zoology 410

The following are works referenced, discussed, or in some fashion consulted or reviewed for this study. Asterisks (****, ***, **, *) indicate the extent a particular source informed this study.

Journals and Periodicals

American Journal of Archaeology (AJA)
American Journal of Science (AJS)
Anatolia Studies
Antiquity *
Archaeology
Astrophysical Journal Letters (AJL)
Biblical Archaeologist (BA)
Biblical Archaeology Review (BAR)
Biblical Review (BR) ***
Bulletin of the American Schools of Oriental Research (BASOR)
Iraq
Journal of Near Eastern Studies (JNES) **
Harvard Theological Review (HTR)
Radiocarbon **
Science
Scientific American (SA) *

Ancient Texts and Histories

Augustine of Hippo. *City of God.* (ca. 418) ****
Caesar. *The Conquest of Gaul.* (51 BC) *
Cicero, Marcus Tullius. Selected works: *De Amicitia, Scipio's Dream, Letters, Treatises on Friendship and Old Age.* (80-43 BC) *
Eusebius. *Chronicles.* (ca. 325) *
Herodotus. *The Histories.* (ca. 446 BC) **
Hesiod. *Theogony.* (ca. 700 BC) *
Homer. *Iliad.* (ca. 700 BC) *
_____. *The Odyssey.* (ca. 700 BC) *
Josephus. *Against Apion.* (ca. 100) ****
_____. *Antiquities of the Jews.* (ca. 100) ***
Julius Africanus. *Extant Writings.* (ca. 232)
Livy. *The Early History of Rome.* (ca. 26 BC) *
Tacitus. *The Germania.* (ca. 100) *
The Rig Veda. (ca. 1700 – 1100 BC) *
Thucydides. *History of the Peloponnesian War.* (ca. 40 BC)

Also

Charles, Robert Henry. *The Ethiopic Version of the Book of Enoch.* Bibliobazaar, 2009.
Cory, I. P. *Ancient Fragments.* 1832. Reprint: Forgotten Books, 2007. **
Matthew, Victor H. and Benjamin, Don C. *Old Testament Parallels: Laws and Stories from the Ancient Near East.* Paulist Press, 1997.
Lumpkin, Joseph B. *The First and Second Books of Enoch: The Ethiopic and Slavonic Texts; A Comprehensive Translation with Commentary.* Fifth Estate, 2009.
Pritchard, James, ed. *Ancient Near Eastern Texts Relating to the Old Testament,* 3rd ed. Princeton University Press, 1969. **
Verbrugghe, Gerald and John Wickersham. *Berossos and Manetho, Introduced and Translated: Native Traditions in Ancient Mesopotamia and Egypt.* University of Michigan Press, 2001. **

Ancient Legends, Myths, and Religion

Angus, Samuel. *The Mystery-Religions and Christianity.* Carol, 1966. *
Cervantes, Fernando. *The Devil in the New World: The Impact of Diabolism in New Spain.* Yale University Press, 1994.
Cumont, Franz. *Oriental Religions in Roman Paganism.* 1911. Reprint: Dover, 1980. *
Durkheim, Emile. *The Elementary Forms of Religious Life.* 1915. Reprint: The Free Press, 1995. ***
Eliade, Mircea. *Shamanism: Archaic Techniques of Ecstasy.* Translated by Willard R. Trask. Princeton University Press, 1951. *
Frazer, Sir James George. *Folk-Lore in the Old Testament: Studies in Comparative Religion, Legend, and Law.* 3 vols. Macmillan, 1919. ***
James, E. O. *The Ancient Gods.* Castle Books, 1960. *
Hays, H. R. *In the Beginnings: Early Man and His Gods.* Putman, 1963. *
Lewis, Mark Edward. *The Flood Myths of Early China.* State University of New York Press, 2006. *
Martin, Charles. *Flood Legends: Global Clues of a Common Event.* Master Books, 2009.
Ringgren, Helmer. *The Religions of the Ancient Near East.* Westminster Press, 1973. **
Rose, H. J. *Ancient Greek and Roman Religion.* 2 vols. Barnes & Noble Books, 1995. *
Sedley, David. *Creationism and its Critics in Antiquity.* University of California Press, 2007. **
Sommer, Deborah, ed. *Chinese Religion: An Anthology of Sources.* Oxford University Press, 1995. *
Walton, John H. *Ancient Near Eastern Thought and the Old Testament: Introduction to the Conceptual World of the Hebrew Bible.* Baker Academic, 2006.

Flood (General and Lore)

Anderson, William Scott. *Solving the Mystery of the Biblical Flood.* Xlibris, 2001.
Chittick, Donald E. *The Puzzle of Ancient Man: Advanced Technology in Past Civilization.* Creation Compass, 1998.
Cohn, Norman. *Noah's Flood: The Genesis Story in Western Thought.* Yale University Press, 1996. ***

Topical Bibliography

Cooper, Bill. *After the Flood: The Early Post-Flood History of Europe Traced Back to Noah*. New Wine Press, 1995.

Filby, Frederick A. *The Flood Reconsidered: A Review of the Evidences of Geology, Archaeology, Ancient Literature and the Bible*. Zondervan, 1970. *

Force, James E. *William Whiston, Honest Newtonian*. Cambridge University Press, 1985. ****

Howorth, Sir Henry Hoyle. *The Glacial Nightmare and the Flood*. 2 vols. 1893. Reprint: Elibron Classics, 2005. **

──────. *The Mammoth and the Flood: An Attempt to Confront the Theory of Uniformity with the Facts of Recent Geology*. General Books, 2010. **

Kang, C. H. and Ethel R. Nelson. *The Discovery of Genesis: How the Truths of Genesis Were Found Hidden in the Chinese Language*. Concordia, 1979.

McDowell, Bruce A. *Noah: A Righteous Man in a Wicked Age*. AMG, 2004.

Pleins, J. David. *When the Great Abyss Opened: Classic and Contemporary Readings of Noah's Flood*. Oxford University Press, 2003.

Stiebing, William H., Jr. *Ancient Astronauts, Cosmic Collisions, and Other Popular Theories about Man's Past*. Prometheus Books, 1984. *

Stone, Michael E., Aryeh Amihay, and Vered Hillel, eds. *Noah and His Book(s)*. Society of Biblical Literature, 2010. **

Velikovski, Immanuel. *Earth in Upheaval*. Doubleday, 1955. *

Young, Davis A. *The Biblical Flood: A Case Study of the Church's Response to Extrabiblical Evidence*. Eerdmans, 1995. ****

Vanished Civilizations and New Age Floods

Hancock, Graham. *Fingerprints of the Gods: The Evidence of Earth's Lost Civilization*. Three Rivers Press, 1995.

──────. *Heaven's Mirror: Quest for the Lost Civilization*. Three Rivers Press, 1998.

Hapgood, Charles. *Maps of the Ancient Sea Kings: Evidence of Advanced Civilizations in the Ice Age*. Adventures Unlimited Press, 1996.

Nur, Amos with Dawn Burgess. *Apocalypse: Earthquakes, Archaeology, and the Wrath of God*. Princeton University Press, 2008.

Schooch, Robert. *Voices of the Rocks: A Scientist Looks at Catastrophes and Ancient Civilizations*. Harmony Books, 1999.

Shrady, Nicholas. *The Last Day: Wrath, Ruin, and Reason in the Great Lisbon Earthquake of 1755*. Viking, 2008.

Wilson, Colin and Rand Flem-Ath. *The Atlantis Blueprint: Unlocking the Ancient Mysteries of Long-Lost Civilization*. Delta, 2000.

Wilson, Ian. *Before the Flood: The Biblical Flood as a Real Event and How it Changed the Course of Civilization*. St. Martin's Press, 2001.

Searches for and Studies of the Ark

Bryce, James. *Transcaucasia and Ararat: Being Notes of a Vacation Tour in the Autumn of 1876*. 1877. Reprint: Elibron Classics, 2005. *

Balsiger, Dave and Charles E. Sellier, Jr. *In Search of Noah's Ark: The Greatest Discovery of Our Time*. DVD. Directed by James L. Conway. Sun Classic Pictures, 1976.

──────. *The Incredible Discovery of Noah's Ark*. Dell, 1995.

Bright, Richard Carl. *Quest for Discovery: The Remarkable Search for Noah's Ark*. New Leaf Press, 2000.

Corbin, B. J., ed. *The Explorers of Ararat and the Search for Noah's Ark*. Great Commission Illustrated Books, 1999. *

Cornuke, Robert and David Halbrook. *Lost Mountains of Noah: The Discovery of the Real Mountains of Ararat*. Broadman & Holman, 2001.

Cummings, Violet M. *Noah's Ark: Fact or Fable*. Creation-Science Research Center, 1972. **

Dawes, June. *Noah's Ark: Adrift in Dark Waters*. Noahide, 2000.

Fasold, David. *The Ark of Noah*. Wynwood Press, 1988.

Montgomery, John Warwick. *The Quest for Noah's Ark: A Treasury of Documented Accounts from Ancient Times to the Present Day of Sightings of the Ark and Explorations of Mount Ararat; Ascent to the Summit of Noah's Mountain*. Bethany Fellowship, 1972. *

Morris, John D. *Adventurers on Ararat*. Creation-Life, 1973.

Navarra, Fernand, ed. with David Balsiger. *Noah's Ark: I Touched It*. Logos International, 1974.

Segraves, Kelly L. *Searching for Noah's Ark*. A Beta Book, 1975.

Wyatt, Ron. *Discovered: Noah's Ark*. World Bible Society, 1989.

Woodmorappe, John. *Noah's Ark: A Feasibility Study*. Institute for Creation Research, 1996.

Young Earth Creationism and Critics

Austin, Steven A., ed. *Grand Canyon: Monument to Catastrophe*. Institute for Creation Research, 1994.

Chaffey, Tim and Jason Lisle. *Old-Earth Creationism on Trial: The Verdict is In*. Master Books, 2008.

Froede, Carl R., Jr. *Geology By Design*. Master Books, 2007.

Gish, Duane T. *Creation Scientists Answer Their Crit-

ics. Institution for Creation Research, 1993.
_____. *Evolution: The Fossils Say No!* Creation-Life, 1973.
Gray, Gorman. *The Age of the Universe: What are the Biblical Limits?* Morningstar Publications, 2000.
Ham, Ken, et al. *A Pocket Guide to Noah's Ark: A Biblical and Scientific Look at the Genesis Account.* Answers in Genesis USA, 2009.
_____, et al. *A Pocket Guide to the Global Flood: A Biblical and Scientific Look at the Catastrophe that Changed the World.* Answers in Genesis USA, 2009.
_____, gen. ed. *The New Answers Book.* Master Books, 2009.
_____. *What Really Happened to the Dinosaurs.* Answers in Genesis, 2001
_____, Jonathan Sarfati, and Carl Wieland. *The Revised Expanded Answers Book: The 20 Most Asked Questions About Creation; Evolution, and the Book of Genesis, Answered!* Edited by Don Batten. Master Books, 2002.
_____, Tim Lovett, Andrew Snelling and John Whitmore. *A Pocket Guide to the Global Flood: A Biblical and Scientific Look at the Catastrophe that Changed the Earth.* Answers in Genesis USA, 2009.
Helfinstine, Robert F. and Jerry D. Roth. *Texas Tracks and Artifacts: Do Texas Fossils Indicate Coexistence of Men with Dinosaurs?* Twin-Cities Creation Science Association, 1994.
MacArthur, John. *The Battle for the Beginnings: Creation, Evolution, and the Bible.* Nelson Books, 2001.
McIver, Tom. *Anti-Evolution: A Reader's Guide to Writings Before and After Darwin.* John Hopkins University Press, 1992. *
Morris, Henry M. *The Bible and Modern Science.* Moody Press, 1968.
_____ and John C. Whitcomb. *The Genesis Flood: The Biblical Record and its Scientific Implications.* Presbyterian & Reformed, 1961. ***
Morris, John D. *Noah's Ark and the Lost World.* Masquerade Books, 1988.
_____. *The Young Earth: The Real History of the Earth – Past, Present, and Future.* Master Books, 1994.
Mortenson, Terry and Thane H. Ury, eds. *Coming to Grips with Genesis: Biblical Authority and the Age of the Earth.* Master Books, 2008.
_____. *The Great Turning Point: The Church's Catastrophic Mistake on Geology – Before Darwin.* Master Books, 2004.
_____. *Millions of Years: and the Downfall of the Christian West.* Answers in Genesis, 2005
Numbers, Ronald L. *The Creationists: The Evolution of Scientific Creationism.* University of California Press, 1992. ***
Oard, Michael. *Frozen in Time: The Woolly Mammoth, the Ice Age, and the Bible.* Master Books, 2004.
_____. *Flood By Design: Receding Water Shapes the Earth's Surface.* Master Books, 2008.
Price, George McCready. *The Fundamentals of Geology and their Bearings on the Doctrine of a Literal Creation.* Pacific Press, 1913. ****
Reed, John K. *Plain Talk about Genesis: A Fresh Look at the PCA Earth History Debate.* Word Ministries and Deo Volente, 2000.
Rehwinkel, Alfred M. *The Flood in the Light of the Bible, Geology, and Archaeology.* Concordia, 1951. **
Ross, Hugh. *A Matter of Days: Resolving a Creation Controversy.* NavPress, 2004.
_____. *The Genesis Question: Scientific Advances and the Accuracy of Genesis.* NavPress, 1998. *
Thompson, Bert. *Creation Compromises.* Apologetics Press, 1995.
Vail, Tom. *Grand Canyon: A Different View.* Master Books, 2003. *
Whitcomb, John C. *The World that Perished.* Baker Book House, 1973.
White, Ellen G. *Patriarchs and Prophets.* Inter-American, 1890.
Whorton, Mark and Hill Roberts. *Guide to Understanding Creation.* Holman Reference, 2008.
Wieland, Carl. *Stones and Bones: Powerful Evidence against Evolution.* Master Books, 1996.
Wise, Kurt. *Faith, Form, and Time: What the Bible Teaches and What Science Confirms about Creation and the Age of the Universe.* Broadman & Holman, 2002.
Young, Davis A. and Ralph F. Stearley. *The Bible, Rocks and Time: Geological Evidence for the Age of the Earth.* InterVarsity Press, 2008.

Local Flood

Bradley, Walter. "Why I Believe the Bible is Scientifically Reliable." In *Why I Am a Christian*, edited by Norman Geisler and Paul K. Hoffman, 175-196. Baker Books, 2003. *
Parrot, André. *The Flood and Noah's Ark.* Translated by Edwin Hudson. SCM Press, 1953. *
Peake, Harold. *The Flood: New Light on an Old Story.* McBride, 1930. **
Ryan, William and Walter Pittman. *Noah's Flood: The New Scientific Discoveries about the Event that Changed History.* Simon & Shuster, 1998.
Snoke, David. *The Biblical Case for an Old Earth.* Baker Books, 2006.

Bible Dictionaries, Encyclopedias, and Reference Books

Bromiley, Geoffrey W., gen. ed. *International Standard Bible Encyclopedia.* 4 vols. Eerdmans, 1979. **

Topical Bibliography

Friedman, David Noel, ed. *Anchor Bible Dictionary*. 6 vols. Doubleday, 1992. ****
Halley, Henry H. *Halley's Bible Handbook*. 1927-1959. Reprint: Zondervan, 1965. **
Hoerth, Alfred J. *Archaeology and the Old Testament*. Baker Books, 1998. *
Smith, Dr. William. *Smith's Bible Dictionary*, rev. ed. Holman Bible, 1884. *
Zondervan with Gordon-Conwell Theological Seminary. *NIV Archaeological Study Bible: An Illustrated Walk Through Biblical History and Culture*. Zondervan, 2005. **

Biblical Text and Interpretation

Ackroyd, P. R. and C. F. Evans, eds. *The Cambridge History of the Bible*. 3 vols. Cambridge University Press, 1970. ****
Anderson, Bernard. *Understanding the Old Testament*, 3rd ed. Prentice-Hall, 1975.
Anderson, G. W., ed. *Tradition and Interpretation: Essays by Members of the Society for Old Testament Study*. Clarendon Press, 1979. *
Archer, Gleason Leonard. *A Survey of Old Testament Introduction*, rev. ed. Moody Press, 1974. *
Baillie, John. *The Idea of Revelation in Recent Thought*. Columbia University Press, 1961.
Bartholomew, Craig, Colin Greene and Karl Moller, eds. *After Pentecost: Language and Biblical Interpretation*. Zondervan, 2001.
_____, C. Stephen Evans, Mary Healy and Murray Rae, **eds.** *"Behind" the Text: History and Biblical Interpretation*. Zondervan, 2003.
Barton, John, ed. *The Cambridge Companion to Biblical Interpretation*. Cambridge University Press, 1998.
Barton, John. *The Nature of Biblical Criticism*. Westminster John Knox Press, 2007.
Beale, G. K. *The Erosion of Inerrancy in Evangelicalism: Responding to New Challenges to Biblical Authority*. Crossway, 2008. *
Bennett, W. H. and Walter F. Adeney. *The Bible and Criticism*. Dodge, 1913. **
Brenton, Sir Lancelot L. C. *The Septuagint with Apocrypha: Greek and English*. Hendrickson, 1986.
Boer, Harry R. *The Bible and Higher Criticism*. Eerdmans, 1975. *
Bruce, Frederick Fyvie. *The Canon of Scripture*. InterVarsity Press, 1988.
Clayton, Charles and Dan McCartney. *Let the Reader Understand: A Guide to Interpreting and Applying the Bible*. P & R Publishing, 2002.
Clements, Ronald E. *One Hundred Years of Old Testament Interpretation*. Westminster Press, 1976. **
Collins, John J. *Science and Faith: Friends or Foes?* Crossway Books, 2003.

Dixon, A. C. and R. A. Torrey. *The Fundamentals: A Testimony to the Truth*. 4 vols. 1919. Reprint: Baker Books, 2003. **
Ellis, E. Earle. *Prophecy and Hermeneutic in Early Christianity*. Eerdmans, 1978. *
Evans, Craig A. *Ancient Texts for New Testament Studies: A Guide to the Background Literature*. Hendrickson, 2005. *
_____ and Emanuel Tov, eds. *Exploring the Origins of the Bible: Canon Formation in Historical, Literary, and Theological Perspective*. Baker Academic, 2008. *
Ferguson, Everett. *Backgrounds of Early Christianity*, 3rd ed. Eerdmans, 2003.
Flint, Peter W., ed. *The Bible at Qumran: Text, Shape, and Interpretation*. Eerdmans, 2001. **
_____ and James VanderKam. *The Meaning of the Dead Sea Scrolls: Their Significance for Understanding the Bible, Judaism, Jesus, and Christianity*. Harper San Francisco, 2002. ****
Friedman, Richard Elliott. *Who Wrote the Bible?* Harper & Row, 1987.
Geisler, Norman L. and William E. Nix. *A General Introduction to the Bible*. Moody Press, 1968.
Grant, Robert M. with David Tracy. *Short History of Interpreting the Bible*, rev. ed. Augsburg Fortress, 1988.
Hauser, Alan J. and Duane F. Watson, eds. *A History of Biblical Interpretation*. Vol. 1, *The Ancient Period*. Eerdmans, 2003.
_____. *A History of Biblical Interpretation*. Vol. 2, *The Medieval Through the Reformation Periods*. Eerdmans, 2008.
Hays, J. Daniel and Donald A. Carson. *From Every People and Nation: A Biblical Theology of Race*. IVP Academic, 2003.
Hayes, John H. *An Introduction to Old Testament Study*. Abingdon Press, 1979. **
Hens-Piazza, Gina. *The New Historicism*. Fortress Press, 2002.
Heschel, Susannah. *The Aryan Jesus: Christian Theologies and the Bible in Nazi Germany*. Princeton University Press, 2008.
Hodge, Archibald A. and Benjamin B. Warfield. *Inspiration*. 1881. Reprint: Baker Book House, 1979.*
Jewish Publication Society. *The Jewish Bible: A JPS Guide*. Jewish Publication Society of America, 2008.
Kaiser, Walter C., Jr. *The Old Testament Documents: Are They Reliable and Relevant?* InterVarsity Press, 2001. **
Keifert, Patrick R. and Alan G. Padgett, eds. *But is it All True? The Bible and the Question of Truth*. Eerdmans, 2006.
Klepper, Deeana Copeland. *The Insight of Unbelievers: Nicholas of Lyra and Christian Reading of Jewish*

Text in the Later Middle Ages. University of Pennsylvania Press, 2007. *

Lancaster, Irene. *Deconstructing the Bible: Abraham ibn Ezra's Introduction to the Torah*. Routledge, 2007. *

Laymon, Charles M., ed. *The Interpreter's One-Volume Commentary on the Bible*. Abingdon Press, 1971. **

Linnemann, Eta. *Biblical Criticism on Trial: How Scientific is "Scientific Theology"?* Translated by Robert Yarbrough, Kregel, 2001. *

Maimonides, Moses. *The Guide for the Perplexed: Unabridged.* circa 1180. Reprint: Bnpublishing.com, 2007.*

Miller, J. Maxwell. *The Old Testament and the Historian*. Fortress Press, 1976.

Moore-Jumonville, Robert. *The Hermeneutics of Historical Distance: Mapping the Terrain of American Biblical Criticism 1880 – 1914*. University Press of America, 2002.

Neill, Stephen and Tom Wright. *The Interpretation of the New Testament, 1861 – 1986*, 2nd ed. Oxford University Press, USA, 1988. *

Popkin, Richard H. *Disputing Christianity: The 400-Year Debate over Rabbi Isaac Ben Abraham of Troki's Classic Arguments*. Humanity Books, 2007. **

_____. *The History of Skepticism from Erasmus to Spinoza*. University of California Press, 1979. ****

Powell, Mark Allan. *What is Narrative Criticism?* Fortress Press, 1990.

Rast, Walter E. *Tradition History and the Old Testament*. Fortress Press, 1972.

Reeves, John C. *Trajectories in Near Eastern Apocalyptic: A Postrabbinic Jewish Apocalypse Reader*. Society of Biblical Literature, 2005. *

Reventlow, Henning Graf. *The Authority of the Bible and the Rise of the Modern World*. Fortress Press, 1985.

_____. *History of Biblical Interpretation*. 2 vols. Society of Biblical Literature, 2009. **

_____. *Problems of Old Testament Theology in the Twentieth Century*. SCM Press, 1985.

Rogerson, J. W. and Judith M. Lieu, eds. *The Oxford Handbook of Biblical Studies*. Oxford University Press USA, 2008.

Rosenthal, Erwin. *Judaism, Philosophy, Culture: Selected Studies by E. I. J. Rosenthal*. Routledge, 2001. *

Ryken, Leland. *The Word of God in English*. Crossway, 2002.

Schleiermacher, Friedrich. *On Religion: Speeches to its Culture Despisers*. 1799. Translated and edited by Richard Crouter. Cambridge University Press, 1996.

*

Sheehan, Jonathan. *The Enlightenment Bible: Translation, Scholarship, Culture*. Princeton University Press, 2005. ****

Silva, Moisés, gen. ed. *Foundations of Contemporary Interpretation, Six Volumes in One*. Zondervan, 1996. *

_____. *Has the Church Misread the Bible: The History of Interpretation in the Light of Current Issues*. Zondervan, 1987.

Sparks, Kenton L. *Ancient Texts for the Study of the Hebrew Bible: A Guide to the Background Literature*. Hendrickson, 2005. *

Stone, Michael E. *Scriptures, Sects, and Visions: A Profile of Judaism from Ezra to the Jewish Revolts*. Fortress Press, 1980.

Thiede, Carsten Peter. *The Dead Sea Scrolls and the Jewish Origins of Christianity*. Palgrave Macmillan, 2003.

Tov, Emanuel. *Textual Criticism of the Hebrew Bible*, 2nd ed. Fortress Press, 2001. *

Turretin, Francis. *The Doctrine of Inspiration*. 1688. Edited and translated by John W. Beardslee III. Baker Book House, 1981. *

Warfield, Benjamin B. *The Inspiration and Authority of the Bible*. Presbyterian & Reformed, 1948. **

Wrede, William. *The Origin of the New Testament*. Bibliobazaar, 2009.

Wright, N.T. *The Last Word: Scripture and the Authority of God – Getting Beyond the Bible Wars*. Harper San Francisco, 2005.

Würthwein, Ernest. *The Text of the Old Testament: An Introduction to the Biblical Hebraica*, 2nd ed. Translated by Erroll T. Rhodes. Eerdmans, 1995.

Zerbe, Alvin Sylvester. *The Antiquity of Hebrew Writing and Literature: or Problems in Pentateuchal Criticism*. 1911. Reprint: by Kessinger, 2009.

Commentary on Genesis

Blenkinsopp, Joseph. *The Pentateuch: An Introduction to the First Five Books of the Bible*. Doubleday, 1992.

Blocher, Henri. *In the Beginning: The Opening Chapters of Genesis*. Translated by David G. Preston. InterVarsity Press, 1984.

Bouteneff, Peter C. *Beginnings: Ancient Christian Readings of the Biblical Creation Narratives*. Baker Academic, 2008.

Boice, James Montgomery. *Genesis Volume 1: Creation and Fall (Genesis 1-11)*. Baker Books, 1982.

Bruggermann, Walter. *Genesis: Interpretation: A Bible Commentary for Teaching and Preaching*. Westminster John Knox Press, 1982.

Buttrick, George Arthur, ed. *Interpreters Bible*. Vol. 1, *General Articles, Genesis, Exodus*. Abingdon

Topical Bibliography

Cokesbury Press, 1952.
Calvin, John. *Genesis.* 1554. Edited by Alister McGrath and J. I. Packer, Crossway Books, 2001. *
Delitzsch, Friedrich. *Babel and Bible: Two Lectures.* Edited with Introduction by C. H. W. Johns. Wipf & Stock, 1902. **
Dembski, William A., Wayne J. Downs and Fr. Justin B. A. Frederick, eds. *The Patristic Understanding of Creation: An Anthology of Writings from the Church Fathers on Creation and Design.* Erasmus Press, 2008.
Driver, S. R. *The Book of Genesis with Introduction and Notes.* Metheun, 1903. *
Garret, Duane. *Rethinking Genesis: The Sources and Authorship of the First Book of the Pentateuch.* Christian Focus, 2000. *
Gibson, John C. L. *Genesis.* 2 vols. Westminster Press, 1981.
Gunkel, Hermann. *The Legends of Genesis.* Translated by W. H. Carruth. Open Court, 1901. ****
Hamilton, Victor P. *The Book of Genesis: Chapters 1-17,* The New International Commentary on the Old Testament. Eerdmans, 1990. ***
Harmon, Nolan B., gen. ed. *The Interpreters Bible,* Vol. 1, *General and Old Testament Articles.* Abingdon Cokesbury Press, 1952.
Henry, Matthew. *Matthew Henry's Commentary on the Whole Bible.* 1706. Reprint: Hendrickson, 1991. *
Jamieson, Robert, A. R. Fausset, and David Brown. *A Commentary – Critical, Experimental, and Practical – on the Old and New Testaments.* 6 vols. 1864. Reprint: Eerdmans, 1945. *
Kidner, Derek. *Genesis: An Introduction and Commentary,* Tyndale Old Testament Commentaries. InterVarsity Press, 1967.
Kselman, John S. "Genesis." In *Harper's Bible Commentary,* gen. ed. James L. May. Harper San Francisco, 1988.
Lewis, Jack P. *A Study of the Interpretation of Noah and the Flood in Jewish and Christian Literature.* Brill, 1978. *
Louth, Andrew with Marco Conti. *Genesis 1-11, Ancient Christian Commentary on Scripture: Old Testament I.* InterVarsity Press, 2001. **
Luther, Martin. *Luther's Works: Lectures on Genesis.* 2 vols. 1536. Edited by Jaroslav Pelikan. Translated by George V. Schick. Concordia, 1960. *
Matthews, Kenneth A. *The New American Commentary: Genesis 1-11:26.* Broadman & Holman, 1996.
Morris, Henry M. *The Genesis Record: A Scientific and Devotional Commentary on the Book of Beginnings.* Baker Book House, 1976.
Moyers, Bill. *Genesis: A Living Conversation.* Doubleday, 1996. *
Newman, Robert C. *Genesis One and the Origin of the Earth.* InterVarsity Press, 1977.

Pfeiffer, Charles F., ed. *The Wycliffe Bible Commentary.* Moody Press, 1962.
Ramm, Bernard. *The Christian View of Science and Scripture.* Eerdmans, 1954. **
Rimmer, Harry. *The Harmony of Science and Scripture.* Eerdmans, 1936. *
Rosenberg, David, ed. *Genesis as it is Written: Contemporary Writers on Our First Stories.* Harper San Francisco, 1996.
Stone, Michael E., Aryeh Amihay and Vered Hillel, eds. *Noah and His Book(s).* Society of Biblical Literature, 2010. **
Waltke, Bruce K. *Genesis: A Commentary.* Zondervan, 2001.
Walton, John H. *The Lost World of Genesis: Ancient Cosmology and the Origins Debate.* InterVarsity Press Academic, 2009.
_____ and Victor Matthews. *The IVP Bible Background Commentary: Genesis – Deuteronomy.* InterVarsity Press, 1997.
Westermann, Claus. *The Genesis Accounts of Creation.* Fortress Press, 1964.
Whorton, Mark and Hill Roberts. *Guide to Understanding Creation.* Holman Reference, 2008.
Youngblood, Ronald, ed. *The Genesis Debate: Persistent Questions about Creation and the Flood.* Thomas Nelson, 1986.

Archaeology and the Bible

Abegg, Martin G., Edward M. Cook and Michael O. Wise. *The Dead Sea Scrolls, Revised Edition: A New Translation.* Harper San Francisco, 2005. *
Albright, William Foxwell. *From the Stone Age to Christianity: Monotheism and the Historical Process.* Doubleday Anchor Books, 1940.
Cline, Eric H. *From Eden to Exile: Unraveling Mysteries of the Bible.* National Geographic, 2007.
Dabney, Robert L. *Discussions.* Vol. 3, *Philosophical.* Springle Publications, 1892. *
Dever, William G. *What Did the Biblical Writers Know and When Did They Know It? What Archaeology Can Tell Us about the Reality of Ancient Israel.* Eerdmans, 2001.
Finegan, Jack. *Light from the Ancient Past: The Archaeological Background of the Hebrew-Christian Religion.* Vol. 1. Princeton University Press, 1959. *
Finkelstein, Israel and Neil Asher Silberman. *The Bible Unearthed: Archaeology's New Vision of Ancient Israel and the Origin of its Sacred Texts.* Free Press, 2001.
Free, Joseph P. *Archaeology and Bible History.* Revised and expanded by Howard Frederic Vos. Zondervan, 1992. *
Hoerth, Alfred J. *Archaeology and the Old Testament.*

Baker Books, 1998.
Kaiser, Walter C., Jr., gen. ed. *NIV Archaeological Study Bible*. Zondervan, 2005.
Kitchen, K. A. *On the Reliability of the Old Testament*. Eerdmans, 2003. **
Mazar, Benjamin. *The Early Biblical Period Historical Studies*. Israel Exploration Society, 1986.
Sheler, Jeffrey L. *Is the Bible True? How Modern Debates and Discoveries Affirm the Essence of the Scriptures*. Harper Collins, 1989.
Thompson, J. A. *Archaeology and the Old Testament*. Eerdmans, 1957.
Vos, Howard Frederic. *Genesis and Archaeology*, rev. and enl. ed. Zondervan, 1985.

The Bible and the Reformation

Glover, Willis B. *Biblical Origins of Modern Secular Culture*. Mercer University Press, 1984. ***
Kristeller, Paul Oskar. *Renaissance Thought and its Sources*. Columbia University Press, 1979. ***
McGrath, Alister. *Reformation Thought: An Introduction*. Blackwell, 1993. ***
——————. *The Intellectual Origins of the Reformation*. Blackwell, 1987. ***
Seebohm, Frederic. *The Era of the Protestant Reformation*. Scribner's, 1906. ***
——————. *The Oxford Reformers: Colet, Erasmus, and Thomas More*. Longmans, Green & Co., 1896. *

The Bible and Science in Modern History

Chadwick, Owen. *The Secularization of the European Mind in the 19th Century*. Cambridge University Press, 1975. **
Dembski, William A., ed. *Darwin's Nemesis: Philip Johnson and the Intelligent Design Movement*. IVP Academic, 2006.
——————. *The End of Christianity: Finding a Good God in an Evil World*. Broadman & Holman, 2009.
Harrison, Peter, ed. *The Cambridge Companion to Science and Religion*. Cambridge University Press, 2010.
Hazard, Paul. *European Thought in the Eighteenth Century: From Montesequieu to Lessing*. Meridian Books, 1967. ***
——————. *The European Mind: The Critical Years, 1680 – 1715*. Yale University Press, 1953. **
Marsden, George M. *The Soul of the American University: From Protestant Establishment to Established Unbelief*. Oxford University Press, 1994. **
Simmons, Geoffrey. *Billions of Missing Links: A Rational Look at the Mysteries Evolution Can't Explain*. Harvest House, 2007.

Smith, Gary Scott. *The Seeds of Secularization: Calvinism, Culture, and Pluralism in America, 1870 – 1915*. Eerdmans, 1985. *
Turner, James. *Without God, Without Creed: The Origins of Unbelief in America*. Johns Hopkins University Press, 1985. ***
Voltaire. *Letters on England*. 1894. Reprint: General Books, 2009. *
Von Fange, Erich A. *In Search of the Genesis World: Debunking the Evolution Myth*. Concordia, 2006.
Wise, Kurt P. and Sheila A. Richardson. *Something from Nothing: Understanding What You Believe About Creation and Why*. Broadman & Holman, 2004.
Youngblood, Ronald, ed. *The Genesis Debate: Persistent Questions About Creation and the Flood*. Thomas Nelson, 1986. *

History of Christian Thought

Bebbington, David. *Evangelicalism in Modern Britain: A History from the 1730s to the 1980s*. Baker Book House, 1989. *
Boettner, Loraine. *The Millennium*. Presbyterian & Reformed, 1958. *
Calvin, John. *Institutes of the Christian Religion*. 2 vols. 1768. Translated by Henry Beveridge. Eerdmans, 1990. **
Chadwick, Henry. *Augustine of Hippo: A Life*. Oxford University Press USA, 2009. ****
——————. *The Early Church*. Penguin Books, 1993. ***
Chadwick, Owen. *The Reformation*. Penguin Books, 1964. **
Coffey, John and Paul C.H. Lim, eds. *The Cambridge Companion to Puritanism*. Cambridge University Press, 2008.
Cragg, G. R. *The Church and the Age of Reason, 1648 – 1789*. Penguin Books, 1990. ***
Dawson, Christopher. *Religion and the Rise of Western Culture: The Classic Study of Medieval Civilization*. Doubleday, 1950. *
Gilson, Etienne. *The Christian Philosophy of St. Thomas Aquinas*. University of Notre Dame Press, 1956.
Gonzalez, Justo L. *A History of Christian Thought*. Vol. 2, *From Augustine to the Eve of the Reformation*. Abingdon, 1987.
——————. *A History of Christian Thought*. Vol. 3, *From the Protestant Reformation to the Twentieth Century*, rev. ed. Abingdon, 1987.
Knowles, David. *Evolution of Medieval Thought*, 2nd ed. Longman, 1989. ***
Lane, Tony. *The Lion Concise Book of Christian Thought*. Lion, 1984. *
Livingston, James C. *Modern Christian Thought*. Vol. 1, *The Enlightenment and the Nineteenth Century*.

Fortress Press, 1997. *

_____, Francis Schussler Fiorenza, Sarah Coakley and James H. Evans, Jr. *Modern Christian Thought.* Vol. 2, *The Twentieth Century.* Fortress Press, 2000. *

Loane, Marcus L. *Makers of Puritan History: Biographical Studies of Alexander Henderson, Samuel Rutherford, John Bunyan, and Richard Baxter.* Banner of Truth Trust, 2009.

Murray, Iain H. *The Puritan Hope: Revival and the Interpretation of Prophecy.* Banner of Truth Trust, 1971. **

Neill, Stephen. *A History of Christian Missions.* Penguin Books, 1964. *

Nuttall, Geoffrey F. *The Holy Spirit in Puritan Faith and Experience.* University of Chicago Press, 1992. ****

Packer, J. I., ed. *Puritan Papers.* 5 vols. P & R Publishing, 1956-1969. **

Southern, R. W. *Western Society and the Church in the Middle Ages.* Penguin Books, 1970. *

Toon, Peter. *Puritans, the Millennium, and the Future of Israel: Puritan Eschatology 1600 to 1660.* James Clarke, 1970. ****

Verduin, Leonard. *The Reformers and Their Stepchildren.* Eerdmans, 1964. **

Vidler, Alex R. *The Church in the Age of Revolution.* Penguin Books, 1961. ***

Witherington, Ben, III. *The Problem with Evangelical Theology: Testing the Exegetical Foundations of Calvinism, Dispensationalism, and Wesleyanism.* Baylor University Press, 2005. *

The Bible in America

Ahlstrom, Sydney. *A Religious History of the American People.* Yale University Press, 1972. ***

Barton, David. *America: To Pray or Not to Pray.* WallBuilder Press, 1994.

Cherry, Conrad, ed. *God's New Israel: Religious Interpretations of American Destiny.* University of North Carolina Press, 1971.

Clark, Glen. *The Man who Talks with the Flowers: The Intimate Life Story of Dr. George Washington Carver.* Macalester Park, 1939.

Conforti, Joseph A. *Samuel Hopkins and the New Divinity Movement: Calvinism, the Congregational Ministry, and Reform in New England between the Great Awakenings.* Christian University Press, 1981. *

Cowing, Cedric B. *The Saving Remnant: Religion and the Settling of New England.* University of Illinois Press, 1995.

Dayton, Donald W. and Robert K. Johnston, eds. *The Variety of American Evangelicalism.* InterVarsity Press, 1991. *

de Tocqueville, Alexis. *Democracy in America.* 1839. Translated by George Lawrence. Edited by J. P. Mayer. Harper Perennial, 2006. **

Dewey, John. *Democracy and Education: An Introduction to the Philosophy of Education.* Free Press, 1916.

Edmondson, Henry T., III. *John Dewey and the Decline of American Education: How the Patron Saint of Schools has Corrupted Teaching and Learning.* ISI Books, 2006.

Federer, William J. *George Washington Carver: His Life and Faith in His Own Words.* Amerisearch, 2003. *

Feiler, Bruce. *America's Prophet: Moses and the American Story.* William Morrow, 2009.

Galloway, Charles B. *Christianity and the American Commonwealth*, 3rd ed. American Vision, 2007.

Geisler, Norman. *Creation and the Courts: Eighty Years of Conflict in the Classroom and the Courtroom.* Crossway, 2007.

Goldman, Shalom, ed. *Hebrew and the Bible in America: The First Two Centuries.* University Press of New England for Brandeis University and Dartmouth College, 1993. **

Hodge, Charles. *Systematic Theology.* 3 vols. Eerdmans, 1968. **

Hughes, Richard T., ed. *The American Quest for the Primitive Church.* University of Illinois Press, 1988. **

Hutchinson, William R. *Errand to the World: American Protestant Thought and Foreign Missions.* University of Chicago Press, 1987. *

Kaestle, Carl E. *Pillars of the Republic: Common Schools and American Society, 1780 – 1860.* Hill & Wang, 1983.

Kidd, Thomas S. *God of Liberty: A Religious History of the American Revolution.* Basic Books, 2010. *

_____. *Protestant Interest: New England after Puritanism.* Yale University Press, 2004.

_____. *The Great Awakening: The Roots of Evangelical Christianity in Colonial America.* Yale University Press, 2007.

Kraus, Michael and Davis D. Joyce. *The Writing of American History.* University of Oklahoma Press, 1985. *

Marsden, George. *Reforming Fundamentalism: Fuller Seminary and the New Evangelism.* Eerdmans, 1987.

_____. *The Outrageous Idea of Christian Scholarship.* Oxford University Press, 1997.

Marty, Martin E. *Modern American History.* 3 vols. University of Chicago Press, 1986-1996. **

Miller, Perry. *Errand Into the Wilderness.* Belknap Press, 1956. *

_____. *The New England Mind in the Seventeenth Century.* Belknap Press, 1939. *

_____. *The New England Mind: From Colony to*

Province. Belknap Press, 1953. *

Moore, E. Ray, Jr. *Let My Children Go: Why Parents Must Remove Their Children from Public School NOW*. Gilead Media, 2002.

Morison, Samuel Eliot. *The Intellectual Life of Colonial New England*. Cornell University Press, 1936. **

Niebuhr, H. Richard. *The Kingdom of God in America*. Harper & Row, 1937. *

Pulliam, John D. and James J. Van Patten. *History of Education in America*. Merrill, 1991.

Ross, Dorothy. *The Origins of American Social Science*. Cambridge University Press, 1991. ****

Schlossberg, Herbert. *Idols for Destruction: Christian Faith and Its Confrontation with American Society*. Regnery Gateway, 1990. *

Shi, David E. *The Simple Life: Plain Living and High Thinking in American Culture*. Oxford University Press, 1985. *

Shortt, Bruce N. *The Harsh Truth about Public Schools*. Chalcedon Foundation, 2004.

Strout, Cushing, ed. *Intellectual History in America: Contemporary Essays on Puritanism, the Enlightenment, and Romanticism*. Harper & Row, 1968.

Tuveson, Ernest Lee. *Redeemer Nation: The Idea of America's Millennial Role*. University of Chicago Press, 1968. **

Urban, Wayne J. and Jennings L. Wagoner, Jr. *American Education: A History*. McGraw-Hill, 1996.

Ussher, Roland Greene. *The Pilgrims and Their History*. Macmillan, 1977. *

Philosophy

Aristotle. *The Works of Aristotle*. 2 vols. ca. 300 BC. Edited by Robert M. Hutchins. University of Chicago, 1952. **

Beardsley, Monroe C. *The European Philosophers from Descartes to Nietzsche*. Random House, 1960.

Becker, Ernest. *The Structure of Evil*. Free Press, 1968.

Bergson, Henri. *Time and Free Will*. Translated by F. L. Pogson. Harper & Row, 1910. *

Born, Max. *Experiment and Theory in Physics*. Dover, 1956. *

Copleston, Frederick. *A History of Philosophy*. 11 vols. Image, 1946-1975. **

Cornford, F. M. *From Religion to Philosophy: A Study in the Origins of Western Speculation*. Harper & Row, 1957. *

Descartes, René. *Descartes: Selections*. Edited by Ralph Monroe Eaton. Scribner, 1927. *

Edwards, Paul, ed. *The Encyclopedia of Philosophy*. 4 vols. Macmillan, 1967. ***

Hartshorne, Charles. *Creative Synthesis and Philosophical Method*. Open Court, 1970. **

Kant, Immanuel. *Immanuel Kant's Moral and Political Writings*. Edited by Carl J. Friedrich. Random House, 1949. *

Lange, Frederick Albert. *History of Materialism and Criticism of its Present Importance*. Philosophical Library, 1879. *

Leibnitz, Gottfried. *Discourse on Metaphysics: Correspondence with Arnauld Modadology*. Translated by George Montgomery. Open Court, 1949. **

_____. *New Essays Concerning Human Understanding*. Translated by Alfred Gideon Langley. Open Court, 1949. *

_____. *Leibniz: Selections*. Edited by Philip P. Wiener. Scribner's, 1951. *

McKeon, Richard, ed. *Selections from Medieval Philosophers*. 2 vols. Scribner's, 1929-1930.

Newlin, Claude M. *Philosophy and Religion in Colonial America*. Philosophical Library, 1962. **

Passmore, John. *A Hundred Years of Philosophy* (1966), Penguin***

_____. *Recent Philosophers*. Open Court, 1985. **

Plato. *The Dialogues of Plato*. ca. 400 BC. Edited by Robert M. Hutchins. Translated by Benjamin Jowett. University of Chicago, 1952. ***

Polyani, Michael. *Science, Faith, and Society: A Searching Examination of the Meaning and Nature of Scientific Inquiry*. University of Chicago Press, 1946.

Randall, John Herman, Jr. *Nature and Historical Experience: Essays in Naturalism and the Theory of History*. Columbia University Press, 1958. *

Saunders, Jason L., ed. *Greek and Roman Philosophy after Aristotle*. Free Press, 1966. *

Schneider, Herbert W. *A History of American Philosophy*. Columbia University Press, 1963. **

Strawson, P. F. *Individuals: An Essay in Descriptive Metaphysics*. Doubleday Anchor, 1963.

Whitehead, Alfred North. *Process and Reality*. Free Press, 1979. *

Philosophy and History of Science

Barbour, Ian G. *Religion and Science: Historical and Contemporary Issues*. Harper San Francisco, 1997. *

Bauer, Alain. *Isaac Newton's Freemasonry: The Alchemy of Science and Mysticism*. Inner Traditions, 2007. *

Berlinski, David. *The Devil's Delusion: Atheism and its Scientific Pretensions*. Crown Forum, 2008. *

Bowler, Peter J. *Evolution: The History of an Idea*, 3rd ed. University of California Press, 2003. *

Brand, Leonard. *Faith, Reason, and Earth History: A Paradigm of Earth and Biological Origins by Intelligent Design*. Andrews University Press, 1997.

Brooke, John Hedley. *Science and Religion: Some Historical Perspectives*. Cambridge University Press, 1991. **

Topical Bibliography

Brown, Colin. *Miracles and the Critical Mind.* Eerdmans, 1984. **

Butterfield, Herbert T. *The Origins of Modern Science 1300 – 1800.* Basic Books, 1965. *

Carlson, Richard F. *Science and Christianity: Four Views.* InterVarsity Press, 2000.

Collins, C. John. *Science and Faith: Friends or Foes?* Crossway, 2003.

Colson, Charles and Nancy Pearcey. *Developing a Christian Worldview of Science and Evolution.* Tyndale House, 2001.

Dawson, J. William. *Points of Contact between Revelation and Natural Science.* Religious Tract Society, 1885.

Fauvel, John, Raymond Flood, Michael Shortland, and Robin Wilson, eds. *Let Newton Be! A New Perspective on his Life and Works.* Oxford University Press, 1988. *

Gay, Peter. *The Enlightenment: An Interpretation; The Rise of Modern Paganism.* Norton, 1966. *

Geivett, Douglas and Gary R. Habermas, eds. *In Defense of Miracles: A Comprehensive Case for God's Actions in History.* InterVarsity Press Academic, 1997. *

Godfrey, Laurie R, ed. *Scientists Confront Creationism.* Norton, 1983. *

Grant, Edward. *Science and Religion, 400 BC – AD 1550: From Aristotle to Copernicus.* John Hopkins University Press, 2004.

Hooykaas, R. *Religion and the Rise of Modern Science.* Regent College Publishing, 1972. **

Horgan, John. *The End of Science: Facing the Limits of Knowledge in the Twilight of the Scientific Age.* Broadway Books, 1996. **

Hume, David. *Dialogues and Natural History of Religion.* 1779. Edited by J. C. A. Gaskin. Reprint: Oxford University Press, 2009.*

Hutchins, Robert Maynard, ed. *Great Books of the Western World.* Vol. 34, *Newton and Huygens.* University of Chicago, 1982.

Klaaren, Eugene. *Religious Origins of Modern Science.* Eerdmans, 1977. **

Kuhn, Thomas. *The Structure of Scientific Revolutions.* University of Chicago Press, 1970. **

Lindberg, David C. and Ronald L. Numbers, eds. *God and Nature: Historical Essays on the Encounter between Christianity and Science.* University of California Press, 1986. ***

_____ and Robert S. Westman, eds. *Reappraisals of the Scientific Revolution.* Cambridge University Press, 1990.

Lindley, John. *The End of Physics: The Myth of a Unified Field Theory.* Basic Books, 1993. **

Lovejoy, Arthur O. *The Great Chain of Being: A Study of the History of an Idea.* 1936. Harvard University Press, 1964.***

Montagu, Ashley, ed. *Science and Creationism.* Oxford University Press, 1984.

Moreland, J. P. *Christianity and the Nature of Science.* Baker Book House, 1989.

Mullin, Robert Bruce. *Miracles and the Modern Religious Imagination.* Yale University Press, 1996. ****

Newton, Isaac. "Newton Project." Edited by Rob Iliffe and Scott Mandelbrote. http://www.newtonproject.sussex.ac.uk (accessed September 16, 2010). **

_____. *Newton's Revised History of Ancient Kingdoms: A Complete Chronology.* Edited by Larry and Marion Peirce. Master Books, 2009.

_____. *Observations upon the Prophecies of Daniel and the Apocalypse of St. John.* 1733. Reprint: Dodo Press, 2007.

Numbers, Ronald L. *Darwinism Comes to America.* Harvard University Press, 1998. *

_____. *Galileo Goes to Jail and Other Myths about Science and Religion.* Harvard University Press, 2009.

Paley, William. *Archdeacon Paley's View of the Evidences of Christianity.* Kay & Troutman, 1851.

_____. *Natural Theology.* 1802. Edited by Matthew D. Eddy and David Knight. Oxford University Press, 2008.

Pierce, Charles Sanders. *The Collected Papers of Charles Sanders Peirce,* vols. 1-8. 1934. Edited by Charles Hartshorne and Paul Weiss. Belknap Press of the Harvard University Press, 1965. ***

Poe, Henry L. and Jimmy H. Davis. *Science and Faith: An Evangelical Dialogue.* Broadman & Holman, 2000.

Popper, Karl R. *Conjectures and Refutations: The Growth of Scientific Knowledge,* 5th ed. Routledge, 2002. *

_____. *The Logic of Scientific Discovery.* 1934. Reprint, 2nd ed.: Routledge Classics, 2002. **

Ruse, Michael. *Evolution-Creation Struggle.* Harvard University Press, 2005.

Snobelen, Stephen David. "Isaac Newton: Theology, Prophecy, Science and Religion." http://www.isaacnewton.org (accessed September 16, 2010). ***

Stove, David. *Darwinian Fairytales: Selfish Genes, Errors of Heredity, and Other Fables of Evolution.* Encounter Books, 1995.

Taylor, Charles. *A Secular Age.* Belknap Press of Harvard University Press, 2007.

Thomson, Keith. *Before Darwin: Reconciling God and Nature.* Yale University Press, 2005. *

White, Andrew Dickson. *History of the Warfare of Science with Theology in Christendom,* Vol. 1. 1895. Reprint: IndyPublish, 2008.**

Williams, Rheinallt Nantlais. *Faith, Facts, History, Science – and How they Fit Together.* Tyndale House,

1973.

Historiography and the Philosophy of History

Anderson, Benedict. *Imagined Communities: Reflections on the Spread and Origin of Nationalism.* Verso Books, 1983. *

Bentley, Michael, ed. *Companion to Historiography.* Routledge, 1997. *

_____. *Modern Historiography: An Introduction.* Routledge, 1999. **

Boia, Lucian, ed. *Great Historians from Antiquity to 1800: An International Dictionary.* Greenwood Press, 1989. *

Breisach, Ernst. *Historiography: Ancient, Medieval, and Modern,* 2nd ed. University of Chicago Press, 1994. *

Butterfield, Herbert T. *The Origin of History.* Basic Books, 1991. **

_____. *The Whig Interpretation of History.* Norton, 1965. *

Collingford, R. G. *The Idea of History.* Oxford University Press, 1946. *

Conkin, Paul K. and Roland N. Stromberg. *Heritage and Challenge: The History and Theory of History.* Forum Press, 1989. **

Evans, Richard J. *In Defense of History.* Norton, 1997. *

Fischer, David Hackett. *Historian's Fallacies: Toward a Logic of Historical Thought.* Harper & Row, 1970. *

Geary, Patrick J. *The Myth of Nations: The Medieval Origins of Europe.* Princeton University Press, 2002. *

Gilderhus, Mark T. *History and Historians: A Historiographical Introduction.* Prentice Hall, 1992. *

Glover, Willis B. *The Biblical Origins of Modern Secular Culture: An Essay in the Interpretation of History.* Mercer University Press, 1984. ***

Grant, Michael. *The Ancient Historians.* Barnes & Noble Books, 1970. **

Green, Anna and Kathleen Troup, eds. *The Houses of History: A Critical Reader in Twentieth-Century History and Theory.* New York University Press, 1999. *

Harvey, Van Austin. *Knowledge and Christian Belief.* Macmillan, 1966. **

Hegel, Georg Wilhelm Friedrich. *The Philosophy of History.* 1831. Translated by J. Sibree. Reprint: Dover, 1956. *

Herder, Johann Gottfried. *Against Pure Reason: Writings on Religion, Language, and History.* Translated and edited by Marcia Bunge. Fortress Press, 1993. **

_____. *On World History: An Anthology.* Edited by Hans Adler and Ernest A. Menze. Translated by Menze and Michael Palma. M. E. Sharpe, 1997. *

Hillard, T. W., R. A. Kearsley, C. E. V. Nixon and A. M. Nobbs. *Ancient History in a Modern University.* Vol. 1, *The Ancient Near East, Greece, and Rome.* Eerdmans, 1998.

Kenyon, John. *The History Men: The Historical Profession in England Since the Renaissance.* University of Pittsburg Press, 1984. *

Kohn, Hans. *The Mind of Germany: The Education of a Nation.* Scribner's, 1960. *

Levinger, Matthew. *Enlightened Nationalism: The Transformation of Prussian Political Culture, 1806 – 1848.* Oxford University Press, 2000. **

Mann, Golo. *The History of Germany since 1789.* Translated by Marian Jackson. Praeger, 1968. *

Meyerhoff, Hans, ed. *The Philosophy of History in Our Time.* Doubleday, 1959. *

Nash, Ronald H. *Christian Faith and Historical Understanding.* Probe Books, 1984.

Pompa, Leon. *Vico: A Study of the 'New Science.'* Cambridge University Press, 1975.

Popper, Karl. *The Poverty of Historicism.* Ark Paperbacks, 1957. *

Rossi, Paolo. *The Dark Abyss of Time: The History of the Earth and the History of Nations from Hooke to Vico.* Translated by Lydia G. Cochrane. University of Chicago Press, 1984. ****

Windschuttle, Keith. *The Killing of History: How Literary Critics and Social Theorists are Murdering Our Past.* Encounter Books, 1996. *

Anthropology, Population, Race, and Genes

Arnold, Matthew. *Culture and Anarchy.* Yale University Press, 1869. **

Aron, Raymond. *Main Currents in Sociological Thought.* Vol. 1, *Montesquieu, Comte, Marx, Tocqueville.* Translated by Richard Howard and Helen Weaver. Anchor Books, 1965. *

_____. *Main Currents in Sociological Thought.* Vol. 2, *Durkeim, Pareto, Weber.* Translated by Richard Howard and Helen Weaver. Anchor Books, 1967. **

Barrett, William. *Death of the Soul: From Descartes to the Computer.* Anchor Press, 1986. **

Blackburn, Robin. *The Making of New World Slavery: From the Baroque to the Modern 1492 – 1800.* Verso, 1997. **

Buck-Morss, Susan. *Hegel, Haiti, and Universal History.* University of Pittsburg Press, 2009.

Burenhult, Goran, gen. ed. *The People of the Stone Age: Hunter-Gatherers and Early Farmers.* Harper San Francisco, 1994.

_____. *Traditional Peoples Today: Continuity and Change in the Modern World.* Harper San Francisco, 1994. *

Cavalli-Sforza, Luigi Luca. *Genes, Peoples, and Languages*. Translated by Mark Seielstad. University of California Press, 2000. ***
_____, Paolo Menozzi, and Alberto Piazza. *The History and Geography of Human Genes*, abridged ed. Princeton University Press, 1994. ****
Childe, V. Gordon. *Man Makes Himself*. New American Library, 1951. *
Darwin, Charles. *The Descent of Man*. 1871. Reprint: Penguin Books, 2004. *
Davis, David Brion. *The Problem of Slavery in Western Culture*. Oxford University Press, 1966. *
Eigen, Sara and Mark Larrimore, eds. *The German Invention of Race*. State University of New York Press, 2006. **
Eliade, Mircea. *The Myth of the Eternal Return: Cosmos and History*. Princeton University Press, 2005. ***
_____. *The Sacred and the Profane: The Nature of Religion*. Harvest Books, 1968. ***
Ellingson, Ter. *The Myth of the Noble Savage*. University of California Press, 2001. *
Eze, Emmanuel Chukwudi, ed. *Race and the Enlightenment: A Reader*. Blackwell, 1997. ****
Fichte, Johann. *Addresses to the German Nation*. Translated by R. F. Jones and G. H. Turnbull. Edited by George A. Kelly. Harper, 1968. ***
Filmer, Sir Robert. *Patriarcha: or, The Natural Power of Kings*. 1680. Reprint: Dodo Press, 2008. **
Gonen, Amiram and Marwin Sanders, eds. *The Encyclopedia of Peoples of the World*. Henry Holt, 1993. **
Gould, Stephen Jay. *The Mismeasure of Man*. Norton, 1996. *
Harris, Marvin. *The Rise of Anthropological Theory: A History of Theories of Culture*, updated ed. AltaMira Press, 2001. ***
Haynes, Stephen R. *Noah's Curse: The Biblical Justification of American Slavery*. Oxford University Press, 2002. **
Heschel, Susannah. *The Aryan Jesus: Christian Theologians and the Bible in Nazi Germany*. Princeton University Press, 2008.
Hobbes, Thomas. *Leviathan*. 1651. Reprint: Dent & Dutton, 1931. **
Hofstadter, Richard. *Social Darwinism in American Thought*. Beacon Press, 1944. **
Isaac, Benjamin. *The Invention of Racism in Classical Antiquity*. Princeton University Press, 2004. *
Jones, Richard and Colin McEvedy. *Atlas of World Population History*. Penguin, 1978. *
Kephart, Calvin. *Races of Mankind: Their Origin and Migration*. Philosophical Library, 1960. *
Kidd, Colin. *The Forging of Races: Races and Scriptures in the Protestant Atlantic World, 1600 – 2000*. Cambridge University Press, 2006. *
Klein, Herbert S. *African Slavery in the Caribbean*. Oxford University Press, 1986. *
Morgan, Lewis Henry. *Ancient Society*. World Publishing, 1963. *
Locke, John. *An Essay Concerning Human Understanding*. 1690. Edited by Alexander Campbell Fraser. Reprint: Dover, 1959.**
_____. *The Reasonableness of Christianity as Delivered in the Scriptures*. 1696. Edited by George W. Ewing. Reprint: Regnery, 1965. ***
_____. *Two Treatises of Government and a Letter Concerning Toleration*. 1824. Reprint: Digireads. com, 2005. *
Lubenow, Marvin L. *Bones of Contention: A Creationist Assessment of Human Fossils*. Baker Books, 1992. *
Lyell, Charles. *The Geological Evidence of the Antiquity of Man*. 1863. Reprint: Dover, 2004. ****
MacDougall, Hugh A. *Racial Myth in English History: Trojans, Teutons, and Anglo-Saxons*. Harvest House and University Press of New England, 1982. *
Olson, Steve. *Mapping Human History: Discovering the Past Through Our Genes*. Houghton Mifflin, 2002. *
Ross, Dorothy. *The Origins of American Social Science*. Cambridge University Press, 1991. ****
Rousseau, Jean-Jacques. *The Social Contract*, rev. ed. 1762. Edited by Charles Frankel. Hafner, 1947. *
Said, Edward W. *Orientalism*. Vintage, 1978. *
Slotkin, J. S. *Readings in Early Anthropology*. Wenner-Gren, 1965. *
Smith, Helmut Walser. *The Continuities of German History: Nation, Religion, and Race across the Long Nineteenth Century*. Cambridge University Press, 2008. *
Tattersall, Ian. *The Fossil Trail: How We Know What We Think We Know about Human Evolution*. Oxford University Press, 1995. ***
Trinkaus, Erik. *The Neanderthals: Of Skeletons, Scientists, and Scandal*. Vintage, 1994. *

Ancient Agriculture and Technologies

Barber, E. J. W. *Prehistoric Textiles: The Development of Cloth in the Neolithic and Bronze Ages*. Princeton University Press, 1991. **
Bulliet, Richard W. *The Camel and the Wheel*. Columbia University Press, 1990. **
Derry, T. K. and Trevor Williams. *A Short History of Technology from the Earliest Times to AD 1900*. Dover, 1960. *
Finley, M. I. *The Ancient Economy*. University of California Press, 1985. **

Heiser, Charles B., Jr. *Seed to Civilization: The Story of Food*, 2nd ed. Freeman, 1981. ****
Heyerdahl, Thor. *Kon-Tiki: Across the Pacific by Raft.* Translated by F. H. Lyon. Washington Square Press, 1984. *
Hodges, Henry. *Technology in the Ancient World.* Barnes & Noble Books, 1970.
Smith, Bruce D. *The Emergence of Agriculture.* Freeman, 1995. *
Williams, Trevor. *The History of Invention: From Stone Axes to Silicon Chips.* Facts on File, 1987.

Languages, Scripts, and Writing Technology

Baur, Laurie. *The Linguistic Students Handbook.* Oxford University Press, 2007.
Benes, Tuska. *In Babel's Shadow: Language, Philology, and Nation in Nineteenth Century Germany.* Wayne State University Press, 2008. ****
Bonfante, Larissa. *Etruscan.* University of California Press, 1990.
Chadwick, John. *Linear B and Related Scripts.* University of California Press, 1987.
Comrie, Bernard, ed. *The World's Major Languages.* 1987. Reprint: Oxford University Press USA, 1990.
_____, Stephen Matthews, and Maria Plinsky. *The Atlas of Languages,* Quarto, 2003. ***
Crystal, David. *The Cambridge Encyclopedia of Language.* Cambridge University Press, 1997. **
Davies, Anna Morpurgo. *History of Linguistics.* Vol. 4, *Nineteenth-Century Linguistics.* Longman, 1992.
Davies, W. V. *Egyptian Hieroglyphs.* University of California Press, 1987. **
Diringer, David. *Alphabet: A Key to the History of Mankind.* Funk & Wagnalls, 1968.
_____. *The Book Before Printing: Ancient, Medieval and Oriental.* 1953. Reprint: Dover, 1982. **
Farrar, Frederic William. *An Essay on the Origin of Language.* 1860. Reprint: General Books, 2009.
_____. *Language and Languages.* 1883. Reprint: Bibliobazaar, 2009.
Friedrich, Johannes. *Extinct Languages.* 1957. Translated by Frank Gaynor. Barnes & Noble Books, 1993.
Gordon, Cyrus. *Forgotten Scripts.* 1968. Revised in 1982 by Basic Books. Barnes & Noble Books, 1993.
Gunn, Giles. *The Culture of Criticism and the Criticism of Culture.* Oxford University Press, 1987. **
Healey, John F. *The Early Alphabet.* University of California Press, 1990.
Hooker, J. T., ed. *Reading the Past.* Barnes & Noble Books, 1990. ****
Houston, S. D. *Maya Glyphs.* University of California Press, 1989.

Jean, Georges. *Writing: The Story of Alphabet and Script.* Translated by Jenny Oates. Harry N. Abrams, 1992.
Moore, Hyatt, ed. *The Alphabet Makers.* Wycliffe Bible Translators, 1991.
Robinson, Andrew. *The Story of Writing.* Thames & Hudson, 1995. ****
Ruhlen, Merritt. *A Guide to the World's Languages.* Vol. 1, *Classification.* Stanford University Press, 1991. **
_____. *The Origin of Language: Tracing the Evolution of the Mother Tongue.* John Wiley & Sons, 1994. *
Ostler, Nicholas. *Empires of the Word: A Language History of the World.* Harper Perennial, 2006.
Sacks, David. *Language Visible: Unraveling the Mystery of the Alphabet from A to Z.* Broadway Books, 2003.
Shanks, Hershel, ed. *Frank Moore Cross: Conversations with a Biblical Scholar.* Biblical Archaeological Society, 1994. ***
Walker, C. B. F. *Cuneiform.* Vol. 3 of *Reading the Past.* University of California Press, 1987. ***
Woodard, Roger D., ed. *The Cambridge Encyclopedia of the World's Ancient Languages.* Cambridge University Press, 2004. ***

Death, Burial, and Archaeological Excavation

Allan, Tony. *Secrets of the Ancient Dead: Deciphering the Past from Tombs, Graves, and Mummies.* Duncan Baird, 2004.
Andrews, Carol. *Egyptian Mummies.* Harvard University Press, 1984.
Barber, Elizabeth Wayland. *The Mummies of Ürümchi.* Norton, 1999. *
Collis, John. *Digging Up the Past: An Introduction to Archaeological Excavation.* Sutton, 2001.
Dix, Jay, Michael Graham and Randy Hanzlick. *Asphyxia and Drowning: An Atlas.* CRC Press, 2000. ***
Pearson, Mike Parker. *The Archaeology of Death and Burial.* Texas A&M University Press, 1999.

Dating and Chronologies

Baillie, M. G. L. *A Slice Through Time: Dendrochronology and Precision Dating.* Routledge, 1997. *
_____. *Tree-Ring Dating and Archaeology.* University of Chicago Press, 1990. ***
Bowman, Sheridan. *Radiocarbon Dating.* University of California Press, 1990. *
de Bourgoing, Jacqueline. *The Calendar History, Lore, and Legend.* Harry N. Abrams, 2001.
Dean, Jeffrey S., David M. Meko, and Thomas W.

Topical Bibliography

Swetnam. "Tree Rings, Environment and Humanity: Proceedings of the International Conference, Tucson, Arizona, May 17-21, 1994." *Radiocarbon* (1996) 3-24.

Ehrich, Robert, ed. *Chronologies in Old World Archaeology*, 2nd ed. University of Chicago Press, 1965. **

──────. *Chronologies in Old World Archaeology*, 3rd ed. 2 vols. University of Chicago Press, 1992. ****

Finegan, Jack. *Handbook of Biblical Chronology*, rev. ed. Hendrickson, 1998. *

Gove, Harry E. *From Hiroshima to the Iceman: The Development and Applications of Mass Spectrometry*. Institute of Physics Publishing, 1999. **

Grun, Bernard. *The Timetables of History*, 3rd rev. ed. Based on Werner Stein. Touchstone, 1975. *

James, Peter. *Centuries of Darkness: A Challenge to the Conventional Chronology of Old World Archaeology*. Rutgers University Press, 1993. *

Jones, Floyd Nolen. *The Chronology of the Old Testament: A Return to the Basics,* 15th ed. Master Books, 2004.

Mazzoni, Stefania. "Elements of the Ceramic Culture of Early Syrian Ebla in Comparison with Syro-Palestinian EBIV." *Bulletin of the American Schools for Oriental Research* 257 (1985): 1-18. **

Nash, Stephen Edward. *Time, Trees, and Prehistory: Tree-Ring Dating and the Development of North American Archaeology, 1914 – 1950*. University of Utah Press, 1999. *

Newton, Isaac. *The Chronology of Ancient Kingdoms,* 1728. **

Renfrew, Colin. *Before Civilization: The Radiocarbon Revolution and Prehistoric Europe*. Knopf, 1973. ***

Smiley, Terah L. and Marvin A. Stokes. *An Introduction to Tree-Ring Dating*. University of Arizona Press, 1996.

Stuiver, Minze and Johannes van der Plicht, eds. "Calibration." Special issue, *Radiocarbon* 40, no. 3 (1998). ***

──────ar and Renée Kra, eds. "Calibration." Special issue, *Radiocarbon* 28, no. 2B (1986). *

──────, Austin Long, and Renée Kra, eds. "Calibration." Special issue, *Radiocarbon* 35, no. 1 (1993). *

Ussher, James. *The Annals of the World,* 1658. ****

Wagner, Gunther A. *Age Determination of Young Rocks and Artifacts: Physical and Chemical Clocks in Quaternary Geology and Archaeology*. Springer, 1995. *

Walker, Mike. *Quaternary Dating Methods*. John Wiley & Sons, 2005. **

Ward, William A. "The Present Status of Egyptian Chronology." Bulletin of the American Schools for Oriental Research 288 (1992): 53-66. ***

World History

Bauer, Susan Wise. *The History of the Ancient World from the Earliest Accounts to the Fall of Rome*. Norton, 2007. *

Breasted, James Henry. *Ancient Times: A History of the Early World [with] an Introduction to the Study of Ancient History and the Career of Early Man*. Ginn, 1935. **

Cheilik, Michael. *Ancient History from its Beginnings to the Fall of Rome*. Barnes & Noble Books, 1969.

Edwards, I. E. S., C. J. Gadd, and N. G. L. Hammond, eds. *The Cambridge Ancient History*. 3rd ed. Vol. 1, Part 1, *Prolegomenon and Prehistory*. Cambridge University Press, 1971. ****

Garraty, John A. and Peter Gay. *The Columbia History of the World*. Harper & Row, 1972. *

H. G. Wells. *The Outline of History*. Revised by Raymond Postgate. Garden City Books, 1949. **

Kinder, Hermann and Werner Hilgemann. *The Anchor Atlas of World History*. Vol. 1, *From the Stone Age to the Eve of the French Revolution*. Anchor Books, 1974. *

McEvedy, Colin. *The Penguin Atlas of Ancient History*. Penguin Books, 1967. *

Roberts, J. M. *History of the World*. Oxford University Press, 1993. *

Saggs, H. W. F. *Civilization before Greece and Rome*. Yale University Press, 1989. **

Shackford, Samuel. *The Sacred and Profane History of the World*. 4 vols. 1727. Reprint: Tolle Lege Press, 2009.

Starr, Chester G. *A History of the Ancient World*, 4th ed. Oxford University Press, 1991. *

Toynbee, Arnold J. *Mankind and Mother Earth: A Narrative History of the World*. Oxford University Press, 1976. ***

Tozer, H. F. *A History of Ancient Geography*. Bilo & Tannen, 1964.

Ussher, James. *The Annals of the World*. 1658. Updated English by Larry Pierce. Master Books, 2003. **

Verbrugghe, Gerald, and John Wickersham. *Berossos and Manetho, Introduced and Translated: Native Traditions in Ancient Mesopotamia and Egypt*. University of Michigan Press, 2001.

History of the Ancient Near East

Dentan, Robert C. ed. *The Idea of History in the Ancient Near East*. American Oriental Society, 1954. *

Edwards, I. E. S, C. J. Gadd, and N. G. L. Hammond, eds. *The Cambridge Ancient History*, 3rd ed. Vol. 1, Part 2, *Early History of the Middle East*. Cambridge University Press, 1971. ****

_____ and E. Sollberger, eds. *The Cambridge Ancient History*, 3rd ed. Vol. 2, Part 1, *History of the Middle East and the Aegean Region c. 1800 – 1380 B.C.* Cambridge University Press, 1971. **

Gershevitch, Ilya. *The Cambridge History of Iran*. Vol. 2, *The Median and Archaemenian Periods*. Cambridge University Press, 1985. *

Hawkes, Jacquetta. *The First Great Civilizations: Life in Mesopotamia, the Indus Valley, and Egypt*. Knopf, 1973.

Keller, Werner. *The Bible as History*. Translated by William Neil and B. H. Rasmussen. Revised with a postscript by Joachim Rehork. William Morrow, 1981. **

Millard, A. R., James K. Hoffmeir, and David W. Baker, eds. *Faith, Tradition, and History: Old Testament Historiography in Its Near Eastern Context*. Eisenbrauns, 1994. *

Moscati, Sabatino. *Ancient Semitic Civilizations*. Putnam, 1960.

Oates, Joan. *Babylon*, rev. ed. Thames & Hudson, 1986. *

Sasson, Jack M., gen. ed. *Civilizations of the Ancient Near East*. 4 vols. Hendrickson, 1995. ****

Van De Mieroop, Marc. *A History of the Ancient Near East ca. 3000 – 323 BC*. Wiley-Blackwell, 2006.

Van Seters, John. *In Search of History: Historiography in the Ancient World and the Origins of Biblical History*. Yale University Press, 1983. *

von Soden, Wolfram. *The Ancient Orient: An Introduction to the Study of the Ancient Near East*. Translated by Donald G. Schley. Eerdmans, 1994.

History of Ancient America

Adams, Richard E. W. and Murdo J. MacLeod, eds. *The Cambridge History of the Native Peoples of America*. Vol. 2, *Mesoamerica*. Cambridge University Press, 2000.*

Ashe, Geoffrey, Thor Heyerdahl, Helge Ingstad, J. V. Luce, Betty J. Meggers, and Birgitta L. Wallace. *The Quest for America*. Praeger, 1971. ***

Davies, Nigel. *The Ancient Kingdoms of Mexico*. Penguin Books, 1982.

Josephy, Alvin M., Jr. *The Indian Heritage of America*. Knopf, 1968.

Katz, Friedrich. *The Ancient American Civilizations*. Translated by K. M. Lois Simpson. Praeger, 1969.

Mallery, Arlington and Mary Roberts Harrison. *The Rediscovery of Lost America*. Dutton, 1979. *

Mason, J. Alden. *The Ancient Civilizations of Peru*. Penguin Books, 1957.

Merrell, James H. *The Indians' New World: Catawbas and Their Neighbors from European Contact through the Era of Removal*. Norton, 1989.

Pauketat, Timothy R. *Cahokia: Ancient America's Great City on the Mississippi*. Viking, 2009.

Rights, Douglas L. *The American Indians in North Carolina*. John F. Blair, 1957.*

Salomon, Frank and Stuart B. Schwartz, eds. *The Cambridge History of the Native Peoples of America*. Vol. 3, *South America*. Cambridge University Press, 2000.*

Sanders, William T. and Barbara J. Price. *Mesoamerica: The Evolution of a Civilization*. Random House, 1968. *

Silverberg, Robert. *The Mound Builders*. New York Graphic Society, 1968. **

Spencer, Robert F., Jesse D. Jennings, et al. *The Native Americans: Ethnology and Backgrounds of the North American Indians*. Harper & Row, 1977.

Starkey, Marion L. *The Cherokee Nation*. J. G. Press, 1999. **

Trigger, Bruce and Wilcomb E. Washburn, eds. *The Cambridge History of the Native Peoples of America*. Vol. 1, *North America*. Cambridge University Press, 1996.**

Wauchope, Robert. *Lost Tribes and Sunken Continents: Myth and Method in the Study of American Indians*. University of Chicago Press, 1962. **

Wax, Murray L. *Indian Americans: Unity and Diversity*. Prentice Hall, 1971.

White, John Manchip. *Everyday Life of the North American Indians*. Indian Head Books, 1979.

Wissler, Clark. *Indians of the United States*. Anchor Books, 1989. *

History of Ancient Europe

Childe, V. Gordon. *The Prehistory of European Society: How and Why the Prehistoric Barbarian Societies of Europe Behaved in a Distinctive European Way*. Pelican, 1958. *

Drews, Robert. *The Coming of the Greeks: Indo-European Conquests in the Aegean and the Near East*. Princeton University Press, 1988. **

Finley, M. I. *The Ancient Greeks*. Penguin, 1977. **

_____. *The World of Odysseus*. Penguin, 1965. **

Franck, Irene M. and David M. Brownstone. *The European Overland Routes*. Facts on File, 1990.

Funck-Bretano, Frantz. *A History of Gaul: Celtic, Roman, and Frankish Rule*. 1927. Barnes & Noble Books, 1993.

Grant, Michael. *The Ancient Mediterranean*. Meridian, 1969. **

_____. *The Rise of the Greeks*. Scribner's, 1987. *

Haywood, Richard Mansfield. *Ancient Greece and the Near East*. David McKay, 1964. *

Jones, Gwyn. *A History of the Vikings*. Oxford Uni-

Topical Bibliography

versity Press, 1973.
Jones, Prudence and Nigel Pennick. *A History of Pagan Europe.* Barnes & Noble Books, 1995.
Niebuhr, Barthold Georg. *The Roman History.* 1827. Reprint: General Books, 2009. *
Owen, Francis. *The Germanic People: Their Origin, Expansion, and Culture.* Dorset Press, 1980.
Powell, T. G. E. *The Celts.* Thames & Hudson, 1980.
Renfrew, Colin. *Archaeology and Language: The Puzzle of Indo-European Origins.* Cambridge University Press, 1987. *
Vana, Adenek. *The World of the Ancient Slavs.* Wayne State University Press, 1983.
Vaughn, Agnes Carr. *The Etruscans.* Barnes & Noble, 1993.

History of the Ancient Orient

Durant, Will. *Our Oriental Heritage.* Simon & Shuster, 1942. *
Gernet, Jacques. *A History of Chinese Civilization.* 1972. Translated by J. R. Foster. Cambridge University Press, 1982. *
Lepsius, Carl Richard. *Letters from Egypt, Ethiopia, and the Peninsula of Sinai. With Extracts from his Chronology of the Egyptians, with Reference to the Exodus of the Israelites. Revised by the Author.* 1853. Reprint: Elibron Classics**.** *
Lum, Peter. *The Growth of Civilization in East Asia: China, Japan and Korea to the 14th Century.* S. G. Phillips, 1969. *
O'Connor, David B. *Abydos: Egypt's First Pharaohs and the Cult of Osiris.* Thames & Hudson, 2009. *
Thapar, Romila. *Early India: From the Origins to AD 1300.* University of California Press, 2002.

Archaeological History, Thought, and Science

Bahn, Paul G., ed. *The Cambridge Illustrated History of Archaeology.* Cambridge University Press, 1996.
_____ and Colin Renfrew. *Archaeology: Theories, Methods, and Practice,* 3rd ed. Thames & Hudson, 2000. *
Barnard, Alan. *History and Theory in Anthropology.* Cambridge University Press, 2000.
Bray, Warwick and David Trump. *The Penguin Dictionary of Archaeology,* 2nd ed. Penguin Books, 1982.
Ceram, C. W. *Gods, Graves, and Scholars: The Story of Archaeology.* Knopf, 1967.
_____. *The First Americans: The Story of North American Archaeology.* Harcourt Brace Jovanovich, 1971.
Daniel, Glynn and C. A. Watts. *The Idea of Prehistory.* Pelican, 1964. **
Darvill, Timothy. *The Concise Oxford Dictionary of Archaeology.* Oxford University Press, 2002.
Drower, Margaret S. *Flinders Petrie: A Life in Archaeology,* 2nd ed. University of Wisconsin Press, 1995. *
Eiseley, Loren. *Darwin's Century: Evolution and the Men Who Discovered It.* Anchor Books, 1958. *
Greene, Kevin. *Archaeology: An Introduction.* University of Pennsylvania Press, 1995.
Hilprecht, Hermann Vollrat with Immanuel Benzinger, Fritz Hommel, Peter Jensen, and Georg Steindorf. *Explorations in Bible Lands during the 19th Century.* Holman, 1903.
Hodder, Ian. *Reading the Past: Current Approaches to Interpretation in Archaeology.* Cambridge University Press, 1991. *
Kelley, Jane H. and Marsha P. Hanen. *Archaeology and the Methodology of Science.* University of New Mexico Press, 1988.
Kennedy, Marv. *The History of Archaeology.* Barnes & Noble Books, 2002.
Lloyd, Seton. *Foundations in the Dust: The Story of Mesopotamian Exploration.* 1947. Thames & Hudson, 1980.
Moorey, P. R. S. *A Century of Biblical Archeology.* Westminister John Knox Press, 1991. **
Nash, Stephen Edward, ed. *It's About Time: A History of Archaeological Dating in North America.* University of Utah Press, 2000.
_____. *Time, Trees, and Prehistory: Tree-Ring Dating and the Development of American Archaeology.* University of Utah Press, 1999. *
Stiebing, William H., Jr. *Uncovering the Past: A History of Archaeology.* Oxford University Press, 1993. *
Thompson, Keith. *The World of the Mastodon: The Golden Age of Fossils in America.* Yale University Press, 2008.
Trigger, Bruce G. *A History of Archaeological Thought.* Cambridge University Press, 1989. ****
Willey, Gordon R. and Jeremy A. Sabloff. *The History of American Archaeology.* Freeman, 1974. **
Wilson, David. *The New Archaeology: How New and Revolutionary Scientific Techniques are Transforming Our Study of the Past.* Knopf, 1974. **

Prehistory and World Archaeology

Bacon, Edward, ed. *Vanished Civilizations of the Ancient World.* McGraw-Hill, 1963. **
Bourbon, Fabio, ed. *The Great Book of Archaeology.* VMB, 2005.
Braidwood, Robert J. *Prehistoric Men,* 7th ed. Scott, Foresman & Co., 1967.
Childe, V. Gordon. *What Happened in History.* Penguin, 1942.
_____. *Man Makes Himself: Man's Progress Through the Ages,* 5th ed. New American Library, 1957.

Clark, Grahame and Stuart Piggot. *Prehistoric Societies*. Pelican, 1970. *
_____. *World Prehistory in New Perspective*, 3rd ed. Cambridge University Press, 1977. *
Cotterell, Arthur, ed. *The Penguin Encyclopedia of Ancient Civilizations*. Penguin, 1980. **
Fagan, Brian M. *People of the Earth: An Introduction to World Prehistory*, 4th ed. Little, Brown & Co., 1983.
_____. *World Prehistory: A Brief Introduction*, 5th ed. Prentice Hall, 2002. *
_____, ed.-in-chief. *The Oxford Companion to Archaeology*. Oxford University Press, 1996. ****
Fairservis, Walter A., Jr. *The Threshold of Civilization: An Experiment in Prehistory*. Scribner's, 1975.
Hawkes, Jacquetta. *Atlas of Ancient Archeology*. 1974. Barnes & Noble Books, 1994.
_____. *The Atlas of Early Man*, rev. ed. St. Martin's Press, 1993. **
Haywood, John. *Historical Atlas of the Ancient World, 4,000,000 – 5,000 BC*. Barnes & Noble Books, 1998.
Lubbock, Sir John. *Pre-Historic Times: As Illustrated by Ancient Remains and the Manners and Customs of Modern Savages*, 6th ed. J. A. Hill, 1906.
McEvedy, Colin. *The Penguin Atlas of Ancient History*. Penguin, 1967. *
Morgan, Lewis Henry. *Ancient Society*. World Publishing, 1963. *
Mithen, Steven. *After The Ice: A Global Human History, 20,0000 – 5,000 BC*. Harvard University Press, 2003.
Oliphant, Margaret. *The Atlas of the Ancient World: Charting the Great Civilizations of the Past*. Simon & Schuster, 1992.
Paul G. Bahn, ed. *Lost Treasures: Great Discoveries in World Archaeology*. Barnes & Noble Books, 2000.
Piggot, Stuart, ed. *The Dawn of Civilization: The First World Survey of Human Cultures in Early Times*. McGraw-Hill, 1961. **
Renfrew, Colin. *Prehistory: The Making of the Human Mind*. Modern Library, 2008. *
Rudgley, Richard. *The Lost Civilizations of the Stone Age*. Touchstone, 1999.
Scarre, Christopher, ed. *The Human Past: World Prehistory and the Development of Human Societies*. Thames & Hudson, 2005.
Scarre, Chris, gen. ed. *Past Worlds: The Times Atlas of Archaeology*. 1988. Reprint: Crescent Books, 1991. **
Wenke, Robert J. *Patterns in Prehistory: Humankind's First Three Million Years*, 3rd ed. Oxford University Press, 1990. *

Old World Archaeology

Amiet, Pierre, Francois Baratte, Christiane Desroches Noblecourt, Catherine Metzger, and Alain Pasquier. *Antiquity: Forms and Styles*. Evergreen, 1981. *
Scientific American. *Old World Archaeology: Foundations of Civilization*. Freeman, 1972. ***
Woolley, Sir Leonard. *The Beginnings of Civilizations*. Mentor Books, 1963.

Archaeology (Ancient Near East)

Algaze, Guillermo. *Ancient Mesopotamia at the Dawn of Civilization: The Evolution of an Urban Landscape*. University of Chicago Press, 2008.
_____. *The Uruk World System: The Dynamics of Expansion of Early Mesopotamian Civilization*, 2nd ed. University of Chicago Press, 2005.
Childe, V. Gordon. *New Light on the Most Ancient East: The Oriental Prelude to European Prehistory*. Norton, 1969. **
Edwards, I. E. S., C. J. Gadd, and N. G. L. Hammond, eds. *The Cambridge Ancient History*, 3rd ed. Vol. 1, Part 2, Early History of the Middle East. Cambridge University Press, 1971. ***
Gordon, Cyrus H. *The Ancient Near East*, 3rd ed. Norton, 1965.
Hole, Frank. *The Archaeology of Western Iran: Settlement and Society from Prehistory to the Islamic Conquest*. Smithsonian Institution Press, 1987. **
Lloyd, Seton. *The Art of the Ancient Near East*. Praeger, 1961.
Meyers, Eric M., ed.-in-chief. *The Oxford Encyclopedia of Archaeology in the Near East*. 5 vols. Oxford University Press, 1997. ****
Nissen, Hans J. *The Early History of the Ancient Near East, 9000 – 2000 B. C*. Translation by Elizabeth Lutzeier with Kenneth J. Northcott. University of Chicago Press, 1988. ***
Olmstead, A. T. *History of the Persian Empire*. University of Chicago Press, 1948.
Rothman, Mitchell S., ed. *Uruk Mesopotamia and Its Neighbors: Cross-Cultural Interactions in the Era of State Formation*. School of American Research Press, 2001.
Saghieh, Muntaha. "Review of Byblos in the Third Millennium B. C.: A Reconstruction of the Stratigraphy and a Study of the Cultural Connections." *Journal of Near Eastern Studies* 51 (April 1992): 141-143.
Sayce, A. H. *The Archaeology of Cuneiform Inscriptions*. Ares, 1907. **
von Soden, Wolfram. *The Ancient Orient: An Introduction to the Study of the Ancient Near East*. Translated by Donald G. Schley. Eerdmans, 1994.

Wilkinson, T. J. *Archaeological Landscapes of the Near East*. University of Arizona Press, 2003.

Archaeology (The Land of the Bible)

Ahlström, Gösta W. *The History of Ancient Palestine*. Fortress Press, 1993.
Ben-Tor, Amnon, ed. *The Archaeology of Ancient Israel*. Yale University Press, 1992. ****
Dever, William G. "The Chronology of Syria-Palestine in the Second Millennium B. C. E.: A Review of the Current Issues." *Bulletin of the American Schools of Research* 288 (1992): 1–22. **
———. "The Peoples of Palestine in the Middle Bronze I Period." *Harvard Theological Review* 64 (1971): 197–226. ****
Hoffmeier, James Karl. *The Archaeology of the Bible*. Lion Hudson, 2008.
Kenyon, Kathleen Mary. *Archaeology in the Holy Land*, 4th ed. Ernest Benn, 1979.
———. *Digging Up Jericho: The Results of the Jericho Excavations, 1952–1956*. Praeger, 1957. ****
Levy, Thomas E., ed. *The Archaeology of Society in the Holy Land*. Leicester University Press, 1998. **
Mazar, Amihai. *Archaeology of the Land of the Bible, 10,000–586 B. C. E.* Doubleday, 1992. ****
Murphy-O'Connor, Jerome. *The Holy Land: An Oxford Archaeological Guide from Earliest Times to 1700*, 4th ed. Oxford University Press USA, 1998.
Stern, Ephraim, ed. *The New Encyclopedia of Archaeological Excavations in the Holy Land*. 4 vols. Carta, 1993. ***
Weinstein, James W. "The Chronology of Palestine in the Early Second Millennium B. C. E." *Bulletin of the American Schools of Research* 288 (1992): 27-46. *
Wright, G. Ernest. *Biblical Archaeology*. Westminster Press, 1962.

Archaeology (Mesopotamia, Arabia, Syria, and Iran)

Akkermans, Peter M. M. G. and Glenn M. Schwartz. *The Archaeology of Syria: From Complex Hunter-Gatherers to Early Urban Societies (ca. 16,000–300 BC)*. Cambridge University Press, 2003.
Amiran, Ruth. "Yanik Tepe, Shengavit, and the Khirbet Kerak Ware." *Anatolian Studies* 15 (1965): 165-167.
Aubet, Maria Eugenia. *The Phoenicians and the West: Politics, Colonies, and Trade*. Translated by Mary Turton. Cambridge University Press, 1994. *
Bermant, Chaim and Michael Weitzman. *Ebla: A Revelation in Archaeology*. Times Books, 1979. *
Braidwood, Linda S., Robert J. Braidwood, Bruce Howe, Charles A. Reed, and Patty Jo Watson, eds. *Prehistoric Archaeology Along the Zagros Flanks*. Oriental Institute of the University of Chicago, 1983.
Burney, C. A. "Excavations at Yanik Tepe, North-West Iran." *Iraq* 23, no. 2 (Autumn, 1961): 138-153.
Burney, C. A. "The Excavations at Yanik Tepe, Azerbaijan, 1961 Preliminary Report." *Iraq* 24, no. 2 (Autumn, 1962): 134-152.
Burney, C. A. "The Excavations at Yanik Tepe, Azerbaijan, 1962: Third Preliminary Report." *Iraq* 26, no. 1 (Spring, 1964), 54-61.
Burney, Charles and David Marshall Lang. *The Peoples of the Hills: Ancient Ararat and Caucasus*. Phoenix Press, 2001. ***
Chahin, M. *The Kingdom of Armenia*. Dorset Press, 1987. *
Chavalas, Mark W. and K. Lawson Younger, Jr., eds. *Mesopotamia and the Bible: Comparative Explorations*. Baker Academic, 2002. ****
Crawford, Harriet. *Sumer and the Sumerians*. Cambridge University Press, 1991. ***
Gray, John. *The Canaanites*. Praeger, 1964.
Gurney, O. R. *The Hittites*. Penguin Books, 1990.
Herm, Gerhard. *The Phoenicians: The Purple Empire of the Ancient World*. Translated by Caroline Hillier. William Morrow, 1975.
Hinz, Walter. *The Lost World of Elam: Re-creation of a Vanished Civilization*. Translated by Jennifer Barnes. New York University Press, 1972. *
Huot, Jean-Louis. *Persia I: From the Origins to the Achaemenids*. Nagel, 1956.
Kramer, Samuel Noah. *History Begins at Sumer: Thirty-Nine Firsts in Recorded History*. University of Pennsylvania Press, 1981.
Lamberg-Karlovsky, C. C. "Dilmun: Gateway to Immortality." *Journal of Near Eastern Studies* 41, no. 1 (1982): 45–50.
Lang, David Marshall. *Armenia: Cradle of Civilization*, 3rd ed. Allen & Unwin, 1980. *
Laughlin, John C. H. *Archaeology and the Bible*. Routledge, 2000.
Leick, Gwendolyn. *Mesopotamia: The Invention of the City*. Penguin Books, 2001.
Lloyd, Seton. *The Archaeology of Mesopotamia from the Old Stone Age to the Persian Conquest*, rev. ed. Thames & Hudson, 1984. *
Macqueen, J. G. *The Hittites and their Contemporaries in Asia Minor*, rev. and enl. ed. Thames & Hudson, 1986.
Mallowan, M. E. L. *Early Mesopotamia and Iran*. McGraw-Hill, 1965.
Markoe, Glenn E. *Phoenicians*. University of California Press, 2000.
Matthiae, Paolo. "New Discoveries at Ebla." *Biblical*

Archaeology, March 1984, 18–32. *

_____. *Ebla: An Empire Rediscovered.* Translated by Christopher Holme. Doubleday, 1981. *

Moore, A. M. T., G. C. Hillman, and A. J. Legge. *Village on the Euphrates: From Foraging to Farming at Abu Hureyra.* Oxford University Press, 2000.

Moscot, Sabatino. *The World of the Phoenicians.* Translated by Alastair Hamilton. Praeger, 1968.

Negev, Avraham. *The Archaeological Encyclopedia of the Holy Land.* Macmillan, 1990.

Piotrovskii, B. B. *Uratu: The Kingdom of Van and its Art.* Translated by Peter S. Gelling. Evelyn, Adams & Mackay, 1967.

Postgate, J. N. *Early Mesopotamia: Society and Economy at the Dawn of History.* Routledge, 1992. *

Potts, D. T. *The Arabian Gulf in Antiquity.* Vol. 1, *From Prehistory to the Fall of the Achaemenid Empire.* Clarendon Press, 1990.

Roaf, Michael. *Cultural Atlas of Mesopotamia and the Ancient Near East.* Facts on File, 1990. ****

Roux, Georges. *Ancient Iraq,* 3rd ed. Penguin Books, 1992. ***

Kramer, Samuel Noah. *The Sumerians: Their History, Culture, and Character.* University of Chicago Press, 1963. ****

Wilhelm, Gernot. *The Hurrians.* Translated by Jennifer Barnes with a chapter by Diana L. Stein. Aris & Phillips, 1989. **

Wooley, C. Leonard. *A Forgotten Kingdom: A Record of the Results From the Excavation of Two Mounds, Atchana and al Mina in the Turkish Hatay.* Norton, 1968. ***

_____. *The Sumerians.* Norton, 1965. **

Woolley, Sir Leonard. *Excavations at Ur: A Record of Twelve Years' Work.* Thomas Y. Crowell, 1954. ****

_____. *Ur of the Chaldees: A Record of Seven Years of Excavations.* Penguin Books, 1930.

Archaeology (Egypt)

Aldred, Cyril. *The Egyptians,* rev. and enl. ed. Thames & Hudson, 1987. *

Bains, John and Jaromir Malek. *Atlas of Ancient Egypt.* Facts on File, 1982.

David, A. R. *The Pyramid Builders of Egypt: A Modern Investigation of Pharaoh's Work Force.* Routledge, 1986. *

Davidovits, Joseph and Margie Morris. *The Pyramids: An Enigma Solved.* Dorset Press, 1988.

Edwards, I. E. S. *The Pyramids of Egypt,* rev. ed. Penguin Books, 1991. *

Emery, W. B. *Archaic Egypt.* Penguin Books, 1961. ***

Gardiner, Sir Alan. *Egypt of the Pharaohs.* Oxford University Press, 1961.

Grimal, Nicolas. *Story of Ancient Egypt.* Blackwell, 1988.

Guillemette, Andreu. *Egypt in the Age of the Pyramids.* Translated by David Lorton. Cornell University Press, 1997.

Hoffman, Michael A. *Egypt Before the Pharaohs: The Prehistoric Foundations of Egyptian Civilization.* 1979. Reprint: Barnes & Noble Books, 1993.

Hoffmeier, James K. *Israel in Egypt: The Evidence for the Authenticity of the Exodus Tradition.* Oxford University Press, 1996.

Lawton, Ian and Chris Ogilvie-Herald. *Giza: The Truth; The People, Politics, and History Behind the World's Most Famous Archaeological Site.* Invisible Cities Press, 2001.

Manchip White, Jon Ewbank. *Ancient Egypt: Its Culture and History.* 1952. Reprint: Dover, 1970.

Redford, Donald B. *Egypt, Canaan, and Israel in Ancient Times.* Princeton University Press, 1992. **

Shaw, Ian M. "Egyptian Chronology and the Irish Oak Calibration." *Journal of Near Eastern Studies* 44, no. 4 (Oct. 1985): 295–317. **

_____, ed. *The Oxford History of Ancient Egypt.* Oxford University Press, 2000. ****

Stead, Miriam. *Egyptian Life.* Harvard University Press, 1986.

Taylor, John H. *Egypt and Nubia.* Harvard University Press, 1991.

Vercoutter, Jean. *The Search for Ancient Egypt.* Translated by Ruth Sharman. Harry N. Abrams, 1986.

Verner, Miroslav. *The Pyramids: The Mystery, Culture, and Science of Egypt's Great Monuments.* Translated by Steven Rendall. Grove Press, 2001.

Ward, William A. "The Present Status of Egyptian Chronology." *Bulletin of the American Schools for Oriental Research* 288 (1992): 53–66. **

Wengrow, David. *The Archaeology of Early Egypt: Social Transformations in North Africa, c. 10,000 to 2,650 B. C.* Cambridge University Press, 2006.

Woldering, Irmgard. *The Art of Egypt: The Time of the Pharaohs.* Translated by Ann E. Keep. Greystone Press, 1963.

Archaeology (Anatolia and the Aegean)

Dickinson, Oliver. *The Aegean Bronze Age.* Cambridge University Press, 1994. *

Gordon, Cyrus J. *Ugarit and Minoan Crete: The Bearing of Their Texts on the Origins of Western Culture.* Norton, 1966.

Hutchinson, R. W. *Prehistoric Crete.* Penguin Books, 1962. **

Lloyd, Seton. *Early Anatolia.* Penguin Books, 1956. **

_____. *Early Highland Peoples of Anatolia.*

Thames & Hudson, 1967. *
Runnels, Curtis and Priscilla Murray. *Greece Before History: An Archaeological Companion and Guide.* Stanford University Press, 2001.
Taylor, Lord Williams. *The Myceneans*, rev. ed. Thames & Hudson, 1983. **

Archaeology (Europe)

Burgess, Colin. *The Age of Stonehenge.* Barnes & Noble Books, 2003.
Childe, V. Gordon. *The Aryans: A Study of Indo-European Origins.* 1926. Reprint: Barnes & Noble Books, 1993. *
———. *The Dawn of European Civilization*, 6th ed. Vintage, 1964. *
Cunliffe, Barry, ed. *The Oxford Illustrated Prehistory of Europe.* Oxford University Press, 1994. ***
Gimbutas, Marija. *The Balts.* Praeger, 1963.
Harbison, Peter. *Pre-Christian Ireland: From the First Settlers to the Early Celts.* Thames & Hudson, 1988.
Mallory, J. P. *In Search of the Indo-Europeans: Language, Archaeology and Myth.* Thames & Hudson, 1989. ****
Mohen, Jean-Pierre and Christieane Eluére. *The Bronze Age of Europe.* Translated by David and Dorie Baker. Harry N. Abrams, 2000.
———. *The World of Megaliths.* Facts on File, 1989. *
Piggot, Stuart. *Ancient Europe from the Beginnings of Agriculture to Classical Antiquity: A Survey.* Aldine, 1965. *
Pitts, Mike. *Hengeworld: Life in Britain 2000 B. C. as Revealed by the Latest Discoveries at Stonehenge, Avebury and Stanton Drew.* Arrow Books, 2001. **
Pryor, Francis. *Seahenge: New Discoveries in Prehistoric Britain.* Harper Collins, 2001. *
Savory, H. N. *Spain and Portugal: The Prehistory of the Iberian Peninsula.* Praeger, 1968.
Souden, David. *Stonehenge Revealed.* Facts on File, 1997. *

Archaeology (Asia)

Allchin, Bridget and Raymond Allchin. *The Birth of Indian Civilization: India and Pakistan before 500 B. C.* Penguin Books, 1968.
Auboyer, Jeannine, Michel Beurdeley, Jean Boisselier, Chantal Massonaud, and Huguette Rousset. *Forms and Styles in Asia.* Taschen, 1994. **
Barber, Elizabeth Wayland. *The Mummies of Ürümchi.* Norton, 1999. *
Barnes, Gina L. *The Rise of Civilization in East Asia: The Archaeology of China, Korea and Japan.* Thames & Hudson, 1999. **
Blunden, Caroline and Mark Elvin. *Cultural Atlas of China.* Facts on File, 1983. **
Chang, Kwang-chih. *The Archaeology of Ancient China*, 4th ed. Yale University Press, 1986. ****
Crump, James and Irving Crump. *Dragon Bones in the Yellow Earth.* Dodd, Mead & Co., 1963. *
Debaine-Francfort, Corinne. *The Search for Ancient China.* Translated by Paul G. Bahn. Harry N. Abrams, 1999.
Fairservis, Walter A., Jr. *Before the Buddha Came.* Scribner's, 1972.
Grousset, René. *The Empires of the Steppes: A History of Central Asia.* Translated by Naomi Walford. Rutgers University Press, 1970.
Imamura, Keiji. *Prehistoric Japan: New Perspectives on Insular East Asia.* University of Hawaii Press, 1996. **
Karnow, Stanley and the editors of Time-Life Books. *Southeast Asia.* Time-Life Books, 1967.
Mallory, J. P. and Victor H. Mair. *The Tarim Mummies: Ancient China and the Mystery of the Earliest Peoples from the West.* Thames & Hudson, 2000. **
Mason, R. H. P. and J. G. Caiger. *A History of Japan.* Charles E. Tuttle, 1972.
Meadow, Richard H., ed. *Harappa Excavations, 1986 – 1990: A Multidisciplinary Approach to Third Millennium Urbanism.* Prehistory Press, 1991. **
Menzies, Gavin. *1421: The Year China Discovered America.* Harper Perennial, 2002.
Mizoguchi, Koji. *An Archaeological History of Japan, 30,000 B. C. to A. D. 700.* University of Pennsylvania Press, 2002.
Nai, Hsai. *New Archaeological Finds in China: Discoveries during the Cultural Revolution.* Foreign Languages Press, 1973.
National Gallery of Art. *The Exhibition of Archaeological Finds of the People's Republic of China.* National Gallery of Art, 1975.
Phillips, E. P. *The Royal Hordes: Nomad Peoples of the Steppes.* McGraw-Hill, 1965.
Rawson, Jessica. *Mysteries of Ancient China: New Discoveries from the Early Dynasties.* George Braziller, 1996. *
Reid, Anna. *The Shaman's Coat: A Native History of Siberia.* Weidenfeld & Nicolson, 2002.
Te-k'un, Cheng. *Studies in Chinese Archaeology.* Chinese University Press, 1982. *
Thaper, Romila. *Early India: From the Origins to A. D. 1300.* University of California Press, 2002.
Yang, Xiaoneng. *The Golden Age of Chinese Archaeology: Celebrated Discoveries from the People's Republic of China.* Yale University Press, 1999. **

Archaeology (Australia and the Pacific)

Bellwood, Peter. *The Polynesians: Prehistory of an Island People*, rev. ed. Thames & Hudson, 1987. **

Buck, Peter. *Vikings of the Pacific*. University of Chicago Press, 1959.

Campbell, I. C. *A History of the Pacific Islands*. University of California Press, 1989. *

Chappell, John, John Head and John Magee. "Beyond the Radiocarbon Limit in Australian Archaeology and Quaternary Research." *Antiquity* 79 (1996): 543–552.

Cook, Captain James. *The Explorations of Captain James Cook in the Pacific: As Told by Selections of His Own Journals, 1768 – 1779*. Edited by A. Grenfell Price. Dover, 1971. *

Goodenough, Ward H., ed. *The Prehistoric Settlement of the Pacific*. American Philosophical Society, 1996.*

Heyerdahl, Thor. *Kon-Tiki: Across the Pacific by Raft*. Washington Square Press, 1973.

_____. *Sea Routes to Polynesia*. Rand McNally. 1968. *

Irwin, Geoffrey. *The Prehistoric Exploration and Colonisation of the Pacific*. Cambridge University Press, 1992.

Mulvaney, John and Johan Kamminga. *Prehistoric Australia*. Allen & Unwin, 1999. *

Oliver, Douglas L. *The Pacific Islands*. Harvard University Press, 1951.

Robequain, Charles. *Malaya, Indonesia, Borneo, and the Philippines*. Longmans, 1964.

Schwartz, Jean-Michel. *The Mysteries of Easter Island*. Translated by Lowell Bair. Avon Books, 1975.

Wyatt Gill, Rev. William. *From Darkness to Light in Polynesia with Illustrative Clan Songs*. 1894. Reprint: Institute of Pacific Studies, University of the South Pacific, 1994.

Archaeology (Americas)

Adovasio, J. M. *The First Americans: In Pursuit of Archaeology's Greatest Mystery*. Random House, 2002.

Chatters, James C. *Ancient Encounters: Kennewick Man and the First Americans*. Simon & Schuster, 2001.

Coe, Michael D., Dean Snow and Elizabeth Benson. *Atlas of Ancient America*. Facts on File, 1986.

Davies, Nigel. *Voyages to the New World*. William Morrow, 1979. **

Dillehay, Thomas. *The Settlement of the Americas: A New Prehistory*. Basic Books, 2000.

Fagan, Brian M. *The Great Journey: The Peopling of Ancient America*. Thames & Hudson, 1987. *

Fiedel, Stuart J. *Prehistory of the Americas*, 2nd ed. Cambridge University Press, 1992. ***

Ford, James A. *A Comparison of Formative Cultures in the Americas: Diffusion or the Psychic Unity of Man?* Smithsonian Institution Press, 1965. ****

Schobinger, Juan. *The First Americans*. Eerdmans, 1994.

Tankersley, Kenneth. *In Search of Ice Age Americans*. Gibbs Smith, 2002.

Taylor, R. E., C. Vance Haynes, Jr. and Minze Stuiver. "Clovis and Folsom Age Estimates: Stratigraphic Context and Radiocarbon Calibration." *Antiquity* 70 (1996): 515–525.

Willey, Gordon R. and Jeremy Sabloff, eds. *Pre-Columbian Archaeology: Readings from "Scientific American."* Freeman, 1980. *

Archaeology (South America)

Bruhns, Karen Olson. *Ancient South America*. Cambridge University Press, 1994.

Burger, Richard L. *Chavin and the Origins of Andean Civilization*. Thames & Hudson, 1995. **

Kaufman, Bernard Barken. *Who Were the Pre-Columbians? Mysteries, Adventures, and Challenges for Today's World*. New World Art, 1992.

Keating, Richard W., ed. *Peruvian Prehistory: An Overview of Pre-Inca and Inca Society*. Cambridge University Press, 1988. **

Meggers, Betty J., Clifford Evans and Emilio Estrada. *Early Formative Period of Coastal Ecuador: The Valdiva and Machalilla Phases*. Smithsonian Institution, 1965. ****

Miller Graham, Mark, ed. *Reinterpreting Prehistory of Central America*. University Press of Colorado, 1993.

Moseley, Michael E. *The Incas and Their Ancestors: The Archaeology of Peru*. Thames & Hudson, 1992. *

Reichel-Dolmatoff, G. *Columbia*. Praeger, 1965.

Vankirk, Jacques and Parney Bassett-Vankirk. *Remarkable Remains of the Ancient Peoples of Guatemala*. University of Oklahoma Press, 1996.

Willey, Gordon R. *An Introduction to American Archaeology*. Vol. 2, *South America*. Prentice Hall, 1971.***

Archaeology (North America)

Birmingham, Robert A. and Leslie E. Eisenberg. *Indian Mounds of Wisconsin*. University of Wisconsin Press, 2000.

Blanton, Richard B., Gary M. Feinman, Stephen A. Kowalewski, and Linda M. Nicholas. *Ancient Oaxaca*. Cambridge University Press, 1999.

Brookes, Samuel O. *The Hester Site: An Early Archaic Occupation in Monroe County, Mississippi*. Mississippi Department of Archives and History, 1979.

Brose, David S. and N'omi Greber. *Hopewell Archaeology: The Chillicothe Conference*. Kent State University Press, 1979.

_____. *Yesterday's River: The Archaeology of 10,000 Years along the Tennessee-Tombigbee Waterway*. Cleveland Museum of Natural History, 1991.

Topical Bibliography

_____., ed. *The Late Prehistory of the Lake Erie Drainage Basin: A 1972 Symposium Revised.* Cleveland Museum of Natural History, 1976.

Coe, Michael D. *America's First Civilization.* American Heritage, 1968. *

_____. *Mexico: From the Olmecs to the Aztecs,* 4th ed. Thames & Hudson, 1994. ***

_____. *The Maya,* 5th ed. Thames & Hudson, 1993. ****

Dacal Moure, Ramon and Manuel Rivero de la Calle. *Art and Archaeology of Pre-Columbian Cuba.* University of Pittsburg Press, 1996.

Dixon, E. James. *Bones, Boats, and Bison: Archaeology and the First Colonization of Western North America.* University of New Mexico Press, 1999.

Fagan, Brian M. *Ancient North America: The Archaeology of a Continent,* 3rd ed. Thames & Hudson, 2000. *

_____. *Before California.* Rowman & Littlefield, 2003. **

Lyttle, Richard B. *People of the Dawn.* Atheneum, 1980. ***

MacDonald, Jerry N. and Susan L. Woodward. *Indian Mounds of the Atlantic Coast: A Guide to Sites from Maine to Florida.* McDonald & Woodward, 1987. *

Markham, Charles W. and Paul K. Kieisa. *The Deere Creek Site: An Early Woodland Camping Locality in Rock Island Country, Illinois.* Northern Illinois Archaeological Research, Vol. 1. Northern Illinois University, 1984.

_____. *Putney Landing: Archaeological Investigations at a Havana-Hopewell Settlement on the Mississippi River West-Central Illinois.* Northern Illinois University, 1988.

McGoun, William E. *Prehistoric Peoples of South Florida.* University of Alabama Press, 1993. *

Meinkoth, Michael C. *Sister Creek Mounds: Middle Woodlands Mortuary Practices in the Illinois River Valley.* University of Illinois at Urbana-Champaign, 1995.

Milner, George R. *The Moundbuilders: Ancient Peoples of North America.* Thames & Hudson, 2004.

Munson, Cheryl Ann, ed. *Archaeological Salvage Investigations at Patoka Lake: Indiana Prehistoric Occupations of the Upper Patoka River Valley.* Indiana University, 1980.

Penny, James S. *Archaeological Investigations in the Turkey Bluffs Fish and Wildlife Area, Randolph County, Illinois.* Midwestern Archeological Research Center, Illinois State University, 1982.

Rouse, Irving. *The Tainos: Rise and Decline of the People Who Greeted Columbus.* Yale University Press, 1992. **

Snow, Dean. *The Archaeology of North America.* Viking Press, 1976. ***

Squier, Ephraim G. and Edwin H. Davis. *Ancient Monuments of the Mississippi Valley* 1848. Edited with introduction by David J. Meltzer. Smithsonian Institution Press, 1998. ***

Stafford, Barbara D. and Mark B. Sant, eds. *Smiling Dan: Structure and Function at a Middle Woodland Settlement in the Lower Illinois Valley.* Kampsville Archaeological Center Research no. 2. Center for American Archaeology, 1985.

Struever, Stuart and Felicia Antonelli Holton. *Koster: Americans in Search of Their Prehistoric Past.* Anchor Press/Doubleday, 1979. ****

Thomas, Cyrus. *Report on the Mound Explorations of the Bureau of Ethnology.* Smithsonian Institution Press, 1894. **

Thomas, David Hurst. *Exploring Ancient Native America.* Routledge, 1999.

Walthall, John A. *Prehistoric Indians of the Southeast: Archaeology of Alabama and the Middle South.* University of Alabama Press, 1980. *

Ward, H. Trawick and R. P. Stephen Davis, Jr. *Time Before History: The Archaeology of North Carolina.* University of North Carolina Press, 1999. **

Weaver, Muriel Porter. *The Aztecs, Maya, and Their Predecessors: Archaeology of Mesoamerica.* Seminar Press, 1972.

Westover, Allan R., Mark E. Esarey, and Joseph S. Phillippe. *Report of Testing at the Columbia Quarry Site, 11-S-629, In FAI-255 Borrow Pit 12, Extension 3, St. Clair County, Illinois.* Illinois State University, 1983.

Willey, Gordon R. *An Introduction to American Archaeology.* Vol. 1, *North and Middle America.* Prentice Hall, 1966. ****

Winters, Howard Dalton. *The Riverton Culture: A Second Millennium Occupation in the Central Wabash Valley.* Illinois State Museum, 1969. **

Archaeology (Africa)

Andah, Bassey W., M. Adebisi Sowunim, A. I. Okpoko, and C. A. Folorunso, eds. *Africa: The Challenge of Archaeology.* Heinemann Educational Books (Nigeria), 1998. **

Bohannan, Paul and Philip Curtin. *Africa and Africans,* rev. ed. Natural History Press for The American Museum of Natural History, 1971.

Clark, Duncan. *African Art.* Crescent Books, 1995. *

Clark, J. Desmond. *The Prehistory of Africa.* Praegar, 1970. **

De Villiers, Marq and Sheila Hirtle. *Sahara: A Natural History.* Walker, 2002. *

Fagg, Bernard. *Nok Terracottas.* Nigerian Museum, 1990. **

Iliffe, John. *Africans: The History of a Continent.* Cambridge University Press, 1995. **

Maquet, Jacques. *Civilizations of Black Africa.* Translated by Joan Rayfield. Oxford University Press, 1972.

McEvedy, Colin. *The Penguin Atlas of African History.* Penguin Books, 1995. *

Oliver, Roland and J. D. Fage. *A Short History of Africa*, 6th ed. Penguin Books, 1988. *

Climatology and Environment

Atkinson, B.W. and Alan Gadd. *Weather.* Weidenfield & Nicolson, 1987.

Bell, Barbara. "The Dark Ages in Ancient History." *American Journal of Archaeology* 75, no. 1 (Jan, 1971): 1–26. ***

Bradley, Raymond S. *Paleoclimatology: Reconstructing Climates of the Quaternary.* Elsevier Academic Press, 1999. *

Burroughs, William J., Bob Crowder, Ted Robertson, Eleanor Vallier-Talbot, and Richard Whitaker. *A Guide to Weather.* City Press, 1996.

Cronin, Thomas M. *Principles of Paleoclimatology.* Columbia University Press, 1999.

Sachs, Aaron. *Humboldt Current: Nineteenth-Century Exploration and the Roots of American Environmentalism.* Viking, 2006.

Saur, James. "The River Runs Dry – Biblical Story Preserves Historical Memory." *Biblical Archaeology Review* 22, no. 4 (July/August 1996): 52. ****

Schneider, Stephen H. and Randi Londer. *The Coevolution of Climate and Life.* Sierra Club Books, 1984. *

Weiss, Harvey. "Beyond the Younger Dryas: Collapse as Adaptation to Abrupt Climate Change in Ancient West Asia and the Mediterranean." In *Confronting Natural Disaster: Engaging the Past to Understand the Future*, edited by Garth Bawden and Richard Martin Reycraft, 75–98. University of New Mexico Press, 2000. **

Cosmology

Barrow, John D. and Joseph Silk. *The Left Hand of Creation: The Origin and Evolution of the Expanding Universe.* Basic Books, 1983.

_____. *The Origin of the Universe.* Basic Books, 1994.

Beatty, J. Kelly, Carolyn Collins Petersen, and Andrew Chaikin, eds. *The New Solar System.* Cambridge University Press, 1999. **

Bell, J. S. *Speakable and Unspeakable in Quantum Mechanics.* Cambridge University Press, 1987.

Caprara, Giovanni, ed. *The Solar System.* Firefly Books, 2003.

Gonzalez, Guillermo and Jay W. Richards. *The Privileged Planet: How Our Place in The Cosmos is Designed for Discovery.* Regnery, 2004. **

Hawking, Stephen with Leonard Mlodinow. *A Briefer History of Time.* Bantam, 2005.

_____. *The Grand Design.* Bantam, 2005.

Kandel, Robert. *Water from Heaven: The Story of Water from the Big Bang to the Rise of Civilization and Beyond.* Columbia University Press, 1998.

Kirshner, Robert P. *The Extravagant Universe: Exploding Stars, Dark Energy, and the Accelerating Cosmos.* Princeton University Press, 2002. *

Lightman, Alan. *Ancient Light: Our Changing View of the Universe.* Harvard University Press, 1991. *

Noyes, Robert N. *The Sun, Our Star.* Havard University Press, 1982.

Ross, Hugh. *More than a Theory: Revealing a Testable Model of Creation.* Baker Books, 2009.

_____. *Why the Universe Is the Way It Is.* Baker Books, 2008.

Scientific American. *Conditions for Life: Readings from Scientific American.* Introduction by Aharon Gibor. Freeman, 1976. **

_____. *Cosmology + 1: Readings from Scientific American.* Introduction by Owen Gingerich. Freeman, 1977.

Weinberg, Steven. *The First Three Minutes: A Modern View of the Origin of the Universe.* Bantam, 1977.

Geology

Ahrens, L. H. *Distribution of the Elements in Our Planet.* McGraw Hill, 1965. *

Aitchison, Stewart. *Grand Canyon: Window of Time.* Sierra Press, 1999.

Allegre, Claude. *The Behavior of the Earth: Continental and Seafloor Mobility.* Harvard University Press, 1988.

Bakewell, Robert and Benjamin Silliman. *An Introduction to Geology.* B & W Noyes, 1839. *

Dalrymple, G. Brent. *The Age of the Earth.* Stanford University Press, 1991. *

Dunbar, Carl O. *Historical Geology*, 2nd ed. John Wiley & Sons, 1960. **

Gohau, Gabriel. *A History of Geology.* Revised and translated by Albert V. Carozzi and Marguerite Carozzi. Rutgers University Press, 1990. *

Gould, Stephen J. *Time's Arrow, Time's Cycle: Myth and Metaphor in the Discovery of Geological Time.* Harvard University Press, 1987. **

Hallam, A. *Great Geological Controversies*, 2nd ed. Oxford University Press, 1989. ***

Inbrie, John and Katherine Palmer Imbrie. *Ice Ages: Solving the Mystery.* Harvard University Press, 1979. **

Johnson, Lucille Lewis. *Paleoshorelines and Prehis-*

Topical Bibliography

tory: An Investigation of Method. CRC Press, 1992. *
Lawrence, David M. *Upheaval from the Abyss: Ocean Floor Mapping and the Earth Science Revolution.* Rutgers University Press, 2002.
Lyell, Charles. *Principles of Geology* 1830 – 1833. Edited with introduction by James A. Secord. Penguin Books, 1997. ****
_____. *Principles of Geology.* Vol. 1. 1830. New introduction by Martin J. S. Rudwick. University of Chicago Press, 1990. ****
MacDougall, J. D. *A Short History of Planet Earth: Mountains, Mammals, Fire, and Ice.* John Wiley & Sons, 1996.
McBirney, Alexander R. *Igneous Petrology*, 2nd ed. Jones & Bartlett, 1984.
McElhinny, M. W. *Palaeomagnetism and Plate Tectonics.* Cambridge University Press, 1973. **
McPhee, John. *Annals of the Former World.* Farrar, Straus & Giroux, 2000.
Merrill, Ronald T., Michael W. McElhinny, and Phillip L. McFadden. *The Magnetic Field of the Earth: Paleomagnetism, the Core, and the Deep Mantle.* Academic Press, 1998.
Oldroyd, David R. *Thinking about the Earth: A History of Ideas in Geology.* Harvard University Press, 1996. **
Oreskes, Naomi, ed. *Plate Tectonics: An Insider's History of the Modern Theory of the Earth.* Westview Press, 2003. *
_____. *The Rejection of Continental Drift: Theory and Method in American Earth Science.* Oxford University Press, 1999. ***
Palmer, Douglas. *Earth Time: Exploring the Deep Past from Victorian England to the Grand Canyon.* Wiley, 2005.
Powell, James Lawrence. *Grand Canyon: Solving Earth's Grandest Puzzle.* Pi Press, 2005.
Price, L. Greer. *An Introduction to Grand Canyon Geology.* Grand Canyon Association, 1999.
Rapp, George, Jr. and Christopher L. Hill. *Geoarchaeology: The Earth-Science Approach to Archaeological Interpretation.* Yale University Press, 1998.
Rudwick, Martin J. S. *Bursting the Limits of Time: The Reconstruction of Geohistory in the Age of Revolution.* University of Chicago Press, 2005. ****
_____. *Scenes from Deep Time: Early Pictorial Representations of the Prehistoric World.* University of Chicago Press, 1992.
_____. *Worlds before Adam: The Reconstruction of Geohistory in the Age of Reform.* University of Chicago Press, 2008. ****
Van Duzer, Chet. *Floating Islands: A Global Bibliography.* Translated and annotated edition of G. C. Munz's *Exercitatio Academica de Insulis Natantibus* (1711). Cantor Press, 2004. ****

Vita-Finzi, Claudio. *Recent Earth History.* Halsted Press, 1973.
Wegener, Alfred. *The Origin of Continents and Oceans.* 1915. Translated by John Biram. Dover, 1966.
Zanger, Eberhard. "Landscape Changes around Tiryns during the Bronze Age." *American Journal of Archaeology* 98 (1994): 189–212. *

Geography

Bryce, James. *Transcaucasia and Ararat: Being Notes of a Vacation Tour in the Autumn of 1876.* 1877. Reprint: Elibron Classics, 2005.
Sobel, Dava and William J. H. Andrewes. *The Illustrated Longitude.* Walker & Company, 2003.
Whitfield, Peter. *The Image of the World: 20 Centuries of World Maps.* Pomegranate, 1994.

Zoology

Cain, A. J. *Animal Species and Their Evolution.* Princeton University Press, 1993. *
Cohen, Claudine. *The Fate of the Mammoth: Fossils, Myth, and History.* Translated by William Rodarmor. University of Chicago Press, 2002. *
Colbert, Edwin H. *Wandering Lands and Animals.* Dover, 1985. ***
Darwin, Charles. *The Origin of Species By Means of Natural Selection: The Preservation of the Favoured Races in the Struggle for Life.* 1859. Penguin Books, *
Dobzhansky, Theodosius, Francis Ayala, G. Ledyard Sebbins, and James W. Valentine. *Evolution.* Freeman, 1977. **
Gould, Stephen J. *Punctuated Equilibrium.* Belknap Press, 2007.
Horner, Jack and James Gorman. *How to Build a Dinosaur: Extinction Doesn't Have to be Forever.* Dutton Adult, 2009.
Mayr, Ernest. *Systematics and the Origin of Species from the Viewpoint of a Zoologist.* 1942. Reprint: Dover, 1964. ***
Rudwick, Martin J. S. *The Meaning of Fossils: Episodes in the History of Paleontology.* University of Chicago Press, 1976. ****
Ward, Peter D. *Rivers in Time: The Search for Clues to Earth's Mass Extinctions.* Columbia University Press, 2000.
Whitefield, Dr. Philip, cons. ed. *The Marshall Illustrated Encyclopedia of Animals: A Comprehensive Guide to Over 2,000 Species of Mammals, Birds, Reptiles, Amphibians and Fishes.* Marshall, 1998. *

ABOUT THE AUTHOR: Philip Ernest Williams has interspersed his career in technology with lengthy studies in the philosophy of science, the history of ideas, biblical studies, and the history of mankind. His book is the product of years of research following his discovery of population patterns in ancient Israel that met his three criteria as archaeological evidence of the Flood. Since his retirement in 1990 from the telecommunications software company he founded, the author has alternated his time researching archaeology and ancient history with the promotion of infrastructure development in poor nations and international community among Christians. He may be contacted at the address below or by writing:

author@christianleadersandscholars.com

To stay abreast of developments, conversations, or schedules for speaking engagements and conferences pertaining to this book, visit the website:

www.christianleadersandscholars.com

Copies of this book can be ordered from the website or by contacting:

Christian Leaders & Scholars Press
PO Box 680847
Charlotte, NC 28216

Telephone: **(704) 374-5231**